I & II
SAMUEL

A COMMENTARY

Library of Biblical Interpretation

I & II SAMUEL

A COMMENTARY

ROBERT P. GORDON

Regency
Reference Library
Zondervan Publishing House
Grand Rapids, Michigan

I & II SAMUEL: A COMMENTARY
Copyright © 1986 by Robert P. Gordon
First published in the United Kingdom by The Paternoster Press

REGENCY REFERENCE LIBRARY is an imprint of Zondervan Publishing House,
1415 Lake Drive, S.E., Grand Rapids, Michigan 49506.

Library of Congress Cataloging in Publication Data
Gordon, R. P.
 1 & 2 Samuel : a commentary / Robert P. Gordon.
  p. cm.
 Includes indexes.
 1. Bible. O.T. Samuel—Commentaries. I. Bible. O.T. Samuel. 1988. II.
Title. III. Title: One & two Samuel. IV. Title: 1 and 2 Samuel.
BS1325.3.G66 1988
222'.407–dc19   88-11565
                       CIP

ISBN 0-310-23022-5

Printed in the United States of America

88 89 90 91 92 / EE / 10 9 8 7 6 5 4 3 2 1

For my Mother
and in memory of my Father

CONTENTS

Preface

The reader should be warned that there are definite limits to what can be achieved in a modest-sized commentary on 1 and 2 Samuel. Not only are there fifty-five chapters to comment upon, but there are also the cascades of secondary literature – now augmented by this commentary – which the commentator must attempt to harness, however little of it he may be able to cite in the actual discussion. (It is a relief not to have to chase and read it all now!) The plan of the commentary is straightforward, so that it should at least be easy to discover what is said, or what is not said, on a particular point. Except where indicated, I have quoted from the Revised Standard Version (OT edn., 1952).

It is a feature of the Samuel narratives that they often stop short just where we might expect a word of censure or a moralizing tailpiece. Lack of space has been partly responsible for my following this good example; but the reader may rest assured that I too am 'against' murder, duplicity and all their evil cronies. Nor have I tried to 'Christianize' 1 and 2 Samuel at every conceivable point. Often, as I have sought to show in the brief introductory section entitled 'David and Christ', it is a question of contrast rather than of comparison; and the only way to arrive at sensible conclusions in this matter is first to appreciate the Old Testament for its own sake – that is, in its own literary, historical, cultural and theological contexts. That is principally what this commentary is about.

On some matters of general introduction, and especially on literary-critical questions, my little volume in the Sheffield 'Old Testament Guides' series (*1 & 2 Samuel* (1984)) can be consulted. (And my thanks to my colleague Graham I. Davies for first mentioning that 'Sheffield are starting a new series' – just when I was wondering what to do with a redundant introduction to 1 and 2 Samuel.) It is as well that we can understand and gain so much from the books of Samuel even while knowing next-to-nothing about the process of their compilation and redaction. I hope that I shall be forgiven for being rather sceptical about some of the views in common currency. Where reliable indicators are lacking I can see no merit in adding to the speculation, and while the dangers of exegesis-in-a-vacuum are obvious, some modern literary theorists would regard that as a happy, and even a necessary, state of affairs.

This is an opportunity to express my gratitude to several friends and mentors who have helped me along the road. Prof. David W. Gooding is to be thanked for his valuable comments on the introductory section on the text, but so much more for his guidance and inspiration at key points ever since my school-days in Belfast where I first made his acquaintance. Prof. John Macdonald, my head of department at Glasgow University during the ten years that I was there, from his wide-ranging interests in the languages and literatures of the ancient near east taught me much that I would probably not have learned otherwise. I first encountered the kindness and the formidable scholarship of Prof. John A. Emerton in 1968 when he was appointed to supervise my dissertation on Targum. Now that I am his colleague I continue to benefit greatly from both. Prof. P. A. H. de Boer of Leiden has put all students of Samuel in his debt by his distinguished work on the Stuttgart edition (*BHS*) of the Hebrew text and on the Peshitta version of Samuel for the IOSOT Peshitta Project which he himself led for many years. Finally in this section, I want to thank David G. Deboys for his expert help with proof-reading.

My wife Ruth typed most of the manuscript of this commentary and is again warmly to be thanked. With Graham and Claire, she has borne cheerfully whatever privations my occupation with articles and books has imposed on them. Since working on the manuscript she has also borne Alasdair Robert (3.10.85), to the great joy of us all.

This commentary is lovingly dedicated to my mother, and to the memory of my father. They above all showed me the path of life, and have demonstrated by their Christian example that 'the kingdom of God is not a matter of talk but of power' (1 Cor. 4:20).

Foxton, Cambridge

CHIEF ABBREVIATIONS

AB	The Anchor Bible
Ackroyd	P. R. Ackroyd, *The First (Second) Book of Samuel* (Cambridge, 1971, 1977)
AI	R. de Vaux, *Ancient Israel* (ET; London, [2]1965)
ANEP	J. B. Pritchard (ed.), *The Ancient Near East in Pictures* (Princeton, 1954)
ANET[3]	J. B. Pritchard (ed.), *Ancient Near Eastern Texts Relating to the Old Testament* (Princeton, [3]1969)
Ant.	Josephus' *Jewish Antiquities*
AOTS	D. W. Thomas (ed.), *Archaeology and Old Testament Study* (Oxford, 1967)
ARI[3]	W. F. Albright, *Archaeology and the Religion of Israel* (Baltimore, [3]1953)
ARM	*Archives royales de Mari*
ASTI	*Annual of the Swedish Theological Institute*
AV	Authorized Version
BA	*Biblical Archaeologist*
BAR	*Biblical Archaeologist Reader*
BARev	*Biblical Archaeology Review*
Barr	J. Barr, *Comparative Philology and the Text of the Old Testament* (Oxford, 1968)
BASOR	*Bulletin of the American Schools of Oriental Research*
BDB	F. Brown, S. R. Driver, C. A. Briggs, *A Hebrew and English Lexicon of the Old Testament* (Oxford, 1906)
BH	Biblical Hebrew
BH[3]	*Biblia Hebraica* (ed. R. Kittel; Stuttgart,[3]1937)
BHS	*Biblia Hebraica Stuttgartensia* (I, II Samuel, ed. P. A. H. de Boer; Stuttgart, 1977)
Birch	B. C. Birch, *The Rise of the Israelite Monarchy* (Missoula, 1976)
de Boer	P. A. H. de Boer, *Research into the Text of I Samuel i–xvi* (Amsterdam, 1938); *idem*, 'Research into the Text of 1 Samuel xviii–xxxi', *OS* 6 (1949), pp. 1–100
Botterweck–Ringgren	G. J. Botterweck and H. Ringgren (eds.), *Theological Dictionary of the Old Testament* (Eng. revd. edn.; Grand Rapids, 1977–.)
Bright	J. Bright, *A History of Israel* (London, [3]1981)
Brockington	L. H. Brockington, *The Hebrew Text of the Old Testament. The Readings Adopted by the Translators of the New English Bible* (Oxford and Cambridge, 1973)
BZ	*Biblische Zeitschrift*

BZAW	Beihefte zur *Zeitschrift für die alttestamentliche Wissenschaft*
*CAH*³	*Cambridge Ancient History* (Cambridge, ³1970–.)
Campbell	A. F. Campbell, *The Ark Narrative (1 Sam. 4–6; 2 Sam. 6)* (Missoula, 1975)
Carlson	R. A. Carlson, *David, the Chosen King* (Stockholm, 1964)
CBQ	*Catholic Biblical Quarterly*
Childs	B. S. Childs, *Introduction to the Old Testament as Scripture* (London, 1979)
CMHE	F. M. Cross, *Canaanite Myth and Hebrew Epic* (London, 1973)
Cody	A. Cody, *A History of Old Testament Priesthood* (Rome, 1969)
Conroy	C. Conroy, *Absalom Absalom! Narrative and Language in 2 Sam 13–20* (Rome, 1978)
Cross–Talmon	F. M. Cross and S. Talmon (eds.), *Qumran and the History of the Biblical Text* (Cambridge (Mass.), 1975)
DJD	*Discoveries in the Judaean Desert of Jordan*
DOTT	D. W. Thomas (ed.), *Documents from Old Testament Times* (Edinburgh, 1958)
Driver	S. R. Driver, *Notes on the Hebrew Text . . . of the Books of Samuel* (Oxford, ²1913)
EQ	*Evangelical Quarterly*
ET	English Translation
ET	*Expository Times*
EThL	*Ephemerides Theologicae Lovanienses*
EvTh	*Evangelische Theologie*
Fs	Festschrift
GNB	Good News Bible
Gottwald	N. K. Gottwald, *The Tribes of Yahweh* (London, 1980)
Grønbaek	J. H. Grønbaek, *Die Geschichte vom Aufstieg Davids (1. Sam. 15–2. Sam. 5)* (Copenhagen, 1971)
GTTOT	J. Simons, *The Geographical and Topographical Texts of the Old Testament* (Leiden, 1959)
Gunn	D. M. Gunn, *The Story of King David* (Sheffield, 1978); idem, *The Fate of King Saul* (Sheffield, 1980)
Halpern	B. Halpern, *The Constitution of the Monarchy in Israel* (Chico, 1981)
Haran	M. Haran, *Temples and Temple-Service in Ancient Israel* (Oxford, 1978)
Hayes–Miller	J. H. Hayes and J. M. Miller (eds.), *Israelite and Judaean History* (London, 1977)

Hertzberg	H. W. Hertzberg, *I and II Samuel* (ET; London, 1964)
HTR	*Harvard Theological Review*
HUCA	*Hebrew Union College Annual*
IBD	*The Illustrated Bible Dictionary* (3 vols.; Leicester, 1980)
ICC	The International Critical Commentary
IDB	*The Interpreter's Dictionary of the Bible* (New York, 1962)
IDBS	*The Interpreter's Dictionary of the Bible: Supplementary Volume* (Nashville, 1976)
IEJ	*Israel Exploration Journal*
IOS	*Israel Oriental Studies*
IOSCS	International Organization for Septuagint and Cognate Studies
Ishida	T. Ishida, *The Royal Dynasties in Ancient Israel* (Berlin, 1977)
JAAR	*Journal of the American Academy of Religion*
JANES	*Journal of the Ancient Near Eastern Society of Columbia University*
JAOS	*Journal of the American Oriental Society*
JB	The Jerusalem Bible
JBL	*Journal of Biblical Literature*
JETS	*Journal of the Evangelical Theological Society*
JJS	*Journal of Jewish Studies*
JNES	*Journal of Near Eastern Studies*
JNSL	*Journal of Northwest Semitic Languages*
Jobling	D. Jobling, *The Sense of Biblical Narrative* (Sheffield, 1978)
JPOS	*Journal of the Palestine Oriental Society*
JQR	*Jewish Quarterly Review*
JRAS	*Journal of the Royal Asiatic Society*
JSOT	*Journal for the Study of the Old Testament*
JSS	*Journal of Semitic Studies*
JTS	*Journal of Theological Studies*
KB	L. Koehler and W. Baumgartner, *Lexicon in Veteris Testamenti Libros* (Leiden, 1953)
KB[3]	L. Koehler and W. Baumgartner, *Hebräisches und aramäisches Lexikon zum Alten Testament* (Leiden, [3]1967–.)
Kennedy	A. R. S. Kennedy, *I & II Samuel* (Edinburgh, 1905)
Kirkpatrick	A. F. Kirkpatrick, *The First (Second) Book of Samuel* (Cambridge, 1888, 1889)
Klein	R. W. Klein, *1 Samuel* (Waco, 1983)
LXX	The Septuagint (A. E. Brooke, N. McLean, H. St. J.

	Thackeray (eds.), *The Old Testament in Greek*, II.I (London, 1927))
McCarter	P. K. McCarter, *I Samuel* (New York, 1980); *II Samuel* (New York, 1984)
McCarthy	C. McCarthy, *The Tiqqune Sopherim* (Göttingen, 1981)
McKane	W. McKane, *I and II Samuel* (London, 1963)
Mauchline	J. Mauchline, *1 and 2 Samuel* (London, 1971)
Mettinger	T. N. D. Mettinger, *King and Messiah* (Lund, 1976)
Miller–Roberts	P. D. Miller and J. J. M. Roberts, *The Hand of the Lord* (London, 1977)
Ms(s)	Manuscript(s)
MT	Massoretic Text
NAB	New American Bible
NCB	New Century Bible
NEB	New English Bible
NERTOT	W. Beyerlin (ed.), *Near Eastern Religious Texts relating to the Old Testament* (London, 1978)
NF	Neue Folge
NICOT	The New International Commentary on the Old Testament
NIV	New International Version
Noth	M. Noth, *The Deuteronomistic History* (ET; Sheffield, 1981)
NS	New Series
NTS	*New Testament Studies*
OS	*Oudtestamentische Studiën*
OTA	*Old Testament Abstracts*
OTG	R. P. Gordon, *1 & 2 Samuel* (Old Testament Guides; Sheffield, 1984)
OTL	Old Testament Library
OTT	G. von Rad, *Old Testament Theology* (ET (2 vols.); London, 1962, 1965)
PEQ	*Palestine Exploration Quarterly*
Peshitta	*The Old Testament in Syriac, Part II, 2* (Leiden, 1978; *Samuel* prepared by P. A. H. de Boer)
POTT	D. J. Wiseman (ed.), *Peoples of Old Testament Times* (Oxford, 1973)
RB	*Revue biblique*
Rost	L. Rost, *The Succession to the Throne of David* (ET; Sheffield, 1982)
RSV	Revised Standard Version
RV	Revised Version
SBL	Society of Biblical Literature

SBT	Studies in Biblical Theology
SBT	*Studia Biblica et Theologica*
Schicklberger	F. Schicklberger, *Die Ladeerzählungen des ersten Samuel-Buches* (Würzburg, 1973)
ScriptHieros	*Scripta Hierosolymitana*
SEÅ	*Svensk Exegetisk Årsbok*
SJT	*Scottish Journal of Theology*
Smith	H. P. Smith, *A Critical and Exegetical Commentary on the Books of Samuel* (Edinburgh, 1899)
STh	*Studia Theologica*
Stoebe	H. J. Stoebe, *Das erste Buch Samuelis* (Gütersloh, 1973)
Stolz	F. Stolz, *Das erste und zweite Buch Samuel* (Zurich, 1981)
SVT	Supplements to *Vetus Testamentum*
Targum	A. Sperber (ed.), *The Bible in Aramaic*, II (Leiden, 1959)
TB	Babylonian Talmud
TB	*Tyndale Bulletin*
TGUOS	*Transactions of the Glasgow University Oriental Society*
TLZ	*Theologische Literaturzeitung*
TOT	W. Eichrodt, *Theology of the Old Testament* (ET (2 vols.); London, 1961, 1967)
TOTC	Tyndale Old Testament Commentaries
TS	*Theological Studies*
TSF	Theological Students' Fellowship
TZ	*Theologische Zeitschrift*
UF	*Ugarit-Forschungen*
Ulrich	E. C. Ulrich, *The Qumran Text of Samuel and Josephus* (Missoula, 1978)
Vannoy	J. R. Vannoy, *Covenant Renewal at Gilgal* (Cherry Hill, 1978)
Veijola	T. Veijola, *Das Königtum in der Beurteilung der deuteronomistischen Historiographie* (Helsinki, 1977)
VT	*Vetus Testamentum*
ZAW	*Zeitschrift für die alttestamentliche Wissenschaft*

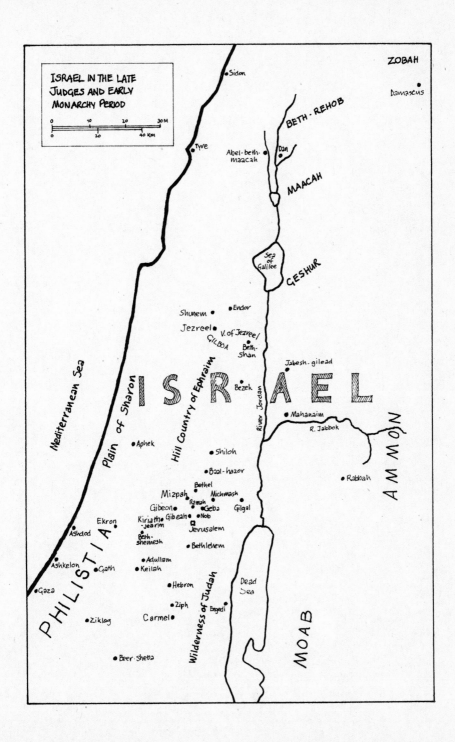

ISRAEL IN THE LATE
JUDGES AND EARLY
MONARCHY PERIOD

ZOBAH

Damascus

Sidon

BETH · REHOB

Tyre

Abel · beth · maacah
Dan

MAACAH

Sea of Galilee

GESHUR

Shunem
Endor
Jezreel
V. of Jezreel
GILBOA
Beth · Shan

Jabesh · gilead

ISRAEL

Bezek

River Jordan

Mahanaim

R. Jabbok

Mediterranean Sea

Plain of Sharon

Hill Country of Ephraim

AMMON

Aphek

Shiloh

Baal · hazor

Rabbah

Mizpah
Bethel
Michmash
Gibeon
Ramah
Geba
Gilgal
Kiriath · jearim
Gibeah
Nob
Ekron
Jerusalem
Ashdod
Beth · shemesh
Bethlehem

PHILISTIA

Ashkelon
Gath
Adullam
Keilah

Gaza

Hebron

Ziph

Wilderness of Judah

Engedi

Dead Sea

Carmel

Ziklag

MOAB

Beer · sheba

Introduction

1 THE BOOKS OF SAMUEL

The books of Samuel are not among the most aptly named in the Old Testament. In the first place, all references to the eponymous hero are confined to 1 Samuel, where he is already being described as an old man in 8:1. After his anointing of David in 16:1–13 he takes little further part in the action. His death is the subject of a short obituary notice in 25:1, and thereafter he makes but a brief posthumous appearance at Endor in 28:12–19. It follows, therefore, that the prophet Samuel can have had very little to do with the recording of the traditions preserved in 1 and 2 Samuel. 1 Chronicles 29:29 does refer us, it is true, to 'the Chronicles of Samuel the seer', but this is for information about the life and times of David, little of which Samuel himself witnessed. In fact, the more interesting point about these 'Chronicles of Samuel the seer' is that they must have stood in the same relationship to the historical Samuel as do the canonical books that bear his name. Quite simply, this is all bound up with the fact that questions of author attribution did not interest the early tradents of the Hebrew scriptures in the way that we may wish they had. A good number of Old Testament books are, properly speaking, anonymous works.[1]

In the Hebrew Bible tradition 1 and 2 Samuel were long reckoned as one book. The third-century Christian scholar Origen, for example, reports the Jewish custom of referring to a single book of Samuel.[2] As we should expect, therefore, the Massoretic notes marking the mid- and end-points of Samuel calculate on the basis of a unified book.[3] A breach was made in this tradition in the fifteenth century, but it was the arrival of the printing-press and the publication of the Bomberg rabbinic Bibles (early sixteenth century) that established the practice of dividing the Hebrew text of Samuel into two separate books. This had long been the convention in Christian circles influenced by the Septuagint and Vulgate. The translators of the Greek Septuagint version of Samuel had divided Samuel-Kings into four 'Books of Reigns' (or 'Kingdoms') more or less corresponding to the divisions with which we are familiar. This catch-all title was modified by Jerome to 'The Books of Kings' – the first books to be translated when he embarked upon his great Vulgate project, as we learn from the preface which he wrote for them, the apologetic *Prologus Galeatus* ('Helmeted Prologue'). It is thus Jerome's influence that can be detected behind the Authorized Version's 'The First (Second) Book of Samuel, Otherwise Called, The First (Second) Book of the Kings.'

In the Hebrew canon of the Old Testament 1 and 2 Samuel are included among the 'Former Prophets' (i.e. Joshua–2 Kings), a subdivision of the prophetic section of the canon. The title 'Former Prophets' as a canonical term is a late coinage[4] and not the most obvious for the books in question,[5] if only because 2 Kings seems almost deliberately to pass over the contributions of most of the 'major prophets' of the eighth and seventh centuries BC. (When Zc. 1:4; 7:12 refer to 'former prophets' it is these pre-exilic preachers who are intended.) In the 'Former Prophets' there is, on the other hand, a great emphasis upon the authoritative character of true prophecy, and upon the necessity of the community's submission to the prophetic word as a precondition to enjoying Yahweh's protection in the land.[6] In this sense Israel's history is a 'prophetic history' – which observation perhaps even allows us to convert the liability of the misnamed book(s) of *Samuel* into an interpretive asset.

The 'Former Prophets' are not quite coterminous with an entity of much more recent vintage (as far as biblical scholarship is concerned), the so-called 'Deuteronomistic History'. This great history-work, comprising Joshua–2 Kings, but also having a specially-augmented book of Deuteronomy for preface, was written, according to its modern advocate Martin Noth, to show how the laws and principles of Deuteronomy applied to Israel's history from the settlement in Canaan until the Babylonian exile.[7] Noth attributed the history to an editor working in Judah in the mid-sixth century BC. For this 'Deuteronomist' the history of Judah as a nation had come to a dead-end, and he wrote principally in vindication of Yahweh's final repudiation of his people. Noth's basic theory, with its rejection of the older view of books individually redacted by the Deuteronomic school, has been enthusiastically received, though his views on such key issues as date, purpose, and provenance have not commanded the same measure of agreement. In general, whereas continental scholars have continued to regard the 'Deuteronomistic History' as essentially an exilic compilation, there is a countervailing tendency in North America to see it as fundamentally a pre-exilic document from the time of Josiah – 'a propaganda work of the Josianic reformation and imperial program', according to the Harvard scholar F. M. Cross.[8] Most would concede, moreover, that at one level or another of the 'Deuteronomistic History' the future of Judah is regarded as at least open-ended: Yahweh has not necessarily cast off his people for ever.[9]

As compared with the other books making up the 'Former Prophets', 1 and 2 Samuel show signs of relatively light Deuteronomistic editing. Some of the more easily recognized 'Deuteronomisms' come in the prophetic speeches in 1 Samuel 7 and 12, and 2 Samuel 7. In the passages from 1 Samuel, for example, the need for, and efficacy of, repentance is stressed in a way which, while not exclusive to the Deuteronomistic school, is suggestive of its influence (1 Sa. 7:3; 12:19–24).[10] This comparative sparseness of Deuteronomistic editorial material may be attributable in part to the circumstance that, in the compilation of Samuel, a number of already-formed narrative blocks were laid end to end – just as was proposed for the Pentateuch a few years ago by the German scholar R. Rendtorff.[11] There are three principal candidates here: the 'Ark Narrative' (1 Sa. 4–6, but also including 2 Sa. 6 according to some), the 'History of David's Rise' (1 Sa. 16:14–2 Sa. 5:10), and the 'Succession Narrative' (2 Sa. 9–20 plus 1 Ki. 1–2, with a small amount of material from earlier in 2 Samuel). The precise demarcation of these narratives from the material surrounding them is a matter of some delicacy, as will become apparent in the next section. Whether it is legitimate at all to treat the last two named as if they originally enjoyed independent status is, in the present writer's opinion, a debatable issue.

The books of Samuel cover the period from the last days of the temple at Shiloh until near the end of David's reign, that is, very approximately, from 1050 to 970 BC. Our main uncertainties relate to the duration of the twilight period at Shiloh represented in 1 Samuel 1–4, and to the length of Saul's reign (cf. on 1 Sa. 13:1). The destruction of Shiloh at some point around 1050 BC was until recently a fairly fixed point in discussions of the period. However, despite the doubts that have been raised, there is still good reason to think that a destruction did occur about this time, and that it is to this that Jeremiah is referring in his famous Shiloh sermons (Je. 7:12; 26:6, 9; *cf.* Ps. 78:60).[12]

Of the changes that overtake Israel between 1 Samuel 1 and 2 Samuel 24 two are especially significant. The first is the eclipse of Shiloh and the eventual transfer of its cultic primacy to Jerusalem, and the second is the conversion of Israel from a tribal league to a unified kingdom capable of exercising imperial power over neighbouring states. These are the tectonic shifts which determine the contours of Judah in particular for the next four centuries.

2 SURVEY

It will now be convenient to highlight some of the main features of 1 and 2 Samuel, observing the same divisions of the text as in the Commentary.

The Shiloh traditions (1 Sa. 1:1–4:1a)

Two major themes are interwoven in this section: the decline of the Shilonite priesthood and the rise to prominence of the prophet Samuel. Of the oral or literary prehistory of the traditions little can be said with any confidence. While it is possible to disengage elements highlighting Eli and his sons from those focused on Hannah and Samuel, this hardly justifies the proposition that they come from distinct, and possibly even unrelated, sources.[13] The contrastive, chiaroscuro portrayal of Samuel and the sons of Eli in chapters 2–3, with alternating sections on the respective parties (Samuel: 2:11, 18–21, 26; 3:1–10, 19–4:1a; Eli's sons: 2:12–17, 22–25, 27–36; 3:11–18), may as easily be the result of a deliberate narrative technique which, whatever the circumstances of composition, has been most successfully applied.

The description of conditions at Shiloh given in chs. 1–2 serves an important purpose in explaining why this old cult centre and repository of the ark of God was set aside, its role and status later to be conferred on 'David's City'. The problem was the corrupt state of the Shilonite priesthood. Eli the chief priest was past his prime, and his two sons, both in holy orders, were scoundrels. It is remarkable, then, that the immediate answer to this situation comes very much in response to a human initiative, for Hannah the mother of Samuel received no angelic visitant or annunciatory oracle. (Eli's blessing, after he had mistaken the suppliant for an inebriate, was not quite in the oracular class, 1:17.) It is this initiative which is commemorated in the name of the son who was born to Hannah. At several points in chs. 1–2 the name Samuel is linked with the Hebrew verb šā'al, meaning 'to ask' (1:20, 27, 28; 2:20). This, we must observe, is in the way of popular etymology, and an exact correspondence between the name and the assumed root is therefore not required.[14] (One of the best examples in this regard is Babel in Gn. 11:9.) The view that, because of the closer connection between šā'al and the name of Saul (meaning 'asked for'), Samuel's birth narrative must be an adaptation of a tradition originally belonging to the Saul cycle fails to do justice to this simple and obvious point.

Two important components of ch. 2 as yet unmentioned are 'Hannah's Song' (vv. 1–10) and the oracle of the man of God (vv. 27–36). Whether or not the former should be classified as a 'royal psalm' will depend very much on the status of verse 10b ('he will give strength to his king, and exalt the horn of his anointed'). A psalm composed in the pre-monarchical period would be unlikely to speak of Yahweh's anointed king, especially since such brushes as Israel had already had with monarchy, within its borders or elsewhere, can hardly be described as inspirational.[15] If, as a few scholars have argued, the psalm derives ultimately from Israel's pre-monarchical holy war tradition, then verse 10b is best regarded as a supplement extending the range of the poem to take account of the advent of the monarchy.[16] (For a good example of this kind of supplementation of a psalm see Ps. 51:18f.)

The introduction of the 'man of God' in verses 27–36 is sometimes regarded as a Deuteronomistic device to permit a statement about the rejection and supersession of the Elide priesthood. However, device or otherwise, there is not very much in these verses – with the possible exception of verse 35 – that could be labelled as distinctively 'Deuteronomistic'.[17] As to the several references in the oracle to developments beyond the immediate horizon, verse 35, in talking of a 'faithful priest', envisages the passing of the priestly succession to Zadok and his house (cf. 1 Ki. 2:35); the Davidic monarchy would be served by the Zadokite priesthood for as long as they both lived. There are also allusions to the deposition of Abiathar, a descendant of Eli (v. 33; cf. 1 Ki. 2:26f.), and, according to some, to the plight of the rural priests who were deprived of their livings by Josiah's centralization policy (v. 36; cf. 2 Ki. 23:8).

The story of Samuel's call in ch. 3 may profitably be compared with the call narratives of various other Old Testament prophets,[18] though a recent study, in attempting – with the aid of near eastern parallels – to relocate Samuel's experience in the area of dream theophany, points out the limitations of such comparisons.[19] At any rate, Samuel receives a call and therewith the authority to speak for Yahweh. And, like some others of the prophetic fraternity, he cuts his teeth on a message laden with warning and judgement. Thus, while ch. 3 begins with a note to the effect that oracle and vision were rare during the last days of Shiloh, it ends with a lofty tribute to a prophet of almost Mosaic proportions with whom Yahweh is pleased to communicate on a regular basis (3:19–4:1a).

The 'Ark Narrative' (1 Sa. 4:1b–7:1)

In 1 Samuel 4–6 everything – even the tragedies that afflict Eli and his family – is subservient to the theme of the ark of God. There are three distinct phases in the story: the loss of the ark in a battle with the Philistines (ch. 4), its pell-mell tour of Philistia (ch. 5), and its return after seven months to the Israelite homeland (ch. 6). It is this single-mindedness as much as anything which warrants the narrative's recognition as an originally independent account of the fortunes of the ark during one particularly troubled period in the early history of Israel.[20] Leonhard Rost's appeal to the distinctive vocabulary of the 'Ark Narrative' as a proof of its independent status has, however, failed to carry weight for the simple reason that the nature of the subject-matter must be taken into account in such evaluations.[21] Perhaps a more significant factor is the total absence of Samuel from these three chapters. Despite the fact that he dominates the scene at the end of ch. 3, no more is heard of him until ch. 7. A reasonable explanation would be that chs. 4–6 form at least the nucleus of a tradition about the ark which once enjoyed a separate literary existence.

Rost also included 2 Samuel 6, which relates how David conveyed the ark from Kiriath-jearim to a specially-prepared tent in Jerusalem, in his 'Ark Narrative'. This has proved a more controversial point, with only Campbell of the fairly recent monographers on the subject agreeing with Rost.[22] The argument from vocabulary is especially weak here since only three or four of Rost's 'characteristic words' are common to 1 Samuel 4–6 and 2 Samuel 6. One particular obstacle to the inclusion of 2 Samuel 6 is the change in names that occurs between 1 Samuel 7:1 and 2 Samuel 6:2–4, i.e. between more or less consecutive verses in the putative ark source. If Baale-judah in 2 Samuel 6:2 is taken as an alternative name for Kiriath-jearim, as it almost certainly should be (cf. Jos. 15:9), this variation within such a short space in a single source would be difficult to explain. There is not necessarily a problem with the names of the custodians of the ark in 2 Samuel 6:3f., as compared with 1 Samuel 7:1, nevertheless Campbell's attempt to explain Ahio in the later passage as a common noun meaning 'his (i.e. Uzzah's) brother' seems very strained.

For Rost the 'Ark Narrative' was composed by a member of the priesthood in the tenth century, in the reign of either David or Solomon, and was intended to outline the previous history of the ark for the benefit of festival pilgrims visiting Jerusalem, where the ark had by then been installed. Campbell accepts the tenth-century dating, but sees the narrative as principally a statement about Yahweh's activity in the recent history of Israel. Yahweh was responsible for the defeat at Ebenezer and for the loss of the ark, and he it was who had made possible the new era which had dawned in Jerusalem.[23]

Miller and Roberts also argue for an early dating, between the defeat at Ebenezer and the installation of the ark in Jerusalem, on the ground that there would have been no point in dwelling on the earlier misfortune once David had started on his conquering way.[24] Later events will have played a part in the shaping of the narrative, but in essence it dates from the era of Saul and David. Miller and Roberts, however, disagree with their predecessors over the starting-point of the 'Ark Narrative', regarding 4:1b as doubly unsatisfactory since Eli and his sons suddenly appear in the story without any word of introduction, and, more problematical still, the standard 'Ark Narrative' describes the débâcle at Ebenezer without giving any clue as to why this judgement was visited upon Israel. Their solution is to annex to the narrative those passages in ch. 2 which are critical of Eli and his family (vv. 12–17, 22–25, 27–36). Neither of these problems, we may note, was likely to vex F. Schicklberger, for whom ch. 4 is basically an old 'catastrophe-account' and chs. 5–6 the real 'Ark Narrative'. The 'catastrophe-account' began life in the northern kingdom, but was brought south after the fall of Samaria in 722/1 BC. Chs. 5–6, with which it was subsequently joined, were composed in the reign of Hezekiah, in the late eighth or early seventh century.[25]

On the theological level the 'Ark Narrative' is making resounding assertions about the power and invincibility of the God of Israel, and about the futility of idol worship. In respect of this latter it bears comparison with the great passages on idolatry in Isaiah 40–46, in which also the element of derision is prominent (with 1 Sa. 5:1–5 compare Is. 40:18–20; 41:7; 44:9–20; 46:1–7).[26] Yahweh's people did indeed suffer defeat twice at the hands of the Philistines,

but that did not mean that Yahweh was inferior to the gods of
Philistia. On the contrary, when the Philistines, acting in accordance with the ancient custom of depositing captured enemy idols
in the temple of one's own god, introduced the ark – for Israel had
no image of Yahweh – into the temple of Dagon, it was greatly to
the embarrassment of the supposedly victorious deity.[27]
Thereafter the ordinary citizens of Philistia felt the weight of
Yahweh's hand upon them as he inflicted plagues on the various
centres to which they brought the ark. It is like the plaguing of
Egypt all over again, and there are direct references to the exodus
story lest we miss the comparison (*cf.* 4:8; 6:6).[28] Yahweh's power
has not diminished, even though the events at Ebenezer seemed to
prove the contrary.

Schicklberger, in an exercise in transposition, reads the 'Ark
Narrative' as a tract written to combat the tide of Assyrian religious
beliefs and practices that had swept into the northern kingdom of
Israel in the late eighth century, as a consequence of the Assyrian
imperial advance. He sees the narrative as specially directed against
the cult of the Mesopotamian plague-god Nergal which was rapidly
winning adherents in the north. The message conveyed in the story
is, on this view, that Yahweh is still associated with the ark, and
that he can, if he chooses, 'out-plague' the pagan plague-gods. This
is, to be sure, a lesson that can be learned from the account, for it
has a certain timelessness about it – and H. Timm, for example,
has pointed out its teaching potential for the generation of the
(Babylonian) exile[29] – nevertheless, the actual historical circumstances reflected in the narrative must be sought three centuries
earlier.

The institution of the monarchy (1 Sa. 7:2–12:25)

Monarchy was a late arrival on the Israelite scene. Even the widely-
accepted 'low chronology' for the exodus and settlement leaves a
hiatus of two centuries before the rise of Saul, Israel's first king.
It was, moreover, a highly controversial development which failed
to win unanimous approval at the start or, it would seem, subsequently. As it happens, 1 Samuel 7–12, which describes the
circumstances in which the monarchy was born, has itself been the
subject of much scholarly debate in the past hundred years. The
basic problem, as it has been conceived, is that the emergence of
Saul as king is associated with several different episodes (or stages),
any one of which would almost suffice for the purpose. At the
same time, the view has persisted that the several narratives are

less than univocal in their estimation of the monarchy and may, indeed, be grouped according as they are pro- or anti-monarchical. The name most conspicuously linked with this approach is that of Julius Wellhausen, who divided 1 Samuel 7–12 into early (9:1–10:16; 11:1–11, 15) and late (7:2–8:22; 10:17–27; 12:1–25) sources, respectively favourable and unfavourable in their attitude to the monarchy.[30] (According to Wellhausen, the 'late' source represented the Deuteronomistic point of view; so negative an attitude towards monarchy would have been inconceivable while the Davidic house still ruled, Wellhausen reckoned, so it must have been the product of the exilic or post-exilic era.) Since the course of the subsequent study of these chapters has been adequately chronicled by a number of scholars,[31] only selective comment is required here.

In an effort to break free from the dominant source-critical theory, a few scholars – notably A. Weiser[32] and H. W. Hertzberg[33] – have argued that the several sections comprised in chs. 7–12 originated at a number of different centres (for example, 8:1–22 at Ramah, 10:17–27 at Mizpah), and were later brought together to form a sequential account in spite of their independent origins. Weiser also differed from Wellhausen and his followers in one other important respect, namely that he regarded the anti-monarchical sentiments in chs. 8, 10 and 12 as belonging to an early, rather than late, stage in the tradition. It may be noted here that the more recent studies by Tomoo Ishida and Frank Crüsemann tend towards a similar conclusion. Ishida observes that immediate opposition to such an innovation as the monarchy was only to be expected,[34] while Crüsemann notes the signs of disaffection towards the central government already in the reigns of David and Solomon.[35] It is hard to disagree with them on this point. Nor does the assumption of editorial (Deuteronomistic?) disapproval of the monarchy require that the disapproval be confined to the later period, for the simple reason that the editor may still be giving a fair representation of the events which he purports to describe.

In point of fact, the question of the stance of 1 Samuel 7–12 *vis-à-vis* the monarchy has generated a considerable amount of discussion in more recent times.[36] Are those sections which Wellhausen attributed to his anti-monarchical source really as critical of the institution as they appear at first sight? Weiser also had something to say on this matter: he contended that the anti-monarchical sections do not oppose monarchy outright, but are set against monarchy 'like all the nations' – even though, as we may note, the phrase 'like all the nations' is used quite neutrally

in the 'Law of the King' (Dt. 17:14). This same question also
exercised H. J. Boecker in his 1969 monograph, in which he sought
to reconcile the supposedly conflicting views of the monarchy in
1 Samuel 7–12 with Noth's hypothesis of a unified Deuteronomistic
History.[37] Boecker's solution was to argue that the anti-monarchical passages are not absolutely opposed to monarchy but do
repudiate forms of kingship which would encroach upon the established sovereignty of Yahweh over his people. In his view the
Deuteronomist even manages to put a brave face on it when he
portrays the monarchy as, despite its unpromising beginnings, a
gracious provision of Yahweh which Israel must be careful not to
forfeit. There is also some toning down of the anti-monarchical
strictures in B. C. Birch's study of 1 Samuel 7–15, in which Birch
posits a pre-Deuteronomistic (prophetic) editor responsible for
most of the work of compilation in 1 Samuel 7–12(15).[38] It was
because the Deuteronomist was not wholly antagonistic to the idea
of monarchy, says Birch, that he was able to include much of the
work of his prophetic precursor with minimal alteration. However,
such attempts at diluting the anti-monarchical content of the likes
of chs. 8 and 12 are unconvincing and are still too dependent
on the two-source theory in the way that they assume a pro-
monarchical – and that almost in a partisan sense – outlook for
the remaining sections, *viz.* 9:1–10:16 and 11:1–15. This is a much
too strong characterization of these last-named, and it serves only
to subsidize a false antithesis. It is noteworthy in this regard that
Baruch Halpern, who introduces his own version of the two-source
theory, nevertheless excludes from his criteria of identification the
supposedly contrasting views of the sources on the issue of the
monarchy.[39] And, whatever else may be said about the historical
reconstruction of the underlying events or process (see below), it
is clear that the dismantling and reassembling of the various
components making up 1 Samuel 7–12 will always tend to create
problems because there is implicit in the exercise a disregard for
that interdependence of plot and narration which is such an obvious
characteristic of these chapters. Thus the hiding of Saul at Mizpah
(10:20–24) is still best explained – despite our ignorance of the
details of the lot-casting procedure – on the basis of his prior
knowledge of his nomination as ruler, as recounted in 9:1–10:16.
It is, moreover, the recognition of such interdependence which
accounts for Halpern's association of 10:17–27 with 11:1–15 in his
'source B'.[40]

The one question which we have not so far considered is the
relationship of our various sections to the historical circumstances

in which Saul actually came to the throne. It has long been the
tendency to give 11:1–15 a special status as the account which most
nearly approaches the events which led to Saul's enthronement,
and this even though such a section as 9:1–10:16 may be regarded
as 'early', and perhaps even dating from Saul's own lifetime
(Ishida). So for the canonical account of a process whereby Saul
became accepted as king there is substituted the idea of Saul's
irruption into public life when Israel, or a part thereof, suddenly
found itself endangered by a Transjordanian neighbour and, the
crisis past, gratefully institutionalized the hero of the hour as the
nation's first king. Now, while the attraction of this reconstruction
is the old familiar of historical probability (as we may now imagine
it), this longstanding consensus seems ripe for at least a gentle
shaking. Study of the offices of judge and king in Israel (and, to a
limited extent, outside) shows that accession to kingship (in particular) commonly involved a *process* of (at least) designation and
confirmation following upon victory either actual or symbolic. So
Halpern concludes with reference to Saul:

> Like the savior-judge, the king-elect was designated by Yhwh.
> Like the savior-judge, he proved his 'charisma' by defeating
> a foe. And, like the savior-judge as Israel's tradition recalled
> him, he assumed power thereafter permanently. The narratives
> of Saul's rise represent historiographic implementations of
> the pattern for a leader's accession. One presumes, however,
> that as Israel's first king, Saul needed historically to conform
> to the same pattern.[41]

Halpern, it is true, finds evidence for this two-tier accession process
in both his 'A' and 'B' accounts of Saul's rise, which leaves us
some distance from a straightforward matching of the narrative
sequence in 1 Samuel 7(8)–12 with the actual events surrounding
Saul's emergence as king. Nevertheless, it is evident that a fresh
evaluation of these chapters is under way, and that the result could
be a more positive regard for the historical worth of some at least
of the material in chs. 8–10, 12. Even so, as Diana Edelman's study
of 1 Samuel 11 shows,[42] the recognition of an accession process in
and out of 1 Samuel 7(8)–12 will not inevitably lead to a more
favourable estimation of these chapters as history-writing. Even
ch. 11 suffers loss of reputation at Edelman's hand: in her view it
is based on archival data, but has been dislodged from its original
context and reworked so as to portray Saul in the manner of the
old judges who, in times of crisis, emerged from relative obscurity

and, in the power of the spirit of Yahweh, rescued their fellow-countrymen from foreign oppression. What is not in question even here, it seems, is the compatibility of 1 Samuel 7(8)–12 with kingship ideology, or with the institutional forms with which the ideology clothed itself, in early Israel. But *how* early is this Israel of which we are speaking? Edelman's suggestion of an accession pattern retrospectively imposed on the tradition appears to assume that the ideology is characteristic of a later phase of Israelite history, whereas Halpern claims to have produced evidence of both ideology and institutional form for the earliest days of the monarchy. If his position can be maintained – as we believe it can – then it is hard to avoid the conclusion that the historical reconstruction which has for long influenced the reading of these chapters is itself the product of an alien ideology.

A brief survey of the several sections making up this montage on the monarchy will highlight some of the more important features of each.

1 Samuel 7:2–17

In outline, the chapter tells how, after a period of national apostasy, the Israelites were challenged by Samuel to 'return to the Lord' and, having done so, experienced a signal victory over the Philistines. The end of the chapter sounds the all-clear: there is peace with the Philistines abroad and with the Amorites at home. Some degree of Deuteronomistic editing of the narrative is usually assumed, though without necessarily treating it as Deuteronomistic through and through, as did Noth. The idea of a basic holy war (or 'Yahweh war') or prophetic tradition subsequently augmented has also been canvassed in several recent discussions of the subject.[43] What can be said with some authority is that the attitude towards the monarchy which is indicated in the chapter is very much in line with the editorial viewpoint expressed in chs. 8–12; for it is an undoubted function of this account of 'Samuel's victory' to show that Israel without a king is perfectly capable of dealing with its enemies. The main point of the elders' demand in the next chapter, that without a king they cannot compete with other nations (8:5, 19f.), is therefore answered before it is raised. 'Hitherto the Lord has helped us!' (7:12).

1 Samuel 8:1–22

Samuel's advanced years and his sons' failure to follow his example in their exercise of public office provide the pretext for the Israelite elders' demand that a king be appointed. Later the question of national security is brought into the discussion (vv. 19f.). Samuel is wholeheartedly opposed to the demand. And so, we may judge, is the author of the passage, for not even his reference to the malpractices of Joel and Abijah can be construed as a gesture of tolerance towards the monarchist position.[44]

The main feature of the chapter is, however, Samuel's unflattering sketch of a typical Israelite king in verses 11–18. Since the Deuteronomistic strictures on kings normally relate to religio-cultic shortcomings, their influence on this passage, which fastens on the social abuses of monarchy, would appear to be minimal. A popular view of Samuel's word-portrait is that it is based on actual experience of the workings of the monarchy in Israel, while for some the finger seems to point specifically at Solomon, under whom some of the less acceptable features of the monarchy first appear (*cf.* 1 Ki. 5:13–16; 11:28).[45] This approach was queried by I. Mendelsohn in a short study comparing what is said in 1 Samuel 8:11–18 with the picture of Canaanite kingship which can be constructed from certain Akkadian texts found on the site of second-millennium Ugarit (mod. Ras Shamra).[46] Mendelsohn's conclusion was that Samuel's sketch of kingly ways could as easily derive from the prophet's own knowledge of the Canaanite city-states which were Israel's neighbours in the late second millennium BC. Mendelsohn's views are often quoted for their interest value, but they have not been as influential as they might have been expected to be. The truth of the matter is that on purely internal criteria it is difficult to date the passage to any particular reign or period with much conviction. This applies as much to attempts to link it with Solomon's reign as to any other, since some of the most characteristic features of his administration are noticeably absent from Samuel's portrait.

1 Samuel 9:1–10:16

When Saul goes in search of his father's lost asses he unexpectedly, but providentially, comes into contact with the prophet Samuel who anoints him privately as king of Israel. Signs of the kingly charisma follow and Saul returns home, but he fails to mention 'the matter of the kingdom' to his uncle (10:16). There is no

debating of the rights and wrongs of the monarchy here; the
decision has been taken (8:22) and the process has been set in
motion. The only possible hint of reservation in the section is its
apparent reluctance to use the normal words for 'king' and 'rule'.
Instead of *melek* ('king') the preferred term is the elusive *nāḡîḏ*,
which is usually translated 'prince' or 'leader' (*cf.* 9:16).[47] Then in
9:17 where we should expect the verb *mālak* ('rule, reign') the
actual choice is *ᶜāṣar* ('restrain' (?)), which occurs nowhere else
with the required sense. So it may be that the passage, at the same
time as it acknowledges the fact of Saul's vocation, seeks to define
it in a way that is compatible with Yahweh's continued exercise of
sovereignty over his people.

The prevailing tendency is to class 1 Samuel 9:1–10:16 as folk
narrative rather than as historical writing, especially as this relates
to the basic theme of providential leading towards a moment of
high destiny. Birch associates the editing of the narrative with
prophetic circles among which it was considered desirable that
Saul's appointment as king should be seen as under prophetic
auspices.[48] As we have noted, Ishida – for whom also the classific-
ation 'folk tale' is valid – argues that the ultimate origin of the
narrative is to be found in Saul's own lifetime: the story took shape
after his rise to power, and has a function equivalent to that of the
birth legends associated with other important historical figures.[49]
Many scholars have difficulty, moreover, in relating the unnamed
seer of the early verses of ch. 9 with the great prophet Samuel,
who is first mentioned by name in verse 14. The usual solution to
this problem is to posit two originally separate traditions, one
describing Saul's visit to a local seer and the other telling of an
interview with Samuel. The view taken in this commentary is that
this 'tension' is a function of the narrator's technique, and that the
anonymity of the seer, like Saul's apparent ignorance of his very
existence, is the narrator's way of dramatizing the young man's
ignorance of the destiny which is shortly to be revealed to him. In
this connection we speak of 'metonymy' (though the term has other
literary significances which are not envisaged here). Something
similar is described by R. Polzin in relation to the angelic appearance to Manoah's wife in Judges 13:

> The situation in which the woman, ignorant of her interlocu-
> tor's identity, was kept ignorant of Samson's future, is related
> to the basic paradox according to which this story is to be
> interpreted. As it progresses, we shall see that Samson himself
> appears to remain ignorant of his delivering role, in spite of

the fact that his mother must have told him at least about the prohibition of the razor.[50]

1 Samuel 10:17–27

In this short report of a national assembly at Mizpah the divine lot falls upon the retiring figure of Saul and he is acclaimed king by most of those present. The section, which is often taken as a narrative continuation of the anti-monarchical ch. 8, actually combines features from the *two* sections immediately preceding. Strong criticism of the people's insistence on having a monarchy (vv. 17–19) is offset by a generous appraisal of Saul himself (vv. 23–27). He is even described as Yahweh's choice as king in verse 24 (contrast 8:18 'whom you have chosen for yourselves'). At the same time, the very act of choosing by lot – more associated with criminal proceedings than with election to public office (*cf.* Jos. 7:16–26; 1 Sa. 14:38–45) – and the emphasis on Saul's physical appearance, as if that were the criterion for kingship, can be read as intimations of trouble ahead. The physical attributes applauded in both 9:2 and 10:23f. will be dismissed as false clues when Saul's successor is being chosen (1 Sa. 16:7).

The proceedings at Mizpah conclude with Samuel's writing up of 'the rights and duties of the kingship' (*mišpaṭ hammᵉlukâ*) in a book which he deposits 'before the Lord' (v. 25). How this book relates to the law-book of Deuteronomy 17:18–20, if at all, is not easy to judge. Any relationship to the 'ways of the king' (*mišpaṭ hammelek*) as described in 8:11–18 can, on the other hand, be ruled out. Z. Ben-Barak finds in this same verse 25 the evidence for a tribal covenant between king and people which was 'the ancient source and prototype of the Israelite monarchic covenants down the generations'. Unfortunately, and despite the air of importance which it exudes, the verse retains a certain degree of mystery and does not permit such a specific inference.[51]

1 Samuel 11:1–15

As far as historical verisimilitude is concerned, this section is the most highly regarded of the three which deal with Saul's elevation to the throne (9:1–10:16; 10:17–27; 11:1–15).[52] When the crisis arises in Transjordan Saul is possessed by the divine spirit and rallies his fellow-Israelites by giving clear indication of what will happen if they fail to appear. But it is not obvious from the passage that the beleaguered Jabesh-gileadites made their appeal directly to Saul, hence the common assertion that ch. 11 does not presuppose the developments described in the two previous sections. There are a couple of reasons for treading cautiously here. First, it is not certainly the case that the Jabesh-gileadite messengers came to Gibeah in the course of a desperate trek through the cities of Israel. Secondly, and more importantly, there is the danger that we may read into the narrative our preconceived ideas as to how Saul must have become king: if the judge-deliverers were propelled into prominence only when a crisis arose, then Saul must conform to the pattern, and any hint of a constitutional process must have been superimposed at a later date. The method of reasoning has only to be stated for its inadequacy to become obvious. Another casualty of this approach is verse 14 – actually verses 12–14 – because of its talk of 'renewal' of the kingdom. And yet in his recent volume Halpern can discuss the renewal of the kingdom as not only a feature of Saul's reign but also of the early monarchic era in general.[53] As noted above, he sees accession as a two-staged affair. First the individual was commissioned by Yahweh to defend the Israelite assembly. 'The appointee, the *nāgîd*, then sallied forth in Yhwh's company, to wreak salvation for his new constituency. After the victory, the celebration of the kingship occurred. The monarchy was "renewed," or confirmed, more permanently.'[54]

1 Samuel 12:1–25

The chapter consists mainly of oration by Samuel and voices the same opposition to the introduction of the monarchy as was heard in ch. 8. Noth reckoned that the whole chapter was specially composed by the Deuteronomist to mark the transition from the judges period to the monarchical era.[55] At any rate, a substantial Deuteronomistic presence in the chapter is generally conceded. The speeches look both forward and back. It is urged that Yahweh's deliverances of his people in the past were their sufficient guarantee of future safety without the expedient of monarchy. But the new reality is faced and an undertaking is given on Yahweh's behalf that, provided the nation does not transgress again, both king and people will be spared. The importance of this undertaking is that the monarchy as the intrusive element in the longstanding relationship between Yahweh and Israel is integrated into that relationship to form part of a new covenantal triad consisting of Yahweh, king, and people.[56]

The section on the monarchy therefore ends as it began, with an assertion of Yahweh's power to protect Israel (12:7–11; *cf.* 7:9–

11) and a condemnation of the alternative which the people of Israel are embracing to themselves (12:12–25; cf. 8:4–22). Even though there is the hope that the relationship between Yahweh and his people will survive the constitutional change which they have sought and won, the request for the new institution is still referred to as 'wickedness', 'this evil', and 'all this evil' (vv. 17, 19f.). In origin, therefore, Israelite kingship is 'of the earth, earthy'. It does not descend from heaven mysterious and fully-formed as in the Mesopotamian version of the origins of kingship.[57] Not even 9:1–10:16, which describes the working of the hidden hand of Yahweh, begins to approach such a conception of the monarchy.

The reign of Saul (13:1–15:35)

Although Saul is king throughout the remainder of 1 Samuel, the account of his reign is, in a sense, confined to this quite short section of three chapters. Ch. 13 begins with a regnal formula of the type used to introduce reigns in 1 and 2 Kings, while, in the absence of a formal marker at the end of ch. 15, there is the distinct impression given that Saul's reign is at an end, that he has in fact 'died'. This is very clearly conveyed by the statement that Samuel 'mourned' for Saul (15:35), and also by a number of other hints in the text. The announcement in 15:28 that Yahweh has torn the kingdom from Saul 'this day' means in this context that his reign is as good as finished. A similar impression is created by the statement, in verse 35, that Samuel never again saw Saul. This is in obvious tension with 19:18–24 and is presumably intended to indicate that all meaningful contact between the two ceased thereafter. Finally, to underline the fact of Saul's 'death', Samuel is commissioned in 16:1 to go to Bethlehem and anoint a new king over Israel. Thereafter David is king-in-waiting, no matter how much Saul dislikes and tries to alter that fact.

 Chs. 13–14 form a single extended narrative dealing with the situation before the battle of Michmash as well as the engagement itself. In view of what many regard as evidence of an underlying sympathy towards Saul in the narrative its basic factuality is not so often called in question. An exception in this regard, nevertheless, is the section 13:7b–15a, in which the prophet Samuel denounces the king for his disregard of a previous instruction (cf. 10:8) and announces Yahweh's rejection of his house. Because these verses appear to be easily detachable from their surroundings and, furthermore, evince a particular interest in the authority of the prophetic word and the necessity for obedience to it, they are often attributed

to a separate – prophetic – source. Their connection with 10:8,
which is undeniable, is also often thought to show them up as
intrusive in their present position. Against this, however, it must
be noted that the whole of 13:3–15a stands in a thematic relationship with 10:1–8, so that the separation of 13:7b–15a from what
immediately precedes is not quite the clean-cut operation that it is
usually thought to be.[58]

If the sources underlying the remainder of chs. 13–14 were
favourably disposed towards Saul, the same cannot be said of the
tradition as it has come down to us. This is especially true of ch.
14, which on the face of it is describing how Saul discharged his
responsibility to expel the Philistines from the land of Israel. Here
the contrast between Jonathan's contribution (vv. 1–15) and the
effect of Saul's intervention (vv. 16–46) is very striking. When
Jonathan and his armour-bearer have done their work there are
twenty Philistine corpses and a panic-stricken camp to show for
it. But as soon as Saul joins in the fray complications set in. He
rashly imposes an oath of abstinence on his men 'until it is evening
and I am avenged on my enemies' (v. 24). The debilitating effect
of this on his warriors and the resultant curtailing of the follow-
up operation are noted in verse 30. A further consequence was
that when the people were at last free to eat they 'sinned' (cf. v. 33)
by devouring the flesh of the captured livestock without draining off
the blood. Saul's *first* altar (v. 35) therefore had to be built in order
to rectify a situation for which he was indirectly responsible. Worst
of all, it transpired that Jonathan, the hero of the day, had fallen
foul of his father's oath and was in danger of forfeiting his life.
He was saved, not by his father but by his fellow-soldiers for whom
the events of the day were a sufficient proof of his good standing
with Yahweh. To say the least, this is a not wholly creditable
performance by Saul.

There are also subtler ways in which Saul is shown to his
disadvantage in the report of the Michmash victory. When, for
example, Jonathan accuses his father of 'troubling the land' with
his ill-judged oath (v. 29), he anticipates the action of verses 40–
42 where Saul starts proceedings to discover who is responsible for
Yahweh's refusal to respond to an oracular inquiry. Saul is thus
judged as the real 'troubler' in the story before ever the problem
with Jonathan comes to a head. On this and a similar kind of
ironical twist in verse 24 see the commentary. It would seem that,
in ch. 14, it is only in the archival summary of verses 47–51 that
Saul is censure-free.

In ch. 15 the issue of obedience as it relates to Saul's tenure of the throne is brought right to the fore. The key word 'obey', for example, occurs five times in verses 19–24 and the whole of the narrative is constructed around this theme. There is nothing in the chapter that can be construed positively of Saul. The objection to him as king is as strong here as is the opposition to the whole idea of monarchy in the overtly anti-monarchical passages in chs. 7–12, which partly explains why ch. 15 is sometimes attributed to the same ('anti-monarchical') source as 8:1–22, 10:17–27 (?), and 12:1–25. (Other factors such as the echoing of the rejection idea of 8:7 in 15:26 are also relevant in this connection.)

Not only is the question of Saul's obedience aired more fully than in 13:7b–15a, the judgement pronounced on him is, as we saw above, more final. The 'neighbour' with whom he is compared unfavourably in verse 28 is, of course, David, and the way is now open for Samuel, as early Israel's king-maker, to anoint a successor (cf. 16:1ff.).[59]

The 'History of David's Rise'

In the previous section we noted that Saul, though king, is not the centre of attention in 1 Samuel 16–31. That honour goes to David, and Saul features to the extent that his path crosses that of David. The one significant exception is the description of Saul's visit to the medium of Endor in ch. 28. But even this episode contributes to the overall theme of David's advance under the aegis of Yahweh, by showing how unfit Saul was to rule. As the Chronicler puts it, 'he was unfaithful to the Lord in that he did not keep the command of the Lord, and also consulted a medium, seeking guidance, and did not seek guidance from the Lord' (1 Ch. 10:13f.).

This centrality of David in the story is recognized in the title 'History of David's Rise' which is sometimes given to a large narrative block with approximate boundaries of 1 Samuel 16 and 2 Samuel 5.[60] In these chapters David's early career is traced from the day that Samuel anointed him in Bethlehem to his installation in Jerusalem as king over all Israel. As to whether such a document as the 'History of David's Rise' ever existed independently of its present setting it is impossible to be sure. It certainly must remain an embarrassment to the theory that the boundary limits of the narrative are so fluid in scholarly discussion. As starting-points, 1 Samuel 15:1, 16:1, and 16:14 are all serious contenders,[61] while at the far end the situation is even more confused because those who prefer to take the narrative beyond 2 Samuel 5:10 do not necessarily have a clear idea as to how much of chs. 6 and 7 should be included. If a narrative has a distinct literary and thematic integrity of its own, then we should not expect that distinctiveness to wear so thin near the edges. And if one writer can advance good reasons for including 2 Samuel 2–4 in the 'Succession Narrative', whither the 'History of David's Rise'?[62]

We shall do well, then, if we dispense with literary-critical discussion and concentrate on theme in 1 Samuel 16 – 2 Samuel 5. At the outset it must be said that these chapters have much more than the recording of traditions about the younger David as their aim. 'Apologetic' is the appropriate term for what is going on, and if the independent origin of the 'History of David's Rise' could be established on thematic grounds, this is its best hope. The reality behind 'David's Rise' is that David, and not a member of Saul's family, became Israel's second king. For some of Saul's supporters, especially among his fellow-tribesmen in Benjamin, this was unforgivable usurpation by David. It did not help, either, that leading members of Saul's family died in violent circumstances which seemed to implicate David as being the obvious beneficiary. This is, apparently, what inspired Shimei's venomous outburst against David as he fled Jerusalem early in the Absalom rebellion: 'Begone, begone, you man of blood, you worthless fellow! The Lord has avenged upon you all the blood of the house of Saul, in whose place you have reigned' (2 Sa. 16:7f.).

'David's Rise' is therefore in the business of defending David against charges destructive of his credibility and potentially subversive of his throne. This may have implications for the dating of the narrative, independent source or not, since the point of producing an 'apology' may as likely be to defend a reigning monarch against criticism as to rehabilitate the memory of one already deceased. Such is the case with the thirteenth century Hittite 'Apology of Ḥattushilish', the purpose of which was to legitimize Ḥattushilish's rule in the face of the fact that he had usurped his predecessor.[63] Ḥattushilish attributes his rise to power to divine favour, just as our narrative stresses at several points that David owed his success to the fact that 'the Lord was with him' (cf. 1 Sa. 16:18; 18:14; 2 Sa. 5:10).

There are specific charges against which the author of these chapters was concerned to defend David. The first was that David was in some way responsible for Saul's defeat (and death) at Gilboa, while the second and third relate to the deaths of Abner and Ish-bosheth, who between them tried to sustain a residual Saulide kingdom in Transjordan.

The defendant's innocence in relation to Saul's death is brought out in a number of ways. First, the fact that David was a vassal of the Philistines at the time of Gilboa, and could easily have ended up fighting his own people in the battle, is attributed to Saul's harrying of him out of Israel (1 Sa. 26:19; 27:1). Secondly, it is made clear that when battle was joined David was far from Gilboa, having been dismissed by his Philistine superiors for fear that he would turn against them at an opportune moment (1 Sa. 29:1–11). Thirdly, when an Amalekite claimed that he had put the dying Saul out of his agony at Gilboa, David rewarded him for his news with a summary execution (2 Sa. 1:1–16). The Amalekite's crime had been to lift his hand against 'the Lord's anointed', which brings us to the fourth point. If David had wished ill on Saul he did not lack opportunity to bring it about. On two occasions, according to our narrative, David had Saul at his mercy and let him go unharmed for the reason that, enemy though he was, he was still 'the Lord's anointed' (24:1–7; 26:1–12). This necessity of David's avoiding blood-guilt for Saul is so important for the narrator that he devotes three chapters to it – even showing at some length how the experience with Nabal the Carmelite can contribute to David's training in non-retaliation (1 Sa. 25).[64] The wider significance of that particular lesson is heavily underlined in a speech by Nabal's wife Abigail: 'And when the Lord has done to my lord according to all the good that he has spoken concerning you, and has appointed you prince over Israel, my lord shall have no cause of grief, or pangs of conscience, for having shed blood without cause or for my lord taking vengeance himself' (1 Sa. 25:30f.).

Although neither Abner nor Ish-bosheth enjoyed the status of 'the Lord's anointed', the text is just as insistent that David was not implicated in their deaths. But it must have looked otherwise to many of his contemporaries – just as it does to some modern critics[65] – who were well aware that the removal of the remaining pillars of the Saulide house must help David to win over the recalcitrant northerners. In Abner's case there was the additional embarrassment that it was Joab, David's right-hand man, who had struck the blow. 2 Samuel 3 responds by describing the circumstances of Abner's death, with laboured emphasis on the cordiality of relations between David and Abner beforehand. It is shown that Abner was already negotiating with David about the transfer of Ish-bosheth's kingdom to David, and that the two had made a covenant (vv. 12f.) Three times (four in LXX) it is said that Abner departed from David 'in peace' (vv. 21, 22, 23, (24, LXX)). And when Joab called Abner back to Hebron 'David did not know about it' (v. 26). Moreover, David's reaction to the news of Abner's death was to declare his own innocence and to call down a curse on Joab and his house. At the funeral David uttered his famous lament, then fasted until sunset. Seven times in seven verses there is mention of 'all the people' as sharing David's grief and approving of his behaviour in the matter of Abner. 'So all the people and all Israel understood that day that it had not been the king's will to slay Abner the son of Ner' (v. 37). (So much for the 'intentional fallacy' in the case of 2 Samuel 3!)

Joab was too powerful a figure, and David was too much indebted to him, for there to have been any possibility of judicial measures against him. However, this did not apply to Rechab and Baanah the murderers of Ish-bosheth. Instead of receiving David's commendation they were executed on the spot, as again David distanced himself from the murder of a rival.

In the light of all this the characterization of 'David's Rise', or at least of a good proportion of the material attributed to it, as 'apology' seems fully justified. There were aspects of David's behaviour, such as his heading of a band of desperadoes during his 'Robin Hood' days in the Judaean wilderness, which seemed to lend credibility to the more serious charges against him. Tomoo Ishida has made the most of this evidence in his depiction of David as a ruthless guerrilla who would go to almost any lengths to relieve Saul of his kingdom.[66] For Ishida, the very defensiveness of 'David's Rise' argues the truth of the opposite case. And yet we must concede that in other respects the narrative is frank and open about David's faults (*e.g.* 1 Sa. 21:1–9; 22:22; 27:8–12). 'David's Rise' is no whitewash, and it is only by reconstructing the story on the subjective basis of hunch and surmise that we shall obtain an alternative, wholly discreditable, view of David.

The question of dating has already been raised in connection with the section's function as 'apology'. Proposed settings range from David's own lifetime down to the reign of Jehu in the late ninth century BC. R. L. Ward maintains that the implicit appeal to the Saulides to accept Davidic rule would make good sense if the narrative was composed before the secession of the northern kingdom.[67] T. N. D. Mettinger, on the other hand, sees Solomon's reign as an unlikely setting because Solomon as the executioner of Joab and Shimei would compare unfavourably with the David who eschewed violence as a means of acquiring the throne.[68] Since, however, it is David who advises Solomon to remove Joab and Shimei in 1 Kings 2:5–9 the point may not be as decisive as

Mettinger imagines. In short, the evidence needed for a reliable dating of 1 Samuel 16 – 2 Samuel 5 does not exist.[69]

The 'Succession Narrative'

So influential did Leonhard Rost's 1926 study of the 'Succession Narrative' become that for a time its unknown author replaced Herodotus as 'the father of history' in the reckoning of many Old Testament scholars. Convinced that later generations, with their idealized picture of the great King David, were incapable of producing the candid portrait given in this narrative, Rost dated it to the reign of Solomon. Rost it was who also popularized the idea that this was a narrative concerned with the issue of succession. Not only did the subject-matter of 2 Samuel 9–20 and 1 Kings 1–2 revolve around this question, there was actually a text for the sermon in Bathsheba's words to David in 1 Kings 1:20: 'And now, my lord the king, the eyes of all Israel are upon you, to tell them who shall sit on the throne of my lord the king after him.' The 'Succession Narrative', then, was written to show how it was that Solomon, and not one of David's other sons, followed his father on the throne. Its vivid portrayals and characterization seemed to confirm its antiquity; its author was personally familiar with some of the persons and events described in his narrative.

When it came to drawing the boundary lines for this exciting piece of eyewitness historiography there was little difficulty in marking its conclusion since 1 Kings 3 begins the account proper of Solomon's reign. The summary of David's military achievements in 2 Samuel 8 also seemed to indicate that the story of the succession could not begin before ch. 9, which tells of David's fulfilment of his promise to his friend Jonathan when he invited Mephibosheth to live at court at royal expense. But because ch. 9 seemed an unlikely beginning to Rost's narrative he cast about for more suitable material in the preceding chapters, finding it in 6:16, 20–23, and 7:11b, 16 – the latter representing a short form of the dynastic oracle in 7:11b–16. The theme of the Davidic succession therefore begins with a reference to the infertility of David's wife Michal, daughter of Saul, and at once excludes the possibility of Davidide and Saulide loyalties converging on any offspring of David and Michal. In the establishment of the dynasty which Yahweh will give to David the rejected house of Saul will have no part.[70]

The entity discussed by Rost has been subjected to the inevitable boundary changes as his work has come under closer scrutiny.

Whereas he himself regarded a few verses in 1 Kings 2 as secondary insertions (vv. 3f., 11, 27b), several scholars take the whole of 2:13–46 as a later addition,[71] with T. N. D. Mettinger also putting 1:41–53 in the same category.[72] A more far-reaching suggestion concerning the *beginning* of the narrative has been made by D. M. Gunn who argues for the inclusion of most of 2 Samuel 2–4 on several grounds, for example that the mention of Abner in 1 Kings 2:5 appears to assume his previous involvement in the story.[73] As with the 'History of David's Rise', the mere fact that the 'Succession Narrative' is capable of such expansion and contraction would seem to be a major obstacle to its recognition as a once-independent narrative. Such a narrative could have been seamlessly woven into the fabric of the 'Deuteronomistic History', but until more convincing evidence is produced the title 'Succession Narrative' will serve best as a convenience-term.[74]

The main qualifications of Rost's position in the past couple of decades have to do with genre and theme. While the literary qualities of the narrative had not gone unnoticed by Rost, the claim that it was partly based on firsthand knowledge of events almost guaranteed single-handed its reputation as a prime example of early Israelite history-writing. If references to source documents were conspicuously absent the proximity of the composition to the events described seemed adequate explanation. Since Rost, however, there have been various attempts to define the genre of the narrative more satisfactorily. Several writers have sought to establish links with Israelite wisdom circles thought to have been responsible for various other Old Testament writings. According to these scholars the 'Succession Narrative' would then have instruction as one of its primary aims. R. N. Whybray sees it as both a wisdom manual and a propagandist novel, and points to certain texts in the ancient Egyptian wisdom tradition as combining these same two interests.[75] F. Crüsemann, noting parallels with the instructions to kings in the book of Proverbs, regards the narrative as principally directed towards Solomon who will be the beneficiary if he follows his father's good example of submitting to sound criticism.[76]

This wisdom connection, it should be said, has so far appealed to only a minority of those who have discussed the narrative in any depth. One of the main supporting arguments, that of vocabulary, may actually qualify as the Achilles' heel of the theory, for some of the occurrences of such key words as 'wise', 'wisdom', and 'counsel' would read most strangely in a narrative intended to commend the merits of 'wisdom' as a concept and a controlling principle of behaviour. Wisdom enables Jonadab to plot the rape of Tamar (2 Sa. 13:3–5), and it is by her wisdom that the wise woman of Abel-beth-maacah persuades her fellow-citizens to behead Sheba and save the town from destruction (2 Sa. 20:22). Again, Solomon was advised by David to deal with Joab in his 'wisdom' – by devising a pretext for his execution (1 Ki. 2:5f.). The idea conveyed by these passages is that 'wisdom' may inspire to quite unprincipled behaviour. It is not enough to say that 'courtly wisdom' in the early monarchy period was basically pragmatic and amoral; in Jonadab's case its exercise is blatantly immoral. Furthermore, almost all the occurrences of the word 'counsel' in the 'Succession Narrative' are related to Ahithophel's advice to Absalom in connection with the rebellion. But, though Ahithophel's counsel was, as usual, impeccable, Yahweh saw fit to overturn it because it ran counter to his own purpose. This is not a perspective on 'counsel' which we should expect to find in a wisdom manual.

The genre of the 'Succession Narrative' has also been defined as 'story' by D. M. Gunn, who describes it as a work of 'serious entertainment' making use of traditional motifs, for example the judgement-eliciting parable, in a way which is more compatible with a literary than a historiographical aim.[77] Gunn and others who have approached the work from this angle – and here we can include the 'soft' structuralism of such as Conroy[78] – have usefully drawn out various themes which are developed to a greater or lesser degree in the text. One effect of these more recent studies has been to play down the importance of the *succession* aspect of the 'Succession Narrative'.[79] From the fact that the narrative is so largely taken up with affairs of the royal family it was easy to conclude that succession must have been the issue of most interest to the author. However, this is not borne out by the text, in which succession is important, but without being central in the way that Rost and many after him thought. If 2 Samuel 9–20 and 1 Kings 1–2 is truly a '*Succession* Narrative' then Solomon must be its hidden hero – fleetingly appearing early on (2 Sa. 12:24f.) and not returning until the final scenes (1 Ki. 1–2). This is a by no means impossible reading of the story, but it seems to constrict it unnecessarily.

At the same time that some scholars were busy restating the theme of the narrative, others were engaged in a search for redactional layers, in pursuit of the thesis that in it contradictory evaluations of David and Solomon exist cheek by jowl. The main names here are Würthwein, Veijola, and Langlamet.[80]

Würthwein, for example, tries to build up a case for an original narrative critical of both David and Solomon, but subsequently redacted to show them in a more favourable light. The basic assumption of these studies is that a text tends to be 'pro' or 'anti' and that if it is candid enough to have both it must be composite. When it is dependent upon the kind of textual dissection practised by Veijola and Langlamet then it is doubly questionable.

The 'Succession Narrative' has frequently been held up as expressive of a new, secularized, view of history, more conscious of historical causation and less dependent upon miracles and other supernatural phenomena than most other parts of the Old Testament.[81] It is noted that references to the involvement of Yahweh in the events of the narrative are few in number, three usually being cited (2 Sa. 11:27, 12:24, and 17:14).[82] Another aspect of the narrative's supposed secularity is the minor role which the cult and cult objects play in the story. There are, certainly, differences of emphasis as between the 'Succession Narrative' and, say, the 'History of David's Rise', or, better still, the 'Samuel Appendix', which relates events of David's reign not included in 2 Samuel 9– 20. But it is easy to exaggerate the differences by (a) failing to note the full number of references in the narrative to Yahweh's involvement (*cf.* also 2 Sa. 12:1, 15; 1 Ki. 2:15), (b) failing to take account of the expressions of traditional piety scattered throughout the narrative (*e.g.* 2 Sa. 14:14; 15:8, 25), and (c) disregarding the implication of a text like 2 Samuel 16:23 for the author's estimation of the importance of the ark of God.[83]

It is hard to discuss with much enthusiasm the dating of a document whose existence has not yet been conclusively demonstrated. Nevertheless, we may at least observe that the Solomonic dating of the chapters in question can no longer be taken for granted, especially if the legitimation of Solomon as David's successor is viewed as anything less than the principal aim of the narrator. The internal evidence, as usual, is not very helpful. In the commentary we have noted the possible significance of 2 Samuel 13:18, as emended by Julius Wellhausen, and we have suggested that certain features of 2 Samuel 19:43–20:2 are most easily understood if the division of the kingdom after Solomon's death was a fact of history at the time of writing.

The Samuel appendix (2 Sa. 21–24)

Various traditions in prose and verse have been brought together in this 'Appendix' to make up a kind of epilogue on David's reign. Since David cuts such a sorry figure in 1 Kings 1–2 their inclusion at this point is more appropriate. The epilogue effect comes not just from the nature of the material in the 'Appendix' but also from the way in which it is structured.[84]

The compiler seems to have arranged his material according to a concentric pattern with pairing of items as follows:

a famine story (21:1–14)
  b warrior exploits (21:15–22)
    c psalm (22:2–51)
    c_1 oracle (23:1–7)
  b_1 warrior exploits and warrior list (23:8–39)
a_1 plague story (24:1–25)

While too much of current Old Testament research is concentrated on the search for such structures – which, of course, seldom fail to emerge provided one looks hard enough – the phenomenon of the 'Geometric Bible' is not entirely an illusion. There are cases like the present one where it may be in order to speak of 'purposeful symmetry'. The purpose in the 'Samuel Appendix' is the linking of David's successes with the benign patronage of Yahweh. In the outer layers we read of famine and plague afflicting the land for the sins of its kings, Saul (21:1–14) and David (24:1–25). With the hero sections (21:15–22; 23:8–39) the theme of David as successful warrior-king is introduced, albeit with a reminder of his physical limitations (21:15–17). Finally, at the centre stand the psalm and poem which ascribe the glory to Yahweh (22:2–51; 23:1–7). (Their juxtaposing, it has been suggested, is modelled on Deuteronomy 32–33, 'The Song of Moses' and 'The Blessing of Moses'.[85]) Yahweh has given victory to his servant in battle and has spoken wonderful things concerning the future of his house (the 'everlasting covenant', 23:5). When account is taken of the structure of the 'Appendix', therefore, it is these psalmodic sections which have the last word on David's reign.

3 SAMUEL AND CHRONICLES

The Chronicler's treatment of the period covered by 1 and 2 Samuel is confined within 1 Chronicles 10–21. This considerable abbreviation of what was undoubtedly his principal source is attributable in the main to the exalted view of David which he wishes to put across. Saul is of interest only as a negative figure who brings about the disaster from which it will be David's responsibility to deliver the nation. Nothing is said, therefore, about Saul's reign, and the Chronicler's account of the kingdom period begins at Gilboa with the deaths of Saul and his sons. In a not uncharacteristic telescoping of history the Chronicler presents this as the end of the house of Saul, *pace* the attempt of his surviving son Ish-bosheth to keep the dynasty afloat in Transjordan. Magnification of David as king and emperor, on the other hand, accounts for the Chronicler's lack of interest in that period of his life which is represented in the 'History of David's Rise'. For the same reason, the tangled family history of David which is the subject of the 'Succession Narrative' has no part in Chronicles.

Even a quite casual comparison of Samuel and Chronicles will be sufficient to show up frequent points of difference, many of a minor nature and some more substantial, between the two. There are three main reasons for this. First, there is the comparatively poor state of preservation of the Hebrew text of Samuel which evidently had its tally of defective readings already by the time of the Chronicler (possibly the fourth century BC.). Sometimes the Chronicler gives the impression of side-stepping a textual crux, as in his report of the capture of Jerusalem (1 Ch. 11:4f.), while at other times we may suspect that his smoother reading reflects not a superior text but an emendation of one already recognized as deficient (*e.g.* 1 Ch. 20:5).

The second point to be borne in mind is that the Chronicler appears to have been using a version of Samuel which might almost be regarded as a different 'text-type' from our standard Massoretic tradition.[86] In Samuel studies there already is the problem that the Hebrew and Greek (Septuagint) traditions occasionally show significant divergences; nor can the Greek be dismissed as the inferior party here. Into this picture we now have to fit the fragments of a Hebrew scroll of Samuel found at Qumran (4QSam[a]), whose text agrees at various points with the Septuagint against the Massoretic Text (and vice versa), and also with Chronicles where it differs from Samuel (*e.g.* 1 Ch. 21:16). Questions of textual corruption apart, then, it is evident that in some respects the text of Samuel consulted by the Chronicler differed from our own. This introduces some slight measure of qualification into the third point that we have to make.

Most of the significant differences between Samuel and Chronicles, however, are the result of the Chronicler's reshaping of inherited material in order to express the ideological tenets and aims which are the hallmark of his work. For example, in his passing over the awkward transition from Saul's reign to David's (see above) he is propounding that Israel's history as controlled by Yahweh moves in a linear progression. This 'continuity theme' has also been noted in connection with his portrayal of Israel as continuously present in the land from the beginning (his 'autochthonous concept').[87] Again, his glorification of David takes the particular form of crediting him with all but the physical building of Solomon's temple. In Chronicles David decides the location of the temple, David prepares the blue-print and amasses the necessary materials, and David organizes the Levites for service in anticipation of the building's completion. This enhanced role of the Levites, over against Samuel-Kings, is already in evidence in the account of the journey of the ark of God to Jerusalem in 1 Chronicles 15:1–16:6. The Chronicler's high opinion of Solomon, who, with his father, is regarded as a twin pillar of the kingdom, is also responsible for some modifications of the 'dynastic oracle' as it is reproduced in 1 Chronicles 17. The disciplinary clause of 2 Samuel 7:14b is omitted as being inappropriate to Solomon, as the Chronicler saw him, and the promise of a perpetual dynasty made in the first instance to David (2 Sa. 7:16) is bound more closely to his son (1 Ch. 17:14).[88]

In all this the Chronicler is ploughing his own furrow; at best some of his traditions can be seen in embryo in Samuel. His wholesale attribution to David of the preparations for the temple-building, for example, may relate in some way to the observation in 2 Samuel 8:11f. that David dedicated all the spoils of his wars to Yahweh.[89] And, while 2 Samuel 24 is silent on the connection between the aversion of the plague at Araunah's threshing floor and the temple location, it may be that the story was preserved principally because of its known link with the tradition of the founding of the temple.

The relationship of Samuel and Chronicles presents a 'synoptic problem' of a kind more familiar to students of the gospels, but one which is not visited with the same degree of complexity. As we match the Chronicler's refashioned accounts against the extant text of Samuel which, our earlier discussion notwithstanding, must

correspond fairly closely to his own *Vorlage*, we can without
difficulty discover some of the principles which governed his
interpretation of history. But it is also salutary to note the degree
of freedom which he exercises in the reinterpreting and reshaping
of established tradition. And unless we make of the Chronicler a
special case, we shall better understand how other biblical historians – including the author(s) of Samuel – might handle the
data and traditions which they likewise inherited.

4 KING DAVID

Amidst all the lionizing and idealizing of David in the Old Testament one of the more puzzling descriptions of him is as 'a man
after God's own heart' (*cf.* 1 Sa. 13:14). Of his entitlement to a
place among the great of the ancient world there can be little
doubt, but how can his inner life and character bear this stultifying
comparison? The David of the books of Samuel is far from being
a plaster saint. Nor is it just that he abused his power in seducing
Bathsheba and contriving the murder – there is no other word for
it – of her husband. Even the eximious David of the 'History of
David's Rise' tricks a priest of Yahweh into believing that he
is on urgent royal business so that he provides him with food
(consecrated bread) and a sword (1 Sa. 21:1–9). Eighty-five priests
and their families lost their lives because of that piece of deception
(1 Sa. 22:11–19). Neither can we admire the way in which David
duped the Philistine king of Gath into thinking that he was flailing
his lord's enemies when all the time he was decimating some of
Judah's more troublesome neighbours, and incidentally preparing
the way for his own take-over of Judah and Israel (1 Sa. 27:8–12).
  The picture does not materially improve when David becomes
king. In the conduct of his military campaigns there are notable
barbarities, while domestically David as father falls far short of
the ideal. Even on his deathbed he cannot relinquish his scheming
ways, and he advises Solomon to devise means of unburdening
himself of Joab and Shimei – for the good of the kingdom, he says
(1 Ki. 2:1–9). It is also true, of course, that the story of David
discloses nobler traits and finer instincts, and perhaps most conspicuously when he is suffering the consequences of his own wrong-
doing. (It is probably no coincidence, then, that the Passion Story
in the gospels has the faintest echoes of David's humiliation during
the Absalom rebellion; see the commentary on 2 Sa. 15:23, 31). In
this respect 2 Samuel 24 would have been a more satisfactory

conclusion to his biography than 1 Kings 1–2, for, under judgement though he is in that chapter, several very commendable features are also apparent.[90]

However, even when all the good has been put down to David's account it is still a very flawed human being, as dependent upon divine mercy as any other, and ostensibly more than most, who fills the pages of Samuel. If, on the other hand, the Hebrew phrase traditionally rendered 'a man after his (*i.e.* God's) own heart' (1 Sa. 13:14) actually means 'a man of his own choice', as has been suggested by McCarter in his commentary, then the emphasis is put where it properly belongs – not on any exalted likeness of David to Yahweh, but on the sovereign will of Yahweh who chose David as the instrument of his purpose. Our attention is then more fully fixed on 'the God of David' (2 Ch. 34:3).

David and Christ

The expectation in Judaism of a coming Davidic king whose achievements would eclipse even those of the great dynast of Israel derived its force ultimately from the Davidic covenant (see below). The looked-for deliverer would be 'a shoot from the stump of Jesse' (Is. 11:1), 'a righteous branch' raised up for David (*cf.* Je. 23:5). And the gospels of Matthew and Luke are at pains to show that our Lord answered to this expectation in a most literal way. He is 'Jesus Christ, the son of David, the son of Abraham' (Mt. 1:1), while Joseph, his adoptive father, is 'of the house and lineage of David' (Lk. 2:4). Both evangelists provide genealogical tables to back up this claim. For the Apocalyptist, who surveys the whole panorama of incarnation and exaltation, our Lord is both the root and the offspring of David (Rev. 5:5; 22:16). In the light of all this the tendency to see David as a 'type' foreshadowing in his life's circumstances the experiences of Christ the promised scion easily developed. In his rejection and subsequent exaltation on the throne David prefigured the one who was crucified but who ascended to heaven in glory. The interpretation of the 'Davidic' psalms as expressions of David's own feelings at various points in his career served to strengthen the comparison, for the David of the psalter is pre-eminently a righteous sufferer, and *the* righteous sufferer identified with the pleas and praise of the psalter as if they were his own.

While, however, it is true that our Lord's descent from David was an important plank in the preaching of the gospel to Jews especially – both in legitimation of his claim to messiahship and

in confirmation that God had fulfilled his word through the prophets (*cf.* Lk. 1:69f.) – the New Testament does not indulge in
wholesale typological comparisons between David and Christ.
Indeed, the limitations of the title 'Son of David' are even pointed
out in a famous passage (Mk. 12:35ff.). But then it is characteristic
of the New Testament's use of the Old that it often favours a
contrastive method of approach as against the comparative emphasis of typology. For sustained use of the contrastive method we
have only to consult the letter to the Hebrews. (When this principle
is applied in the area of practical Christian experience it simply
means that things 'written for our instruction' (Rom. 15:4) are not
necessarily written for our imitation, and may as readily serve for
our admonition; *cf.* 1 Cor. 10:6.) In the following paragraphs, then,
we shall briefly examine three points of contrast between Christ
and David as they are suggested by New Testament writers.

The first is obvious and unavoidable. It concerns a contrast
between Christ and David which must have been made with great
conviction and, we may be sure, with considerable effect by the
early Christians. On the day of Pentecost Peter preached to his
Jerusalem audience from three Old Testament passages, of which
Psalm 16, taken at face value as a 'Psalm of David', was the *pièce
de résistance.*

> For thou wilt not abandon my soul to Hades, nor let thy
> Holy One see corruption (Ps. 16:10 quoted in Acts 2:27).

If David is speaking of the experience of death and resurrection,
as Peter assumes he is, then this cannot be autobiographical.
Everyone knew where to find 'David's Tomb' in Jerusalem, so he
himself did 'see corruption'. This same contrast between Christ
who did not see corruption and David who did is made in Paul's
synagogue address in Pisidian Antioch (Acts 13:35–37). Again, if
we look further into Acts 2 we find David contrasted with the
ascended 'Lord' of Psalm 110:1, for 'David did not ascend into the
heavens' (vv. 34f.). So, although the Davidic descent of Christ and
his resurrection may be closely linked in New Testament summaries
of the gospel (*cf.* Rom. 1:3; 2 Tim. 2:8), the relationship of Christ
to David in the matter of resurrection is inevitably and expressly
contrastive.

The second point of contrast concerns the presentation of Christ
as king in Matthew's gospel. In ch. 21 the evangelist recounts our
Lord's entering into Jerusalem to the acclaim of a crowd hailing
him as the 'Son of David'. He did this, we are told, in fulfilment

of the prophecy in Zechariah 9:9 ('Tell the daughter of Zion, Behold your king is coming to you' (Mt. 21:5)). At the temple he forcibly removed the money-changers and pigeon-sellers who had no proper conception of what the temple stood for (vv. 12f.). Then comes a verse which seems almost to stand in isolation: 'And the blind and the lame came to him in the temple, and he healed them' (v. 14). Few of the commentaries stop over this statement, and yet it yields a significant clue about Matthew's understanding of Jesus as 'Son of David'.

The evangelist apparently has 2 Samuel 5 in mind as he describes the entry into Jerusalem. In 2 Samuel 5 David captures Jerusalem, the last of the Canaanite strongholds to fall to the Israelites. The account, which is brief and very obscure on a couple of points, quotes a saying about the blind and lame being sufficient to ward David off, so well was the city fortified. But Jerusalem was captured after David had challenged his men to smite the inhabitants, including 'the lame and the blind, who are hated by David's soul' (v. 8). The episode concludes with the observation, 'Therefore it is said, "The blind and the lame shall not come into the house."'

Even without resolving the problems of the Hebrew of 2 Samuel 5 it is possible to see how closely Matthew's cameo is related to David's capture of Jerusalem. When David takes the city the lame and blind earn his disfavour such that an interdict barring them from 'the house' (i.e. the temple) is associated with the occasion. By contrast, when the 'Son of David' enters the city a thousand years later he makes a point of receiving representatives of these two disadvantaged categories in the temple, where he heals them. This act of mercy can, moreover, be seen as a counterpart to the expulsion of the merchandizers as described in verses 12f. In relation to the latter Zechariah 14:21 is not actually quoted but it is difficult not to think that the evangelist had it in mind: 'And there shall no longer be a trader in the house of the Lord of hosts on that day.' When, therefore, the Lord comes to his temple the extortioners are driven out and the afflicted are brought in. Furthermore, in the quotation from Isaiah 56:7, which envisages the temple as 'a house of prayer for all peoples', there is a hint of the larger blessings of the gospel which, in a way which the ancient prophet could not have foreseen, brought both the Israelite outcast and the foreigner into the joyous experience of the worship of God (Is. 56:3, 8). The point of the reference to the blind and the lame in Matthew 21:14 is, therefore, to show how our Lord's exercise of his kingly power differs from David's. He comes to bless, and it is to him as 'Son of David' that the needy – the blind (Mt. 9:27;

20:30f.), and even a Canaanite mother (Mt. 15:22) – apply for mercy.

The reference to the Canaanite woman leads us naturally into the third point, for which a brief consideration of the opening verses of the letter to the Romans will be necessary. First we should recall that Jewish expectation in the first century AD centred on a Davidic ruler who would restore the sovereignty of Israel as in former times. David himself had won many military successes as a result of which,

> Foreigners came cringing to me;
> as soon as they heard of me, they obeyed me
>
> (2 Sa. 22:45).

And in a number of Old Testament passages the ultimate triumph of the Davidic king is depicted in similar terms (*e.g.* Pss. 2:7–9; 72:11).

How, then, does the New Testament deal with this kingly, conquering aspect of the 'Son of David'? Romans 1:1–6 appears to be a key passage in this regard. There Paul speaks of the gospel as that which God 'promised beforehand through his prophets in the holy scriptures' and which concerns Jesus Christ whose descent is from David (vv. 1–3). Further, Paul defines the purpose of his apostolic calling as being 'to bring about the obedience of faith . . . among all the nations' (v. 5). If we were to look for a possible Old Testament matrix for this association of ideas – as verse 2 rather suggests we should! – Genesis 49:10 deserves close attention.

> The sceptre shall not depart from Judah,
> nor the ruler's staff from between his feet,
> until he comes to whom it belongs;
> and to him shall be the obedience of the peoples.

The text is 'prophecy' in the sense that it comes among Jacob's last words to his sons, telling of what would befall them 'in days to come' (Gn. 49:1). It refers, moreover, to the Judahite supremacy among the tribes of Israel, and to a great Judahite ruler to whom even the Gentile nations would submit. The word translated 'obedience' is rare but, despite earlier uncertainty (*cf.* AV 'gathering'), the meaning is fairly secure.[91] More to the point is the fact that an important strand of Jewish exegesis represented by the Aramaic Targums – written translations ultimately deriving from the oral renderings of the synagogue – understands the last line of Genesis

49:10 to refer to the obedience of the nations to the Davidic king.[92] This does not quite achieve the distinction of being a *topos* in the Targums, nevertheless the idea is occasionally picked up elsewhere in the Targumic tradition, for example at Isaiah 11:10 where, instead of the nations 'seeking' the root of Jesse, as in MT, the Targum has 'him shall the kingdoms obey'. Compare also MT and Targum at Jeremiah 30:9.

We need not posit direct dependence by Paul on a Targum in order to justify the suggestion that he interpreted Genesis 49:10 in the same way and that this interpretation has a great deal to do with the theme of 'the obedience of the Gentiles' in Romans (see also 15:18; 16:19, 26). It is in these terms that Paul sums up the purpose of the Gentile mission. How may Christians living in the imperial capital submit to the Davidic king proclaimed in the gospel? Paul answers by qualifying the 'obedience' of Genesis 49:10 with a genitive: it will be by the obedience *of faith*.[93] This is a very different kind of submission from that required by David, just as the present manifestation of Christ's rule differs *toto caelo* from David's earthly exercise of kingship. The same point is made in a different way in Revelation 5:5f. There the seer's attention is directed to one described as 'the Lion of the tribe of Judah', a title in obvious debt to Genesis 49:9. The lion symbolized kingly might and majesty; the main feature of Solomon's magnificent throne was its lion figures (*cf.* 1 Ki. 10:19f.). However, what the New Testament seer saw was 'a Lamb standing, as though it had been slain' (Rev. 5:6). The Davidic king has triumphed, but not in the Davidic way.

As a final point we must note that, although there are basic contrasts between our Lord's exercise of his sovereignty and David's, this is not the complete story. In the end the Lamb of the Apocalypse does battle with the rebellious forces of the earth and prevails because he is 'King of kings and Lord of lords' (*cf.* Rev. 17:14; 19:11–21). Since apocalyptic is not to be dismissed as a 'strange child' of revelation this is an essential element in our understanding of the church's Lord. The Christ of the gospel who has displayed the love and forgiveness of God to the unworthy citizens of this world has not abdicated from his position as the judge of mankind or from his responsibility as the final destroyer of evil.

The Davidic covenant

From the beginning, it would seem, the ruling house in Judah was
the subject of a remarkable dynastic promise announced to its
founder through the prophet Nathan. The classic formulation of
this 'covenant' between Yahweh and David comes in 2 Samuel 7,
while there are several poetic compositions which have it as their
major theme, notably the 'last words of David' in 2 Samuel 23:1–
7, and Psalms 89 and 132. Although 'covenant' is the appropriate
term, the search for literary models and analogues in other near
eastern literature has ranged much more widely to include, for
example, the Egyptian 'royal novel', Mesopotamian 'prophecies',
Hittite and Assyrian royal land-grants, as well as the inevitable
vassal treaties.[94]

The distinguishing feature of this 'covenant' is Yahweh's unconditional undertaking to preserve the Davidic house in perpetuity
and without regard to the worthiness of the occupants of David's
throne in Jerusalem. If David's son did misbehave then he would
be subject to the fatherly discipline of Yahweh, though without
ever standing in danger of being disinherited as Saul had been
(2 Sa. 7:15). Soon, however, the kingdom was divided and the
house of Judah found itself being governed by a succession of
Davidides who, with rare exceptions, were at best shadows and at
worst parodies of the kingly ideal enshrined in the Davidic kingship
ideology. For Isaiah of Jerusalem the house of David, as represented by the weak-kneed Ahaz, was guilty of wearying both
men and God (Is. 7:13). It is Isaiah who speaks in positively
messianic terms of the new ruler of the fourfold name who would
restore the lost glory of David's throne (Is. 9:6f.). Whether he was
saluting the accession of Hezekiah in the exalted language of
Davidic ideology or expressing a less immediate hope, it remains
true that a great gulf separated present reality from the realization
of the ideal. This is also the thinking behind Isaiah 11:1 where
expectation centres on a 'shoot from the stump of Jesse', as if to
suggest that, rather than the perpetuation of the Davidic line, what
is needed is a new beginning. Elsewhere in the Old Testament there
are even signs of a conditionalizing of the covenant terms, as in
1 Kings 9:6–9, where disregard of Yahweh's commandments will
result in the destruction of the temple and expulsion from the land.

When the tragedy of exile finally came, the everlastingness of
the 'everlasting covenant' seemed to have been illusory. An addendum to Psalm 89 bewails the fact that the enduring covenant which
the psalmist had been extolling has been decisively set aside:

Lord, where is thy steadfast love of old,
   which by thy faithfulness thou didst swear to David?
                                             (v. 49).

How could an unconditional covenant suddenly convert to being
conditional? That was the problem for those who witnessed the
Babylonian destruction, and for those who subsequently tried to
make sense of the 'Davidic hope'. Opinion is divided as to what
exactly was in the mind of the compiler or redactor responsible for
the tailpiece to the 'Deuteronomistic History' in 2 Kings 25:27–30,
but the probability is that in the rehabilitation of Jehoiachin in
Babylon someone thought to see a fore-gleam of the returning
glory of the Davidic kingdom.[95] For the period immediately after
the return from Babylon we have the prophecies of Haggai, who
seems to have expected a restoration of Davidic fortunes under
Jehoiachin's grandson Zerubbabel (cf. Hg. 2:20–23). Even the
Chronicler (or his redactor), whose eschatology has often been
represented as of the realized variety, still troubles to extend the
Davidic genealogy well into the fourth century, as if the 'Davidic
hope' was not exhausted by the 'Davidic institutions' about which
he himself had written.[96]
   Monarchy did eventually return to Judah, in the form of the
Hasmonaean dynasty in the second and first centuries BC, but it
was no improvement on the tarnished Davidic model which had
been destroyed in 587 BC. It was those loyal to traditional Jewish
teaching who were most offended by some of the policies of the
Hasmonaeans and who at times suffered most from them. They
were not the hoped-for saviours of Israel. On the other hand, the
exposition of God's kingly rule that was offered by Jesus Christ –
the *autobasileia* ('kingdom in person'), to use Origen's fine coinage[97] – differed so radically from preconceived ideas about the
great 'Son of David' as almost to ensure his rejection by the mass
of the people. The utopian conditions which the prophets had
associated with the coming of the greatest Davidide (cf. Is. 11:1–
10; Je. 23:5f.) did not materialize either during or after our Lord's
public ministry. But, for all that, the consistent witness of the New
Testament is that in him the 'Davidic hope' finds its fulfilment.
His descent is from David (Rom. 1:3; 2 Tim. 2:8), he is the root
and offspring of David (Rev. 5:5; 22:16), and to him will be given
'the throne of his father David' (Lk. 1:32). His rule, though not
now visibly displayed, will far transcend the bounds of any national

kingdom when 'the kingdom of the world has become the kingdom of our Lord and of his Christ' (Rev. 11:15).

David and the Psalter

Already in the Old Testament David is celebrated as both a musician and a composer of psalms. For the former see 1 Samuel 16:18, 23, 2 Chronicles 29:27 and Nehemiah 12:36, for the latter 2 Samuel 22:1, 23:1. Later tradition considerably magnified this facet of his activity, so that an apocryphal psalm text found at Qumran can make him the author of 3,600 psalms and four hundred and fifty 'songs', the latter mainly for liturgical use.[98] It seems probable, too, that in Hebrews 4:7 the phrase 'in (RSV "through") David' is equivalent to 'in the Psalter' – Psalm 95 quoted there is not 'Davidic' in the Massoretic tradition, though it is in the Septuagint – in keeping with a tendency to link the psalms generally with David's name.[99]

The main point which we have to consider here concerns the various superscriptions to the psalms, which not only associate them with David but also relate them to particular experiences and circumstances in his life (Pss. 3, 7, 18, 30, 34, 51, 52, 54, 56, 57, 59, 60, 63, 142). There are several factors to be borne in mind before reading these or any other psalms as guides to the inner workings of David's mind in specific situations. First, the expression $l^e\underline{d}\bar{a}wi\underline{d}$, traditionally rendered 'of David', may also mean 'for David' or 'about David'. (The Hebrew $li\underline{d}i\underline{d}i$, 'for my beloved', in Is. 5:1 is comparable with the first alternative.) The mention of David in the superscription is, therefore, not necessarily a statement of authorship. Secondly, the superscriptions to the psalms are almost certainly later additions. (So convinced of this point were the NEB translators that they omitted them altogether.) They are, nevertheless, older than the Greek translation of the Psalter, and in one case, Psalm 18, the superscription was probably in existence by the time of the final redaction of the 'Deuteronomistic History' (mid-sixth century BC), since it is included with the version of the psalm in the 'Samuel Appendix' (see 2 Sa. 22:1).[100]

It is also a consideration that the superscriptions do not always agree with the information given in Samuel-Chronicles. The title to Psalm 34 refers to David's feigning of madness 'before Abimelech', whereas the Philistine king in question in 1 Samuel 21 is called Achish. Confusion of the names of the Philistine contemporaries of Abraham and David is the obvious explanation (Gn. 20:2). The title of Psalm 60 is also problematical in that it refers to Joab's slaughter of twelve thousand Edomites in the Valley of Salt, following engagements with Aramaean kingdoms north of Israel. This is seriously discrepant with what is reported in 2 Samuel 8:13 and 1 Chronicles 18:12. All in all, it seems most prudent to treat the superscriptions as sources of information about the way in which the 'Psalms of David' were read at a fairly early stage in their transmission, rather than as authoritative statements on the authorship and circumstances of composition of each of the 'Davidic' psalms. This is not to deny that 'David spoke', but just to acknowledge that the situation is more complex than it might at first appear.

5   THE TEXT

I

For some reason the books of Samuel have suffered more in the process of transmission than perhaps any other part of the Old Testament.[101] Although the problem passages represent only a very small proportion of the aggregate text, the unsatisfactoriness of MT has long been felt, which explains, for example, Julius Wellhausen's frequent recourse to the LXX ('Septuagint') in his 1871 commentary. Many since then have acknowledged a similar debt to the LXX. This reputation of the Greek has received a further boost with the discovery of fragments of three Hebrew scrolls of Samuel in the outstandingly productive Cave 4 at Qumran.

The scrolls represented by these fragments have been given the sigla 4QSam[a-c] (where 'Q' stands for Qumran and 4 is the number of the cave). The vast majority of the fragments actually belong to one scroll, 4QSam[a], and all together will be published, after an abnormally long gestation period, in an *editio princeps* being prepared by F. M. Cross in collaboration with his former pupil E. C. Ulrich. In 1953, soon after the initial discovery, Cross published two columns of 4QSam[a],[102] and our knowledge of this scroll has been considerably enhanced by the publication in 1978 of Ulrich's dissertation, *The Qumran Text of Samuel and Josephus*, in which a great number of readings, hitherto undisclosed, are discussed.[103] (Often enough these 'readings' are more in the nature of pregnant lacunae; see below.) A number of fragments of 4QSam[b] were published by Cross in 1955,[104] and those of 4QSam[c] by Ulrich in 1979.[105]

Study of the text contained in the fragments soon showed that at many points it differed significantly from the Massoretic tradition, being in not infrequent agreement with the LXX where it diverged from MT. What had previously been surmised by scholars was now supported with firm textual evidence: the apparent 'deviations' of the LXX from MT were for the most part already in the LXX *Vorlage* and were not the invention of the Greek translator(s). It also became apparent that at the end of the first millennium BC there existed texts of Samuel containing elements which, in the Massoretic tradition, are found only in Chronicles.

Cross characterizes 4QSam[a] and 4QSam[c] – both dated to the first century BC – as Palestinian and expansionist, whereas 4QSam[b], which he dates to the third century BC, is fuller than MT without being expansionist in the same way as its cave-mates. Cross asserts, indeed, that the Massoretic tradition, as far as Samuel is concerned, 'is wholly absent from Qumrân'.[106] This Massoretic tradition, he notes – and not without a touch of hyperbole – is 'riddled with haplographies',[107] that is, in addition to the more run of the mill corruptions to which it has fallen prey. It was the LXX, or strictly the retroversion of its Greek into Hebrew, which had brought the haplographic phenomenon to light. The longer readings of the LXX too often occur where an MT omission by homoioteleuton can be postulated for MT to be able to escape suspicion. The only alternative would be to accuse an early editor with expansionist tendencies of having deliberately constructed his additions to create the impression of haplography in the parent text.[108] Even where an omission by MT cannot be put down to straightforward haplography the superiority of the 4QSam[a] (and LXX) reading may be all too evident, as in 1 Samuel 1:24 where MT includes the statement 'and the boy was a boy' (*wehanna'ar nā'ar*), refined in RSV to 'and the child was young'.[109] Now while B. S. Childs holds out the hope of finding protein value even in this canonical husk,[110] we have at the same time the confirmation in 4QSam[a] of the fuller LXX reading: 'and the boy (was) *with them. And they brought (him) before the Lord, and his father killed the sacrifice as he did year by year before the Lord. And she brought* the boy . . .' This is a notable difference between MT and 4QSam[a]/LXX, though the mere fact that the longer reading was originally in the MT tradition means that it does not of itself provide evidence of a text-type different from MT (see below).[111]

At this point we may note a few other places where 4QSam[a] (+ LXX) offers readings which on the face of it are superior to MT. At 1 Samuel 1:24 the scroll confirms the reading 'a three-year-old bull' (MT 'three bulls'), already known from the LXX and Peshitta.

The addition of '(two) wave-offerings (of bread)' in 1 Samuel 10:4 relieves a grammatical incongruence and adds something to the sense. It is likely that the words 'and the Egyptians oppressed them' have fallen out of MT by haplography at 1 Samuel 12:8; they are in the LXX and apparently were in 4QSam[a]. The 4QSam[a] and LXX plus at the end of 2 Samuel 13:21 – 'but he did not grieve the spirit of Amnon his son because he loved him; for he was his firstborn' – is probably omitted from MT by haplography. The missing words recall 1 Kings 1:6, where it is observed that David was similarly indulgent towards Adonijah. While in theory an expansion based on the Kings reference could be argued, it seems unlikely. A clause directly paralleled in another passage comes in 2 Samuel 13:27: 'and Absalom made a feast like the feast of a king'. (Spacing as much as anything indicates the scroll's agreement with the LXX here.) Of the LXX reading S. R. Driver had remarked: 'The words may, indeed, be an addition, suggested by a reminiscence of I 25, 36: at the same time an express notice of the feast prepared by Absalom is quite suitable, and their omission may be due to *homoioteleuton*'.[112] At 2 Samuel 18:9 4QSam[a] has the verb which genuinely can be translated 'was left hanging', though a defence of MT (lit. 'was placed, put') has also been made.[113]

However, 4QSam[a] has its own crop of errors – errors often enough shared with LXX – whether it is a double rendering at 1 Samuel 2:24, a question of congruence at 1 Samuel 8:16, or transposed letters and confused sense at 2 Samuel 7:23.[114] Moreover, in a number of cases where MT and 4QSam[a] + LXX are in dispute the choice is between two equally plausible readings, which means that literary and other subjective factors come into prominence. At 2 Samuel 24:17, for example, the scroll and the LXX have 'and I *the shepherd* have done wrong', and the italicized words are adopted by NAB and favoured also by Ulrich on the ground that they match the antithetical 'but these (are) the sheep'.[115] Long ago, however, S. R. Driver branded the addition in the Greek as 'an unnecessary explanatory gloss'.[116] Presumably if Driver had been aware of the existence of the 'gloss' in a Hebrew manuscript he would not have fundamentally altered his opinion. There is also the case of 2 Samuel 11:18–25 in the LXX – the Qumran fragment apparently covers only verses 16–20[117] – where there is a ponderous repetition of a speech which Joab originally put into the mouth of David and which the LXX puts into David's mouth as well. But whereas the LXX is followed by JB and NEB, it is castigated by

D. W. Gooding as expansionist and disruptive of the narrative momentum of the passage.[118]

The major conclusion of Ulrich's preliminary investigation of 4QSam[a] is that its text has a particular affinity with the LXX. En route it emerges that some of the scroll readings are paralleled in Josephus' Bible text and also in the Greek Lucianic tradition represented by the minuscules b o c_2 e_2.[119] There was already evidence to show that Lucianic readings existed in Bible texts long before the time of the Antiochene martyr Lucian (d. AD 312).[120] Whether this 'proto-Lucianic' text reflects the Old Greek tradition[121] or represents an early, and light, revision of the same,[122] its importance is now well-established. This is especially true for the latter part of 2 Samuel (in the βγ section of 'Reigns') since Barthélemy's discovery that from 2 Samuel 11:2[123] Codex Vaticanus presents a text which has been revised towards the proto-Massoretic Hebrew tradition of the first century AD as part of the so-called *kaige* revision.[124] In such circumstances the Lucianic readings cited in Brooke-McLean-Thackeray are an essential tool for the recovery of the earliest Septuagint text.[125]

Important methodological modifications of Ulrich's approach have been proposed by the Israeli scholar E. Tov,[126] who also notes in passing the extent to which Ulrich's presentation of the evidence has to be taken on trust pending the publication of an authoritative edition, including photographs, of the fragments. Many of Ulrich's reconstructions depend in part or in whole upon the counting of letter-spaces in lacunae, and upon the retroverting into Hebrew of the relevant LXX text. Tov also warns that Ulrich's analysis of the substantial number of *disagreements* between 4QSam[a] and the LXX betrays a partisan zeal in the way that it tends to play down their importance: 'If, for the sake of argument, the agreements between 4Q and the LXX should also have been subjected to value judgments, their number also would have been reduced.'[127] He further questions the wisdom of taking statistical account of those agreements of 4QSam[a] and the LXX against MT where the latter has suffered from mechanical error. Again, more attention could have been paid to the unique readings of 4QSam[a], claims Tov, and he bows out of his critique of Ulrich with the observation that, for all the agreements between 4QSam[a] and LXX, they with MT make up three independent sources.[128] As to this last point, we might even go so far as to say that, on the available evidence, the presentation of 4QSam[a] and LXX as a coalition against MT risks seriously distorting the picture of the textual transmission of the books of Samuel.

In spite of all the enthusiasm which the Qumran fragments have generated, one distinguished Septuagintalist, Père Dominique Barthélemy, has unambiguously stated his preference for the MT of Samuel.[129] Barthélemy is well aware of the mutilations which MT has sustained, and he makes allowances for theological 'retouches' as well; nevertheless he argues for the integrity of MT as a literary text. Whatever the merits of the Qumran-type texts, they were transmitted by scribes with a penchant for innovation: they harmonized, explained pregnant expressions, and built midrashic interpretations on 'versets ruinés'. MT's transmission, on the other hand, was regulated according to conservative literary principles, which means that MT has a basic 'literary honesty' about it.

So the evidence as we have observed it encourages neither an attitude of Massoretic fundamentalism nor the wholesale adoption of every Qumran neologism. The practical implications for text-critic and commentator alike are aptly summed up by D. W. Gooding: 'If the Masoretic text is not automatically to be regarded in any disputed case as representing the original, neither is the Septuagint, not even when it happens to be supported by some non-Masoretic Hebrew manuscript. One must judge each case on its merits.'[130]

It is largely on the basis of his work on Samuel that F. M. Cross has developed his 'theory of local texts' by way of explaining the kinds of textual divergences that have been noted above.[131] Cross apportions the main text-types to three distinct geographical areas: Palestine (the Qumran fragments), Babylonia (the proto-Massoretic text), and Egypt (LXX; strictly the unrevised 'Old Greek').[132] The Palestinian and Egyptian text traditions are thought to have parted company at an early stage, while the Babylonian text is believed to have been reintroduced into Palestine late in the pre-Christian era. When the rabbinic authorities set about the standardization of the text of the Hebrew Bible it was the Babylonian version which received their imprimatur.[133]

Despite the ordered appearance that Cross's theory lends to what otherwise looks like a formless waste, it has not won many adherents beyond his immediate sphere of influence in North America. There is nothing to connect the development of the Massoretic tradition specifically with Babylonia,[134] nor does the LXX necessarily represent an Egyptian text tradition, since the LXX text could have been imported into Egypt from Palestine early in the second century BC.[135] It has also been objected that a theory which distinguishes text-types largely on the basis of their individual characteristics is not being self-consistent when it propounds that the character of the regional text traditions may vary from one section to another.[136] Moreover, it apparently is possible for books representing the same text-type to originate in different places.[137] Finally, the exposition of the theory has been hampered by a lack of precision in the use of some basic technical terms,[138] as also by the simplistic assumption that the 'text-types' supposedly identified were the only ones ever to have existed.[139]

II

In this section we shall briefly discuss two passages of special interest for the way in which they raise the problem of short and long texts.

1 Samuel 11

One of the most striking features of 4QSam[a] is its inclusion of several lines of additional text at the beginning of 1 Samuel 11. These have been hailed by F. M. Cross, who drew attention to them in a paper read in Vienna in 1980, as 'missing verses' of the chapter in question.[140] In purporting to give the background to Nahash's attack on Jabesh-gilead the additional material reflects a tradition already known from Josephus' *Antiquities* vi. 5.1. The Qumran version reads as follows:

> And Nahash king of the Ammonites grievously oppressed the Gadites and Reubenites and gouged out all their right eyes and brought ter[ror and dread] upon Israel. There was not left a man among the Israelites beyond the Jordan whose right eye Nahash king of the Ammonites did not gouge out. However, seven thousand men fled before the Ammonites and came to Jabesh-gilead. And it came to pass after a month that Nahash the Ammonite went up and encamped against Jabesh-gilead . . .

Nahash's ultimatum to the Jabesh-gileadites therefore threatened them with the same treatment as he had inflicted upon the Gadites and Reubenites. Cross makes out a good case for the originality of the extra lines, noting, for example, that in the shorter MT version Nahash is introduced merely as 'the Ammonite', in contravention of the universal Deuteronomistic practice.[141] He also anticipates possible criticisms of his position – criticisms which have been put for all that by A. Rofé, who judges the 4QSam[a] plus to be late and midrashic.[142]

The first and obvious question requiring an answer before the authenticity of the additional material can be established is, How could these lines have been omitted even in accident-prone Samuel? Cross thinks that 'the omission of the passage by parablepsis, the scribe's eye jumping from one paragraph break to another (both with Nahash as subject), is an entirely adequate explanation of the loss of the paragraph'.[143] P. K. McCarter, who is no less enthused by the prospect of extra lines of holy writ, speaks simply of 'an extraordinary case of scribal oversight'.[144] He rightly points out that haplography cannot be blamed in this instance. While, therefore, we must concede with Cross that strange things do happen in the copying out of texts, his 'parablepsis' is a name, not a diagnosis.

A further issue is raised by the position of the words 'and it came to pass after a month' in the fragment. (Substantially the same reading (corresponding to MT 'but he (= Saul) was as one keeping silent') is found in the LXX, even though it does not have the above-mentioned 4QSam[a] plus.) The whole sentence to which the clause belongs – at first omitted by the Qumran scribe but inserted before he had proceeded more than a few words – comes at the end of the additional material and so is understood by Cross to pinpoint the Ammonite attack on Jabesh-gilead as taking place one month after the refugees had fled there. Josephus, on the other hand, has the time reference at the beginning of his report of Nahash's Transjordanian activity, which means that it refers back to the election of Saul in 10:17–27: Nahash's attack came a month later. Cross assumes that Josephus must be in error and conjures up a theory involving both dittography (vertical) and haplography (homoioteleutic) to explain Josephus' misconstruction. There is an important point at issue here, for if Cross is right then the LXX is wrong in linking the time reference with Saul's election, and so are those modern versions which have followed the LXX's lead. It may be, however, that all that precedes the time reference in 4QSam[a] is intended to be parenthetical; McCarter even thinks that the syntax of the plus requires this explanation.[145]

One of the points in favour of 4QSam[a], in Cross's opinion, is that it provides an explanation for the Ammonites' interest in Jabesh-gilead, which was somewhat to the north of the area which they disputed with Israel. Rofé claims that the plus merely answers that question by posing another: why did Nahash perpetrate his barbarities against Gad and Reuben in the first place? This objection had, in fact, been anticipated by Cross who suggested that the Transjordanians could have been in breach of a treaty with the Ammonites. But this kind of discussion can go on a long time without necessarily being very conclusive. We might, for example, consider the possible relevance of Nahash's answer in 11:2, in which he says that by gouging out the right eyes of the citizens of Jabesh-gilead he would 'thus put disgrace upon all Israel'. But according to the Qumran text he had been assiduously doing this throughout southern Transjordan.

Finally, the Qumran addition's function as 'background' could as easily be an indication of its secondariness as of its originality. For it is possible that as 'background' its purpose is to explain not why Nahash attacked Jabesh-gilead but why the inhabitants of that city were so eager to make a treaty with him. As the story is told in MT, they could be accused of unseemly haste in their rush to win vassal status, without even making an appeal for help from their brother Israelites as they soon were forced to do anyway. But if Nahash had been striking terror into much of southern Transjordan, then their behaviour was more easily excused. The wise course for the present, therefore, is to reserve judgement on the status of these additional lines in 4QSam[a].

1 Samuel 17–18

The most notorious divergence between MT and the LXX in the books of Samuel is in their respective accounts of the contest between David and Goliath, and its sequel, in 1 Samuel 17–18.[146] The Greek version is much shorter and is often preferred as being neater and more consistent. It is composed of the following verses: 17:1–11, 32–40, 42–48a, 49, 51–54; 18:6–8a, 9, 12a, 13–16. The LXX thus lacks that entire section in which David is sent on his errand to the battle-front to discover news of his brothers (17:12–31), and also the scenes in which Saul inquires about David's background and, with Jonathan, salutes the young conqueror of Goliath (17:55–18:5). It has occasionally been mooted that the LXX represents an abridgement of a fuller account of the dimensions of MT, but more often MT is taken as a conflation of two separate traditions about David's victory over Goliath. The earlier, represented by the LXX and the parallel portions in MT, follows on naturally from 16:14–23 where David enters Saul's service and becomes his armour-bearer. When the Philistines encamped at Ephes-dammim and Goliath issued his challenge David was on the spot to volunteer. MT's version, on the other hand, seems to set up a tension with 16:14–23 by its inclusion of 17:12–31 and 17:55–58. In the former David is, initially at least, back with the sheep, while in the latter Saul addresses him as if they had no previous acquaintance with each other. Further points made in support of the view that MT is conflate are that 17:12 reads as if David is appearing for the first time, and that 17:15 reads too obviously like a harmonistic note aimed at reconciling 17:12–31 with 16:14–23.

There are two distinct issues that must be kept separate here. The first is that of conflate accounts. Despite assertions to the contrary, the phenomenon of composite narrative does occur in near eastern literature and in biblical literature in particular.[147] (The most obvious biblical examples are provided by the 'synoptic gospels'.) To say that MT is 'composite' in 1 Samuel 17–18 – if it is – is to imply nothing about its status as scripture, nor does it, for that matter, imply the 'superiority' of whatever earlier strand may have gone into the making of such a composite narrative. The second issue is the one which literary criticism may be able to illuminate, viz. whether, in 1 Samuel 17–18, the LXX (or its *Vorlage*) represents just such an earlier strand or is an abridged version of MT.

It is certainly surprising to find the LXX version relating how David took his shepherd's staff and wallet into his encounter with Goliath (17:40) – this in a version whose alleged superiority over MT partly consists in the fact that it has David securely installed in Saul's court since 16:14–23. Should he not have been finished with his shepherd gear if he was full-time in Saul's service? The most that can be said for the LXX on this particular is that it may have suffered contamination from that part of the tradition which is peculiar to MT. This is a theoretical possibility, but once we begin to defend the LXX's priority along these lines the hypothesis becomes virtually unverifiable. (Contamination is more or less ruled out in McCarter's reconstruction of the textual development of 1 Samuel 17–18: 'a complete, alternative account of David's arrival and victory over Goliath was interpolated somewhat heavy-handedly into some manuscripts of the completed story after the distinctive textual traditions had already begun to develop.'[148])

One other point which seems to support the abridgement view of the LXX deserves brief mention. In 1 Samuel 20:8 Jonathan refers to a 'covenant of the Lord' into which David and he have entered, and the reference is as much part of the LXX text as of MT. The difficulty for the LXX unfortunately is that its omission of 18:1–5 has left us unaware of this important factor in the relationship between the two.

We have already noted the difficulty in harmonizing 16:14–23 with 17:1–58, but the resolution of the problem by adopting the shorter LXX version merely introduces problems of a different sort. Of the positive merits of the longer MT text in terms of plot development and narrative skill nothing has been said. But a discussion of these would, we believe, also produce evidence in favour of its originality. Finally, if the LXX is indeed to be regarded as an abridged version of MT then we may assume that it was tensions of the kind noted at the beginning of this paragraph which induced someone – whether at the Hebrew or Greek stage it is hard to say – to prune the narrative in so drastic a manner.[149] Some of the 'omissions', it must be said, seem to indicate a cavilling and unimaginative approach to the business of story-telling.

ANALYSIS

1 Samuel

1 THE RISE OF SAMUEL (1:1–4:1a)

Birth and dedication (1:1–2:10)
The decline of Shiloh (2:11–4:1a)

2 THE ARK OF GOD (4:1b–7:1)

The ark captured (4:1b–22)
Victus victor (5:1–12)
The return (6:1–7:1)

3 THE INSTITUTION OF THE MONARCHY (7:2–12:25)

Victory at Mizpah (7:2–17)
The request for a king (8:1–22)
Saul anointed king (9:1–10:16)
The second Mizpah convocation (10:17–27)
The relief of Jabesh-gilead (11:1–15)
Samuel's speech (12:1–25)

4 THE REIGN OF SAUL (13:1–15:35)

Preparations for war (13:1–23)
Victory at Michmash (14:1–52)
Saul and the Amalekites (15:1–35)

5 DAVID AND SAUL (16:1–31:13)

David of Bethlehem (16:1–23)
The Valley of Elah (17:1–58)
After the battle (18:1–30)
David evades death (19:1–24)
David and Jonathan (20:1–42)
David at Nob and Gath (21:1–15)
The destruction of Nob (22:1–23)
Saul seeks David (23:1–29)
David spares Saul (24:1–22)
Nabal and Abigail (25:1–44)
David in Saul's camp (26:1–25)

David flees to Gath (27:1–12)
Saul at Endor (28:1–25)
The Philistines muster (29:1–11)
Attacking the Amalekites (30:1–31)
The death of Saul (31:1–13)

2 Samuel

6   DAVID KING OF JUDAH (1:1–4:12)

The Amalekite messenger (1:1–16)
David's lament (1:17–27)
Civil war (2:1–32)
The death of Abner (3:1–39)
Treachery against Ish-bosheth (4:1–12)

7   DAVID KING OF ISRAEL (5:1–20:26)

The capture of Jerusalem (5:1–25)
The installation of the ark (6:1–23)
The dynastic promise (7:1–29)
David's campaigns (8:1–18)
Mephibosheth, son of Jonathan (9:1–13)
Ammonites and Aramaeans (10:1–19)
David and Bathsheba (11:1–27)
Nathan's parable (12:1–31)
Amnon, Tamar, and Absalom (13:1–39)
The wise woman of Tekoa (14:1–33)
Absalom rebels (15:1–37)
David's flight to the Jordan (16:1–23)
Hushai prevails (17:1–29)
The death of Absalom (18:1–33)
The king returns (19:1–43)
Sheba's secession (20:1–26)

8   THE SAMUEL APPENDIX (21:1–24:25)

The Gibeonites and the family of Saul (21:1–14)
Encounters with Philistine heroes (21:15–22)
A psalm of thanksgiving (22:1–51)
The last words of David (23:1–7)
'The Three' and 'The Thirty' (23:8–39)
Census and plague (24:1–25)

1 SAMUEL

1   The Rise of Samuel (1:1–4:1a)

The convergent themes of this section are the decline of the Shilonite priesthood and the rise of the prophet Samuel. While precise chronological data are not given, it is clear that the story begins late in what is generally known as 'the period of the judges', *i.e.* some time around the middle of the eleventh century BC. The ark of God, associated with Bethel at a late point in the book of Judges (20:26–28), is now at Shiloh which, therefore, has claim to be regarded as the chief Israelite sanctuary during this period. But, as our narrator would have us understand, it was the worst of times when Samuel was called to be a prophet. Shiloh and its worship were in the hands of the miscreant sons of Eli, Hophni and Phinehas (1:3), whose misdeeds will soon be brought into causal connection with the loss of the ark of God to the Philistines and (in all probability) the destruction of the Shiloh sanctuary (3:11–14). Indeed, one of the most conspicuous features of these three chapters is the heavily underlined contrast between the exemplary conduct of the young Samuel and the rascality of Hophni and Phinehas. The latter, as we shall discover, are marked out for destruction as surely as the former is destined for honour.

BIRTH AND DEDICATION (1:1–2:10)

A new era – the era of the monarchy – is about to be born, and the story fitly begins with the birth of the man who would be remembered above all for his part in the making (and in one case the unmaking) of the first two kings of Israel.

Elkanah's family (1:1–8)

1. Elkanah's pedigree, like his dual marriage (v. 2), suggests that he was a man of means. *Ramathaim-zophim*: both NEB and NIV follow the LXX in taking *zophi(m)* as indicating the clan to which Elkanah belonged: 'a Zuphite from the hill country of Ephraim'.[1] Ramah, the usual name for Samuel's home-town (*e.g.* v. 19), is presumably the town mentioned in 9:5f. and located in 'the land of Zuph'. *Ramathaim* (ostensibly a dual form meaning 'twin heights') invites comparison with the Arimathea of the gospels (*e.g.* Mt. 27:57). The form of the name in the LXX is 'Harmathaim'.[2]

2. Monogamy was not *de rigueur* in ancient Israel (*cf.* Dt. 21:15–17), but economic and eudemonistic considerations will have ensured that Elkanah's situation was the exception rather than the rule. *Hannah* is mentioned first because of her role in what follows; it is also, perhaps, a fair inference that she was Elkanah's first wife and that, because of her barrenness, she had to share her husband's affections with the depressingly fecund *Peninnah* (compare, after a manner, Abraham's siring of Ishmael, Gn. 16:1–4).

3. Three annual pilgrim-festivals are stipulated in the Pentateuchal laws (Ex. 23:14–17; 34:23; Dt. 16:16), but this says little about Israelite observance in the period of the judges. Judges 21:19–24, referring to 'the yearly feast of the Lord at Shiloh' (v. 19), mentions vineyards and dancing in such a way as to suggest that it is the autumn vintage festival which is in view; this originally agricultural celebration was given a historical significance in commemoration of the wilderness wanderings of the Israelites.[3] However, other agrarian and religious festivals, doubtless with regional variations, may be safely assumed for this period, though hardly to the tune of the fifty or sixty festivals per annum celebrated in Egyptian Thebes.[4] Nothing more than a family observance (*cf.* 20:6) may be implied by Elkanah's yearly trip to Shiloh, for that matter.[5] Since the title *Lord of hosts* makes its canonical début here it may have been specially connected with the Shiloh sanctuary; this cannot, however, be advanced beyond the conjectural. The significance of this ancient title is hard to pin down, mainly because of the ambivalence of *hosts*, which may mean either supernatural hosts, whether heavenly bodies (*cf.* Jdg. 5:20; Is. 40:26) or angelic beings (*cf.* Jos. 5:14f.), or the hosts of the armies of Israel (*cf.* 17:45).[6] F. M. Cross, claiming formulaic parallels in the Ugaritic texts, holds that the original meaning was 'He who creates the (heavenly) armies' – a creation formula which was also recognized as 'an

appropriate name of the god who called together the tribes to form
the militia of the League, who led Israel in her historical wars'.[7]
In practice the ancient Israelite may have contrived to enjoy the
best of both worlds. Whether Cross's theory of origins is correct
is, however, a different question, since the usual explanation of the
title as exhibiting a simple construct (*i.e.* genitival) relationship is
by no means as indefensible as Cross assumes.[8] In view of our
reference above to the autumn festival, it is noteworthy that the
end-time prospectus in Zechariah 14 envisages the nations making
annual pilgrimage to Jerusalem 'to worship the King, the Lord of
hosts, and to keep the feast of booths' (v. 16).

The ancient city of Shiloh is represented by the modern Seilūn,
a ruined site about twenty miles north of Jerusalem. Shiloh was
one of several important sanctuary cities in the pre-monarchical
period (*cf.* Jos. 18:1; Jdg. 18:31), owing its importance at this time
to the presence of Israel's prime cultic object, the ark of the
covenant (*cf.* 3:3). There the priestly family of Eli regulated the
worship. Perhaps too much can be read into the fact that only the
three principals are mentioned; the priests of Nob who officiated
at that sanctuary in succession to the house of Eli numbered more
than eighty a couple of generations later (22:18). *Hophni* and
Phinehas – as with some others of the priestly connexion, their
names are Egyptian, probably as a legacy from Israel's earlier
history[9] – are described as the *priests of the Lord*, either because
Eli was by now superannuated, or, possibly, because already at
this stage the narrator wishes to strike an ominous note in relation
to the ensuing narrative.

4. The next few verses (4b–7a) give an impression of what went
on during the family's annual visit to Shiloh, viz. a religious ritual
conferring no detectable spiritual benefit on Peninnah (*cf.* v. 7) and
serving merely to accentuate Hannah's plight. It is a far cry from
the festal ideal of joyous family celebration commended in such a
reference as Deuteronomy 16:14. The distribution of *portions* by
Elkanah was in accordance with the worshipper's right to a share
of the flesh of his sacrificial animal, as was the case with the 'peace
offering' (or 'communion offering') in the priestly tariff (Lv. 7:11–
18).

5. RSV *although* represents a slightly free rendering of the reading
presupposed by the LXX. MT *'appāyim* should mean 'face', but
it fits ill in this context. Various unsatisfactory solutions have been
proposed.[10] The LXX, reading *'epes (kî)*, yields a sense which
cannot be bettered in the circumstances: 'and to Hannah he gave
one portion; however, Elkanah loved Hannah more than the other

(= Peninnah)'. Some of the alternative explanations favour the
view that Elkanah must have given Hannah a special portion for
Peninnah to have reacted as she did; all that is lacking is a suitably
convincing explanation of *'appāyim*. AV 'worthy portion' goes
back to the Targum's 'choice portion' but, in spite of Deist's best
efforts, it still looks as if the Targum is guessing (so Driver).[11] The
Peshitta's 'double (portion)' (*cf.* RV, NIV) may owe more to
assonance than to lexicography.

6–8. The domestic tensions created by plural marriage (*cf.* Dt.
21:15–17; perhaps also Ecclus. 26:5f.) are reflected in the fact that
the word translated *rival* (6) also served as a technical term for
'rival wife' in Syriac and Arabic; compare the use of the cognate
verb to express the same idea in Leviticus 18:18. For *irritate* (6)
NEB has 'humiliate', which betrays a debt to Arabic,[12] while
McCarter's 'complain aloud' reproduces an Aramaic nuance. The
raw material for both explanations is already on view in Driver,
Notes, p. 10, and little is to be gained by departing from RSV. For
all his express sympathy and devotion (8) Elkanah is unable to
control the situation, so that all hinges on Hannah's initiative, and
on the appropriate divine response, in the next phase of the story.

The birth of Samuel (1:9–20)

9. Hannah's initiative is marked by the double-duty *rose* which can
express decisive action as well as mere physical movement (*e.g.* Ex.
32:1). The mention of *Shiloh*, frequently rejected as superfluous,
may also be intended to formalize the turn of events. Plausible
emendations of MT *bešilōh* ('in Shiloh') are not lacking, the main
contenders being Wellhausen's 'boiled flesh' (*bešēlā*), Kittel's 'in
the dining hall' (*ballìškâ*),[13] and McCarter's 'privately' (*baššelî, cf.*
2 Sa. 3:27); nevertheless, the versional support for MT is very
strong. Functional or otherwise (see on v. 3), Eli is here called *the
priest*, though in point of fact his position would originally have
been that of chief priest (*cf.* 'Ahimelech the priest' in 21:2, *etc.*, as
also 'Jethro the priest of Midian' in Ex. 18:1).[14] The term 'high
priest' occurs but infrequently in the Old Testament and is commonly regarded as late (though an equivalent title appears already
in a Ugaritic text of the second millennium BC[15]). Perhaps more
significantly, the proportions of the Samuel narrative, which deals
in what is essentially family history at this stage, favour the use of
the simpler term. A more substantial shrine than the Pentateuchal
'tent of meeting' is suggested by the mention of a *doorpost* and the

designation *temple* (*cf.* 3:3); doors are also mentioned in 3:15.[16] These implications of permanence are not recognized, however, in the tradition to which the Davidic promise is wedded in 2 Samuel 7:4–29, while for the author of Psalm 78 the Shiloh sanctuary was 'the tent where he (*i.e.* God) dwelt among men' (v. 60).

10, 11. Hannah prays *de profundis*.[17] Her request is for a *son* – strictly the Hebrew expression ('seed of men') is epicene – and she makes what is effectively a Nazirite vow on his behalf.[18] It is possible that the longer text of the LXX represents a Hebrew manuscript tradition which contained the word 'Nazirite'; 4QSam[a] attests a reading of similar proportions but is too fragmentary to permit absolute certainty.[19] For the hair-style and for further details of the Nazirite vow see Numbers 6:1–21. The full Nazirite vow also involved abstention from strong drink (Nu. 6:3f.); the LXX – and almost certainly 4QSam[a] – includes this as an additional undertaking here. Samson's Naziriteship is formulated in the same terms in Judges 13:5, 7.[20] Not a temporary commitment, which is the norm in Numbers 6, but a lifelong consecration to God is envisaged in both instances.

12–16. The aged priest, whose eyesight was by now seriously deficient (*cf.* 3:2; 4:15), easily mistook the tremulous form for a drunken woman; but the LXX has Eli's servant deliver the rebuke!

15. RSV *sorely troubled* is actually a better equivalent of the variant reflected in the LXX (lit. 'hard of day'; *cf.* Jb. 30:25); MT should, in the light of a similar expression in Ezekiel 3:7, be translated 'obstinate' (lit. 'hard of spirit'). But since the less nocuous 'persistent' seems an unlikely utterance on Hannah's lips the LXX may preserve a superior reading.[21] NEB goes out on a limb with 'I am *a sober person*'.

16. 'Worthlessness' and 'confusion' are two of the meanings which have been proposed for the somewhat opaque *beliyā'al* which occurs in the expression 'daughter of *beliyā'al*', here represented by *base woman* (*cf.* NEB 'degraded', NIV 'wicked woman'). In the Old Testament the word attracted various synonyms in the semantic field of 'evil', finally achieving personification in the intertestamental era as the prince of evil (so Beliar/Belial in 2 Cor. 6:15). That respect for the priestly office, despite its glaring faults, which is implied in the loyalty of Elkanah's family to the Shiloh sanctuary also marks Hannah's reply to Eli's accusation.[22]

17. Eli could still invoke a blessing as befitted a priest of the Lord (*cf.* Nu. 6:22–27; Dt. 10:8), and indeed this is the only passage which actually shows a priest blessing an individual worshipper.[23]

Form-critically Eli's answer corresponds to the 'oracle of salvation' sought by the Israelite petitioner at the sanctuary (*cf.* Klein). *your petition which you have made*, which translates two occurrences of the root *šā'al* ('ask'), anticipates the word-play in verses 27f.

18. While her response is conventionally phrased, the relationship of *favour* (*ḥēn*) to the name Hannah would be obvious to a Hebrew reader. Her taking of food (contrast v. 8) signals her confidence that her request has been heard. The LXX provides a location for the repast with an addition which can be reconstructed to mean, 'and she entered the dining hall' – this doubtless referring to a room adjoining the sanctuary (*cf.* 9:22). Whether this forms a likely sequel to the statement that she *went her way* is a moot point; the LXX plus has been dubbed a rabbinic-type gloss by one competent judge of such matters.[24]

19. *Ramah*, a contraction of Ramathaim (see v. 1), is the regular name for Samuel's city. It is not surprising, in view of the meaning of the name ('height'), that a number of Old Testament sites were so called, or that several identifications of this particular Ramah have been proposed. The location usually favoured is the modern er–Rām, five miles north of Jerusalem. The divine beneficence is expressed in *remembered*, which in Old Testament parlance does not imply a prior forgetting, but rather, a superintendence of events towards their desired, or promised, conclusion (*e.g.* Ex. 2:24).

20. So is born the prophet Samuel, albeit the observation is usually lost in a welter of discussion about the meaning of his name. The difficulty is that the explanation of the name is framed, per popular etymology, in terms of the root *šā'al* ('ask'), whereas the strictly scientific etymology has to be traced elsewhere; 'Asked of God' (AVmg) is most unlikely as the original meaning.[25] Worthier candidates are 'Name of El' (or 'His Name is El') or 'El is exalted',[26] where El is a divine name which was in vogue in pre-Israelite Canaan, as may be seen from Melchizedek's blessing Abraham in the name of El Elyon ('God Most High') in Genesis 14:19. For discussion of the view that verses 27f. give the etymology of *Saul's* name see the Introduction (section II). At the least this conflict of etymological interests – which also drew comment from mediaeval critics[27] – serves as a reminder that in the books of Samuel 'the real deliverer is not the first king, but the last judge'.[28]

Presentation at Shiloh (1:21–28)

21–23. According to the law of the vow (women's regulations) in Numbers 30:6–15, a husband had power of confirmation or veto of any vow undertaken by his spouse. However, in the Hannah story this is a mere technicality inasmuch as Elkanah happily plays second fiddle, not only accepting his wife's vow but even, according to a variant reading in verse 23 (see below), invoking divine assistance towards its fulfilment. His own *vow* (v. 21) is less perspicuous; with *sacrifice* in close attendance it possibly relates to a votive offering promised to God in return for some undisclosed favour (*cf.* Lv. 7:16f.; 22:17–23), but the text is a trifle uncertain.[29] Whether Elkanah's vow is to be seen as in any way related to the birth of Samuel – husband having been caught up in wife's votive fervour? – can only be surmised.[30]

22. Weaning might take place as late as the third or fourth year (*cf.* 2 Macc. 7:27). Thereafter the boy Samuel was to be taken to Shiloh to *appear in the presence of the Lord*, or, as the text may have said originally, 'that we (or possibly "he") may see the face of the Lord', for the scribal practice, apparently established at a very early stage in transmission, was to disinfect this once acceptable anthropomorphism.[31] 4QSam[a] has an additional line which is without versional parallel, though it may be reflected in Josephus (*Ant.* v. 10. 3): 'and I will dedicate him as a Nazirite for ever, all the days of (his life)'; NAB characteristically treats it as original.[32]

23. MT *his word* reads strangely in view of the fact that God has already fulfilled Hannah's wish, whereas NEB's 'your vow' (lit. 'word') has the support of 4QSam[a], LXX, and Peshitta. The first two actually have a periphrasis, 'that which has gone out of your mouth', which corresponds to the wording of Numbers 30:2(3) in relation to the fulfilling of vows. According to this reading God is implored to assist Hannah in the fulfilment of her vow at the appropriate time. And since *establish* is the word used in Numbers 30:13f. in connection with the husband's overall responsibility for his wife's vows, the clause is also confirmatory of what immediately precedes. Normally in the Old Testament God is seen confirming his own word (*e.g.* Dt. 9:5), so that MT 'his word' may have been influenced by the common usage or, alternatively, may have been motivated by a euphemistic concern to avoid the suggestion that God would establish the word of 'a mere mortal woman',[33] though in the latter case account would have to be taken of such references as Isaiah 44:26 and Jeremiah 28:6.

24. When the time for presentation came a votive offering of generous proportions accompanied the family to Shiloh. The emendation of MT 'three bulls' (*cf.* AV) to *a three-year-old bull* (*cf.* 'the bull', v. 25) is now almost universally accepted, being encouraged by 4QSam[a], LXX, and the Peshitta.[34] As in Genesis 15:9, it is a question of maturity and, therefore, of cultic acceptability.[35] Supplementation of votive offerings with amounts of *flour* and *wine*, though not quite on this scale, is laid down in Numbers 15:8–10. Properly speaking *the child was young* should be 'the child was a child'. However, not even on the analogy of 'boys will be boys', nor from a consideration of the other connotations which the Hebrew *na'ar* may bear in other contexts,[36] can MT be defended. The longer LXX text is supported by 4QSam[a], and the reconstructed original reads in translation: 'and the boy was with them. And they came before the Lord, and his father killed the sacrifice as he did year by year before the Lord, and she brought the boy . . ..'[37]

25, 26. Hannah again evinces that respect for divinely-appointed authority noted earlier (see on v. 16). It is a principle of conduct warmly commended in a church context by New Testament writers (*e.g.* 1 Thes. 5:12f.; 1 Tim. 5:17–19).

27, 28. There are four occurrences of the root *šā'al* ('ask') in these verses, culminating in *lent* (28) – for the one verb, with appropriate modifications, expresses the two ideas. Since *lent* is *šā'ûl*, corresponding exactly to the Hebrew form of the name of Israel's first king, the pressure to divorce both the etymology of verse 20 and the Nazirite elements in the story from the historical personage Samuel is at its greatest at this point.[38] Again the reader is referred to the Introduction (section II).

Hannah's thanksgiving (2:1–10)

In its exuberant, sometimes defiant, ascription of universal might to Yahweh God of Israel this psalm, prototype of the Magnificat (Lk. 1:46–55), ranges far beyond the contemplation of Hannah's plight and vindication. Only in verse 5, indeed, does the subject of barrenness and birth-giving definitely materialize, though verse 1 may make its contribution. (The LXX, in an additional bicolon at verse 8, praises God as the respondent of vows ('granting the vow to the vower'), thus echoing a feature of the preceding narrative (*cf.* 1:11).) Throughout its several movements the psalm focuses on the illimitable power of God as it is deployed in the reversal of human fortunes. The climax is reached with an assertion of universal sovereignty and a declaration that the same divine power is at work for the good of God's earthly vicegerent the king. It is mainly because of this concluding note that the psalm, in all respects a worthy candidate for the canonical Psalter (*cf.* Ps. 113), has sometimes been classed with the so-called 'royal psalms' (*e.g.* Pss. 45, 72). Attention has also been drawn to the militaristic moments in the poem, in pursuit of the thesis that the composition was originally made in celebration of an Israelite victory over an external enemy.[39] Whatever the original life-setting, the sentiments expressed fit the Hannah story well and, by virtue of their universality, make an ideal introit to the history of the early monarchy as recounted in the books of Samuel.[40] For further comment of a general nature see the Introduction.[41]

1. God is the ground of rejoicing as he is the object of praise. The vacuous *my strength is exalted* in RSV arises from a half-interpretation of the biblical figure (lit. 'my horn is exalted'). Both strength and pride (*cf.* NEB 'hold my head high') are symbolized in the animal horn. In a couple of passages (*e.g.* 1 Ch. 25:5 (MT)) the exalting of the horn signifies the granting of offspring (*cf.* McCarter, p. 71), but, while the idea has obvious appeal here and cannot be excluded, the more usual significance is favoured by both the immediate context and the parallel in verse 10. In the third colon the literal sense is of a mouth opened wide in an expression of derision (AV 'my mouth is enlarged'; *cf.* Is. 57:4). The mention of *enemies*, who make frequent appearance in the Psalter, invites us on this occasion to recall the description of Peninnah as Hannah's 'rival' (*ṣārâ*) in 1:6, even though the usage there borders on the technical.

2. There are intimations of pure monotheism here (*cf.* Is. 45:21f.), though the LXX is not so complaisant, reading 'there is none *holy* besides thee' in the second (third in LXX) line. *rock*, more titular than metaphorical, is a common appellation of God in the Old Testament (*e.g.* Dt. 32:4, 15, *etc.*, in a section which has various parallels with 'Hannah's Song'). Those who have the God of Israel as their 'Rock' find protection and security in him (2 Sa. 22:3, 32f.).[42] Thanks to Isaiah 8:14 ('a rock of stumbling') and associative texts in Isaiah 28:16 and Psalm 118:22 the figure assumed a messianic significance which is reflected in the New Testament (*e.g.* 1 Pet. 2:6–8).

3. The weighing of *actions* is tantamount to the adjusting of human behaviour and circumstances (NEB, a trifle strongly, 'he governs all that men do'). In verses 4f. God is seen adjusting the balance in favour of the weak and disadvantaged.

5. In a curious way the statement about the *full* falling on

hard times anticipates the parting shot of the man of God who
prophesied the downfall of Eli's house (see v. 36). *ceased*
(*ḥāḏellû*): the existence of a second root *ḥ-d-l*, meaning 'to be fat,
well-nourished', has to be recognized (*cf.* NEB 'grow strong').[43]
At the end of the second colon there is a word (*'aḏ*) which is given
short shrift in some versions (RV waxes bold with 'Yea') but which
has plausibly been explained as meaning 'food'.[44] The hungry are,
therefore, to be 'fattened with food'. *seven* expresses the poetic
ideal, whereas in fact Hannah had five other children in addition
to Samuel (v. 21).

6. *Sheol*, the resting-place of the flaccid shades, is also part of
God's domain.[45] It does not stand in this instance for 'critical
illness' (*pace* Mauchline). While it is true that resurrection is not a
central dogma of the Old Testament, there is more chance of
establishing its true place in Israelite thinking if texts such as this
are not silenced by scholarly presupposition before they have had
the opportunity to speak.[46] NEB 'he can bring the dead up again'
strikes a blow for freedom.

7, 8. Since God founded the world (8b) he has the right to
intervene in the social order.[47] The *ash heap* is 'the mound of dung
and other rubbish, now called a *mezbele*, or "place of dung," which
accumulates outside an eastern town or village, and on which
beggars sit, asking alms of passers-by, and, by night, often sleep'
(Driver, *Notes*, p. 26). For exaltation to the heavenly throne itself,
in a Christian context, see Revelation 3:21.[48]

Hebrew cosmology represented the earth as supported by *pillars*
(*cf.* Jb. 9:6; Ps. 75:3), but this word is less certain, hence 'foundations' in NEB, NIV.[49] The Peshitta talks about 'the depths of the
earth' in what is, perhaps, no more than a guess. McCarter (p. 73)
tries a different tack with 'the straits of the earth', a reference to
the subterranean waters upon which the world is founded (Ps.
24:2) and where God was thought to enter into judgement with
mankind.[50] In that case 'straits of the underworld' would be
preferable, since BH *'ereṣ* occasionally means 'underworld'. Verse
8b reads entirely differently in the LXX whose version looks like
an attempt at harmonization with the story of Hannah in 1:9–11:
'He grants the vow to the vower, he has blessed the years of the
just.'[51]

9. Those *faithful* to God are kept from harm (*cf.* Pr. 3:26), but
the wicked 'sink into silence and gloom' (NEB). This *darkness* is
the nether gloom which engulfs the wicked at death and which
may be experienced already in this life (Ps. 35:6). The Targum
introduces Gehenna, which is really a later idea, in characteristic

exegetical overkill. NIV joins the final colon with the first in verse
10 to obtain the not unsuitable observation that those who pit
their strength against God will be destroyed.

10. Since *adversaries* often has a legal connotation it agrees well
with the depiction of God as the judge of the earth. *against them*
(*'ālāw*) may conceal a divine name, probably in the form *'elî*
and meaning 'Exalted One' (*cf.* NEB 'the High God').[52] RSV is
satisfactory, but it remains the case that there are various places
in the Old Testament where the occurrence of this divine name,
attested in the Ugaritic texts and comparable with the long-estab-
lished *'elyôn* ('Most High', as in Gn. 14:18–22), is suspected.[53] The
king mentioned in the final bicolon must be a member of the ruling
Davidic house (see the Introduction); at a later stage both *king*
and *anointed* will have been interpreted along the lines of messianic
idealism. *anointed* (*mᵉšîḥô*), which has become anglicized as 'Messiah', recalls the initiatory act by which the king was appointed to
his task (*cf.* 10:1; 16:13) and a special sacrosanctity conferred upon
him (*cf.* 26:9). *power* is properly 'horn' (*cf.* on v. 1); thus by a neat
inclusio the psalmist's vindication betokens the exaltation of the
reigning monarch.[54]

THE DECLINE OF SHILOH   (2:11–4:1a)

The section poignantly illustrates the theme of 'Hannah's Song' as
it is epitomized in 2:7b, 'he brings low, he also exalts'. For it is
under the auspices of God who has determined the ruin of Hophni
and Phinehas that Samuel makes his mark. To emphasize these
contrasting fortunes the narrator inserts brief progress reports on
the boy Samuel (2:11b, 18, 21b, 26; 3:1; 3:19–4:1a) in what is
otherwise an account of the last days of the Elide priesthood.

A right abused (2:11–36)

11. *ministered* translates the verb *šārēṭ*, commonly used of priestly
service.

12. For *worthless men* (lit. 'sons of Belial') see on 1:16. *they had
no regard* is a fair rendering of BH *yāḍa'* but will not suit in 3:7;
AV 'they knew not the Lord' therefore has merit. The LXX,
however, represents a slightly different text in which verse 12b joins
with 13a: 'they did not know (regard?) the Lord or the priest's due
from all the people who sacrificed'. This has the advantage of

giving MT *mišpaṭ* the same nuance as in a similarly oriented clause in Deuteronomy 18:3.

13–16. There are two schools of thought. RSV apparently endorses the view that verses 13f. as well as 15f. describe a deviation from the proper procedure. The occurrence of *Moreover* (*gam*) at the beginning of verse 15 does seem to assume malpractice in what precedes, yet the same verse makes it clear that only *raw* meat was acceptable to the priests who conducted affairs in the way deprecated. While the latter consideration appears the more weighty, there is good reason for caution. Nevertheless, NEB nails its colours to the mast with 'This should have been their practice' for the more factual *So they did* in verse 14. Accepted procedure or not, the practice outlined in verses 13f. has little in common with the regulations on priestly perquisites in, for example, Leviticus 7:31–36. The priests' subsistence at Shiloh depended more on 'pot luck', perhaps in the belief that the hand of God decided the trident's catch; according to a reconstructed addition in 4QSam[a] at verse 16 the priest had to be content with his catch 'whether bad or good'.[55]

15, 16 describe an undoubted abuse, for the fat of a sacrifice was regarded as the portion of the deity (*cf.* Lv. 3:16) and was consumed by humans on pain of death (Lv. 7:22–25).[56] Despite all this Eli's sons insisted on having their cut even before the fat had been separated off or had been burned on the altar (*cf.* v. 29). If even the ordinary worshipper had his sensibilities shocked by this behaviour, there was no excusing the priests who were supposed to instruct the people in these very matters (*cf.* Mal. 2:7).

17. A hint of the judgement that will fall (*cf.* Gn. 6:5; 13:13). AV interprets *the men* to mean people in general: 'men abhorred the offering of the Lord' (*cf.* NEB's 'general contempt'); but this hardly reckons with the definite article. The word is absent from 4QSam[a] and the LXX and, following so soon after *the young men*, also in reference to Eli's sons (*pace* McCarter[57]), may be intrusive in MT.[58] *offering* (*minḥâ*), the term for the cereal offering (Lv. 2:1–16) and other bloodless sacrifices, can also cover animal sacrifices (*e.g.* Gn. 4:4).

18–21. More heartsome is the story of the acolyte Samuel. He wears a *linen ephod*, probably a loincloth, in accordance with priestly custom (*e.g.* 22:18); there is no talk of lower age-limits for priestly service in this story where grown men have failed (*cf.* Nu. 8:24–26; 1 Ch. 23:24–32). A more substantial outer *robe* (19) was supplied for his growing frame when his mother made her accustomed visits to Shiloh. As with the midwives in the Exodus

story (Ex. 1:21), Hannah's faithfulness was rewarded with the gift
of a family (*cf*. Ps. 127:3). Significantly, this prosperity is connected
with Eli's priestly blessing, and the relationship between the aged
priest and Elkanah's family fulfils the ideal of a happy co-operation
between priesthood and people which is so desiderated in verses
12–17.

20. *give*: 4QSam[a] and the LXX have 'repay' (*cf. BHS*). A
difference of only one letter is involved and a case can be made for
either reading as far as idiom is concerned. The variant, however,
fits the Hannah story particularly well. The root *šā'al* gets a double
billing in *the loan which she lent*. MT is problematical, in fact, but
RSV has the support of 4QSam[a] and the LXX for *lent*, which is
in any case the expected sense (see Ulrich, pp. 72f.).

22–26. Eli, apprised of his sons' rascality, ineffectually remon-
strates, though the ineffectiveness is not put down to his extreme
old age – 4QSam[a] anticipates 4:15 with the information that Eli
was now ninety-eight years old – but to divine counteraction (25b).

22. *to all Israel* recalls verse 14 and appears at first blush to
support the view that verses 13f. form part of the charge against
Eli's sons. But 4QSam[a] and the LXX have 'to the children of
Israel', which weakens the comparison; it may even be that MT
represents a later editorial attempt to highlight the cross-reference.
The mention of the female personnel who *served* at the *tent of
meeting* excites interest: (1) in form it closely parallels Exodus 38:8;
(2) the reference to the Shiloh sanctuary as a tent of meeting is
generally held to jar with the facts as given (see on 1:9);[59] (3) this
half-verse is absent from 4QSam[a] and from part of the LXX
tradition. At the least our two references seem to preserve a
tradition about female ancillary staff who performed menial duties
in the pre-monarchical sanctuaries; whereas the degeneracy of Eli's
sons would have been more at home with the cultic prostitution
which was a feature of Canaanite sanctuary worship.[60] *served*
(*ṣābā'*) is a word which occasionally describes the service of the
Levites (Nu. 4:23; 8:24), but it is most often used of troops
assembling for battle, hence, incorrectly, AV 'assembled' (mg.
'assembled by troops'). The Targum and Peshitta compound the
Elides' wickedness by venturing the information that the women
came to say their prayers. (At Exodus 38:8 (LXX 26) the LXX
confides that they were fasting – an observation perhaps not
unconnected with their willingness to relinquish their mirrors!)

24. *spreading abroad* is the likeliest rendering of MT *ma'aḥirîm*,
though it is not without difficulty. AV, RV 'ye make the Lord's
people to transgress' strains the syntax too much.

25. The general sense is clear despite some uncertainty about the meaning of *God will mediate for him*.[61] High-handed sin against God, unlike offences against one's fellow, leaves no room for mediation. The sense in which God mediates is probably in those offices and institutions of arbitrament which are acknowledged as divinely-appointed.[62] The nuances *mediate* and *intercede* are conveyed by different conjugations of the verb *pālal*; in the former case 'arbitrate' would arguably be an improvement on *mediate for him* (*cf.* Ex. 21:22 where RSV 'as the judges determine' fills out a Hebrew term based on the same root and meaning 'after assess- ment' (NEB)). The present reference to God as arbiter parallels Exodus 22:7f. where again the subject is the settlement of disputes.[63] That the Old Testament offers instances where human intercession did assuage God's anger for outrages against himself (*e.g.* Ex. 32:7–14) is of no account in the light of the following statement about the destiny of Eli's sons. For the biblical writers it is enough that human destinies are woven within the context of divine providence for them to be regarded as the out-working of the divine will. The general principle is stated in Isaiah 45:7 ('I make weal and create woe') and the parade example is the Pharaoh of the exodus (*cf.* Ex. 7:3, 13, *etc.*). Human accountability is not thereby excluded; on the contrary, it is assumed that the cause of the downfall of Hophni and Phinehas was their own wilful rejection of God (*cf.* Lk. 7:30).

26. In contrast with what has just been recounted the narrator pays Samuel what is, as Luke 2:52 shows, the highest of compliments.

27–36. The doom-laden message concerning the destruction of his family is not announced to Eli directly, but through an unnamed *man of God* (*cf.* 1 Ki. 13:1ff.). Even Samuel may hear messages from God (3:11–14), but apparently not Eli (*cf.* 3:1). In these verses there is set forth the rationale for the disinvestiture of the house of Eli and its eventual replacement by the Zadokite family which, after the rustication of Abiathar to Anathoth for his complicity in the Adonijah rebellion (1 Ki. 2:26f.), exercised a priestly monopoly in the Jerusalem temple for as long as the monarchy and state lasted.

27. *man of God*, as in most of its occurrences, is virtually a synonym for 'prophet' (*e.g.* 2 Ki. 1:9); the New Testament usage is more generalized (1 Tim. 6:11; 2 Tim. 3:17). This anonymous figure is often regarded as the mouthpiece of the Deuteronomistic historian (*cf.* Klein). God's revelation of himself to Eli's ancestors is traced back before the exodus and Sinai to Egypt itself in order to emphasize the fact that it was slaves upon whom he chose to confer the high honour of priesthood. By *house of your father* the Aaronide family is indicated, as the next verse implies.[64] It is true that Moses was the recipient of revelation at that stage in the Israelites' history and it is also the case that, in the Pentateuch, he exercises priestly functions in advance of Aaron (*e.g.* Lv. 8, at the installation of Aaron and his sons), but this in no way justifies seeing a reference to him in this verse.[65] *subject to* asks a lot of the preposition *l*e, even though the meaning of MT is clear enough; 4QSam[a] and the LXX show, however, that the word 'slaves' has been accidentally lost from MT.

28. A summary of the chief duties of the priesthood. *to go up*, like its converse in Leviticus 9:22, probably means that the priests ascended the altar by means of steps; compare the reference to steps in the description of Ezekiel's altar of burnt offering (Ezk. 43:17). The earliest regulation on the subject, in the 'Book of the Covenant' (Ex. 20:22–23:33), actually prohibits the construction of altar steps from considerations of modesty (Ex. 20:26); the later relaxation of the rule may be connected with the sartorial modification mentioned in Exodus 28:42.[66] There is no reason why the burning of *incense* should not have formed part of Israelite cultic ritual at this time, so that NEB 'to burn sacrifices', while linguistically possible, is an unnecessary precaution.[67]

The *ephod* mentioned here is to be distinguished from Samuel's linen ephod of verse 18, even though the verb 'to bear' (so MT for RSV *to wear*) is used in 22:18 in connection with the linen ephods worn by the priests of Nob. The high priest's *ephod* was a more elaborate item made all the more distinguished by the so-called 'breastpiece of judgement', containing the oracular devices Urim and Thummim, which was attached to it (*cf.* Ex. 28:5–30). From other references in Samuel we learn that an ephod was consulted for the purpose of obtaining oracular decisions, which suggests a correspondence, in part or in whole, with the high priestly vestment (*cf.* 23:6; 30:7f.).

In recognition of their service to God and his people, the priests had been allocated specific parts of the offerings which the ordinary Israelite worshippers brought to the sanctuary (*cf.* Lv. 2:3, 10; 7:31–36; Nu. 18:8). It is a right which, *mutatis mutandis*, Paul claims for those who are engaged in the ministry of the gospel (1 Cor. 9:13f.; *cf.* 1 Tim. 5:17f.). *offerings by fire* assumes in the traditional manner a link between MT *'iššê* and BH *'ēš*, 'fire' (*cf.* LXX), but the translation is singularly unsuited to some of the offerings designated by the term; the 'bread of the presence' (*cf.*

Lv. 24:7–9), for example, was in no sense a fire-offering. It is noteworthy that two of the ancient versions, the Targum and the Peshitta, prefer a more general term meaning 'offering', 'present', and that several alternative explanations in more recent times have tended in the same direction (*cf.* NEB 'food-offerings').[68]

29. Eli is challenged with the fact that, despite these generous arrangements made on the priests' behalf, he has connived at his sons' unprincipled behaviour. That the ultimate responsibility is his is underlined by the occurrences of *honour* in verses 29f. RSV *look* follows the LXX, now confirmed by 4QSam^a, in reading *tabbît* for MT *tib'aṭû* ('you (pl.) kick'). However, MT 'Why do you kick at my sacrifice and my offering?' not only makes reasonable sense, it also offers a parallel to Deuteronomy 32:15 where over-nourishment leads to the same physical act of defiance. The suitability of the variant favoured by RSV depends to some extent on what one does with MT *mā'ôn* at the end of the clause. The emendation to *me'ôyēn* ('eyeing'), apparently accepted by RSV, produces a suitable meaning but runs up against the problem that the word, if it is indeed a participle, is out of place at the end of the clause in MT.[69] McCarter (p. 87) follows F. M. Cross in proposing a more drastic treatment of MT which brings it nearer to the LXX. The problem, in the present writer's view, still awaits a solution. AV, RV 'in my habitation' and NIV 'for my dwelling' agree with the Targum in seeing an ordinary occurrence of BH *mā'ôn* ('dwelling', here in reference to God's earthly house as in 2 Ch. 36:15; Ps. 26:8), but to achieve this they have to supply both the preposition and the suffix.

30. The promise of perpetual priestly office (*cf.* Ex. 29:9; Nu. 25:10–13) is revoked because of Eli's failure. *honour* (*cf.* v. 29) points the finger at Eli himself. This is an interesting statement for the way in which the seemingly unconditional promise suddenly assumes a fragile conditionality; it suggests that the tension between the conditional and the unconditional which is sometimes apparent in the Old Testament's exposition of covenant and promise, for example in the Deuteronomistic historian's treatment of the Davidic promise, can be overstated. *go in and out* (lit. 'go about') means 'conduct oneself' (*cf.* the New Testament use of *peripatein*, 'to walk'); here it virtually means 'serve' (so NEB).[70]

31–34. Eli's failure is treated as a covenant breach, with the threatened judgement expressed in language redolent of the curses which were a common feature of ancient treaty (covenant) texts and which were designed to discourage nonconformity.

31, 32. Not immediate extinction, but something only marginally

preferable, is the prospect for the Elide family. *strength* (31) is lit.
'arm', which makes better sense of *cut off*. Verses 31b–32a (*so that
. . . upon Israel*) are not represented in 4QSam[a] or the LXX and,
in view of the difficulties which they raise, are not favourably
regarded by a number of textual critics.[71] One of the problems is
that Eli, despite his approaching demise, is addressed as if he would
live long enough to witness, and to envy, the better times forecast
for Israel (32). If verse 32a is original, and not just a corrupt
variant of verse 29a, the meaning is much as in RSV, except that
in distress should be eliminated; Eli, meaning the remnant of his
house, would have cause to envy Israel in the day of her prosperity,
as when Abiathar began Solomon's reign by being banished to
Anathoth (1 Ki. 2:26f.). Moreover, as both verses 31 and 32 say
in MT, the scourge of untimely death would dog the descendants
of Eli.

33. Any survivor from the first onslaught of the divine retribution
would eke out his days in misery. So RSV and NEB, *etc.* But the
reference may be more specific, requiring translation along the
lines of, 'One man of you I shall not cut off from my altar, but it
will be to weep . . . ' Even with the RSV rendering, however, it is
possible to see a reference to Abiathar, who escaped the slaughter
(*cf. sword*) of the priests of Nob (22:17–20) but who was unfrocked
by Solomon because of his support for Adonijah (1 Ki. 2:27, 35).
to weep out his eyes and grieve his heart fails to convey the idea of
decrepitude suggested in the original. In the first place, *weep out*
should give way to 'wear out', and, secondly, the wording is
strongly evocative of the curse formula of Leviticus 26:16 (*cf.* Dt.
28:65), where it is a question of the morbid effects of certain
diseases threatened on the community should it turn aside from
God's statutes and commandments. MT has 'your eyes' and 'your
heart', but RSV's preference for the LXX variants is vindicated by
4QSam[a].[72] *by the sword of men*, for MT 'as men', enjoys the same
patronage.[73] MT can barely be construed to mean 'in the flower
of their age' (AV, RV; *cf.* NIV), even though it would be a fitting
reprise of what is said in verses 31f. NEB stays with MT and, by
a change of vowel points, produces 'weaklings'. It is more likely
that *beḥereḇ* ('by the sword of') has fallen out of MT.

34. Though Eli will not live to witness all this, he will have to
endure a confirmatory *sign* in the double tragedy of the deaths of
Hophni and Phinehas (*cf.* 4:11, 17).

35. It is sometimes suggested that the prophecy concerning the
faithful priest pointed, in the first instance, to Samuel, particularly
since MT *ne'emān*, occurring twice in *faithful* and *sure*, is the word

translated by 'established' in 3:20. However, the simple distinction between priest and prophet which is evident in the two verses must not be overlooked. It is almost certainly Zadok whose preferment is thus announced, for it was the Zadokite priestly family which held office under the aegis of the *anointed* Davidic kings (*cf.* 1 Ki. 2:35). Moreover, even the phraseology of this verse hints at the Davidic connection (*cf.* 13:14; 2 Sa. 7:16; Acts 13:22). Not only the ideal of the *faithful priest*, as in traditional Christian interpretation, but also that of the *anointed* king is fulfilled in Christ, from the standpoint of the New Testament (*cf.* Rom. 1:1–6).

36. Extreme penury such as is not even described in connection with the cashiering of the rural priests of the high places during the Josianic reforms (2 Ki. 23:8f.) will also befall the Elides. The punishment is obviously meant to fit the crime as it is described in verses 15f.

The Lord calls Samuel (3:1–4:1a)

The contrasting accounts of Samuel and of Eli and family now appear momentarily in conjunction. Samuel, progressing under the tutelage of the aged priest, is initiated into the mysteries of prophecy only to find that his first sermon is one of judgement and doom. But in that respect too he is one of the prophets (*cf.* Is. 6:9–13; Je. 1:5–19). The doom is for Eli and his house, yet Israel is not without hope; before the chapter is finished and the judgement narrative begun, Samuel is functioning as the mouthpiece of God to his people. The location (sanctuary) and time (night) provide no justification for treating this as an incubation oracle (see on 28:6), since it is of the essence of the story that the oracle was as unexpected as it was unpalatable.[74]

1. When prophets were rare and visionaries few God bypassed the established priesthood and disclosed his intentions concerning that same priesthood to a novice. *word* and *vision* were the prime means by which God communicated with his servants the prophets and, through them, with his people, so that their absence might be construed as a sign of disfavour (*cf.* Ps. 74:9; La. 2:9; Am. 8:11; Mi. 3:6f.). There might also be social and moral consequences, as the likelier version of Proverbs 29:18 teaches (see RSV). The word translated *frequent* (*niprāṣ*) is itself rare enough to create slight uncertainty, but RSV cannot be far off the mark.[75]

3. The outer compartment of the sanctuary was illuminated by a night *lamp* (*nēr*; *cf.* Ex. 27:20f.; 30:7f.; Lv. 24:1–4). Since the regular term for the seven-branched lampstand of the tent of meeting is *menôrâ* (*cf.* Ex. 25:31–40), a distinction between the two is often assumed; however, the two terms are brought into association in Leviticus 24:2, 4, with reference to the one luminary. Only by a misreading of Exodus 27:20f. (// Lv. 24:2f.) could it be imagined that the lamp envisaged there was to burn perpetually, for 'continually' is qualified by 'from evening to morning' (v. 21). Comparative iconographical studies certainly do not encourage the view that the *menôrâ* is a late priestly invention.[76] While Samuel's sleeping arrangements *within the temple* turned out to be an embarrassment to some ancient guardians of orthodoxy, something similar may be implied in the statement that the young man Joshua 'did not depart from the tent (*sc.* of meeting)' (Ex. 33:11). Blushes are spared, nevertheless, if Samuel slept in an adjacent room or area, as Driver (p. 42) suggests and as the Targum takes pains to explain ('and Samuel was sleeping in the court of the Levites and the voice was heard from the temple of the Lord'). Even the Massoretic punctuation of the verse, by putting the half-way pause (*'athnaḥ*) after *lying down*, reflects unease at the plain sense of the text.[77] Well away from profane gaze, the *ark of God* – soon to be the focus of the narrative (chs. 4–6) – was housed in the inner chamber of the sanctuary. It is not necessarily to be inferred that the voice issued from the ark (*cf.* v. 10).

4–7. RSV's repetition of the name in verse 4 (*cf.* fn.) has the agreement of the LXX and (probably) 4QSamᵃ and parallels MT at verse 10. The LXX, omitting 'and (Samuel) arose', also has the repetition in verse 6. It is a not unfamiliar feature of narratives of divine communication and self-disclosure, whether Jacob's 'visions of the night' (Gn. 46:2) or Moses' call (Ex. 3:4). 'Almost a tragicomic figure' (McCarter, p. 100) is not the best description of Eli in this sequence; it is Samuel's inexperience which delays his response to the divine caller.

9, 10. It could be that the omission of 'Lord' in Samuel's response (10) is meant to underline what is said in verse 7, but part of the LXX tradition omits the word in verse 9 as well. *the Lord came and stood* is plain fare in comparison with Eliphaz's eerie scene-setting for his audition (Jb. 4:12–16), yet numinous feelings are no substitute for an encounter with God, just as Eliphaz's trite couplet (Jb. 4:17) is no match for a word from God.

11–14. A tersely-worded confirmation of the message of the man of God (2:27–36). Again Eli is blamed for tolerating his sons' misbehaviour (*cf.* 2:29f.).

12. *all that I have spoken* includes 2:27–36 but need not be limited to it.

13. *punish* shows up a rare shade in the verb *šāpaṭ* which more often means 'judge', as in the formula 'judged Israel forty years' (4:18), with reference to Eli. There may be, then, an ironic touch here. As the RSV footnote indicates, MT has 'blaspheming for themselves' instead of the presumed original *blaspheming God.* Scribal piety is responsible for this defacing of the original.[78] The change involved merely the omission of the initial letter and, since there are other cases where the quiescent *'aleph* has been intruded or extruded with similar intent, there need be no hesitation in following the LXX, RSV, NEB, *etc.*[79] Close verbal parallels are provided by Exodus 22:28 and Leviticus 24:15.

14. The doom of the house of Eli is sealed by an awful oath of disinvestiture. For an altogether more positive interposition of a divine oath, conferring perpetual priesthood on a Davidic scion, see Psalm 110:4. *expiated* may connote either cleansing or the payment of a ransom price, more probably the latter in this case. The cognate noun (*kōper*) means 'ransom', 'price of a life' (*BDB*; *cf.* Ex. 21:30 where the commutation of the death penalty to a 'ransom' is allowed in certain circumstances).[80] In the sacrificial realm, it is the blood of the animal victim, representing its life, which makes atonement for the offerer (Lv. 17:11). So also in the Christian economy, 'The price was paid in precious blood' (1 Pet. 1:19, NEB). As for Eli's house, they have despised 'sacrifices and offerings' (*cf.* 2:29) and need not think that these will now have any efficacy on their behalf (so Stoebe). The alternative rendering, 'the guilt of Eli's house in the matter of sacrifice and offering shall not be expiated' (*cf.* NEB), makes a cross-reference to 2:15f. No matter, the sin of the Elides is in the category 'high-handed' and therefore inexpiable (Nu. 15:30f.; *cf.* Heb. 10:26); priestly sins of inadvertence were, on the other hand, the subject of a more merciful provision (Lv. 4:3–12).

15–18. A not unsympathetic presentation of Eli. He obviously suspects that the interview – here called a *vision* (15; *cf.* 'appeared' in v. 21) – bodes ill for him and his family. Samuel, on the other hand, seeks to carry on business as usual (*opened the doors*); he will be a reluctant prophet.[81] *do so to you and more also* (17) is a conventional form of adjuration which does not specify the penalty for non-compliance; a gesture may have been enough. Once informed, Eli acknowledges the sovereign authority of God irrespective of the consequences for himself. 'Eli was memorable for the passive virtues. He could bear much, though he could dare little.'[82] The same acquiescence would be required of the whole nation of Judah when engulfed in the disaster of the Babylonian destruction and deportations (La. 1:18).

19, 20. Samuel embarks on a prophetic career which satisfies the Deuteronomic criterion of authentic prophecy (Dt. 18:21f.).[83] *his words* (19) are surely Samuel's (*cf.* 9:6), notwithstanding the occasional attempt to refer them to Yahweh.[84] *from Dan to Beersheba* (20), *i.e.* within the traditional limits of Israel to the north and south (*cf.* 2 Sa. 17:11), Samuel's status as a prophet was acknowledged, though a more circumscribed jurisdiction is attributed to Samuel the judge in 7:15–17. For *established* (20) see on 2:35. *prophet* (*nābî'*) is an old Semitic term reportedly in use already in the third millennium BC at Ebla (in modern Syria)[85] and with rough equivalents in the second millennium Akkadian texts found at Mari on the mid-Euphrates.[86] However, while the concept of the prophetic oracle was known outside Israel in pre-Mosaic times, and subsequently, there is nothing in the extant texts to compare with the developed religious, ethical, and social concerns of the classical prophets of Israel.

21. Now instead of infrequent vision (v. 1) Shiloh is distinguished as the place where God regularly appears to his servant (*cf.* NEB 'continued to appear' for *appeared again*). Our narrator is thus careful to trace Samuel's career to its zenith before letting us see Israel at its nadir (ch. 4). For the moment Shiloh's reputation is enhanced and all seems to be well, but tragedy supervenes.

2 The Ark of God (4:1b–7:1)

Much more than the exactions of God from Eli's house is resolved in this remarkable account of the calamitous – for all concerned – forfeiture of the ark of God to the enemies of Israel. As the podium of the invisible divine throne (*cf.* on 4:4), the ark was symbol and guarantee of the divine presence among the people of Israel. No intimation of its loss has so far been given, though 3:11 might be enlisted in retrospect. More to the point, this episode in the history of the ark becomes a parable of exile *and* restoration as the captive ark wreaks havoc and its own release, having turned Dagon into Humpty-Dumpty in the process. As noted in the Introduction, these chapters are often taken to represent the core of an originally independent composition which celebrated the awesome exploits of the ark before its sedentarization in Jerusalem. If so, the obvious connections between ch. 4 and what precedes make it unlikely that 4:1b represents the start of the original 'Ark Narrative', whatever else may be said on the subject. Moreover, the claims of outstanding antiquity entered on the narrative's behalf by some recent interpreters are perhaps more an attestation of its descriptive power than a statement of empirical fact.

THE ARK CAPTURED (4:1b–22)

1. The first sentence of ch. 4 belongs with 3:19–21. There is no suggestion that the Israelites mustered at Samuel's behest; indeed, the longer text of the LXX, favoured by NEB, states that it was the Philistines who initiated the hostilities.[1] The Philistines were a Mediterranean people, mentioned as one of the 'Sea Peoples' in

Egyptian texts from the reign of Rameses III (twelfth century BC), who finally settled on the coastal belt of land south of the plain of Sharon at about the same time as the Israelites were laying claim to regions east and north. In the Old Testament they are mainly associated with the five cities of Gath, Ashdod, Ashkelon, Ekron, and Gaza (the 'Philistine pentapolis').[2] Since such a limited terrain was incapable of satisfying the territorial ambitions of both incoming groups conflict was unavoidable. *Ebenezer* and *Aphek* lay at the southern end of the plain of Sharon, to the west of the hill country of Ephraim, from which it may be judged that the Philistines were intent on furthering their interests in the area to the north of their established territory. *Aphek*, the later Antipatris, is mentioned in various non-Israelite texts and may confidently be identified with a site (mod. Ras al-'Ain) on the river Yarkon. Less certain, but not without its attractions, is the identification of *Ebenezer* with 'Izbet Ṣarṭaḥ, the site of an Iron Age I settlement discovered during a survey of the Sharon plain in 1974 and yielding, among other items of interest, an inscribed ostracon from the period of the judges.[3]

2. *spread* (*wattiṭṭōš*) is uncertain, but as good as the alternatives ('clashed', 'fluctuated', 'deployed') which have so far been suggested.[4] If *thousand* here means '(military) unit', as seems likely, then the loss may have been smaller than it appears at first sight.[5]

3. It was a defeat for all that, and an explanation had to be found (*cf.* Jos. 7:7). The elders' conclusion is not that Yahweh had absented himself from the field of battle, nor that he had been unable to deliver them, but that he had actually intervened on the side of the enemy. This is more than to say that to Yahweh belongs the general apportioning of victory and defeat, as in 2 Kings 5:1 ('the Lord had given victory to Syria'). As is evident from the cultic invocations preserved in Numbers 10:35f. (*cf.* Ps. 68:1), at one stage the ark played a leading role in the Israelites' military undertakings (*cf.* 2 Sa. 11:11).[6] So it is agreed that it will accompany the warriors in their next encounter with the Philistines. While several titles for the ark are to be found in chs. 4–6, reference to the *covenant* is confined to the account of the preparations for the second engagement (vv. 3, 4, 5), as if to suggest that this 'messenger of the covenant' was bound to disappoint expectations once battle was joined (*cf.* Mal. 3:1f.).[7] *that he may come among us* views the ark as mediating the divine presence (*cf.* v. 4; 2 Sa. 7:1–6). Thus the verse brings together two aspects of the ark ideology which are sometimes regarded as immiscible, *viz.* the ark as container of the tablets of the Sinaitic covenant and the ark as a divine dwelling-place.[8] But since the Hebrew for *ark* is in the masculine gender it is as likely that the reference is to the ark itself as the agent of deliverance (so the Peshitta and some modern versions).

4. While the verb in question (*nāśā'*) may serve even when the ark is transported on the 'new cart' (2 Sa. 6:3), the more common usage and the example of the ancient versions favour the substitution of 'carried' for *brought*. Behind the reference to the carrying of the ark in 2 Samuel 6:13 lies the assumption that this was the proper means of conveyance (*cf.* Dt. 10:8; Jos. 3:6; 6:6; 1 Ki. 2:26); see on 2 Samuel 6:3. BH *nāśā'* has a distinct cultic usage, occurring also in connection with the ephod (see on 2:28) and the ceremonial carrying of images (Is. 46:7; Am. 5:26(?)). *enthroned* is a legitimate rendering of MT *yōšēḇ*,[9] though by far the commonest meanings of this verb are 'sit' and 'dwell' (*cf.* AV, RV). As in Ezekiel's vision of the sapphire throne (Ezk. 10:1; *cf.* Ezk. 1:22–26), the *cherubim* have a supporting role, here in relation to the invisible divine throne. The idea is represented extensively in the iconography of the ancient near east, in which hybrid figures incorporating animal and human characteristics flank palace entrances or, as in a much-quoted ivory carving from eleventh-century (?) Gebal (Byblos), royal thrones.[10] The description of God as *enthroned on the cherubim* is particularly apposite in view of the association of the ark with the cherub figures which overlooked it in the inner compartment of the sanctuary (Ex. 25:18–22; 1 Ki. 6:23–28; 8:6f.). It is not to be inferred from all this that God's presence is limited to an earthly 'dwelling', for 'the throne in the holy of holies is but a model of the throne on high'.[11] *Hophni and Phinehas* are in charge of the ark; well might Eli tremble (v. 13).

5. At first the signs are good: exhilaration in the Israelite camp and enervation among the Philistines (vv. 7f.). The *mighty shout* (*tᵉrûᶜâ*) doubles here as an expression of joy and as a battle-cry; for the latter compare the use of the cognate verb in 17:20, 52, *etc.*[12]

6. In terms of Old Testament genealogy *Hebrews* (*'iḇrîm*) is a patronymic based on the name of Eber (*'ēḇer*), the great-grandson of Shem (*cf.* Gn. 10:21–25; 11:10–17). As a surrogate for 'Israelite(s)' it tends to occur on the lips of non-Israelites (*e.g.* Ex. 2:6) or of Israelites addressing non-Israelites (*e.g.* Jon. 1:9). The question as to whether some of the occurrences of 'Hebrew' have a social, as distinct from an ethnic, connotation is much debated, with the answer depending to a large extent on the relationship, if any, between BH *'iḇrî* and the Akkadian *ḫabiru* (same as the Egyptian *ᶜpr.w*), which occurs in texts of the second millennium as the name for an assortment of peoples who appear to have remained on the periphery of the larger socio-economic communities of the near east.[13] If the case for linking the two terms were stronger then 'Hebrew' would carry some suggestion of social inferiority or even of political dependence (cf. v. 9 and see on 13:3).

7. *A god* makes express the connection between the ark and the divine presence. There may be the further thought that the Philistines regard the ark as the equivalent of an image, which is exactly how they treated it when it came into their hands (cf. 5:2).[14]

8. Apart from the obvious parallel of the plague episodes in the next chapter, there are various other features of 1 Samuel 4–6 which recall the exodus story. Here, as in 6:6, a direct comparison is made. Alas, the Philistines are not cast as the most accurate of historians! In Exodus the plagues are located in Egypt, not in the wilderness, and partly for that reason some scholars have favoured the minor emendation of MT *bammiḏbār* to *ûḇaddāḇer* (or *ûḇᵉmô ḏāḇer*): '(with every sort of plague) and with pestilence'. LXX *'and* in the wilderness' may preserve a superior reading, or – just as likely – eases the historical problem by inserting the conjunction.[15]

9. Using standard formulae, the Philistines 'psych' themselves for battle (cf. 2 Sa. 10:12; 13:28). (When Paul applies the idea to Christian attitude and conduct he adds, 'Let all that you do be done *in love*' (1 Cor. 16:13f.).)

10, 11. This time the 'plague' – for *slaughter* (10) represents another nuance of the word used in verse 8 – is on Israel; even *the ark of God* may become 'deceptive words' (cf. Je. 7:4) and, in impious hands, will function neither as palladium nor *deus ex machina*. Again the number of casualties would be considerably smaller if the Hebrew *'elep* may mean '(military) unit' as well as *thousand* (cf. on v. 2). *foot soldiers* were all that the Israelite tribal militia was capable of mustering at this stage; only under the monarchy, and not really until Solomon, did Israel maintain an effective chariot force (1 Ki. 4:26; 10:26; though see 2 Sa. 8:4 for David's reign). Verse 11 records the fulfilment of the sign given in 2:34 in the prophetic impeachment of Eli's house, yet even this is overshadowed by the notice of the capture of the ark.

Nothing is said about the fate of Shiloh in the wake of this disaster, but Jeremiah seems to be referring to this period when he holds up to his contemporaries the destruction of the Shiloh sanctuary as an awful warning against defection from God (Je. 7:12–15; 26:6). Psalm 78:60–64, in linking the abandonment of Shiloh with the slaughter of its priests, also appears to have

this occasion in mind. Finally, the circumstance that the Elides'
successors are found at Nob (21:1–9; 22:9–19) may be an indication
that Shiloh suffered in a follow-up operation by the Philistines
after their success at Ebenezer. Both the archaeological evidence,
which had previously seemed compatible with an eleventh-century
destruction of Shiloh, and the historical implications of Jeremiah's
'Shiloh sermon' have been subjected to reinterpretation in more
recent times, nevertheless the traditional view has much to be said
in its defence.[16] In the interests of clarity it is well to distinguish
between the destruction of the Shilonite sanctuary and the town of
Shiloh which, whatever its treatment at the hands of the Philistines,
revived sufficiently to produce a few worthy citizens in later generations (cf. 1 Ki. 11:29; Je. 41:5).

12–18. Some of the most memorable scenes in Hebrew narrative
revolve around the figure of the messenger (e.g. 2 Sa. 1:2–16; 18:19–
33; Jb. 1:13–19). The narrator skilfully creates an air of suspense
in the build-up to Eli's death, partly by means of narrative retardation (e.g. v. 15) and partly by repetition of the verb 'come' (vv.
12, 13 (twice; 'when he arrived' is lit. 'and he came'), 14).

12. It was a 'mini-marathon' of close on twenty miles that the
Benjaminite ran that day.[17] As the bringer of bad tidings he bears
the customary signs of mourning (cf. Jos. 7:6; 2 Sa. 1:2, 11f.;
13:31).[18] A Targumic gloss reflecting the rabbinic belief in the
co-inherence of all things biblical discloses that Saul, also from
Benjamin (9:1f.), accompanied the runner.[19]

13. Visual details are lost on the pathetic old priest who, blind
(v. 15) but *watching*, waited for news of the ark of God. Despite
his flaws and foibles he has this in his favour – he has a concern
for the ark, a concern which overrides even paternal instinct (v.
18). It is ironical that Eli should fear for the ark when it was
capable of striking terror in the hearts of Israel's enemies (cf. vv.
7f.). The alternative suggestion that Eli feared *because of* the ark,
lest it bring judgement upon his sons in whose charge it was, is
grammatically possible but does not agree so well with the tenor of
the section (e.g. v. 18).[20] NEB, reviving a suggestion of Wellhausen,
repoints MT *mᵉṣappeh* (*watching*) to read 'to Mizpah'. However,
while this would explain why Eli was the last to hear the report of
the messenger – for Mizpah lay to the south of Shiloh and Ebenezer
to the west – it leaves unexplained why the trepid Eli should have
been on the Mizpah side of town in the first place.[21] The LXX's
'by the gate watching the road' reflects a smoother text than MT
and could be original.

15. The reference to Eli's age and condition at this point slows up the movement of the story, just as it probably was intended to do. To treat the verse as interpolative is to miss the point (*pace* Smith, McCarter).

16, 17. The messenger is a fugitive. Four clauses, climaxing in the mention of the *ark*, sum up the day's calamities (17). *slaughter* (*maggēpâ*) is another word which, appropriately enough in the context of 1 Samuel 4–6, may mean 'plague' (so 6:4; *cf.* on vv. 10f. above).

18. The verse associates Eli with the judges of the book of Judges, though there is scarcely warrant for Hertzberg's surmise that Eli's name may have originally appeared in a list of minor judges which survives in Judges 10 and 12.[22] All the same, and despite the silence of the preceding narrative on the subject, Eli may have fulfilled a role comparable with that of the minor judges. Priesthood and judgeship were not necessarily incompatible, as Cody rightly concludes from such references as Exodus 18:13–26 and Deuteronomy 17:8–13.[23] Something broader than mere judicial function is indicated by *judged*, and the Hebrew *šōpēṭ* ('judge') may profitably be compared with the *šāpiṭum* ('governor') of the Mari texts.[24] *side (of the gate)*: here BH *yăḏ* may possibly denote one of the parallel walls making up the gateway (so McCarter). In that case Eli fell from the top of the gateway wall, with the barely avoidable consequence described. But Klein thinks that McCarter's explanation is suspect.

19, 20. Phinehas' wife, sent into premature labour by the baleful tidings, also becomes a casualty of Ebenezer. The curiously indirect way in which her *death* is broached in verse 20 suggests that it is to be taken for granted – a further instalment of the judgement on Eli's family.[25]

21, 22. The tragedy of Israel, bereft of the divine presence, is encapsulated in the name *Ichabod* which may mean 'No glory' (*cf.* Josephus, *Ant.* v. 11. 4) or, since it is apparently of the same construction as the name Jezebel (Heb. *'î-zeḇel*), 'Where is the glory?'. In the latter case there would be a formal parallel with the lamentation for absentee gods (of the vegetational-seasonal variety) which is a feature of Canaanite cult mythology as reflected in the Ugaritic epic texts.[26] *departed* can be justified as a translation of *gālâ*, but it obscures the fact that this is a story of exile; in most of its occurrences the verb means 'go into exile'.[27] The appositeness of the reference will not have been missed by those of a later generation who suffered the loss of their temple and the inconvenience of deportation following the Babylonian depredations.

Then too it entailed, as Ezekiel saw in his visions, a withdrawal of the divine glory (Ezk. 10:18f.; 11:22f.).

VICTUS VICTOR (5:1–12)

'Then the Lord awoke as from sleep . . .' Thus does Psalm 78:65 recall the happenings of this chapter in which God, freed of the encumbrance of his wayward devotees, stirs himself to execute judgement on Philistia and its gods, as on Egypt at the exodus. The Philistine gods are represented by Dagon who, to judge from the other Old Testament references to him (Jdg. 16:23; 1 Ch. 10:10), may have been head of the Philistine pantheon. In the Ugaritic texts he is described as the father of Baal who, of course, appears as the arch-enemy of Yahweh at many points in the Old Testament. Above and beyond the 'grim humour' (Ackroyd) which pervades the story is the assertion of God's sovereignty over the domain of Dagon and his colleagues – a sovereignty which extends right into Dagon's den (vv. 1–5). The same kind of claim and the same derisive air are extensively present in Isaiah 40–55 (*e.g.* 44:6–20). McCarter imaginatively entitles this section 'The Harrowing of the Philistines', presumably drawing inspiration from a later 'harrowing', also in circumstances of weakness and defeat (1 Pet. 3:18–22; *cf.* Col. 2:15).

1, 2. It was common practice in the near east for victorious armies to carry off enemy idols and install them in the temple of their chief god in symbol of the latter's sovereignty over the subject people and its gods.[28] Because Israel's worship was image-less (aniconic) their enemies had to make do with substitutes, whether the ark as on this occasion, or the sacred temple vessels as at the time of the Babylonian exile (*e.g.* Ezr. 1:7). *Dagon* was a Semitic god worshipped in Mesopotamia already in the third millennium BC.[29] When the Philistines settled in Canaan they quickly adopted local deities into their pantheon, perhaps by identifying them with suitable candidates from among their ancestral gods. The result is that hardly anything is known about Philistine religion in its pre-Canaanite phase; the gods with whom they are associated in the Old Testament, *viz.* Dagon, Ashtoreth, and Baal-zebub, are all Semitic gods. Dagon's name is almost certainly connected with a Semitic root meaning 'grain' (*cf.* Hebrew *dāḡān*), which would make him a vegetation deity.

3. As the ark begins to show itself 'a terrible guest'[30] Dagon suffers the first of his two 'defeats' in the presence of a superior power. Nothing is said of the workings of that mysterious power; only its effects are described. Dagon, far from being 'an image that will not move' (Is. 40:20), measures his length on the ground, a worshipper himself.[31]

4. A worse fate follows. God's judgement falls in the night, just as in his final assault on the gods of Egypt (Ex. 12:12; *cf.* Nu. 33:4). It is not inappropriate in this setting to think of the *head* and *hands* as trophies of war (*cf.* 17:54; 31:9f.).[32] Campbell notes a contrast between the 'powerless severed palms of Dagon' and Yahweh's 'oppressive hand' in 5:6-12.[33] *the trunk of Dagon* probably conveys the right sense, though MT has 'only Dagon was left to him'. It is possible that a word meaning 'body' or 'trunk' and similar in form to the name 'Dagon' has fallen out of MT. NIV offers 'only his body remained'.

5. The ridicule implicit in the story so far is heightened by the observation, perhaps as much satirical as aetiological,[34] that the untrodden *threshold* of the Ashdod temple is witness to this unseemly episode in the career of Dagon. Sanctuary thresholds were commonly treated with respect in the ancient world because they marked the boundary dividing sacred from profane. Instead of *threshold* (*miṗtān*) some prefer 'platform' (so NEB), but it is questionable whether the priests would have been expected to tread on the plinth in any case.[35] The reference to *leaping* (*cf.* the LXX addition here) over the *miṗtān* in Zephaniah 1:9, if it reflects the same custom, would tend to support RSV. *to this day* indicates a significant interval between the loss of the ark and the writing of the present narrative. For similar references in connection with the ark see 6:18 and 2 Samuel 6:8. Dagon was worshipped at Ashdod until at least the middle of the first century BC (*cf.* 1 Macc. 10:83-85; 11:4).

6. Now in the mention of *the hand of the Lord* (*cf.* vv. 7, 9, 11) the involvement of Yahweh in the discomfiting of Ashdod is expressly stated (*cf.* on v. 3).[36] While MT notes only an affliction of *tumours* at this point, the LXX, with its reference to mice, anticipates 6:4f., 11; NEB follows the Greek Pied Piper with its additional clause, 'and their territory swarmed with rats'. Despite a fair amount of discussion of the pathology of this plague it is hard to improve upon the old suggestion of an outbreak of bubonic plague in which *rattus rattus* would have played his accustomed role of carrier.[37] Another view, as old as Josephus (*Ant.* vi. 1. 1), is that the Philistines were afflicted with dysentery.[38]

8. The *lords* (*s^erānîm*) of the Philistines were the governors of the five cities of the Philistine confederacy listed in 6:17 (*cf.* 6:4).

The word has frequently been compared with the Greek *tyrannos* (popularly 'tyrant'), in illustration of the Mediterranean prehistory of the Philistines; both words may be related to the Hittite royal title *tarwanas*, for which the meaning 'judge' has been suggested.[39] As the ark moves on to *Gath* and then to Ekron (v. 10) the story begins to read like a parody of a victory tour, in which the roles of victor and vanquished are reversed. And despite the silence of the text on the matter, the contest motif – Yahweh versus the gods of Philistia – is not necessarily abandoned after verse 7 (*cf.* 6:5). Ekron, for example, is associated at a later date with the worship of Baal-zebub (2 Ki. 1:3).

9, 10. *panic* (*meḥûmâ*) denotes that divinely-induced confusion which was wont to befall the enemies of Israel when Yahweh entered the lists on behalf of his people (*cf.* Zc. 14:13). *us . . . us* (10): actually MT has 'me . . . me', in accordance with Hebrew idiom whereby a city may speak on behalf of, or as one of, its citizens; so also 'my people' for RSV *our people*. Daube, comparing Pharaoh's utterances in Exodus 8:8, *etc.*, sees a reflex of the exodus narrative in MT 'me and my people', on the supposition that the words are more appropriate on the lips of Pharaoh; but he over-looks the idiomatic factor.[40]

11, 12. RSV *deathly* (11) should, as McKane noted, be 'deadly'; it is just a matter of correct English usage.[41] Phraseologically the statement that the Ekronites' cry *went up to heaven* (12) finds its closest parallel in Exodus 2:23 (*cf.* Driver, McCarter), but a truer comparison is with the anguished cries of the Egyptians forced to release their Hebrew slaves because of Yahweh's punitive inter-vention (*cf.* Ex. 11:6; 12:30).

THE RETURN   (6:1–7:1)

It is a little surprising that there has been no involvement of the Philistine priesthood in the story so far; the appeals of the suffering population have been directed to the city rulers (*cf.* 5:8, 11). In fact the role of the priests and diviners, as this chapter shows, is to relieve Philistia of its agony by counselling submission before Israel's God.

1. *seven months*: the first of three time references (*cf.* 7:2; 2 Sa. 6:11) emphasizing the enormity of the loss suffered by Israel when the ark was taken.

2. Hardly anything is said about the mechanics of divination in the Old Testament which, indeed, is more concerned to discourage its practice in Israelite society (*cf.* Dt. 18:10–14). *diviners* (*qōsᵉmîm*) represents a root which is characteristically associated with the heathen prophet Balaam (Nu. 22:7; 23:23; Jos. 13:22). That the priests and diviners were, like Balaam, outsiders engaged for a particular occasion and need has even been inferred from their apparently disinterested discussion of Philistia's troubles, but they do eventually get round to identifying with the afflicted populace (v. 9).

3. The experts advise that compensation be paid to Israel's God. This is the basic notion in *guilt offering* (*'āšām*), which is especially appropriate where the offence is assessable in monetary terms (Lv. 5:15f.); *cf.* NEB 'a gift . . . by way of indemnity'.[42] There is an obvious parallel between this 'spoiling of the Philistines' and the exodus tradition (*cf.* Ex. 3:21f.), but Daube makes an additional comparison with the law of release for the Hebrew slave who was not to be sent away *empty*(-handed) (Dt. 15:13f.); so the ark of God emerges from its period of 'slavery'.[43]

4, 5. The prescription smacks of sympathetic magic, with the sending away of the plague models (*tumours, mice*) symbolizing the banishment of the plague from the land. German commentators (Hugo Gressmann, Hertzberg) not unnaturally think of the homeopathic principle of *similia similibus curantur* – curing like with like – formulated by Samuel Hahnemann. There is a superficial resemblance to the making of the bronze serpent in Numbers 21, the chief difference being that there the serpent is itself the agent of healing. These models are in gold because they are also an offering and an indemnity to the God whose property has been violated.[44] *give glory* (5): compare Joshua's advice to the convicted Achan (Jos. 7:19).

6. The priests and diviners are made to speak in the manner of the great prophets (or of a Balaam?) as they cite the classic error of the Egyptians whose obduracy of old had only intensified their own sufferings, at the same time as it enhanced the reputation of the God of the Israelites (*cf.* Ex. 10:1f.; 14:17f.). See on 4:8.

7–9. Since natural instinct would incline the cows to head back home to their offspring, the logic of this scheme was that only a strong impulse from a superior power would send them off in the direction of Beth-shemesh. (Klein finds a rough analogy in Elijah's dousing of his burnt-offering on Carmel (1 Kgs. 18:33f.).) If that happened the Philistines' miseries could confidently be attributed to the Israelites' God. The *cart* (7) must be *new*, *i.e.* not previously used for a profane purpose, if it was to be a fit conveyance for the ark. That the cows had never borne the *yoke* is doubly significant in that it confirms the absence of human interference in their movements and also looks to their future sacrificial role (v. 14; *cf.* Nu. 19:2 of the purificatory 'red cow'). Certain points of similarity between this account and a Hittite plague ritual, which involved the despatching of a ram toward the territory of an enemy god, have already been noticed by Miller–Roberts and therefore call for no further comment here.[45] The parallel holds particular interest because of the possible connection of the Philistines with Anatolia. The word translated *box* (*'argaz*, 8) is often assumed to be a Philistine loan-word but may as likely be homespun Semitic, possibly meaning 'pouch' or 'bag'.[46] *Beth-shemesh* ('house of the sun', 9), represented by the modern Tell er-Rumeileh, lay about twelve miles to the west of Jerusalem in an area bordering on Philistine territory. Archaeologists have unearthed a considerable amount of evidence of Philistine influence, in the form of pottery remains, in this period (*i.e.* just before 1000 BC).[47]

12, 13. Contrary to what might have been expected of them, the cows moved off towards Beth-shemesh, albeit making a noise about it. The reference to wheat harvesting in the *valley* (13) of Sorek (*cf.* Jdg. 16:4), in which Beth-shemesh was located, shows that it was early summer (May-June).

14, 15. An impromptu sacrificial ceremony was held in the field of the otherwise unknown *Joshua*, the Philistines having provided both combustibles and offering. According to the strict letter of priestly law it should have been a male animal that was offered (*cf.* Lv. 1:3). It might be inferred from verse 14 that the *great stone* served as an altar (*cf.* Ex. 20:25), but this is gainsaid in verse 15 – by a later editor in the opinion of many scholars[48] – and according to verse 18 the stone is remembered primarily as the resting-place of the ark. *Levites* (15), the sole custodians of the ark according to Pentateuchal law (*cf.* Nu. 3:27–32; Dt. 10:8), are seldom mentioned in the books of Samuel – a fact which has been highly influential in modern scholarly reconstructions of the history of Israelite religion.[49] A still larger question concerns the hiatus between the elaborate cult and ritual outlined in the Pentateuch and the meagre cultic apparatus described in the books dealing with the pre-monarchical period. At the same time, it is certainly no embarrassment to the present reference to Levites that Beth-shemesh is listed among the Levitical cities in Joshua 21:16 (*cf.* 1 Ch. 6:59), for it is unlikely that the Levites were introduced here merely because of the special status of Beth-shemesh.

16. The Philistine *lords*, who have been watching from a distance (v. 12), return in the knowledge that their reparation offering has been accepted. They make for *Ekron*, the city most recently afflicted by the plague (*cf.* 5:10).

17, 18. Whereas there are five *golden tumours*, one for each of the cities of the Philistine pentapolis listed here, it seems to be implied that the number of golden *mice* was greater, to take account of the full number of Philistine settlements.[50] A few small points require clarification in verse 18. *The great stone*: RSV's emendation of MT *'āḇēl* (meaning either 'meadow' or 'brook'; AV transliterates as a proper name) to *'eḇen* ('stone') is doubtless correct. The occurrence of the verb *'āḇal* ('mourn') in verse 19 may account for the error, while little credence may be given to the suggestion that the stone was renamed 'Great Mourning' because of the tragedy about to be recounted.[51] *beside which* would be better translated 'upon which' (*cf.* v. 15). *witness* (*'ēḏ*) involves repointing MT *'aḏ* ('as far as') and is thoroughly defensible.

19. Even in Israelite territory the ark brings destruction. The reason for the slaughter is not clear since RSV *looked into*, though paralleled in Jewish tradition as it is reflected in the Targum, goes beyond the natural sense of the original.[52] A reading peculiar to the LXX supplies one or two of the deficiencies of the standard text and is followed by NEB: 'But the sons of Jechoniah did not rejoice with the rest of the men of Beth-shemesh . . .' Next there is the number killed – 50,070 according to MT – which seems impossibly large for a town of, at most, a few thousand inhabitants. RSV's omission of 'fifty thousand men', which comes in most awkwardly after *seventy men* in the original, is almost universally accepted (*cf.* NEB, NIV against AV, RV). Josephus gives the smaller number without further comment (*Ant.* vi. 1. 4).[53] The basic point at issue in this verse is that God will brook no irregularity in his people's treatment of the sacred ark (*cf.* 2 Sa. 6:6f.).

20. McCarter, who joins Josephus in attributing the slaughter to the absence of proper priestly supervision at Beth-shemesh, interprets *stand before* in relation to priestly service, as in Judges 20:27f., *etc.* Another possible interpretation is suggested by the very similar form of words used in Exodus 9:11, according to which the Egyptian magicians were not able to 'stand before Moses'. In this case the men of Beth-shemesh would be acknowledging the overwhelming power of Yahweh, rather than overlooking the obvious expedient of hiring a priest.

21. Not only was *Kiriath-jearim* a near neighbour of Beth-shemesh (*cf.* Jos. 15:9f.), both its location (*cf.* on 7:1) and the variant names by which it is known are compatible with sanctuary status. A previous connection with the worship of Baal is probably

indicated in the alternative forms Baalah (Jos. 15:9), Kiriath-
baal (Jos. 15:60), and Baale-judah (2 Sa. 6:2). The most likely
identification of the site is with Tell el-'Azhar, eight miles west of
Jerusalem.[54] This association of Kiriath-jearim ('city of (the) for-
ests') with the ark may be commemorated in the reference to 'the
fields of Jaar (Heb. *ya'ar*, "forest")' in a psalm composed in praise
of the ark (Ps. 132:6).

7:1. The location of Abinadab's house *on the hill* may account
for the depositing of the ark there, since in this period the 'high
place' as a centre of worship was not regarded unfavourably (*cf.*
9:12f.). While *Eleazar* is a good Levitical name, first borne by a
son of Aaron (Nu. 3:32), this was an *ad hoc* appointment in the
manner of Judges 17:5. The suggestion that Eleazar was the original
'faithful priest' of 2:35 would appear to elevate him above his
proper station.[55]

3   The Institution of the Monarchy (7:2–12:25)

For an institution which promised so much, the Israelite monarchy turned out to be a costly failure. Hence it is fitting that, as the circumstances of its birth are rehearsed *in extenso* in the next six chapters, the uncomfortable question of legitimacy should continually be pressing for answer. It was a development which set prophet and people at variance, and the tensions are faithfully represented in the narrative. Saul, caught in the middle, is sympathetically treated by the narrator, whose sense of fairness – no doubt reflecting the attitude of his sources – has frequently, indeed, been taken to indicate ambivalence toward the monarchy itself. But when the dust of argument has settled the overall view of the text is not in doubt; it is frankly antagonistic. And yet, if the monarchy is a monument to human weakness it is also a symbol of divine grace, for Israel may put her disobedience behind her and look confidently ahead if only she will maintain covenant obedience to her God (12:20–24).

VICTORY AT MIZPAH   (7:2–17)

As has been noted in the Introduction, while this chapter makes no overt reference to the monarchy it is anything but silent on the issue. Its message is simply that when Israel owes allegiance to God a king is *de trop*. In a military encounter which is presented as a test case, Samuel, by priestly-prophetic mediation, taps that divine power which, unaided, puts enemies to flight and makes Israelite armies all but non-combatant. Samuel is here depicted at the height of his powers (contrast 8:1) and in the exercise of his threefold role of prophet, priest, and judge; the comparison with Moses in Exodus 17–18 is well taken in this regard.[1] Notices of further military successes by Israel (vv. 13f.) and of Samuel's administrative circuit (vv. 15–17) round off the account. In short, everything is under the control of Yahweh and his chosen representative. To ask for a king in these circumstances would, it is implied, be an impertinence.

2, 3. The return of the ark of God to Israelite territory did not mark the end of the Philistine oppression. Still, it was all of twenty years before 'there was a movement throughout Israel to follow the Lord' (NEB). And even then Samuel challenged the people as to the genuineness of their repentance; *with all your heart* is emphatically placed in MT to make this point. Undivided allegiance to the one God (*cf.* Dt. 6:4f.) entails the rejection of all rivals (Ps. 16:2, 4) – for the real agent of *foreign* oppression in the land is their adherence to the cults of Baal (*cf.* v. 4) and Ashtart. This is sermon enough, with its echoes of Joshua's farewell (Jos. 24:14f., 23) and of Judges 10:6–16, yet G. E. Mendenhall wants to see Deuteronomy 32:1–43 as the full text of Samuel's speech on this occasion.[2] Whereas all that can be said is that similar sets of circumstances are reflected in both chapters.

4. The Israelites by their repentance fulfil the third element in that scheme of apostasy-oppression-repentance-deliverance which is outlined for the period of the judges (Jdg. 2:11–23) and which is, to a degree, exemplified in this chapter. That repentance avails in the bleakest of situations is a tenet of the 'Deuteronomistic History' of which the books of Samuel form a part.[3] Various fertility deities of both sexes may be comprehended in *Baals* and *Ashtaroth*. In the first instance Baal denotes the West Semitic storm god Hadad, but the term is used in the Old Testament for an indeterminate number of hypostases and manifestations. Ashtart (Astarte) was the female counterpart of Baal and, with her interests in love, fertility, and war, also had attractions for the Philistines (*cf.* 31:10).

5. *Mizpah* was an important rendezvous for the Israelite tribes in the pre-monarchical period (*cf.* Jdg. 20:1; 21:1, 5, 8; 1 Sa. 10:17). It was to here, many centuries later, that Judas Maccabaeus resorted at a critical moment, apparently in hope of a re-enactment of Samuel's famous victory (1 Macc. 3:46). Tell en-Naṣbeh, eight miles north of Jerusalem, is the probable site of Mizpah.[4]

6. Before Samuel's prayer of intercession the assembly at Mizpah gives ample evidence that the precondition of confession and repentance has been met (*cf.* Ps. 66:18). The pouring out of the water *before the Lord* may simply have formed part of the self-denial of the occasion as the participants solemnly proclaimed their abstention from even this necessity of life.[5] If there is a ritual significance it is not clear what it is; comparisons with water rites in extra-biblical sources, for example in connection with the Festival of Tabernacles, are not very helpful. At the same time, a fertility significance, in that the God of Israel, and not Baal or Ashtart (*cf*. v. 4), is acknowledged as the true source of life and fertility, may lie beneath the surface.[6] So it was that when Ahab king of Israel defected to Baal-Melkart and the fertility religion of Canaan the Lord of history made devastating riposte as God of nature (1 Ki. 16:31f.; 17:1; *cf*. Ho. 2:5–9). David's water libation on a later occasion is best seen as a spontaneous gesture in response to a notable display of loyalty by three of his captains (2 Sa. 23:16). *judged* may imply the kind of function described in Exodus 18:13–27, but see the note on 4:18.

7–9. By their reaction to the report of the Israelite convention at Mizpah the Philistines create the circumstances in which the promised deliverance (v. 3) can be achieved. Not being in a state of military preparedness, the assembled Israelites are the more appreciative of Samuel's good offices (8). Ironically, they are no less dependent even when they have appointed their own means of salvation in the person of their first king (*cf*. 12:19–23). *a sucking lamb* (9): in priestly law an animal became eligible for sacrifice on its eighth day (Ex. 22:30; Lv. 22:27). Ideas of expiation and intercession merge here, since a basic function of the *burnt offering* was to make atonement (Lv. 1:4; *cf*. 2 Sa. 24:25; Jb. 1:5; 42:8).

10, 11. The 'answer' (*cf*. v. 9) comes in the form of a thunderclap and the Philistines are reduced to a state of discomfiture familiar from other stories in the holy war tradition of the Old Testament (*e.g.* Jos. 10:10; Jdg. 4:15, where the verb *hāmam* ('throw into confusion') is also featured).[7] This divine thundering recalls the imagery of the storm theophany by which God's activity is described in a number of texts (*e.g.* Ex. 19:16; Ps. 29). The result is that Israelite participation is limited to a second phase mopping up of fugitives (11). Since this is the sole mention of *Beth-car* it can only be surmised that it lay west of Mizpah and in the general direction of Philistia. The identification with Lower Beth-horon, favoured by some, assumes the corruption in MT of a relatively well-known name.[8]

12. There is more to the naming of the commemorative *stone* than the acknowledgement that the victory had come from God. *Ebenezer*, as the name linked with Israel's earlier defeats by the

Philistines (*cf*. 4:1; 5:1), announces the reversal of these indignities; it is a symbol of reintegration. (Geographical considerations render it unlikely that this Ebenezer is the same as that mentioned in ch. 4.) *Hitherto* may mean no more than that God's help against the Philistines was experienced along the way as far as Ebenezer. However, in the present setting (see the introductory comments above on 7:2–17) it is tempting to entertain a temporal significance: until this point in Israel's history Yahweh has been her helper. The question soon to be resolved (ch. 8) is whether Yahweh would be allowed to continue that help within the old theocratic framework, or would be set aside as Israel sought to go it alone. *Jeshanah* is the name of a town on the border between Judah and Israel (2 Ch. 13:19). MT has 'Shen' ('crag'),[9] but RSV has support in the ancient versions (LXX, Peshitta).

13, 14. The victory at Mizpah is viewed as decisive in driving the Philistines back on their heels and preventing them from troubling Israel during the remainder of Samuel's life. Thus Samuel's tenure as judge conforms to the pattern observed in Judges 2:18: 'Whenever the Lord raised up judges for them, the Lord was with the judge, and he saved them from the hand of their enemies all the days of the judge . . .'. The somewhat idealized picture of domestic stability and of territorial integrity is manifestly intended to demonstrate the sufficiency of the old theocratic order which is about to be called in question. To that end, no account is taken of Philistine garrisons in Israelite territory (*cf*. 10:5; 13:3), nor of the confrontations between the Israelites and Philistines that were a feature of Saul's reign (*cf*. 14:52). *the hand of the Lord* (13) sounds like an echo from the story of the ark's visit to Philistia (5:6, 7, 9, *etc*.). *from Ekron to Gath* (14) delimits a stretch of border territory which was freed from Philistine control during this period (*cf*. NEB). The *Amorites* here represent the pre-Israelite inhabitants of Canaan (*cf*. 2 Sa. 21:2), and as such a potential threat to Israelite security from within.[10]

15–17. Finally, a summary of Samuel's activities as judge-administrator which links him with three venerable Israelite cities, all of them more or less within the Benjaminite tribal ambit at this time (*cf*. Jos. 18:21–28). The LXX understands *places* (16) in its more specialized sense of 'sanctuaries'. Even *Ramah* could become a place of sacrifice and enjoy unaccustomed prominence thanks to its most famous son (17). Shiloh, as we should judge from ch. 4, was no longer a centre of worship or administration.

16. The site of the ancient sanctuary town of *Bethel* (*cf*. 10:3) is indicated by the modern Tell Beitîn, ten miles north of Jerusalem.

The exact whereabouts of *Gilgal*, which certainly cannot be very far from Jericho (*cf.* Jos. 5:9f.), is not known.

17. *Ramah*: see on 1:19 (*cf.* 25:1).

THE REQUEST FOR A KING   (8:1–22)

At several points towards the end of the book of Judges the reader is reminded that in those days Israel lacked a king (17:6; 18:1; 19:1; 21:25). The significance of this observation is spelled out in two of these references with the additional comment that 'every man did what was right in his own eyes' (17:6; 21:25), and we are left to conclude that only the advent of monarchy would bring an end to the lawless years. In the same book, however, we are told of Gideon's uncompromising stand when, in the euphoria following his victory over the Midianites, he was invited to found a dynasty: 'I will not rule over you, and my son will not rule over you; the Lord will rule over you' (Jdg. 8:23). A similar estimation of the monarchy, finding it incompatible with the theocratic ideal, is expressed in 1 Samuel 8. Monarchy was not indigenous to Israelite society, and it is surely no coincidence that Abimelech, the engineer and, initially, the beneficiary of the short-lived Shechemite experiment in monarchy, was Gideon's son by a Canaanite concubine (Jdg. 8:31; *cf.* 9:1–57). When, therefore, the Israelite elders came asking Samuel for a king he, as spokesman for Yahweh, offered stalwart resistance. And even if there are signs of a more positive attitude toward the monarchy in chs. 9–11, as has often been maintained (though see the Introduction), it remains the case that the first word (8:11–18) and the last (12:1–25) are with Samuel, and that he saw the new development as ill-disguised apostasy.

1, 2. Late in life Samuel conducted his own little dynastic experiment when he appointed his sons to succeed him in the office of judge. That *Joel* and *Abijah* functioned in Beer-sheba, in the south of Judah, agrees well with the depiction of Samuel as a national figure in these chapters, though it takes us well beyond the range of Samuel's movements as summarized in 7:16f. Both sons' names contain short forms (*yô* and *yâ*) of the divine name Yahweh, as befitted the offspring of an ardent Yahwist like Samuel.

3. 'Now these men afford us an evident example and demonstration, how some children are not of the like dispositions with their parents' (Josephus, *Ant.* vi. 3. 2, tr. Whiston). It was no consolation that Joel and Abijah were practising their deceits away down in Beer-sheba; judges, then as now, were supposed to be incorruptible (*cf*. Ex. 18:21; 23:8; Dt. 16:19), and Samuel himself could claim an impeccable record in this regard (12:3–5).

4, 5. Unintentionally, therefore, Samuel had given a handle to those in Israel who were hankering after the prestige and security that institutionalized leadership seemed to promise. If he could *appoint* once (v. 1), he could do it again (5). The elders had a pretext in the malpractices at Beer-sheba, but the real motivation behind their request was an aspiration to nationhood on the same basis as Israel's neighbours. *like all the nations* (5; *cf*. v. 20) provides a point of contact with the Deuteronomic 'Law of the King' in Deuteronomy 17:14–20 (especially v. 14).

6. Since *govern* is lit. 'judge' in verses 5f. (contrast 'reign' in the divine speech in v. 9), the elders momentarily sound as if they want to put new wine into an old bottle. Samuel, they discover, has no liking for the new wine. His response, however, is based not on his own predilection but on a word from God in answer to prayer.

7–9. The popular dissatisfaction is not with Samuel, except insofar as he is God's representative (*cf*. Jn. 15:20). The people of Israel are chafing at God's exercise of his sovereign rights over them just as they have been inclined to do since the time of the exodus – witness their frequent lapses into idolatry (8).[11] Thus, in explanation of how the monarchy failed despite its being under divine auspices, the section emphasizes that this institution came not as a gift but as a concession from Yahweh. Firmly attached, moreover, is a stern prophetic warning (9; *cf*. vv. 11–18). Let Israel beware lest in its quest for justice it institutionalizes injustice, is the burden of the message.[12] *ways* translates *mišpāṭ*, which in many other contexts has the meaning 'justice'; we are probably to think of both senses here.

10. Hebrew readers, ever alert to word-play, would naturally find an allusion to Saul in *asking* (*šō'ᵃlîm*), which comes from the verb *šā'al*, the assumed base of Saul's name (Heb. *šā'ûl*, 'requested').

11–18. An unflattering word-portrait of kingly ways which could as easily derive from contemporary – not to speak of antecedent – non-Israelite models as from subsequent Israelite experience of its own monarchies. See the Introduction.

11, 12. Monarchy will mean the conscription of the young for military and corvée duties.[13] The acquisition of *chariots*, begun under David (*cf*. 2 Sa. 8:4), was stepped up in Solomon's reign (*cf*. 1 Ki. 4:26; 10:26–29), which is one reason why many scholars are inclined to see a retrojection of conditions under Solomon in these verses. The employment of 'runners' is a form of vanity particularly associated with ambitious young charioteers like Absalom (2 Sa. 15:1) and Adonijah (1 Ki. 1:5). 'Runners' (Heb. *rāṣîm*) is also used without reference to chariots to denote 'bodyguard', as perhaps in connection with Saul's retinue (22:17; *cf.* 1 Ki. 14:27f.; 2 Ki. 10:25).

14, 15. Saul's plea for loyalty among his entourage in 22:7 is based upon this 'kingly' practice of confiscating private property and giving it in fief to servants of the royal house. Exacting of harvest tithes (15) was, as Mendelsohn has shown, not unknown in neighbouring states.[14] In Israel the practice could readily be seen as an encroachment upon Yahweh's prerogative in view of the place which tithing had in the religious sphere (*cf.* Lv. 27:30–32). The tithing of flocks is mentioned in verse 17. *servants* in this context can refer to high-ranking officials like Jehozerah 'servant' of Hezekiah, whose seal impression still survives.[15]

16. In favour of RSV *your cattle* (*beqarekem*; *cf.* LXX), as against MT 'your young men' (*baḥûrêkem*), is the fact that the latter are covered in verses 11f. Weinfeld introduces the additional consideration that in some near eastern documents of release and exemption the royal work-force is represented by the triad slaves, oxen, and asses.[16]

17. The enslaving of an Israelite by a fellow-Israelite is forbidden in the so-called 'Holiness Code' (*cf.* Lv. 25:39f.), and was a sufficiently delicate matter for the editor of 1 Kings to draw out the distinction between Solomon's corvée impositions on the people of Israel and actual enslavement (1 Ki. 9:22; *cf.* 1 Ki. 5:13–16).

18. If a particular *day* is in question – and biblical usage is far from requiring that it be so[17] – the assembly that confronted Rehoboam at Shechem (1 Ki. 12:1ff.) might be regarded as the historical counterpart to what is envisaged here. *your king, whom you have chosen for yourselves*: compare God's reference to Israel as 'your (*i.e.* Moses') people, whom you brought up out of the land of Egypt', following on their worshipping of the golden calf (Ex. 32:7).

21. God does not need informants, but Israel needed an intermediary.

22. Samuel's position elicits sympathy; he does not recognize the divorce, yet has to perform the remarriage. It is something of a historical enigma, yet there is no reason to discount Samuel's role as king-maker or his opposition to the new constitution. Furthermore, if some sort of *modus vivendi* is to be achieved the new king will have to be, in some sense, God's choice as well as the people's choice. Samuel's dismissal of the company, now described as *the men of Israel*, prepares the way for this adoptive fiction.

SAUL ANOINTED KING   (9:1–10:16)

The arguments have been heard and Samuel, on Yahweh's instruction, has conceded the point: Israel will become a monarchy. When the prophet next assembles the people it will be to present to them their 'undoubted king' (10:17–27). This would, in many respects, be the next logical step, but first we are treated to a leisurely account of a young man's mission to retrieve lost asses and of his momentous meeting with a man of God. Apparently as ignorant of the existence of the holy man as he is of his own high destiny, the young Saul is, nevertheless, led unerringly on to his meeting with Samuel by an unseen divine hand. The inconvenience of the lost asses, like all the fortuitous conjunctions of verses 3–14, turns out to be serving a higher purpose. It is a small matter that the Old Testament lacks a word for 'providence' when it can subscribe so heartily to the concept in a passage like the present one.

1. This story is not quite of the 'rags to riches' variety, however surprising the choice of Saul as king may have been to himself or his contemporaries. In the first instance the genealogy bespeaks a measure of respectability (*cf.* 1:1),[18] and, secondly, Kish is described as a *gibbôr ḥayil*, which means either that he belonged to a warrior élite or, more probably, that he was a *man of wealth* (*cf.* Boaz, Ru. 2:1). This latter is confirmed by the reference to servants and asses in verse 3.

2. If a king is to be distinguished by his physical appearance then Saul is every inch a king (*cf.* 10:23f.). *handsome* as a translation of MT *ṭôḇ* could be bettered, since the word suggests more than Adonis looks; 'impressive' (NIV) or 'fine' would be nearer the mark. Nevertheless, even in this praiseful introduction Humphreys is aware of a 'discordant subtone' inasmuch as '1 Sam 9:1–2 corresponds most closely to words about another doomed potential king, namely Absalom (2 Sam 14:25–6)'.[19]

3, 4. The Hebrew need not be taken to mean that all Kish's asses had gone missing (*cf.* McCarter and NEB 'some asses'). Since the exact whereabouts of *Shalishah* and *Shaalim* are matters for conjecture, it is difficult to reconstruct the itinerary of verse 4 with any degree of conviction. *Shalishah* could be the same as the Baal-Shalishah mentioned in 2 Kings 4:42 and apparently located in the vicinity of Gilgal. If *the land of Shaalim* is not identical with 'the

land of Shual' in 13:17 a connection with the similar-sounding Shaalbim (*cf*. Jdg. 1:35; 1 Ki. 4:9) is a reasonable alternative.

5, 6. Ironically, when the goal of the real mission is within sight Saul decides to turn back. He is a dutiful son – a *pius Aeneas* – whose inward spirit matches his outward appearance in attractiveness. But *the land of Zuph* is Samuel's territory (*cf*. on 1:1) and now is the time for the servant – a *fidus Achates*? – to make a critical intervention (*cf*. 2 Ki. 5:13). Actually the servant is more in the 'Jeevesian' mould, able to offer just the right information and the requisite item (v. 8) to keep his master in business. At this stage the talk is of a *man of God*, later of a seer (vv. 9, 11), and Samuel is not named until verse 14. Principally for this reason it is often assumed that Samuel did not figure in the original version of the story and that Saul's interview was with a minor village seer. However, as we have suggested in the Introduction, it is possible that Saul's ignorance and Samuel's anonymity represent by a kind of metonymy the young man's complete unawareness of what lies ahead of him. The terms in which the *man of God* (*cf*. 2:27) is recommended are assuredly not unworthy of a Samuel, and this particularly of the testimonial that *all that he says comes true* (*cf*. 3:19 and the Deuteronomic criterion of true prophecy in Dt. 18:22).

7, 8. It was customary to take a present when one went to seek the help of a seer (*cf*. 1 Ki. 14:3; 2 Ki. 5:5, 15; 8:8). It has even been suggested that *we bring* (*nābî'*) represents a folk etymology for the Hebrew *nābî'*, 'prophet': a prophet is 'one to whom we bring a gift'.[20] *present* (*teśûrâ*) may be derived from a verb meaning 'to see' and therefore more precisely defined as an 'interview fee'; a good Akkadian parallel can be adduced.[21] Providentially the servant has a piece of *silver* with which to pay for the intelligence which they seek; nothing can stand in the way of Saul's meeting with Samuel.

9. An explanatory aside which would come more naturally after verse 11. The narrator, or a later editor, accounts for the use of the apparently outmoded term 'seer' (*rō'eh*) which has given way to the more common 'prophet' (*nābî'*).[22] This should not be taken to mean that *nābî'* is a late invention – the related term *na-bi-u-tum* is said to occur in texts of the third millennium from the Syrian city of Ebla[23] – nor is it the case that *rō'eh* fell out of use in the later period, for it occurs several times in Chronicles (*e.g.* 1 Ch. 9:22). In terms of the developing narrative the verse is intended to ease the transition from local clairvoyant to the mighty Samuel.

10. The *city* is without doubt Ramah (*cf*. on 1:19).

11–14. Here the narrative pace quickens. Ramah was 'a city set

on a hill'. Elevation was desirable in the interests of defence, while
proximity to a source of water was essential for the existence of
an ancient city. The spring or well was usually outside the walls
of the city and visits by the womenfolk were normally made in the
evening (cf. Gn. 24:11); the woman of Samaria was an exception
(Jn. 4:6f.). There is no need to infer from Samuel's recent arrival
(12) that this was not his home-town, particularly in view of his
peripatetic habits as described in 7:16f. Again the overruling of
providence is evident, for the two travellers have arrived just in
time for a feast at which, unaware of it as they are, Saul will be
guest of honour. It was a small, local celebration of a kind which
must often have taken place in Israel (cf. 20:29). The *high place*
(bāmâ) was a local shrine centred on an artificial mound or
platform, often located in an open space outside a city.[24] By no
means an exclusively Israelite institution, it nevertheless played a
major part in the folk religion of Israel throughout its history, and
even long after the completion of Solomon's temple (*pace* 1 Ki.
3:2). Because of the tendency of the religion of the high place to
assimilate some of the worst aspects of pagan ritual and mores it
came under heavy fire from the prophets of the classical period
(cf. Ho. 10:8; Am. 7:9) and is denounced repeatedly in the books
of Kings. This tradition of the prophet Samuel's association with
a high place is, therefore, of particular antiquarian value.

15, 16. Samuel's ear has been 'uncovered' (cf. MT) – the idea is
of the head-gear being drawn back to permit a word in secret – so
that he knows in advance of Saul's arrival (cf. 1 Ki. 14:5) and of
the hidden purpose behind it. The reader (or hearer) also now
knows that those earlier, disappointed travels have been closely
supervised (*I will send*, 16). Kings, no less than priests and altars,
were anointed with fragrant oil in token of their consecration to a
divinely-assigned task (cf. on 2:10). There is no need to attribute
Saul's anointing to the solicitude of an editor writing in a period
when the rite had truly – so the hypothesis – become standard
practice.[25] In the 'History of David's Rise' (see the Introduction)
it is Saul's status as 'the Lord's anointed' which deters David from
dealing him a premature death despite the provocations offered.

Saul is to be anointed *nāḡîḏ* (RSV *prince*), a title which on
purely etymological grounds should mean 'designated one', in this
case 'king-designate'.[26] (The more specific 'crown prince'[27] requires
that the term was not used in royal contexts until some time later.)
Some scholars prefer 'military commander',[28] with the possible
corollary that the usage goes back to pre-monarchical times when
it referred to the commanders of the Israelite tribal militia.[29]

There is the further question whether the choice of *nāḡîḏ* here deliberately puts limits on Saul's role in the new constitution (we might compare Ezekiel's use of *nāśî'* ('prince') in preference to *meleḵ* ('king') when referring to Zedekiah).[30] The fact that an established ruler (*pace* McCarter) can be called a *nāḡîḏ* (*e.g.* 25:30) has been urged against this view, nonetheless it is noteworthy that the root *m-l-k* (whence 'king', 'rule', *etc.*) goes unrepresented until 10:16. See on verse 17. At any rate, it is a military role that awaits this *nāḡîḏ*: the Philistines once again need to be driven back home. *for I have seen . . .*: *cf.* Exodus 3:9.

17. *rule* is barely possible as a rendering of the verb *'āṣar* ('restrain', 'control'). McCarter's 'muster' hardly passes. If this is intended as a straightforward statement about Saul's authority to rule we might have expected the common verb *mālaḵ*, were it not for the consideration discussed in connection with verse 16.

18. *Tell* (*haggîḏâ*) is one of several occurrences of the root *n-g-d* which give the *nāḡîḏ* theme a stereophonic effect in this section (*cf.* vv. 6, 8, 19; 10:15, 16).[31]

19, 20. The contrast that is made between what is on Saul's mind (19; *cf.* 1 Ki. 10:2) and the problem of the asses (20) assumes higher, and as yet undisclosed, preoccupations. *all that is desirable* (*cf.* Hg. 2:7 (MT)) bids him consider the wealth, not to be measured in asses, that kingship will confer. But the phrase is ambiguous, and NIV 'to whom is all the desire of Israel turned?' (*cf.* AV, NEB) is at least as likely: Saul is to become the focus of Israelite hopes against the reality of Philistine aggression.

21. Self-deprecation of this sort belongs to a worthy line of tradition which includes Moses (Ex. 3:11) and Gideon (Jdg. 6:15). But it could take extreme (*cf.* 10:21f.) and thoroughly debilitating forms (*cf.* 15:17). Benjamin was indeed the smallest of the tribes and was at one point in sordid opposition to the rest (*cf.* Jdg. 19–21). Somewhat in compensation, however, this little tribe was strategically placed, and from the time of David on could claim Israel's most important city. Thus it was that a later Saul could preen himself on his Benjaminite origin (Phil. 3:5). *family* should be 'clan' (so also 'the *clan* of the Matrites' in 10:21). The clan formed the middle tier in the three-tiered structure of family–clan–tribe in ancient Israelite society.[32] As we have seen (*cf.* on v. 1), Saul's family was not in the depressed class. All things considered, the motif of the ennobling of the lowly is probably not so prominent in this verse as is sometimes suggested.

22. The visitors are given the places of honour, and the meal takes on the character of a coronation supper (*cf.* 2 Sa. 15:7–12;

1 Ki. 1:9f.(?)).[33] This high place had an adjoining dining *hall* (*liškâ*) such as the LXX (*Vorlage*) associates with the Shiloh temple at 1:18. The same word is used for various ancillary rooms abutting the temples in Jerusalem (*e.g.* Je. 35:2, 4; Ne. 10:38f.).

23, 24. The reserved *portion* is proof to Saul of Samuel's precognition. *took up* (*wayyārem*, 24) is properly a technical term for the separation of designated portions from the sacrifice (*cf.* 'the thigh of the priests' portion' (*šôq hatterûmâ*), Ex. 29:27).[34] Saul is therefore receiving tokens of the new status which is about to be conferred upon him. *upper portion* presumably means 'thigh', which is what two of the ancient versions (Targum, Peshitta) have. But the word (consonantally *h'lyh*) is peculiar[35] and may conceal a reference to the 'fat tail' (*'alyâ*) which was considered a delicacy and, in priestly law, was reserved for God alone (Lv. 3:9, *etc.*). It is even possible that the difference between *'alyâ* and the present reading is the work of a scribe desirous of extricating Samuel and Saul from an infringement of priestly regulations, since the change involves merely the substitution of one guttural consonant for another.[36] *See*: the general sense of the rest of the verse is possibly as in RSV, but there are textual problems which defy solution.[37]

25–27. Saul, like the covenanting Gerarites of Genesis 26:30f., spent the night after the feast at his host's and left the next morning. *a bed was spread for Saul*: MT 'and he spoke with Saul' is plainly inferior; apart from textual considerations – and MT contains several indications of its own inferiority in the remainder of verse 25 and into verse 26 – the private interview does not come until 10:1ff. NIV's decision to stay with MT betrays remarkable timidity.

10:1. The anointing of Saul is a private affair (*cf.* 9:27) and will remain so (*cf.* v. 16) until it has been demonstrated publicly that he is God's own nominee (vv. 17–27). That he is such is emphasized here in the association of the anointing with God: Samuel 'pours' and God 'anoints' (contrast 9:16; 16:3, 12f.). For the inward change corresponding to the external act see verses 6, 9f. and compare 16:13f. Samuel's kiss may betoken nothing more than affection; in view of the textual uncertainty at Psalm 2:12 (despite AV, NIV), the kiss of homage must be regarded as a slightly doubtful entity in the Old Testament (1 Ki. 19:18 and Ho. 13:2 relate to idolatry). The apparent circumscription of Saul's office in the use of *prince* (*nāgîd*; see on 9:16) is the more noticeable in the longer LXX text, perhaps original, adopted in RSV. Apart from the repetition of *prince*, the verb translated 'rule' in 9:17 (*q.v.*) is presupposed in *reign*. Even under the new constitution Yahweh will not relinquish his claim upon Israel whom he has chosen as his *heritage* (*cf.* Dt. 32:8f.); Saul's proper station will therefore be that of vicegerent.

2–6. The sign of verse 1 is in three parts (*cf.* 'signs', vv. 7, 9). Signs also feature in the commissioning of Moses (Ex. 4:1–9), but, whereas his three signs were intended to convince the Hebrew slaves that God had at last provided a deliverer, Saul's signs are primarily for his own encouragement.

2. *Rachel's tomb* was near Ramah (*cf.* Je. 31:15), where we may assume Saul's meeting with Samuel to have taken place (*cf.* on 9:10). The original text of Genesis 35:19f. (*cf.* 48:7) may have envisaged a location between Bethel and a Benjaminite, as distinct from Judaean, town of Ephrath. *Zelzah* is mentioned only here and is sometimes thought to conceal an occurrence of the verb *ṣālaḥ*, translated 'come mightily upon' in verse 6 (*cf.* v. 10); the LXX, for example, has the men 'leaping'. Mauchline, on the other hand, suggests that the name was coined after 'a memorable occasion of spirit-possession there'.

3, 4. The second sign involved the receiving of a gift from *three men* who were on their way to Bethel laden with sacrificial offerings. The mere fact of the gift – two 'wave-offerings' of bread according to 4QSam[a] and the LXX[38] – is significant (*cf.* 'present' in v. 27), while the circumstance that the bread was intended for holy use may hint at the sacral character of Saul's appointment as the anointed ruler of Israel. *Tabor* (3), evidently a Benjaminite locality, is not to be confused with the more northerly site in the plain of Jezreel (1 Ch. 6:77, *etc.*). The alternative proposals 'oak of Deborah' (*cf.* Gn. 35:8) and 'oak of Bahurim' (*cf.* LXX Mss and 2 Sa. 17:18) are hardly necessary.

5, 6. The most impressive sign was the third. Saul, having encountered a prophetic ensemble at *Gibeathelohim* ('Gibeah' in v. 10 and probably the same as 'Gibeah of Saul' in 11:4), would also come under the control of the divine spirit and join them in their ecstatic display.[39] *prophesying* (5) in this context virtually means 'ecstasizing in the manner of the "prophets"' (*cf.* on 18:10). Music also features as an aid to inspiration in 2 Kings 3:15.[40] For prophesying (in whatever sense) as an initial manifestation of the Holy Spirit in the early church compare Acts 2:17f.; 19:6. From this experience Saul would emerge *another man* (6), equipped in the manner of Gideon and Jephthah for deeds of valour (*cf.* Jdg. 6:34; 11:29). The prophetic band described here was representative of an element in the Israelite prophetic movement which distinguished itself by its irrational, ecstatic tendencies.[41] Ecstatic prophets of this sort were inclined to operate in groups which

attached themselves to cult centres (*cf. high place*, 5). Samuel was
the leader of one such guild according to 19:18–24. While Israelite
prophecy is most nearly contiguous with Canaanite prophecy in
this area of ecstasy, it can also be said that increased knowledge
of the phenomenon of prophecy in the ancient near east leaves
little room for the view, once popular among the historians of
religion, that Israelite prophecy was derived from the Canaanite
model and was merely ecstatic in origin.

garrison (5) could be 'prefect' or 'governor' (*cf.* NEB). Whichever
we prefer, the mention of the Philistines could be significant. The
point of the reference may be that Saul's empowering by the divine
spirit is directly related to the Philistine menace which it will be
his task to remove.[42]

7. *whatever your hand finds to do*: a specific opportunity will be
provided by the Ammonite attack on Jabesh-gilead (11:1ff.).
Others, however, relate these words directly to the challenge of the
Philistine presence as in the previous verse.[43] As Yahweh's anointed, Saul may be assured of the divine presence and help in his
forthcoming endeavours; and in this the possession of the spirit of
Yahweh is crucial (*cf.* v. 6; Acts 10:38). *God is with you*: the claim
that 'God was with David' will be something of a leitmotiv in the
'History of David's Rise' (*e.g.* 16:18; 18:14), explaining both his
survival and his successes against all the opposition of Saul. Saul
starts out with the same promise, but fails to capitalize on it.

8. Since this verse connects with 13:7b–15a, by which time Saul
has a son of warrior age, its present position is sometimes explained
as an editorial device to show that from the beginning Saul's rule
was to be exercised within the constraints imposed by the prophetic
authority of Samuel.[44] However, as noted in the Introduction
(section II), the verses preceding (esp. vv. 5–7) are also involved in
this relationship with 13:7b–15a. At any rate, the freedom implied
in verse 7 has limits; there is a tree of knowledge in Saul's Eden
(*cf.* Gn. 2:16f.).

9–12. The surprise of some of Saul's acquaintances at seeing him
in the company of the ecstatics is encapsulated in a proverb
which has been subjected to various attempts at explanation. Two
counterbalancing points have to be borne in mind: that Samuel is
identified with a band of ecstatics in 19:18–24, and that prophets
of this kind were not always held in the highest regard in Israel
(*cf.* 2 Ki. 9:11; we may also compare the use of the word 'prophesying' for Saul's raving in 18:10). The proverb itself need not express
a negative evaluation of either Saul or the prophets, though the
response of the bystander in verse 12 could be interpreted to the

detriment of the latter. On balance, it seems likely that the onlookers are puzzled by Saul's fraternizing with nonentities (thus *And who is their father?*). The honorific sense of *father* as occasionally applied to prophets by their disciples (*e.g.* 2 Ki. 2:12) would also suit this interpretation: these men are insignificant and they lack a reputable leader.[45] Another suggestion is that when Saul's right to 'prophesy' is challenged (11) the response is made that, since heredity is not the determining factor, Saul has as much right as anyone else (12).[46] The note on the saying's proverbial status, together with its recurrence in a quite distinct setting in 19:24, attests its popularity as a way of pinpointing uncharacteristic behaviour by an individual.

13. The mention of *the high place* is cryptic enough for NEB to pick up Wellhausen's emendation to 'home'. But since the ecstatics had recently been to the high place there is no good reason to deny Saul his visit. It is not hard to imagine some private act of devotion in the light of his recent experiences.

14–16. A short exchange which, while leaving unexplained the involvement of Saul's *uncle* (*cf.*, perhaps, 14:50f.), confirms that what has transpired will remain a secret – even to Saul's intimates – until the public declaration of Yahweh's will at the Mizpah convocation (vv. 17–27).[47] Samson's reticence about his feat of strength (Jdg. 14:6) affords only a superficial parallel, since it stems from other considerations which become apparent as that story progresses (*cf.* Jdg. 14:9, 16). *the kingdom*: *cf.* on 9:16.

THE SECOND MIZPAH CONVOCATION   (10:17–27)

To this point Saul's appointment has been kept secret; now, in response to the earlier demand of the tribal elders (8:4–22), Samuel convenes a public assembly at which Saul can be presented as God's choice as king. But the new ruler will not necessarily be welcomed on Samuel's say-so, and the process of election by lot will have to be undergone so that there will be no doubt as to whom God favours. Even with this precaution there will be some who will question the appropriateness of the choice (v. 27).

If, in its attitude to the monarchy, the section appears to be striking discordant notes this is largely because its opposition to monarchy as such is tempered by enthusiasm for Saul as an individual. The prophetic charge of ingratitude and lack of trust in God still stands, but if Israel must have a king then only the best will do. It is therefore not a little fitting that the episode of

the lot-casting which stands between the prophetic condemnation
(vv. 18f.) and commendation (vv. 24f.) is itself tinged with ambiguity, for, although it can be read as a straightforward affirmation
of Saul's divine election, the fact is that the two other accounts of
the procedure in the Old Testament concern the identification of
individuals whose behaviour was detrimental to the common good
(*cf.* Jos. 7:14–18; 1 Sa. 14:38–42).

Here too, as in the earlier scenes in this review of kingship,
Samuel takes the lead, and the role of the prophet is seen as
determinative in the fashioning of the new constitution. Nor at the
end does this 'rejected' old man slip quietly back to Ramah. Far
from it! It is he, and not king Saul, who sends the people away
'each one to his home' (v. 25).

17. Samuel, having finally acceded to the demand of the monarchist lobbyists, had sent them home to await further developments
(8:22). When the appropriate time comes it is again to *Mizpah* that
he calls them (*cf.* 7:5f.).

18, 19. A denunciation out of the classic prophetic mould,
reminding the hearers of God's beneficence to them and upbraiding
them with their own inconstancy.[48]

18. *Thus says the Lord* is the so-called 'herald (or "messenger")
formula' beloved of the canonical prophets. God's claim upon
Israel (*the God of Israel*) is based primarily upon that delivering
act by which he liberated their forefathers from Egypt. That
deliverance becomes the *point d'appui* of many a prophetic remon-
strance with the people of Israel (*cf.* 12:8; Jdg. 6:8f.).[49] Now,
however, God's ability to deliver is being called in question. On
the evidence of north-west Semitic dialects the word translated
kingdoms occasionally means 'kings' (as here where the accompanying participle is masculine), just as the converse is sometimes true
(*e.g.* Is. 60:16).

19. *this day* by no means implies that this occasion was at one
time identified with that described in 8:4–22. The term simply
focuses on the present reality of the people's defection from God.[50]
What they will perforce learn is that to reject their God is to reject
their saviour (*cf.* Is. 45:15, 'O God of Israel, the Saviour').

20, 21. A more detailed reconstruction of the process by which
Saul came to be identified as Yahweh's choice is not possible.[51]
Joshua 7:14–18, in its account of the unmasking of Achan, is just
as concise. From the description of the roughly analogous occasion,
involving Saul and Jonathan, in 14:38–42 a more extensive use of
the oracular devices Urim and Thummim could be inferred. The
Matrite *family* (better 'clan', as in 9:21) is known only from this

reference.[52] The clause beginning *finally he brought* is restored on the basis of the LXX and agrees well with the parallel in Joshua 7:17. On the surface it looks as if it was possible for the lot to fall upon someone in his absence, though this impression may be attributable to the compressed nature of the narrative.[53] Saul, at any rate, cannot be accused of canvassing for election, no matter how tenaciously he clung to office once he had been installed.

22. Further inquiry reveals his whereabouts: in a fit of bashfulness (*cf.* 9:21) he had taken refuge among the convention *baggage*. (A Targum text says that he had slipped off for some quiet prayer and Bible study.)[54]

23, 24. Saul's physical appearance seemed in retrospect to have intimated the high honour to which he was now called (*cf.* Ps. 45:2). The same attitude to physical build – to be repudiated soon enough (*cf.* 16:7) – is reflected in the story of Athtar ('he of the kingly pretensions') in the Ugaritic epic 'Baal and Mot':

> He sat on the seat of mightiest Baal,
> (but) his feet did not reach the footstool,
> his head did not reach its top.[55]

And he was deemed unfit to reign on mount Zaphon. Here Samuel speaks admiringly and in terms which do not exactly encourage the promotion of a rival. Now for the first time since his introduction in 9:1f. Saul is called 'king'; significantly, it is the people who acclaim him so (see on 9:16 and *cf.* 1 Ki. 1:25, 34, *etc.*).

25. The constitutional *rights and duties* (both for MT *mišpaṭ*) of the king are proclaimed in the hearing of the people before being committed to writing and deposited in a sanctuary (*before the Lord*; *cf.* Dt. 31:26; Jos. 24:26).[56] A similar concern for the exercise of kingly justice lies behind the Deuteronomic requirement that the Israelite king provide himself with a copy of the Deuteronomic laws which it was his duty to obey and to enforce (Dt. 17:18–20; *cf.* 2 Ki. 11:12; Ps. 40:7). In his administration of justice the king was expected to be especially vigilant on behalf of the socially disadvantaged who often had no other champion. The cold reality, however, was too frequently as depicted in Samuel's earlier speech where 'the *mišpāṭ* of the king' has a decidedly negative connotation (*cf.* 8:9, 11).[57] Z. Ben-Barak thinks that we have here a covenant between king and people that became 'the ancient source and prototype of the Israelite monarchic covenants down the generations'.[58]

The ceremony ended, Samuel dismisses the people (*cf.* 8:22); he is still a man of authority.

26. Saul, for his part, did not immediately set about fulfilling Samuel's low expectation of the monarchy by building a palace and establishing a court. Instead he returned home to Gibeah and to his former interests (cf. 11:5). But he has the support of a group of henchmen who have felt a divine impulse to join him, perhaps in anticipation of the war of liberation that was bound to come.

27. No editorial reservations, or hints of reservations, are expressed at this point. The only dissentients at Mizpah were certain 'fellows of the baser sort' (MT 'sons of Belial'; cf. on 1:16) whose praise would have been condemnation. They bring no token of homage, but Saul – as reported in MT – held his peace. The concluding sentence in RSV makes good enough sense (MT lit. 'he was as one holding his peace'), nevertheless the superior reading of 4QSam[a] and the LXX should be adopted and joined with 11:1 to read: 'About a month later (Nahash the Ammonite went up)' (cf. NEB, NAB).[59]

THE RELIEF OF JABESH-GILEAD (11:1–15)

Saul's chance to show his military prowess and confound his critics came a month after the Mizpah assembly when the beleaguered inhabitants of Jabesh-gilead in Transjordan appealed for assistance against their Ammonite attackers. It was another of those occasions when the Ammonites, whose territory lay east and south of the Jabbok river,[60] sought to establish their claim to the Israelite-occupied land of Gilead which stood between them and the Jordan (cf. Jdg. 11:4–33). Judging their situation to be hopeless, the men of Jabesh-gilead would have sued for peace had it not been for the impossible condition laid down by the Ammonite king.

Saul is a transitional figure in this chapter. At its conclusion he is king by popular acclaim, but the mode of inspiration by which he wins that acclaim shows him to be one with the great charismatic judge-deliverers who have preceded him (see on v. 6). How much his success owed to his newly-acquired authority may be debated (cf. on v. 7); that all hinged on the empowering of the divine spirit is the undoubted view of our author. In its present setting, therefore, chapter 11 – in other respects so positive about Saul and the monarchy – may be heard to say that the old constitution was still sufficient for Israel's crises. For it was largely under its rules that this victory was won.

1. *Jabesh-gilead*, situated as it was in Transjordan, was vulnerable to this kind of attack from the Ammonites when they were in one of their expansionist moods. The ancient site is probably represented by Tell Abū Kharaz, about twenty-two miles to the south of the Sea of Galilee.[61.] Little else is known of Nahash, beyond that he later maintained friendly relations with Israel in David's reign (*cf.* 2 Sa. 10:2). The loose tribal federation that was Israel in this period is evident in the way in which the men of Jabesh-gilead make their own treaty proposals to the Ammonites.[62] They request a vassal treaty which, while putting them in a relationship of inferiority and servitude to Nahash, would ordinarily have entitled them to certain privileges, notably the protection of their liege lord against attack by other powers for as long as they remained loyal to him.[63] *Make a treaty* translates literally as 'cut a treaty', as frequently in the Old Testament; treaty (and covenant) ceremonies often involved the symbolic killing ('cutting') of animals (*cf.* Gn. 15:9–11, 17; Je. 34:18f.).

2. Nahash, however, has no aspirations to being a humane conqueror. According to a tradition preserved in 4QSam[a], and also known to Josephus, the Ammonites had been systematically reducing the Israelite population of Transjordan – the tribes of Gad and Reuben – to slavery by the very means described in this verse.[64] Josephus observes, 'and this he did, that when their left eyes were covered by their shields, they might be wholly useless in war' (*Ant.* vi. 5. 1, tr. Whiston). A later example of this kind of savagery comes from the time of the Babylonian conquest of Judah, when Zedekiah had both his eyes removed as the punishment appropriate to a rebellious vassal (2 Ki. 25:7; *cf.* the story of Samson, Jdg. 16:21).

3. Ammonite arrogance before Israelite impotence leads Nahash to agree to a stay of execution while the emissaries of Jabesh broadcast the city's predicament west of the Jordan. But if no old-style deliverer has arisen to repel the Philistines there, what chance is there of one coming to challenge Nahash? Neither here nor in the following verses is it explicitly indicated that hopes were automatically pinned on Saul, though that may well have been the case.

4, 5. Judges 21 preserves a tradition of a long-standing amity, strengthened by intermarriage, between the inhabitants of Jabesh-gilead and *Gibeah*, so that the messengers' visit to Saul's home-town need cause no surprise. Nor should the tearful outburst which greeted the news of the siege and its threatened sequel. Saul, however, was out in the fields, presumably ploughing (*cf.* Elisha, 1 Ki. 19:19) or threshing,[65] when the messengers arrived. He is no less a king for his agrarian pursuits (*cf.* Rom. 12:16, RSVfn.),[66]

and even in better times his will be a cut-price court (*cf.* 22:6).
Gibeah (meaning 'hill', 4), which remained Saul's capital throughout his reign, is almost certainly to be identified with the modern
Tell el-Fûl about three miles north of Jerusalem; a small fortress
dating back to the time of Saul has been uncovered.[67]

6, 7. Saul, possessed by *the spirit of God*, gives vent to his fierce
indignation at the plight of his fellow-Israelites in Jabesh-gilead.
The description differs hardly at all from the experiences of Othniel,
Gideon, Jephthah, and Samson (*cf.* Jdg. 3:10; 6:34; 11:29; 14:19),
and Saul appears for the present to have more of the charismatic
'judge' than the constitutional monarch. However, his symbolic
act and accompanying message do seem to presuppose a certain
amount of authority on his part.[68] The dismemberment of the
oxen (7) – superficially resembling the gruesome treatment of the
concubine's corpse in Judges 19:29f. – evokes the world of
execration and treaty curse where the threat was directed not so
much at the individual's property as at the individual himself.[69]
The thought of this worse exaction may well have contributed to
the wholehearted response to the summons, for, as the 'Song of
Deborah' reminds us in connection with a previous Israelite victory,
a good turn-out of the tribes in time of crisis was not easily achieved
(*cf.* Jdg. 5:15–17). Samuel's name invests the summons with added
authority irrespective of whether the old prophet himself could any
longer be considered a combatant. Nevertheless, the words *and
Samuel* are often treated as a secondary insertion, even though we
may seriously question whether there ever was a written form of
the tradition which did not have them.[70]

8. If the name *Bezek* is preserved in the modern Khirbet Ibziq,
situated about fifteen miles north-east of Nablus, it follows that
Saul mustered his men at a northerly point almost opposite Jabesh-
gilead, on the near side of the Jordan. The old distinction between
north and south which became institutionalized after the death of
Solomon is reflected in the separate totals given for *Israel* and
Judah (*cf.* 2 Sa. 24:9). *thousand* probably denotes a military unit
(*cf.* on 4:2).

11. Attack in *the morning watch* (*cf.* Ex. 14:24) was certain to
catch the enemy off guard. The night was divided into three
watches – compare the 'middle watch' of Judges 7:19 – so that the
third watch would have extended from two in the morning until
six (approx.).[71] Saul's division of his troops into *three companies*
was conventional strategy for the time (*cf.* 13:17; Jdg. 7:16; 9:43).

12, 13. The dissidents of Mizpah (10:27) have to eat their own
words, and would have suffered a much worse fate (*cf.* Lk. 19:27)

had it not been for the gracious intervention of Saul.[72] The *deliverance* (13) is ascribed to God who has given his answer to the 'How?' of Saul's opponents, and in so doing has declared his willingness to act on Israel's behalf despite the constraints imposed by the introduction of the monarchy. As for Saul, he has won his spurs and the right to the united loyalty of his subjects.

14, 15. This renewal ceremony, so soon after the Mizpah convention (10:17–27), perhaps forms part of an accession process which was standard for Israelite kings (see the Introduction). Even so, a large number of scholars see this occasion as the first public acclamation of Saul as king and regard the word *renew* – and indeed the whole of verse 14 – as an editorial attempt to harmonize the Gilgal coronation (15) with the preceding Mizpah narrative. Vannoy's equation of the *kingdom* with Yahweh's kingly rule over Israel gets round this particular problem, but leaves a lot to be read into the text.[73] The assembly at Gilgal has a more overtly ritual character than the earlier one at Mizpah, perhaps in recognition of the fact that now for the first time the people are united in their expression of allegiance to Saul. Nor should it be forgotten that they had a victory to celebrate. Despite the absence of covenant terminology in verse 15, it has been maintained that the Gilgal ceremony focused on the ratification of a covenant between king and people before Yahweh.[74] But this depends on how we read ch. 12 and, indeed, on whether we recognize it as an account of proceedings at Gilgal (see below). We should, in any case, note the fateful part played by Gilgal in Saul's history as king (*cf.* 13:7–15; 15:12–33). *peace offerings* were especially appropriate to occasions of joy and celebration (*cf.* Dt. 27:7), parts of them being made available for consumption by the worshippers themselves (*cf.* on 1:4).[75]

SAMUEL'S SPEECH (12:1–25)

This chapter, consisting mainly of oration by Samuel, formally marks the end of the period of the judges in the speechifying way that is characteristic of the 'Deuteronomistic History'. It could be read as a report of exchanges between Samuel and the assembled company at Gilgal (*cf.* 11:15), though it is sometimes seen as a free-standing narrative which reiterates previous condemnations of Israel's 'great wickedness' in demanding a king, while yet giving an assurance of God's continuing proprietary interest so long as they and their king keep faith with him.

First, however, Samuel solicits from his audience a character reference which is doubly significant. Whereas the tribal elders had used the venality of the prophet's sons as a pretext for constitutional change, Samuel ensures that on this occasion the spotlight falls on himself and his record of probity in public affairs. The concept of hereditary judgeship noticeably has receded, and Samuel takes his place in a distinguished line of 'saviours' whom God has raised up, and would continue to raise up, if only the people had a heart for theocracy. But even more pointed than this is the contrast between Samuel's testimonial and the earlier sketch of the typical king (8:11–18) who would 'take' and 'take again', as if by constitutional right. This latter is what the people have embraced to themselves, and they must not be allowed to forget how different things might have been.

If this is Samuel's valedictory,[76] he would go out with a bang, not a whimper (cf. vv. 16–18); but, in fact, he is no Isaiah retiring, however temporarily (Is. 8:16–18), from the rigour of the prophetic yoke. He still has influence with God, as proved by the unseasonable thunder-shower (v. 18), and will appoint himself a two-fold ministry – a blue-print for successors in the prophetic office – of intercession and instruction (v. 23).

Again we have the spectre of the covenant as various scholars discover signs of a covenantal structure – Deuteronomistic superstructure maybe – in this chapter.[77] And covenant or not, the fact remains that the Samuel speeches meet head on the problem of the covenantal relationship between God and Israel, so seriously jeopardized by the people's wilful choice of a king but now, in the goodness of God, reconstituted so that people and king may have another chance.

1, 2. These verses have 8:1–22 for background: Saul is king and the people have had their way (cf. 8:22). Samuel alludes (2) to the two factors on which the tribal elders had based their plea for change, viz. his advanced years and his sons' unsuitability for office, 'indicating neither acceptance nor rejection of their legitimacy as a basis for the establishment of kingship'.[78] (A Targumic addition to MT suggests that the sons had 'amended their ways' in the meantime!) the king walks and I have walked are in counterpoise, inviting us to contrast 'the ways of the king', as outlined in 8:11–18, with the open book of Samuel's judgeship.

3, 4. The occurrences of the verb 'take' set up the contrast with the expropriative tendencies of the typical king (cf. 8:11, 13–17). Ironically, the king, as God's anointed, is mentioned here in his capacity as chief justiciary and upholder of the nation's laws. The highly serviceable *ox* and *ass* were among the most valuable possessions that a person might own, hence their inclusion in the decalogal prohibition on covetousness (Ex. 20:17); compare Moses' *apologia* in Numbers 16:15. The idea of justice being blindfold meant the exact opposite of impartiality to the ancient Hebrew: 'a bribe blinds the officials, and subverts the cause of those who are in the right' (Ex. 23:8; *cf.* Dt. 16:19). Instead of this reference to blindness by subornation the LXX has a notable variant: 'Or from whose hand have I taken a bribe *or a (pair of) sandal(s)*?' (*cf.* also Ecclus. 46:19, summarizing this section). Sandals in this context may signify something paltry (*e.g.* Am. 2:6; 8:6) or, according to a very different line of interpretation, may represent token payments made in order to validate certain legal transactions.[79]

6–15 A résumé of Israelite history, showing how God had savingly interposed on his people's behalf when they repented of their faithlessness (vv. 9–11). The hearers are then rebuked for their inability, or unwillingness, to extrapolate on collective past experience, as they faced the latest threat to their security. Such summaries of salvation-history were an integral part of Israel's worship (*e.g.* Ps. 78), and are equally at home in the New Testament where Christ is seen as their end-point and culmination (*e.g.* Acts 13:17–23).[80] Here, however, the element of historical retrospection could be attributed to a covenantal emphasis in the speech, since the historical summary was a regular feature of the ancient treaty-covenant.

6. The point at issue is God's ability to provide deliverers as in the days of the judges, hence his designation as *the Lord . . . who appointed Moses and Aaron*; they were two of 'the gifts bestowed by Yahweh'[81] upon his people Israel (*cf.* Eph. 4:11).

7. *plead with you*: NEB 'put the case against you' is more to the point, since Samuel is now in the role of prosecuting counsel before the bar of God. The required forensic nuance is also lacking in RSV's *saving deeds* for MT *ṣidᵉqôṯ*; 'righteous acts' (NIV) is better, and takes account of the fact that God's covenant faithfulness involves disciplinary, as well as salvific, acts (*e.g.* v. 9).

8. 'The Hexateuch is 1 Samuel 12:8 writ large' (J. A. Sanders).[82] Salvation-history begins with the exodus, whether the preacher be Samuel or Paul (*cf.* Acts 13:17). *made them dwell* has Moses and Aaron for subject and therefore cannot be pressed too literally. The LXX's 'and he (*sc.* the Lord) made them dwell' does not present the same difficulty. There is no need to join Ahlström in constructing a pre-Deuteronomic tradition about Moses and Aaron which attributed to them the role fulfilled by Joshua in the canonical book bearing his name.[83]

9–11. The dismal and recurring pattern of apostasy–oppression– repentance–deliverance in the book of Judges (*cf.* Jdg. 2:11–23) is miniaturized here.

9, 10. Three agents of oppression familiar from Judges are listed: Sisera (Jdg. 4–5), the Philistines (Jdg. 3:31; 10:7; 13–16), and the Moabites (Jdg. 3). In verse 10 defection to the pagan worship of Canaan is epitomized in the mention of *the Baals and the Ashtaroth* (see on 7:4 and *cf.* Jdg. 2:13; 10:6).

11. *Jerubbaal* is the lesser-known name of Gideon (*cf.* Jdg. 6:32). For *Barak* (so LXX, Peshitta) the Hebrew actually has 'Bedan', a name which does not occur in the Judges roll of honour. A few writers prefer to retain MT on the assumption that a tradition independent of Judges may be preserved here. On the other hand, a reference to Barak would correspond nicely to the mention of Sisera in verse 9. There are several other explanations, of which only the most recent, by Y. Zakovitch, need be reported.[84] Zakovitch identifies MT 'Bedan' with the Gileadite of 1 Chronicles 7:17 and both of these with the (Gileadite) hero Jephthah of Judges 11–12. The existence of *Jephthah* in MT here is then explained as a gloss on the less familiar name, and Zakovitch thinks that the 'gloss' was subsequently misconstrued as referring to a separate individual.

The third-person reference to *Samuel* in a speech delivered by him sounds a trifle odd, even though some account of his role as deliverer in the recent past might be considered essential to the point of the argument. If the speech is a free composition of such things as Samuel was likely to have said on an occasion like this the problem is, of course, less acute (*cf.* 7:13f.). Emendation to 'Samson' (*cf.* LXX Mss, Peshitta) is ill-advised.

12. The Ammonite offensive against Jabesh-gilead (11:1ff.) is reviewed as one more occasion when Israel might have experienced deliverance through a saviour-figure in the succession of the judges. But the possibility was spurned (*cf.* 8:19; 10:19). As a summary of recent events the verse appears to stand history on its head, for the issue of the monarchy had been thrashed out before Nahash even set out for Jabesh-gilead (*cf.* on 10:27). Clearly it is the integration of the Ammonite attack, the latest threat to Israelite security, into the scheme of oppression and (potential) deliverance which has produced the apparent anomaly. At the same time, we must admit the possibility that an independent tradition concerning the origins of the monarchy is reflected here, especially in view of the corroboration by 4QSam[a] of Josephus' reference to Ammonite barbarities in Transjordan prior to the investment of Jabesh-gilead (see on 11:2).[85] This to some extent vindicates Vannoy's claim that 'it is not at all impossible that the threat of attack from Nahash was already a matter of concern at that time (*sc.* ch. 8)'.[86] See, however, the Introduction ('The Text').

13. *you have chosen* (*cf.* 8:18) adopts a more negative view of Saul's election than 10:24 (*cf.* Dt. 17:15), where the choice is made by Yahweh himself.

14, 15. These two verses correspond to the blessing and curse sections in an ancient covenant. Strangely, verse 14 gives no indication of what the blessing consequent on obedience will be, so that RSV has to supply epexegetically the words *it will be well* (*cf.* NEB 'well and good'). Most probably this is a syntactical matter (ellipsis), though it is possible to find something ominous in the absence of a 'hopeful apodosis'.[87] *and your king* (15), with some support from the LXX, replaces the indefensible 'and your fathers' of MT. The translation 'as it was against your fathers' (*cf.* v. 7) has advocates ancient (Targum, Peshitta) and modern (Stoebe, Vannoy, NIV), but it is doubtful whether the Hebrew will stretch that far.[88]

16–18. What is primarily an expression of Yahweh's displeasure – coincidentally reinforcing the sanction threatened in verse 15 – serves also to validate Samuel's claim to a unique standing with Yahweh. Since the *wheat* (17) was harvested in May-June (*cf.* 6:13), early in the dry season, the unnatural occurrence of *thunder and rain* was readily acknowledged as having a supernatural origin (*cf.* 6:9).[89] *greatly feared the Lord and Samuel* (18): more important than the momentary awe is the lesson that even under the monarchy there can be no derogation of prophetic authority, granted that there will be some redefining of the prophet's function (v. 23).

19. Samuel has attained the proportions of a Moses and is asked to fulfil a similar mediatorial role (*cf.* Ex. 20:19; 32:11–13). The two were remembered as intercessors *par excellence* (*cf.* Je. 15:1; Ps. 99:6). That the people speak of *your God* (contrast 7:8) is as much an admission of guilt (*cf.* 15:30) as an acknowledgement of Samuel's favoured status.

20–22. All is not lost, provided that Israel maintains covenantal loyalty and does not compound its offence by resorting to idolatry. For *vain things* (*tōhû*, 21) as applied to idolatrous images see Isaiah 41:29 ('wind and *emptiness*'). Moreover, even though Israel has proved unworthy of God's kindness there is still the consideration that God, in making special choice of her (*cf.* Ex. 19:5f.; Dt. 28:9; 29:13), has put his own reputation (name) at stake. That is why

the refrain, 'and you (they) shall know that I am the Lord', is so
constant in the book of Ezekiel, for to Ezekiel's contemporaries it
appeared that the reputation of Israel's God had been laid in
Babylonian dust.

23. Prophetic intercession is regarded as essential to Israel's
continued prosperity; only when her doom is sealed is a prophet
told to desist (Je. 11:14; 14:11). Samuel's ministry of intercession
and teaching, exercised independently of the offices of state,
becomes the norm for those who followed him in the prophetic
succession. These are 'the irreducible aspects of the prophetic office'
(McCarter, p. 219).

24, 25. Yet responsibility devolves ultimately upon the people
themselves. They have been witnesses of the delivering power
of God (*e.g.* 11:1–15), but cannot presume upon divine mercy
indefinitely. *swept away* (25) is more than a dark hint at the fate
of exile.

4 The Reign of Saul (13:1–15:35)

The title for this section makes a deliberate point, for although Saul remains king of Israel until his death on Gilboa, as recorded at the end of 1 Samuel, he immediately yields prominence – in terms of the narrative – to David from the moment that the latter is introduced in 16:1ff. However, the narrator prepares us for this shift of emphasis with his various hints, at the end of ch. 15, to the effect that we are bidding farewell to king Saul. It is all neatly summed up in the way that Samuel mourns for Saul (15:35) and is then instructed to anoint a new king (16:1).

Considerable military successes are attributed to Saul in 14:47f., and the accounts of two of them form the backbone of the section which we are discussing. Nevertheless, the dominant feeling in chs. 13–15 is not of success, but of failure. For the biblical writer (or compiler) the victories are immaterial as compared with the importance of understanding why Saul did not earn Yahweh's approval so as to be able both to deliver Israel in its time of greatest danger and also to establish a dynasty that would earn the loyalty of its grateful subjects. So the prophet Samuel makes two appearances (13:8–15; 15:10–35) to upbraid Saul for his disregard of Yahweh's word and to announce Yahweh's rejection of him. It is an irreversible decision by Yahweh and there are immediate consequences (cf. 16:1ff., 14); Saul's rule under Yahweh's aegis ends with ch. 15.

PREPARATIONS FOR WAR   (13:1–23)

The Philistines' presence in Israel during this period will have been
patchy but disabling nonetheless. As the topography of the chapter
indicates, the tribal territory of Benjamin, Saul's own tribe, was
by no means exempt from Philistine encroachments: if Saul is to
be king he will have to lay claim to his kingdom. The chapter is
largely given over to scene-setting – the disposition of the respective
forces and the decimation, wrought by fear, in Saul's ranks before
ever battle is joined. For the resolution we shall have to wait until
the next chapter. But in the meantime, in a dark passage describing
an interview between Saul and Samuel at Gilgal (vv. 7b–15a),
sentence is passed on Saul for failing to heed the word of Yahweh.

There are problems of topography in the chapter that are
occasioned in no small way by the easy confusion of the names
Geba and Gibeah.[1] It may suffice here to note that Geba was closer
to Michmash (see on v. 16), and that Gibeah lay a few miles to
the south-west of Geba.

1. The accession formula, a commonplace in 1 and 2 Kings (*e.g.*
1 Ki. 15:1f.; 16:8), is in this instance incomplete.[2] MT as it stands
would have Saul one year old at his accession, which is absurd,
and would limit his reign to two years, which is highly improbable.
The round figure of forty years for his reign is given in Acts 13:21
and in Josephus' *Antiquities* (vi. 14. 9), though the latter elsewhere
suggests twenty (*Ant.* x. 8. 4). Despite the acceptance of MT 'two
years' by a number of scholars,[3] a much longer term is certainly
indicated by the available data in 1 Samuel 9–31.[4] NEB's totals of
fifty for Saul's age and twenty-two for his reign are traceable to
the 'abbreviation theory' of Sir Godfrey Driver who collected
evidence to show that already in antiquity numerals were sometimes
represented by letters of the alphabet – a practice which assuredly
would have made them more than a little accident-prone.[5]

2. Prior to the monarchy, the Israelites looked to their citizen
militia in times of crisis, but Saul's establishment of a cadre of
three thousand men (for 'thousand' see on 4:2) provides Israel
with a standing army (*cf.* 14:52). The immediate concern was the
expulsion of Philistine forces from the very heart of Saul's kingdom,
for all the places mentioned here were in Benjaminite territory.
Michmash (mod. Mukhmās) lay a few miles to the south-east of
Bethel.

3, 4. This was not the only time that an initiative by Jonathan
was the signal for bold action by his father (see 14:20). In spite of
the popular attribution in verse 4, it is unnecessary to conclude

that the narrator has credited Jonathan with an exploit of his father's because of a bias against Saul (*cf.* on 2 Sa. 8:13).[6] Whether it was a Philistine *garrison* (RSV) or governor (NEB) that suffered Jonathan's attentions is difficult to tell from the word itself. See on 10:5. *Let the Hebrews hear!* should possibly be emended on the basis of the LXX to read 'The Hebrews have rebelled!' (*cf.* NEB), now as an expression of Philistine indignation at what Jonathan had done.[7] *Hebrews* is most often used of Israelites by non-Israelites in the Old Testament (*cf.* v. 19; 4:6,9). See on 4:6. In the expectation of Philistine counter-measures there was a general muster of Israelites at *Gilgal* (4), situated somewhat to the east of Michmash, in the direction of the Jordan. With the mention of Gilgal the scene is set for a confrontation which is even more decisive for Saul than that with the Philistines (vv. 10–14; *cf.* 10:8).

5–7a. *Beth-aven* ('house of iniquity', 5) is the name given pejoratively to Bethel by the prophet Hosea (*e.g.* 4:15; *cf.* Am. 5:5). A Beth-aven in the vicinity of Ai is distinguished from Bethel in Joshua 7:2, and is favoured by Stoebe (p. 244) here.[8] The odds being thus piled high against the Israelites, they began to seek refuge in caves and crevices just as when the Midianites and Amalekites came 'like locusts for number' in the time of Gideon (Jdg. 6:2, 5). *holes* (6): MT has 'thickets' and the emendation by RSV is unnecessary. Some Israelites fled to Transjordan where the Philistines were unlikely to follow. (Elijah could even feel secure there from king Ahab of Israel (1 Ki. 17:1–7).)

7b–15a. An interval of many years separates the events of this chapter from the occasion of Saul's anointing in ch. 10, yet there is the closest literary link between the instruction given in 10:8 and this meeting of Samuel and Saul. Plainly the earlier verse is meant to key the whole question of Saul's exercise of kingship, and of his failed dynastic hopes (*cf.* vv. 13f.), to the issue of obedience. Only if Saul meets the requirement of obedience to Yahweh's commandment as revealed through the prophet will he be judged worthy to rule. It was a prophetic perspective on kingship that continued to challenge Israel's rulers as long as there was an Israelite kingdom.

8–12. Although each day sees the Israelite ranks further depleted by the enemy of fear, Saul avoids decisive action in accordance with Samuel's instruction. We might then feel entitled to ask, What has he *not* done? And it is as hard as that to pinpoint Saul's fault, unless we conclude that his obedience was in the letter rather than in the spirit. If his fault was to usurp Samuel's priestly prerogative by precipitately offering the appointed sacrifices (*cf.* 10:8), nothing is made of it in the prophet's speech of censure; nor, in the light of such references as 14:33–35; 2 Samuel 8:18; 20:26; 1 Kings 3:3; 8:62f., is this to be expected.[9] (Other issues are involved in Uzziah's censing in the temple (2 Ch. 26:16–21).) Albright's explanation of Samuel's 'recorded harshness and refusal to compromise' on an occasion like this as stemming from 'unhappy experiences as a boy in Shiloh' bids fair to put the psychiatrist on the couch![10] Saul's concern that he had not entreated Yahweh's favour (12) could be pious or prudential; no king liked going into battle without first seeking favourable omens.

13. Whatever the precise infringement, the issue is that of Saul's obedience to Yahweh. Herein lies the answer to the question which must have occurred to the thinking Israelite: If God allowed Saul to rule in the first place, why did he not permit him to establish a dynasty? David, after all, did not suffer disqualification for any of his sins. The verse is important for the way in which it allows the theoretical possibility of a Saulide dynasty – as if to say that Saul was *not* doomed from the start.

14. Saul may have sons – and we already know of Jonathan – but there is no future for his house. It is Shiloh and the Elides all over again (*cf.* 2:30–36). Now Yahweh will appoint his own nominee (lit. 'has sought out *for himself*'; contrast 'make a king *for them*' in 8:22). The decision, being irrevocable, is fitly stated in the 'prophetic perfect' (*has sought out . . . has appointed*). *a man after his own heart* suggests likemindedness, whereas the idiom more probably means 'a man of his choice';[11] see on 2 Samuel 7:21. The reference is, of course, to David. For *prince* (*nāgîd*) see on 9:16.

The formal account of Saul's reign has barely begun, but already the die is cast. Samuel's denunciation at Gilgal is 'put before the period of Saul's reign like a clef on a music stave' (Hertzberg).

15a. According to the longer text of the LXX, which may be original (*cf.* NEB), Samuel merely departed from Gilgal, whereas it was Saul and his men who headed for Gibeah.[12]

16–18. The cities of *Geba* and *Michmash* lay on either side of a valley, with only a couple of miles separating them. However, with but a fraction of his force still in the field, Saul was in no position to check the Philistine raiding parties operating out of Michmash. David in his fugitive days could command as big a following as Saul had now (*cf.* 23:13). *Ophrah* (17) figures among the Benjaminite cities in Joshua 18:23; the usual identification is with the modern eṭ-Ṭayibeh, five miles north of Michmash. *the land of Shual*: see on 9:4. The Beth-horons (Upper and Lower) were situated some miles to the west of Michmash, while *the valley of Zeboim*

('Hyenas'), as the explanatory *toward the wilderness* suggests, lay to the east or south-east.

19–22. Saul and his men are at even more of a disadvantage than we had suspected, for the Israelites had for some time been effectively disarmed by a Philistine ban on craftsmen whose skills might be used against them. It is often assumed that the Philistines had learned the secret of iron-working in their earlier travels, possibly in Anatolia, and wanted to deny the Israelites this expertise. But this is probably to read too much into the text.[13] With a similar end in view, Porsenna ruled that the citizens of Rome were to use iron solely in the manufacture of agricultural implements (Pliny, 34. 139).[14] The reference to the Canaanites' iron chariotry in Judges 1:19 and the special attention which the Babylonian conquerors of Judah paid to 'craftsmen and smiths' (2 Ki. 24:14, 16) provide further historical side-lights from the Old Testament itself.

21, 22. This closed-shop arrangement also provided the Philistines with additional revenue. Although there are one or two unresolved difficulties in these verses, the sense has been greatly improved since the recognition that MT *pîm* (perhaps *payim* originally) preserves the sole Old Testament reference to a weight equivalent to two-thirds of a shekel (*cf.* NEB).[15] Various weights inscribed with the letters *PYM* have been found on Judaean sites such as Gezer and Lachish, as well as in the vicinity of Jerusalem, during the present century.[16]

The effectiveness of the Philistines' policy was now to be seen in the depleted, ill-equipped band that remained with Saul and Jonathan. Only a ruse like that carried out by Jonathan in ch. 14 could save the situation for the Israelites.

23. Meanwhile a Philistine garrison was posted in a forward position to guard the pass of Michmash (*cf.* NEB).

VICTORY AT MICHMASH (14:1–52)

In the previous chapter there have been indications enough of the extent of Israelite subservience to the Philistines even during the reign of Saul. How the Israelites won temporary respite is the story of ch. 14. The achievement ('a smashing victory' (John Bright)) was, moreover, sufficiently notable for the compiler of these traditions to append in verses 47f. a list of sweeping successes against various of Israel's neighbours. Yet while this is as positive a presentation of Saul as we find in 1 Samuel 13–31, the credit for the victory at

Michmash is shown to have belonged principally to Jonathan; as
far as Saul's personal contribution is concerned this might aptly
be entitled 'A Chapter of Errors'. But there are also hints of the
good in Saul: in fact, he is his enigmatic self at Michmash.[17]

1. The information given in 13:19–22 precludes the possibility
of a set-piece between the Israelites and the Philistines. On the
other hand, Jonathan is properly armed (13:22) and sees the
advance positioning of the enemy garrison (13:23) as a challenge
to action. Saul has no part in the stratagem; he is as ill-informed
as the rest of the army (*cf.* v. 3). Are we to see this lack of
communication between father and son in the light of their subsequent turbulent relationship? Even in the present chapter filial
respect and paternal affection are not overwhelmingly present.
young man (na'ar): see the comment on 2 Samuel 2:14; 'attendant'
or 'squire' would be appropriate here.

2, 3. Saul at this time was holding court in the vicinity of
Gibeah; his *pomegranate tree* may have much the same judicial-
administrative significance as the tamarisk tree in 22:6 or Deborah's
palm in Judges 4:5. If so, MT *yôšeḇ* (RSV *staying*) might be
translated 'sitting', as in these other references. *Migron* cannot be
the place of the same name in Isaiah 10:28 since a location north
of Michmash is clearly indicated there (the section traces the
southward march of an Assyrian army). As has long been observed,
it takes only a slight rearrangement of the letters in *at Migron* to
produce the reading 'on a threshing-floor', which, on the analogy
of 1 Kings 22:10, would fit the context well. From the Ugaritic
Aqhat legend McCarter quotes the case of Danel who sat under a
great tree, on a threshing-floor, as he judged the causes of the
widow and orphan.[18] Apart from the loyal six hundred Saul has
the services of Ahijah, complete with Shilonite pedigree and, more
importantly, the oracular *ephod* (see on 2:28). This information is
important to the development of the story (vv. 18f., 36–42), but
the way in which Saul is linked with the failed house of Eli is
perhaps also suggestive when we consider that the fate of Saul's
house is strikingly prefigured in the downfall of Eli's family.

4, 5. The meanings of the names *Bozez* and *Seneh* can only be
guessed at. 'Shining' is possible for the former (*cf.* NEBfn.), while
'Bramble-bush' for *Seneh* is likely because of the close similarity
to the '(burning) bush' (*seneh*) of Exodus 3:2, *etc.*

6. What sets Jonathan apart from the rest – including his father –
is his faith in Yahweh's ability to deliver Israel regardless of
circumstances. The same conviction nerved David for the contest
with Goliath when things had reached a similar impasse (17:37).

uncircumcised is a standard epithet of contempt for Philistines in
Judges-Samuel (*e.g.* Jdg. 14:3). Since most of Israel's neighbours
practised circumcision (*cf.* Je. 9:25f.), though without the covenantal associations cherished in Israel (Gn. 17:9–14), the Philistines'
uncircumcision is usually regarded as evidence that they were not
indigenous to the Semitic world.

8–10. Unlike Gideon (Jdg. 6:34–40; 7:9–15), Jonathan does not
so much seek a sign as appoint himself one. Moreover, it is a sign
shot through with irony, for the garrison will unwittingly pass on
Yahweh's instruction to his servants. *the Lord has given* (10; *cf.* v.
12) is precisely the meaning of Jonathan's name which, as it
happens, is given in the full form *yᵉhônāṯān* in verses 6, 8 as
against the shorter *yônāṯān* elsewhere in the chapter.

11. *Hebrews*: see on 4:6. By the insertion of an extra consonant
Hebrews (*'ibrîm*) can become 'mice' (*'akbārîm*), hence Moffatt's
famous 'Look at the mice . . .!' But MT presents no problem.
holes: see 13:6.

12. *show you a thing* makes an innocuous suggestion, whereas
NIV interprets their shout as a challenge ('teach you a lesson').

13, 14. Whether taken by surprise or not, the garrison falls easy
prey to Jonathan and his armour-bearer who, in customary fashion
(*cf.* 2 Sa. 18:15), dispatches his master's victims after him. *within
as it were* . . . (14) represents difficult Hebrew which NEB revises
slightly so as to read: 'like men cutting a furrow across a half-acre
field'.[19]

15. Now it is the Philistines' turn to panic; the root used to
describe the Israelites' reaction in 13:7 ('followed trembling') occurs
three times here in description of the Philistines' plight (*panic*
(twice), *trembled*). *a very great panic* is lit. 'a panic of (from) God'.
The superlative force of *'ᵉlōhîm* ('God') in certain instances is
undeniable, but the Hebrew is also making a point about the source
of the Philistines' discomfiture.

16. McCarter points out the improbability of Saul's watchmen
being able to spectate from *Gibeah* and therefore prefers to read
'Geba'. It is part of the more general problem created by these
similar-looking names, as noted in the introduction to ch. 13.

18. Saul prepares to consult the divine oracle before committing
his men. According to MT he asks his padre for *the ark of God*,
which poses a difficulty. The ark did accompany the Israelite army
into battle on occasion (*cf.* ch. 4), but it is not normally associated
with oracular consultation (though Jdg. 20:27 might be cited). A
still greater problem consists in the fact that the ark was in limbo
in Kiriath-jearim (7:1f.; *cf.* 2 Sa. 6:1–3; 1 Ch. 13:3) during this

period. The reading of the LXX therefore has obvious advantage:
' "Bring the ephod." For it was he who bore the ephod before
Israel on that day' (cf. NEB, NIVfn.).[20] Oracular decisions were
usually obtained from the ephod, which included the sacred lots
Urim and Thummim (see on 2:28 and on v. 41 of this chapter),
and Ahijah's 'wearing' of the same is mentioned already in verse
3. Finally, the attendant verb *bring* (*higgîš*) occurs twice elsewhere
in 1 Samuel in connection with the ephod (23:9; 30:7). There is no
obvious explanation for the alteration of 'ephod' to 'ark'; Kennedy's suggestion of editorial disapproval of the ephod (as also,
allegedly, at 1 Ki. 2:26) fails to fit the facts.[21]

19, 20. But the signs on the battle-field are good enough for Saul
not to feel the need of other signs, so Ahijah's services are dispensed
with. Saul appears as a man who gets flustered when under
pressure; his command (19) could be construed as disrespect for
things sacred, though there is contrary evidence in the chapter
(vv. 31–35). If the Israelites are ill-equipped (13:22), Philistine
weapons – and hands – can do their work for them (20; *cf.* Jdg.
7:22).

21. For some Israelites subjection to the Philistines involved
military service; whether as mercenaries or otherwise we cannot
tell. Their denomination as *Hebrews* could imply a looser ancestral
or political tie to the main Israelite tribes, but more probably
reproduces the name by which they were known to the Philistines
(*cf.* on 13:3). They added to the Philistines' ills by turning into an
Israelite fifth column. (With David as their improbable ally the
Philistines might have found history repeating itself at Gilboa, had
not Achish of Gath been overruled by the Philistine commanders
(29:4).)

22, 23. The faint-hearted took courage, and the result of the
encounter was a great deliverance (see on v. 24) for Israel. *Beth-
aven* (see on 13:5) was a few miles to the north-west of Michmash.
The longer text of the LXX in verse 23 says that the fighting spread
to every city in the hill-country of Ephraim. At any rate, there was
good opportunity for the kind of mishap that is now described.

24–30. This section relates the circumstances in which Saul
imposed, and Jonathan broke, an oath that, though well-meant,
was pregnant with mischief.

24. *distressed* (reading *niggaś*) described the state of the Israelites
before Jonathan's bold venture (13:6). It may also denote conditions of Egyptian-type oppression requiring divine intervention
and deliverance (*cf.* v. 23). It is ironic, then, that on this particular
day it is the *bêtise* of the king of Israel that brings a measure of

'oppression' upon the Israelites. However, it has to be said that the grounds for translating the Hebrew conjunction w^e (usually 'and') by *for* at the beginning of the next clause are slight. The whole of the verse could be a flashback to an earlier stage in the day's fighting, when Saul reacted to his men's 'distress' by imposing the oath.[22] The point of the fast was, we may assume, to secure Yahweh's continued help. Saul was late in joining the fray, but now that he is involved he will make a proper job of it, though, as events turn out, his contribution has the opposite effect. By his rash imprecation he causes problems for Jonathan (vv. 24–30; 40–45), the army (vv. 31–35), and the whole mopping-up exercise.[23]

25, 26. A temptation scene. There is honey in plenty and the bees have gone (*cf.* LXX).[24] But the *oath* (26) tended to be taken seriously throughout the ancient near east inasmuch as it was reckoned to carry divine authority.[25] So the army (a frequent sense of BH *'am*, 'people') left the honey untouched. For a good illustration of 'fear of the oath' in a non-Israelite context see the Nuzi text translated in *ANET*[3], p. 220 (lawsuit). (When Shukriya and Kula-hupi shrank from taking the 'oath of the gods' their evidence was rejected.)

27, 28. Jonathan, acting in ignorance of the prohibition, shows the folly of it. *his eyes became bright*: he was refreshed (*cf.* NEB); see also Psalm 13:3 (Heb. 4); Ezra 9:8; Proverbs 16:24. The antithesis between what was (fatigue, 28b) and what might have been (reinvigoration, 27b) is underlined by the assonance in the key verbs *'ārar* ('curse', 24, 28) and *'ôr* ('be bright', 27, 29).[26]

29. *troubled* (*'ākar*): an 'ominous' word in the Old Testament (S. R. Driver).[27] It is best-known from the story of Achan in Joshua 7, and its occurrence here gives pause in view of the further parallels with the Achan story in verses 37–42 (*q.v.*). In reality the lot-casting in those verses is to determine who has 'troubled' Israel – for the divine oracle has been reduced to silence (v. 37) – whereas now, by clever pre-emption, Jonathan, who is technically guilty (v. 42), lays the charge against his father. 'Troubling the land' is akin to 'troubling Israel' in Ahab's accusation against Elijah (1 Ki. 18:17f., where also the question of responsibility is disputed by the protagonists).

30. Their enforced abstinence has rendered the warriors incapable of capitalizing on their earlier successes.

31–35. This time it is the ranks who are in breach of a cultic regulation, and again the problem arises out of Saul's incapacitating oath.

31. As the Philistines are driven back towards their own territory the pursuit extends to *Aijalon*, a good twenty miles west of Michmash.

32. At evening when the oath had expired (*cf.* vv. 24, 34 ('that night')) the hungry warriors pounced on the enemy's livestock, omitting, in their haste, to drain off the blood of the animals.[28] In priestly law the blood represents the life force of the animal and the blood of sacrificial animals is thus viewed as having atoning efficacy (*cf.* Lv. 17:11). Animal blood was therefore not for human consumption, as is stressed at a number of points in the Pentateuch (Gn. 9:4; Lv. 7:26f.; 17:10–13; 19:26; Dt. 12:16, 23–27).[29]

33, 34. Saul as king and upholder of cultic order (*cf.* Dt. 17:18f.) gives instructions for a large *stone* to be brought so that when the animals are sacrificed the blood may be easily drained away.[30]

35. So Saul raised his first altar not as an expression of gratitude for the day's victory (*cf.* Ex. 17:15f.), but to make amends for the infringement just described. NIV strikes a slightly reproachful note with 'it was the first time he had done this'; it may be a not unfair representation of the author's intention.

36–46. The worst consequences of Saul's oath are reserved for Jonathan who, apart from the intervention of the army (v. 45), would have lost his life. And as if one oath had not brought mischief enough, Saul reinforces it with two others specifically binding Jonathan to his fate (vv. 39, 44). Small wonder that some critics read between the lines in search of evidence of a deadly rivalry between father and son before ever David set them at loggerheads!

36, 37. Saul's stirring words carry the army, but Ahijah advises caution. Where there is the prospect of collecting Philistine scalps Saul's interest in oracular consultation noticeably wanes (*cf.* v. 19). For the type of question put to the oracle compare 23:11f.; 30:8. The withholding of an answer (37) was a certain indication that Yahweh was displeased (*cf.* 28:6).

39. Has Saul an inkling of Jonathan's guilt or is this unconscious irony? If, as some claim, Saul was manipulating the oracle in order to procure Jonathan's death the narrator maintains a discreet silence.[31] More probably we are to think of the blind, unreasoning consistency of a man whose moral and religious instincts are badly confused. The silence of the people contrasts with their ready responses in verses 36, 40 and prepares us for the startling intervention in verse 45.

40–42. The sacred lot operated by a process of elimination and the process could be long, as in the story of Achan (Jos. 7), or short, as here.[32] In verse 41 RSV wisely follows the fuller text represented by the LXX.[33] The precise nature of the *Urim* and *Thummim* remains a mystery. That they were stones – black and white, according to one theory[34] – seems the most likely view. *Urim* could be connected with a Hebrew verb meaning 'curse' (*'ārar*) and *Thummim* with a root signifying 'perfection' (*t-m-m*), in which case the two would represent the negative and positive responses that could be obtained by consultation.[35] However, the true etymology may yet have to be discovered.[36] The high priest's ephod described in Exodus 28 had a 'breastpiece of judgement' in which the Urim and Thummim were kept. See also on 10:20f.[37]

43. *Tell me*: cf. Joshua 7:19. Jonathan admits to an offence that is utterly trivial and accepts a punishment that is out of all proportion. Is he making a point by baldly stating the two side by side? He certainly does not try to emulate the acceptance speech of Jephthah's daughter when she found herself in a similar situation (Jdg. 11:36f.). Indeed, NIV turns the last clause into a question: 'And now must I die?'

44. Saul superimposes oath upon oath (*cf.* v. 39). Supreme judicial authority was vested in him as king, but it has been argued that on this occasion he was merely acting within the jurisdiction of the pre-monarchical war-leader in Israel (*cf.* Joshua's role in the Achan crisis in Jos. 7).[38]

45. The people find the whole thing too preposterous and counter with an oath of their own. Saul's kind of curse was not irrevocable; when the mother of the Ephraimite Micah unwittingly cursed her son she was pleased to convert it into a blessing (Jdg. 17:1f.).[39] *ransomed* could imply commutation to a monetary fine, as in the case of unfulfilled vows (*cf.* Lv. 27:1ff.),[40] but may mean no more than that the people saved Jonathan by their timely intervention. They did, in any event, prevent Saul from drowning victory in tragedy; to them the course of the day's events made it very clear where, and upon whom, God's favour lay. Saul had been thwarted by them and soon he would fear them (15:24).

47, 48. Whereas the chapter has so far shown ambivalence towards Saul the war-leader, there now follows a summary of his campaigns in terms wholly favourable to him. (Contrast the reference to his Amalekite campaigning in v. 48 with the account given in ch. 15.) The list more or less boxes the compass; the same six kingdoms are named as tributaries of David in 2 Samuel 8:12. *Zobah* was an Aramaean state to the north of Damascus (*cf.* 2 Sa. 10:6ff.). The advantage over the *Philistines* was short-lived (*cf.* v. 52), and by the end of Saul's reign they posed as great a threat as ever to Israel's sovereignty.[41] It has been suggested on the basis of the information given in 1 Samuel that in his campaigns Saul had the simple strategic aim of securing the centre, south, and north of the country against outside interference.[42]

49–51. Details of Saul's family. Even though verse 49 does not list all his sons – Abinadab (31:2) is not mentioned – it would be surprising if there were no reference to Ish-bosheth, who ruled for a short time in Transjordan after his father's death (2 Sa. 2–4). But, in fact, *Ishvi* may be a variant form of his name (*cf.* NIVfn.).[43] *uncle* (50) refers to Ner, as the next verse indicates (*cf.* 9:1); Saul and Abner were cousins.[44] *commander*: one of the few official appointments mentioned in connection with Saul's reign (*cf.* on 21:7).

52. *attached him*: David is a case in point (*cf.* 16:14–23; 18:2); see also 8:10–12.

SAUL AND THE AMALEKITES   (15:1–35)

In the short pericope 13:7b–15a obedience was the stone on which Saul stumbled; here it is the rock that crushes him. As the executor of Yahweh's will and purpose he was given a task which, from all we know about him (*e.g.* 14:36; 2 Sa. 21:2), should have proved highly congenial. But, in spite of very specific instructions from Samuel, Saul failed in his commission, showing scant regard for both the prophetic word and the awesome institution of the 'ban' (see on v. 3). So the earlier performance at Gilgal is confirmed as disobedience, and as not out of character for the self-willed king of Israel. Saul, as this chapter in particular would have us understand, was a man in contention with Yahweh in a way that David, for all his lurid sins, never was. Since the rebel is now pronounced a reject, as the result of a reciprocating act of Yahweh (vv. 23, 26), the mourning and the breach (v. 35) come long before their time. Saul is dead while he still lives.

1. Samuel stands erect as he delivers Yahweh's directive to Saul; in the Hebrew *me* comes first in his speech. In the reference to the prophet's anointing of Saul there is also the suggestion that this too is a momentous occasion. And in *hearken* the question of obedience is immediately brought to the fore.

2, 3. The Amalekites were a nomadic ((?) *cf.* v. 5) tribe living mainly in the Judaean Negev and often acting detrimentally to Israelite interests (*e.g.* Jdg. 3:13; 6:3–5, 33; 7:12). Israelite hostility towards these southern neighbours was traced back to the time of the exodus when the fugitives from Egypt found themselves under

attack from the Amalekites at Rephidim (Ex. 17:8–13). In consequence of that first encounter Israel was committed by Yahweh to
unremitting war against Amalek (*cf.* Ex. 17:14–16; Dt. 25:17–19).
utterly destroy (3) renders a technical term meaning 'put to the
ban' (*ḥērem*, 'ban'), which involved the setting aside of people
and, usually, possessions as Yahweh's 'spoil'. In practice that
meant destruction for everyone and everything included within the
scope of the 'ban' (*cf.* Jos. 6:17). The 'ban' is cited in Deuteronomy
20:16–18 as an important factor in the Israelite conquest of Canaan.
As an institution it was not peculiar to Israel, being attested, for
example, in the Moabite Inscription, where Mesha king of Moab
records that he put the Israelite city of Nebo under a 'ban' ('for I
had devoted-it-to-destruction to Ashtar-Chemosh').[45] See the note
at the end of this chapter.

4. *Telaim* is probably the same as Telem in Joshua 15:24, listed
among the cities of Judah 'in the extreme South'. *Cf.* on 27:8.
thousand: see on 4:2.

5. These nomads, as they are usually described, are linked with
a *city*, which term certainly implies something more substantial
than an encampment. *in the valley* (*bannaḥal*): McCarter, comparing Ezekiel 47:19; 48:28, favours a reference to the 'Brook of Egypt'
(*naḥal miṣrayim*), the modern Wadi el-'Arish, about fifty miles
south of Gaza.

6. The *Kenites*, a Midianite phratry of metal-workers, were living
among the Amalekites at the time of the Israelite settlement,
according to the likelier reading of Judges 1:16.[46] Israel's experience
of the Kenites at the time of the exodus contrasted strongly with
their reception by the Amalekites. In Exodus the story of the
Amalekites' defeat (17:8–16) is followed by a report of the meeting
between Moses and his Kenite father-in-law Jethro, the latter
having come out to congratulate him on the liberation of the
Hebrew serfs from Egypt (Ex. 18:1–12). It is doubtful, however,
whether the occurrence here of *ḥesed* (RSV *kindness*), occasionally a word of covenant association, is sufficient ground for postulat-
ing an actual treaty relationship between Israel and the Kenites.[47]
As at Jericho, then, the 'ban' was applied with some degree of
discrimination (Jos. 6:17).

7. A comprehensive-sounding defeat was inflicted, though
Amalek lived to fight again (30:1f.). *Havilah*, also mentioned with
Shur in Genesis 25:18, cannot be located with any precision. *Shur*
was a wilderness region in north-west Sinai, *east of Egypt*.

8, 9. The 'ban' is still more selectively applied by Saul (*cf.* v. 6).
He may have thought that kings deserved special treatment – an

extension of the principle of preserving *the best*! Compare Ahab's sparing of his 'brother' Ben-hadad (1 Ki. 20:30–34, 42). The fateful word is *spared*, which represents a direct contravention of the instruction in verse 3, and significantly, in view of Saul's subsequent attempt to shift the blame (v. 15), responsibility is laid at the door of *Saul and the people* (9).[48]

Agag is a name, or title (*cf.* Pharaoh, Candace), occurring also in Numbers 24:7 and perhaps perpetuated in the adjectival 'Agagite' used to describe – perhaps vilify – Haman in the book of Esther (3:1, *etc.*).

11. When the Old Testament speaks of God 'repenting' (Heb. *niham*) it is usually a question of withholding or mitigating judgement (*e.g.* 2 Sa. 24:16), whereas here it is the reversing of what is intended for good – for which Genesis 6:6f. provides a rare parallel.[49] 'Repent' when used of God is, of course, anthropopathic; yet it conveys an important truth about a God who is not impassive or static, but dynamic in his interaction with his creation. We are probably to assume that Samuel's anger was directed against Saul, though there may also have been an element of annoyance at having to perform the disagreeable task of pronouncing sentence on him.[50] *cried* is suggestive of an attempt at intercession, a characteristic role of the great prophets (*cf.* Gn. 20:7; Ex. 32:11–14; Je. 15:1).

12. After his victory over the Amalekites Moses raised an altar (Ex. 17:15f.); Saul in a fit of apparent self-congratulation erects a stele (lit. 'hand'; *cf.* Absalom's monument, 2 Sa. 18:18).[51] *Carmel* (mod. Khirbet el-Karmil, nine miles south of Hebron) would have been a convenient stopping-place for Saul as he returned from his Amalekite expedition; it is not to be confused with the famous mountain of the same name (see also 25:2). Thereafter Saul proceeded to *Gilgal*, which fact seems to lend substance to his claim that he intended to offer sacrifices from the spoil that had not been destroyed (*cf.* vv. 15, 21).[52] But see on verse 19. (An additional sentence in the LXX states that he was already sacrificing when Samuel arrived.)[53] Gilgal is a place of destiny for Saul, whether in connection with the inauguration of his kingship (*cf.* 11:14f.) or – twice (*cf.* 13:7–15) – with its prophesied termination.

13. *I have performed*: the assertion suffers from the disadvantage of being contradicted by the prior statement of Yahweh in verse 11.

14. Samuel's reply takes the form of a poetic couplet and should perhaps, therefore, be set out in the same way as verses 22f.

What then is this bleating of sheep in my ears?
And the lowing of oxen that I hear?[54]

The theme of the tell-tale sound recalls Joshua's little saying in Exodus 32:18.

15. Saul tries to slough responsibility for the sparing of the animals; the terms in which he replies certainly suggest that he was aware of what a 'ban' entailed. He also offers the defence that the intention was to sacrifice, so that no personal gain was involved. If *'your* God' sounds a little defiant at this point (*cf.* v. 21), it has a different tone in verse 30.

16. Whatever Samuel sought during his night of prayer (v. 11), he was given a message of unmitigated doom to deliver.

17. Saul's self-deprecation (*cf.* 9:21) should not have been allowed to affect his view of the high office to which he had been called.

18. *sinners*, an unusual way of referring to a national enemy of Israel, expresses the special opprobrium attaching to the Amalekites. Compare the reference to 'the iniquity of the Amorites' in Genesis 15:16. Although distinct from the pre-Israelite population of Canaan to whom the rigours of the 'ban' were first applied (Dt. 20:16–18), they are branded as archetypal enemies and worthy of the same treatment.

19–21. Obedience is the key issue, and again it is pressed. Whereas Saul has held up the sacrifices as evidence of good faith, Samuel accuses him of self-interested plundering (with *swoop* compare 'flew' in 14:32). *and do what was evil*: this becomes a standard form of censure in the books of Kings (*e.g.* 1 Ki. 15:26, 34). Saul, nevertheless, insists that he has obeyed orders, and attempts to maintain his innocence by dividing the responsibility between himself (20) and the army (21).

22, 23. The so-called 'writing prophets' also inveighed – in verse – against abuses of the sacrificial system whereby the externalities of the cult took precedence over the religion of the heart (Is. 1:11–15; Ho. 6:6; Am. 5:21–24; Mi. 6:6–8). But verse 22, while stating a general principle, is here offering a very specific reply to Saul's defensive talk about his sacrifices at Gilgal. His sin (23) is classed with *divination* and *idolatry* – the consultation and worship of other deities – because it is no less an affront to the unique authority of Yahweh.[55] *idolatry* is represented by *terāpîm*, which functioned as household gods (Gn. 31:30) and as aids to divination (Ezk. 21:21). *rejected . . . rejected*: Yahweh's *quid pro quo* (*cf.* v. 26; Dt. 31:16f.; Ho. 4:6, *etc.*). In contrast with 13:7b–15a, there is no reference to the dynastic question, in this verse or in the denunciations that follow; nevertheless the point should not be pressed too much, as if the respective narratives were orientated to the separate issues of Saul's dynasty (ch. 13) and Saul's personal rule (ch. 15).[56]

24, 25. *sinned* (24): compare 26:21 and Pharaoh's (insincere) confession (Ex. 10:16f.). Saul cuts a pathetic figure as he appeals to Samuel for forgiveness and seeks his good offices to achieve his reinstatement with Yahweh (25).

26–28. But Samuel's adamant refusal underlines the finality of the rejection that Saul has brought upon himself. As the prophet turns to leave, Saul grasps his robe in a desperate act of supplication that becomes an unintentional acted parable.[57] Samuel interprets the torn robe as symbolizing the wrenching of the kingdom from Saul (*cf.* Ahijah's prophecy to Jeroboam, 1 Ki. 11:29–33). *this day* (28) is final and leaves no room for further argument. Again (*cf.* 13:14) there is reference to a successor: the kingdom is earmarked for a *neighbour* of Saul's, not named (contrast 28:17) but very soon to be introduced. The next phase of the narrative will reveal who that *neighbour* is, and how he came to be in Saul's entourage (16:14–23). *who is better*: *cf.* Esther 1:19.

29. *Glory*: the only occurrence of BH *nēṣaḥ* as a divine title, though it is listed as an attribute in 1 Chronicles 29:11; compare also the use of *kāḇôḏ* ('glory') in Jeremiah 2:11.[58] Too much can be made of the surface tension between the statements, in verses 11 and 29, concerning the possibility or impossibility of God's repenting. When God issues a decree that is plainly intended as irrevocable, as in the rejection of Saul, then, says our text, there is no possibility of that decree being rescinded (*cf.* Nu. 23:19).

30, 31. Samuel – a man (v. 29)! – relents, even though Saul's preoccupation is now with saving face.[59]

32. How Agag came and what he said are both elusive. For *cheerfully* (*ma'aḏannōṯ*) we could read 'in fetters' on the basis of Job 38:31. NEB 'with faltering step' (*me'ōḏannîṯ*) is also feasible and has the agreement of the LXX. RSV gives a straightforward translation of Agag's observation, but it is not replete with meaning and there is room for conjecture. As it stands, Agag is voicing the untimely sentiment that he need no longer fear for his life. The LXX presents a slightly different text, 'Would death have been so bitter?'; Agag ruefully remarks on the preferability of dying with his people to being singled out for this special treatment by Samuel.[60]

33. Samuel's sentence has a verse rhythm (*cf.* NIV and see on v. 14). *hewed* (*šāsap*): a rare word, just as is the form of execution; 'death by slicing' was more characteristic of the Chinese Sung

Dynasty than of ancient Israel.[61] Nevertheless, Samuel appears to have conducted the execution in a ritual way *before the Lord*.

34, 35. Samuel and Saul no longer have business in common, and a meeting like that recorded in 19:24 does not come into the reckoning. Since AV was chided a long time ago for departing from its 'usual fidelity' in giving 'came no more to see' for *did not see* (*lō' yāsap̄ lir'ōṯ*),[62] it is disappointing to find NIV trying to square the circle with 'did not go to see'. The bald statement in the original is quite simply 'occasioned by the theological urgency of showing Saul rejected'.[63] *grieved*: 'mourned' would be as appropriate for BH *'āḇal*, not least in the present context which treats Saul's rejection as his virtual demise. Samuel's grief over Saul casts light on the private emotions of a prophet who, like others of his calling, had to deliver messages which were no more palatable to themselves than to those to whom they brought them. On the other hand, there was no shortage of time-serving mantics willing to tell the likes of Ahab what he wanted to hear (1 Ki. 22:6).

A note on the 'ban'

The institution of the 'ban', like the whole concept of the holy war, is far removed from the Christian code of the New Testament and must be seen in the context of the provisional morality of the Old Testament. Its very existence outside Israel (*cf.* on 15:3) would point to such a conclusion. But it is not simply a pagan idea that has nothing to say to the Christian believer, for within the Old Testament it is viewed strictly as the execution of God's judgement on nations and societies that are morally irredeemable (*cf.* Gn. 15:16). It was also a double-edged concept, in that Israelite communities were not exempt from the same treatment (Dt. 13:12–18). Nor is the notion of community sin being punished on a community scale wholly alien to the New Testament (*cf.* Lk. 10:12; 19:41–44).

Nevertheless, as subsequent history has shown, the exterminatory 'ban' has been a concept riddled with irony for the descendants of those Israelites who cherished the tradition of Jericho and Ai. The Christian is certainly under no obligation to strain argument or morality in defence of a principle of rough justice, with all its attendant injustice; but, equally, he must affirm the truth that God has never abdicated his responsibility of judging the impenitent, whether they be individuals or nations (*cf.* Heb. 10:29; 12:25). As to the possibility of a Christian being the agent of judgement, Luke 9:51–56 gives the appropriate answer; however lacking in textual

authority are the words relegated to footnote status in RSV at
verse 55, they are exceedingly Christian nonetheless.

In an age when the patronage of Christ and his church is claimed
for all kinds of extreme behaviour, the need for the Christian to
distance himself from the *damnosa hereditas* of the 'ban' is all the
more apparent. But how, then, shall we 'slay the Amalekite' in the
late twentieth century? The answer can best be framed along the
lines of Ephesians 6:12 ('we are not contending against flesh and
blood, but against the principalities, against the powers . . .'), and
in keeping with the broad concept of 'spiritual warfare' in the New
Testament – anticipated, to be sure, in the Old Testament itself.
That very old tradition – still fostered in some circles – of spiritualiz-
ing Amalek to represent 'the flesh', in a distinctly Pauline sense of
the term, was, for all its quaintness, applying just this insight.[64]
And it is a tradition which might even claim to have a toe-hold in
the Hebrew text itself, when it speaks of '*the sinners*, the Amalekites'
(15:18). 'The flesh', at any rate, constitutes an enemy against which
the Christian is bound to wage a 'perpetual warfare' (Ex. 17:16;
Gal. 5:16–21).

Finally, our attitude to the 'ban', with its emphasis on individual-
izing and interiorizing, finds very agreeable matter in C. S. Lewis's
conclusions on the imprecatory psalms: 'From this point of view
I can use even the horrible passage in 137 about dashing the Babylonian babies against the stones. I know things in the inner
world which are like babies; the infantile beginnings of small indul-
gences . . .'[65]

5 David and Saul (16:1–31:13)

By the end of ch. 15 Saul's rejection by Yahweh is established as irreversible. For the remainder of 1 Samuel Saul is still the king of Israel, but it is equally apparent that the focus is now on the man who, against all adversity – and not least adversity of Saul's own devising – will replace him on the throne. David, the man in question, steps immediately into view in ch. 16, with the account of his anointing by Samuel, and he is the undoubted hero of all that ensues. There is, in these chapters, a fair amount about Saul's emotional state and the actions to which it drove him, but mainly insofar as these impinge on the story of David and the question of the succession.

This section forms part of what has become known as the 'History of David's Rise', thought to be an apologetic work composed to defend David against slanderous charges of complicity in the deaths of key members of the Saulide family during the early part of his career. That this is a fair reading of these chapters can scarcely be questioned, even if the independent status of the narrative, and its allegedly early date, are points in need of more substantiation. For further discussion see the Introduction.

DAVID OF BETHLEHEM (16:1–23)

The chapter is in two topically distinct, and yet closely related, parts. In the first (vv. 1–13), Samuel is told by Yahweh to stop grieving for Saul, and to go to Bethlehem, where he will anoint his successor. The unexpectedness of Yahweh's choice from among the sons of Jesse only underlines the fact of Saul's rejection, for the criterion which set Saul apart from the rest of Israel is expressly repudiated at the outset of Samuel's little ceremony (v. 7).

But David, once anointed as Israel's next king, is not left to while away the waiting years among the sheepfolds, and in the second main division of the chapter (vv. 14–23) we learn how it came about that the young Bethlehemite was introduced to Saul's court, firmly ensconcing himself in the king's favour in the process. There will be many twists in the story of David's progress towards the throne, and not a few crisis-points, yet all is told in the knowledge that God can put his men where he wants them to be, whether the route is direct, or ever so circuitous. 1 Samuel 16:14–23 is, in this matter of David's arrival at court, difficult to reconcile with certain aspects of the following narrative in ch. 17, and especially with Saul's apparent unfamiliarity with David prior to his encounter with Goliath in the valley of Elah. The most probable explanation lies not in strained arguments about Saul's mental state during previous meetings of the two, but in the compiler's use of traditional material, relating to David, which could be pressed into service to illustrate some of his leading themes concerning the rise to prominence of Jesse's son.

1. The previous chapter ends in bathos as Samuel, so formidable in the public execution of his duties, welters in private grief for Saul (v. 35). But Yahweh has rejected Saul and disapproves of the inordinate mourning; Samuel has made kings tremble, yet 'he too stands in need of the divine corrective word'.[1] The mission on which he is sent takes him some way beyond the limited circuit of 7:16f.; Bethlehem is six miles to the south of Jerusalem. *for myself*: this king is Yahweh's choice, in contrast with Saul, who, though officially Yahweh's nominee (see 10:24), was appointed in response to public clamour (*cf.* 'for us' (8:5), 'for them' (8:22)).

2, 3. The anointing of a rival to the reigning monarch was a dangerous business (*cf.* 2 Ki. 9:3), so it is not surprising that Samuel blanched when given his instructions. As later events proved, Saul could no more tolerate a rival than the next man; some of his attempts to eliminate David are distinctly in the Herodian style. However, Samuel was given a pretext for his trip – an ironical pretext in the light of the preceding disagreement between Samuel and Saul (15:15, 21). We may assume that there was a sanctuary at Bethlehem in this period.[2] A *heifer* was acceptable as a 'peace offering' (or 'communion offering') in priestly law (Lv. 3:1). Compare also the killing of the two milch cows as a burnt offering at Beth-shemesh, on the occasion described in 6:14f.

4, 5. The sight of Samuel and his heifer (presumably) occasions thoughts of a disciplinary visit in the minds of the Bethlehemite elders. Prophets, and the prophet Samuel as much as any, came to be associated in the popular mind with tidings of doom and judgement. *consecrate yourselves* (5): though nothing more is heard of the elders, the implication certainly is that they witnessed David's anointing. They were to perform whatever purificatory acts were necessary before they could participate in the sacrifice. At the least, this would probably involve ritual washing (*cf.* Ex. 19:10; Nu. 8:21).

6, 7. *Eliab* has a physique similar to that of Saul, and therefore the same appeal for conventional views of kingliness. *I have rejected him*, in recalling verse 1, makes the comparison with Saul unmistakable – and does nothing at all for Eliab's candidature.

8–10. Jesse is credited with eight sons (*cf.* 17:12). 1 Chronicles 2:13–15 gives the names of seven, and, somewhat to our confusion, includes David in the seven ('David the seventh', v. 15). There is not much likelihood that the Elihu mentioned in 1 Chronicles 27:18 completes the octave, since that is probably a variant for Eliab (*cf.* LXX). (It would be surprising if a brother who is not even listed in the genealogy in 1 Ch. 2 held the position of tribal officer for Judah. As the eldest of Jesse's sons, Eliab, on the other hand, might well have fulfilled this role.) *Shammah* (9): several forms of the name occur; *cf.* also Shimeah (2 Sa. 13:3, 32) and Shimei (2 Sa. 21:21).

11. *sit down* (*nāsōb*): in later Hebrew the verb *sābab* can denote reclining at table, and so probably here, as a couple of the ancient versions already suggest. The sacrificial meal is to be delayed until David's arrival.

12. David was handsome – doubtless to be interpreted as a sign of divine favour (*cf.* Ex. 2:2; Acts 7:20) – without having the physical proportions of a Saul or an Eliab (*cf.* 17:42(?)).

13. David is anointed, but to what task? It is a quasi-private appointment, the significance of which, as far as the narrative is concerned, is known only to Samuel. Since more than kings were anointed in ancient Israel, the onlookers may, or may not, have drawn the appropriate conclusion. As with Saul (10:1, 9), the external application of oil was followed by an affusion of the spirit of Yahweh, to equip the anointed for the task laid upon him (*cf.* Is. 11:2; 61:1). There is some uncertainty about the meaning of David's name – of which he is the sole bearer in the Old Testament – especially since the supposed Akkadian cognate *dāwidūm*, previously thought to mean 'commander', has fallen on hard times.[3]

A connection with the Hebrew *dōḏ*, and a meaning 'beloved' (or even 'uncle'), still remains feasible.[4]

14. Saul, bereft of the spirit of Yahweh, falls victim to bouts of Kierkegaardian melancholia here attributed to an evil spirit from Yahweh. ('Whom God wants to destroy he first drives mad.') Psalm 51:11 ('take not thy holy Spirit from me') may well reflect a psalmist's fear of Saul-like dereliction. Saul's evil spirit is on a par with the lying spirit in Ahab's prophets (1 Ki. 22:21–23), and as difficult to accommodate in traditional Christian theology. In part, the answer lies in the tendency of the Old Testament to trace both good *and* evil back to Yahweh (*cf.* Jb. 2:10), which, whatever other difficulties it hazards, steers well clear of the pitfall of dualism.[5] But we must also allow that a traditional manner of speaking may not be intended to carry the amount of theological freight that we may wish to impose upon it. How much, for example, is intended in the statement in Judges 9:23 that 'God sent an evil spirit between Abimelech and the men of Shechem'? Or are we to suppose that in 1 Samuel 16 Saul's servants (vv. 15f.), and then David (v. 23), self-consciously seek to thwart the work of God?

15–17. Saul's melancholia actually creates the circumstances in which Yahweh's appointee is brought into the court circle.[6] The servants are well aware of the soothing effect of music on people suffering from Saul's complaint.

18. The young man gives an irresistible account of David's qualifications – and one which anticipates some of the later action. At this stage David was hardly describable as *a man of valour* and *a man of war* (*cf.* 17:33, 39).[7] *of good presence*: NIV 'fine-looking' is better. With *the Lord is with him* there begins a refrain which recurs at intervals throughout the so-called 'History of David's Rise' (*cf.* 18:14, *etc.*, and see the Introduction).

19. Saul, acting in the regal way outlined in Samuel's 'portrait of a king' (*cf.* 8:11–18), summons David to the palace.

20. *an ass laden with bread*: lit. 'an ass (*ḥᵃmôr*) of bread', which could be idiomatic or textually deficient. NEB 'homer' (Heb. *ḥōmer*) represents a dry measure, perhaps originally meaning 'ass-load', and involves minimal alteration of the text. McCarter, following the LXX, prefers 'omer' (Heb. *'ōmer*), which was a much smaller measure than the homer.[8]

21. *entered his service*: lit. 'stood before him', which may refer either to the initial presentation, as here, or to more permanent service, as in verse 22 (where 'remain in my service' is lit. 'stand before me'). For the latter sense compare Elijah's reference to 'the

God of Israel . . . before whom I stand' (1 Ki. 17:1). Saul immediately takes to David, as soon will his son Jonathan (18:1) and the population at large (18:16). It seems unnecessary, however, to read into *loved* the connotation of a political or legal commitment, even though the word may bear this sense when used of more overtly political liaisons, as, for example, between overlord and vassal.[9] There is no reason to think that the position of *armour-bearer* was merely honorific; on the contrary, the appointment, like everything else in verses 21–23, assumes David's continued presence at the palace.

23. *Cf.* 18:10; 19:9. An apocryphal psalm from Qumran (11QPs[a] 27) includes among David's compositions four 'songs for making music over the stricken' – evidently suggesting that Saul had the benefit of words as well as music.[10] The same idea is expressed in Robert Browning's *Saul*.

THE VALLEY OF ELAH   (17:1–58)

The Philistines, by now inveterate enemies of Israel, have massed for attack, but prefer to settle the issue in a relatively bloodless way, provided that Israel will put up a representative to try conclusions with their vaunted champion. What is at stake, as is clearly stated, is nothing less than Israelite – and, theoretically, Philistine – sovereignty (v. 9). Saul, appointed king in the first instance to deal with the Philistine menace (*cf.* 9:16), is found wanting on this occasion, and Israel is without a champion. The account of how David stepped into the breach and confounded everyone by his famous victory is justly regarded as a classic short story in its own right. As to whether David is justly credited with the victory see on 2 Samuel 21:19. At this point we merely note the two factors which made the heroic possible, viz. David's zeal for the reputation of Israel's God – 'that all the earth may know' (v. 46) – and his utter trust in God's ability to preserve him against all odds (vv. 37, 45–47). His victory that day in the valley of Elah made a national hero of him, as well as entitling him to the hand of the king's daughter in marriage; but it also evoked jealous feelings in Saul, thus indirectly setting in motion the events which fill the rest of 1 Samuel. On the relative merits of the Hebrew and Septuagintal versions of chs. 17–18 see the Introduction ('The Text').

1, 2. Again the Philistines make an incursion into Israelite territory. *Socoh* and *Azekah*, mentioned together in Joshua 15:35

in a list of lowland towns belonging to Judah, were situated in the
Shephelah, some miles west of Bethlehem. The name *Socoh* survives
in the modern Khirbet Shuweikeh. *Azekah*, perhaps best-known
for its appearance on Lachish ostracon no. 4 ('we cannot see
Azekah'), lay to the north-west of Socoh; the site may be represented by the modern Tell ez-Zakariyeh. *Ephes-dammim* (*cf.* Pas-
dammim, 1 Ch. 11:13) cannot be located with certainty. The valley
of *Elah* (meaning 'terebinth') is identified with the Wadi es-Sant,
which debouches on the Philistine plain further west.

3. The scene is set for a classic encounter – or for stalemate, as
it actually works out. There is no mention of Philistine armoured
divisions as at Michmash (*cf.* 13:5); this is to be the story of a duel.

4–7. Goliath's armour and weapons are described in detail to
enhance our appreciation of David's valour when, unprotected, he
advanced against this intimidating hulk, with his trusty sling in his
hand.[11] *champion* is perhaps too specific for *'îš-habbēnayim* (lit.
'man-of-the-between'). In the Qumran *War Scroll* the term denotes
skirmishers who operate between the lines, though this is no
guarantee that such was the original meaning.[12] *Goliath* is perhaps
a name of Anatolian origin, but not necessarily so.[13] His height of
six cubits and a span would come out at about nine feet six inches,
if we reckon with a cubit of slightly under eighteen inches.[14] While
this is not impossible, it has to be noted that, for MT *six cubits*,
both 4QSam[a] and the LXX have 'four cubits', which would make
him about six feet six inches, and formidable enough by contemporary standards.

5. The description starts with the head, which also happens to
be the champion's weak point (*cf.* v. 49); he could have done with
a visor. *five thousand shekels of bronze*: about 125 pounds.

6. *greaves* are mentioned only here in the Old Testament, though
they were commonplace in the Aegean world, and figure in the
panoplies of the Trojan heroes of the *Iliad*.[15] *javelin* for MT *kîḏôn*
is a disputed rendering (*cf.* NEB 'dagger'). 'Sword' and 'scimitar'
have had strong advocacy in recent years, and it is clear that at
Qumran *kîḏôn* signified a sword of some sort.[16] *between his shoulders* (*bên kᵉṯēp̄āyw*) is preferable to 'among his weapons', the
alternative favoured by a few scholars and underlying NEB 'one
of his weapons . . .'.[17]

7. *weaver's beam*: according to Yadin, the leash- or heddlerod
of a loom.[18] The comparison is then not with the size of the rod –
which is unremarkable – but with the loops or leashes of cord that
were attached to it. There are illustrations of Egyptian and Aegean
javelins which were 'slung' by this means, and ballistic tests suggest

that performance over against the ordinary method of propulsion was considerably improved. *six hundred shekels*: about fifteen pounds. The mention of *iron* is noteworthy (*cf.* on 13:19–22).

8–11. Representative combat is rare in the Old Testament, so that it is fitting, in a way, that a non-Israelite should be the instigator of this particular contest.[19] An episode of a similar character, involving two groups of 'knights' from opposing sides, is described in 2 Samuel 2. Then, from extra-biblical sources, there is the duel recounted in the Egyptian 'Tale of Sinuhe', in which Sinuhe defeated a mighty man of Retenu (an ancient Egyptian name for Palestine).[20] And there are other instances from the Aegean world and thereabouts, typified in the combat scenes in Homer's *Iliad*.

8. In the preliminary to the ancient duel the taunt has an honoured place. Goliath actually says, 'Am I not *the* Philistine?', which NEB tries to reproduce in, 'I am the Philistine champion.' But, if the Philistine preens himself, he also insults the ranks opposite by calling them 'slaves' (*'ăḇāḏîm*; RSV 'servants') of Saul (*cf.* NEB).

9. Philistine submission to Israel did not, of course, come about on the terms proposed by Goliath.

10. *defy* recurs in the chapter (vv. 25, 26, 36, 45), and, in view of its use in connection with other Israelite-Philistine exchanges (2 Sa. 21:21; 23:9), obviously touched on a point of national honour (*cf.* also 'reproach' (*ḥerpâ*), from the same root, in v. 26 and in 11:2).

12. Enter the hero! He is introduced as if for the first time, either because the narrator has drawn upon a new source at this point, or perhaps as a matter of narrative technique. Stories told in the folkloristic mode sometimes reflect the view that a hero is more of a hero if he is an 'outsider'.[21] *Ephrathite* has two distinct usages: (i) as a gentilic for 'Ephraimite' (*cf.* 1:1); (ii) denoting a sub-phratry within the tribe of Judah, as here (*cf.* Ru. 1:2). These latter Ephrathites lived in Bethlehem and environs (*cf.* 1 Ch. 4:4). *eight sons*: *cf.* on 16:8–10. *advanced in years*: better than MT 'advanced among men', but not without its own problems.[22]

13. *Cf.* 16:6–9.

15. A verse designed to explain how David, who, according to 16:21, had been appointed armour-bearer to Saul, was not in the Israelite camp when Goliath was issuing his challenge.

17, 18. Already the picture of David anointed 'in the midst of his brothers' (16:13) might have evoked a comparison with the highly-favoured Joseph of the Genesis narratives. Now his errand to the battle-front is a detail reminiscent of Joseph's fact-finding mission to Dothan (Gn. 37:12ff.); in both cases the errand leads to an unforeseen encounter with destiny. *token* (*'arubbâ*, 18): some material evidence that all is well with them.

19–24. David arrives in time to hear Goliath issue his daily challenge. *David heard* (23), but his reaction was totally different from that of Saul and his warriors when they heard the Philistine (v. 11).

20. *war cry*: see on 4:5.

25–27. Whereas Saul's generous incentives have so far failed to produce a hero from the Israelite ranks, David immediately shows himself not a little interested.

25. *will give him his daughter*: a common motif in this kind of story, though where Saul is the father there are unexpected complications (*cf.* 18:17–27). *free* (*ḥopšî*) does not suggest prior servitude, as in some other of its occurrences (*e.g.* Ex. 21:2, 5, *etc.*; Dt. 15:12). While the Akkadian term *ḥupšu*, descriptive of a certain social class, offers a possible cognate, it does not necessarily help towards a precise definition of the Hebrew word. We should probably think in terms of exemption from taxation (*cf.* NIV) and similar obligations to the crown;[23] alternatively, it has been suggested that the hero's family were to live as pensioners of the royal house.[24]

26. *reproach*: *cf.* 11:2. *uncircumcised*: see on 14:6. The God of Israel is a *living God* in contrast with the lifeless idols and venerated nonentities of the nations (*cf.* Jos. 3:10; 1 Thes. 1:9). In pagan religion, as a Hebrew prophet pointed out in a devastating satire, it was the idol that was carried, whereas the God of Israel undertook to *carry* and to save (Is. 46:1–7).

28–30. Like Joseph (*cf.* on vv. 17f.), David was not necessarily a favourite with his brothers. Eliab, the eldest of the family (16:6), laces his advice with contempt for David's pastoral calling. Whether or not we read his speech against the background of 16:1–13 – the anointing of David in preference to Eliab and the rest – will depend on how we envisage the process of compilation of the narrative. Eliab's anger is the anger of a man who feels small because of the Israelite army's inability to deal with Goliath, and he particularly resents looking small in the eyes of his young brother. If David had indeed come hoping to see some action he would have been disappointed.

29. *Was it not but a word ?*: NIV 'Can't I even speak?' is excellent.

33–36. Saul sees David's inexperience as too much of a handicap, but the Bethlehemite is not quite the greenhorn that the king has imagined. There is no incompatibility between the description of David as a *youth* (33) and the earlier statement that Saul appointed him as his armour-bearer (16:21);[25] it is actual military experience that is in question. To judge from the numbers of Old Testament references to them, lions, especially, were not uncommon in the Palestine of the Israelite period. Here David claims a level of success beyond that of the proverbial shepherd of Amos 3:12. Since bears generally do not grow beards (35; *cf.* 34), there is something to be said for the LXX's 'throat';[26] 'throat' (*gārôn*) could easily have been corrupted to *beard* (*zāqān*) in the Hebrew square script.

34. *used to keep sheep*: but David, according to MT, has just come from the sheepfold and he still has his shepherd's gear (v. 40). Since the Hebrew can tolerate it, we must therefore render with NIV, 'Your servant has been keeping . . .'

37. The same faith in Yahweh that inspired Jonathan's deed of valour (14:6) is found in David.

38–40. David cannot be turned into an armadillo at the drop of a helmet; even experienced fighters would not necessarily possess a *coat of mail* (38), as Stoebe notes on the basis of the booty list of Tuthmosis III from Megiddo.[27] *staff* (40): see on verse 43. In a skilled hand the *sling* could be a deadly weapon. According to Judges 20:16 the tribe of Benjamin could at one time count on the services of seven hundred left-handed slingers every one of whom 'could sling a stone at a hair, and not miss'. Compare also the ambidextrous Benjaminites mentioned in 1 Chronicles 12:2. The sling was commonly deployed in near eastern armies, the evidence in the case of Egypt going back to the beginning of the second millennium BC.[28]

41. *shield*: the *ṣinnâ*, larger than the ordinary *māḡēn* (*cf.* 1 Ki. 10:16f.).

43, 44. In the best traditions of the duel, the action is prefaced by an exchange of 'speeches'. Goliath's generalizing *with sticks* (and no more) indicates that he is unaware of David's lethal long-range weapon.[29] The LXX's 'with a staff and stones' aims at exactitude, but misses the point: the stones are not visible.[30] To be left as carrion was a horrendous thought to any Israelite contemplating death (*cf.* Je. 8:1f.; 16:6), but David returns the compliment with interest (v. 46).

45. A *sword* (*ḥereḇ*) as such has not previously been mentioned among Goliath's weaponry; see, however, verse 51. The description of Yahweh as *the God of the armies of Israel* explicates the title *Lord of hosts*, where *hosts* is capable of at least two other interpretations (*cf.* on 1:3). With verse 45 the theme of defiance is articulated

for the last time in the chapter (*cf.* on v. 10), and RSV *whom* makes
for a fitting climax in that it is not the Israelite army (v. 10), nor
Israel (v. 25), nor even the armies of the living God (vv. 26, 36),
but Yahweh himself who has been affronted. However, the relative
could refer to the armies of Israel as having been defied by Goliath
(*cf.* NEB 'which').

46, 47. David's eschewing of conventional armour will ensure
that the glory goes to Yahweh to whom it belongs. Then it will be
evident to all that the God of Israel is far from being powerless
against his foes; for it is Yahweh's standing that is in question
when the Philistines extend their hegemony to Israelite territory.
As for the giant's original proposal (v. 9), David will have none
of it (v. 46).

48, 49. Acting swiftly, David finds his mark before his opponent
has time to change tack; the surprise has worked. Goliath is
prostrated like Dagon before the ark (5:1–5), and will likewise
suffer decapitation (v. 51).[31]

50. The narrative flow is interrupted so that the real significance
of the day's victory over the Philistines can be underlined. Since
David prevailed in such an unconventional way the unspoken
suggestion is that it must have been with Yahweh's co-operation
(*cf.* vv. 45–47).

51. The champion's head is removed as a trophy; compare the
Romans' treatment of Theudas' head after he was arrested for
trying to divide the waters of the Jordan (*Ant.* xx. 5. 1). *killed*:
'despatched' as in 14:13 (RSV 'killed').

52. Routed, the Philistines head for the home ports of Gath
(LXX; MT *Gai*) and Ekron. *Shaaraim* is listed in the company of
Socoh and Azekah, plot-points at the beginning of this chapter
(v. 1), in Joshua 15:35f. Beyond that its location is not known.

54. Since Jerusalem was not in Israelite hands at this point we
must assume that Goliath's skull was brought there at a later
date[32] – like other prizes of war (*cf.* 2 Sa. 8:7). *his armour*: later
the giant's sword is found at the sanctuary in Nob (21:9; *cf.* 31:10
(Saul's armour)), but this scarcely requires that *his tent* originally
referred to Yahweh's tent-shrine. Nor have we grounds for
assuming that the Nob shrine was a tent.

55–58. Saul's curiosity about David's parentage presumably
relates to the incentives of verse 25, in particular the promise of
his daughter in marriage and the according of privileged status
to the hero's family. Nevertheless, in the light of Saul's prior
acquaintance with David (16:18–23) we should have expected Saul
to speak differently both to (*cf. young man*, 58) and about him.

The conclusion that 16:14–23 and 17:55–58 stem from independent traditions concerning David's début at court is therefore not unreasonable.[33]

AFTER THE BATTLE   (18:1–30)

As a result of his victory over Goliath, David is lionized by the population at large, and the king's own son is so impressed as to present his robe and armour to the young hero. With all this concentration on David, however, the seeds of insecurity and jealousy are sown in Saul's heart, and they produce a tragic harvest. Whereas all Israel love David, Saul is set on his destruction. But he finds that whatever he tries to do against him is frustrated; the curse is turned into blessing, because God is with David.

1–3. Jonathan, no mean combatant himself, generously acknowledges the conqueror of Goliath and instigates a mutual alliance that will be crucial for David's physical survival at court, to speak of nothing else. *loved him as his own soul* (1, 3) does not exactly replicate Leviticus 19:18, which is concerned with the ordinary, everyday relationships of community life. Encouraged by the reference to a *covenant* of amity in verse 3, some scholars discover in *loved* (1, 3) a political nuance such as 'love' has in some ancient treaty texts which prescribe the relationship appropriate to treaty partners.[34] However, in this chapter everyone – apart from Saul, that is – loves David (vv. 16, 20, 22)! This particular consideration tends to be overlooked when David and Jonathan's relationship is presented in a less worthy light.

4. Jonathan divests himself of his *robe* and *armour* – and invests David with these symbols of his own princely status. It is hard not to find here some recognition already on the part of Jonathan that David, and not he, was to be the next ruler of Israel (*cf.* 20:13–17; 23:17f.). This is a virtual abdication by Jonathan, the crown prince.[35] The rest of the story, as it affects the two, will hint at a certain merging of their roles. Although the monarchy was in its infancy, and the question of succession had not yet arisen, the hereditary principle was such a well-established feature of near eastern monarchies that Jonathan must originally have held some expectation of succeeding his father on the throne.[36] But that he soon relinquishes in favour of someone with greater endowments than his own.

5. The first of three reports of David's popularity in Israel (*cf.* vv. 16, 30). His appointment to an army command was enthusiastically

received by the men themselves (*the people*), and even by his
potential rivals among Saul's 'servants'. ('*ebed* ('servant') is frequently used for palace ministers and the like; 'minister' itself, of
course, originally meant 'servant'.)

6, 7. The returning hero is treated to the Israelite equivalent of
the Roman 'triumph', as the women chant their victory song – in
the best exodus tradition (*cf.* Ex. 15:20f.). Unfortunately, their
celebratory couplet contained an injudicious variation on the usual
theme, and an implacable jealousy was stirred in Saul. 'Thousand'
and 'ten thousand' occasionally appear in poetic parallel in Hebrew
(and Ugaritic) poetry (*cf.* Ps. 91:7; 144:13; Mi. 6:7), but always for
cumulative effect. However, by apportioning the figures to Saul
and David as they did, the women seem to make an invidious
comparison. *instruments of music* (6): BH *šālîš* seems to be derived
from *š-l-š* ('three'), hence the footnoted alternatives, 'triangles' and
'three-stringed instruments', in RSV. This is the only occurrence of
the word, as denoting a musical instrument, in the Old Testament.

8, 9. Saul has discovered who his 'neighbour' (15:28) is.

10, 11. 'Jealousy is cruel as the grave' (Song 8:6). The language
of verse 10 is noteworthy. *rushed* (*ṣālaḥ*) describes the accession
of the divine spirit upon Saul after his anointing by Samuel (10:10),
and *raved* is the word rendered 'prophesied' in the same verse.
There are, then, similarities between the external manifestations of
spirit-possession on these two occasions, no matter how different
the underlying causes and significance (*cf.* 2 Ki. 9:1–3, 11; Je.
29:26). Saul's *spear* functions as a symbol of his kingly authority
(*cf.* 22:6; 26:7), but for David it has a more sinister association (*cf.*
19:9f. and see on 26:22).

12–30. Having failed in his murder attempts, Saul tries other
ploys to reduce David to size (vv. 12–16), or to have him eliminated
altogether (vv. 17–30), yet they are counter-productive (vv. 15f.,
30).

12–16. His fear was probably inspired by David's capacity for
survival (*cf.* v. 11), which Saul attributed not to youthful lissomness
but to Yahweh's presence with the young man (*cf.* vv. 28f.). (Twice
in these verses (12, 14) David's *leitmotiv* is heard: *the Lord was
with him* (see on 16:18).) David is therefore stellenbosched, to the
rank of section commander, in the hope that his popularity will
dwindle.[37] However, this change only brought him into closer
contact with the soldiery, and into greater favour with them. It is
all faintly reminiscent of Pharaoh's predicament in Exodus 1:12–
22; *cf.* also Genesis 50:20. *went out and came in before* (13, 16) is
an expression for leadership in battle (*cf.* 29:6; Nu. 27:17). *loved*

(16), to judge from a possibly analogous use outside the Old Testament, may connote a political attachment or loyalty such as would normally exist between a king and his subjects.[38] If so, Saul might well feel envious. See, however, the comment on verses 1–3.

17. The promise of the king's daughter to the conqueror of Goliath (*cf.* 17:25) is finally to be redeemed, but she will come with strings attached. David must prosecute the war against the Philistines, and Saul hopes to lead the mourning for his lost hero. Saul is more concerned about his personal position than about the nation's security. Not only has David become a pawn in Saul's deadly game, so also has the king's own daughter. *the Lord's battles*: not a source of danger, but the ground of David's dynastic hope, according to Abigail's speech (25:28).

18, 19. David's reply perhaps contains a little more than the conventional self-effacement of the lowly called of a sudden to higher things (*cf.* 9:21),[39] for he speaks in the same vein to Saul's servants in verse 23. It is unlikely that he shrank from the thought of further military engagement with the Philistines (see vv. 26f.). At the last minute, however, and out of sheer contrariness, Saul bestowed his daughter on someone else. *Meholathite* (19): from Abel-meholah in the Jordan valley, some miles to the south (?) of Beth-shan. The male offspring of this marriage suffered a grim execution at the hands of the Gibeonites, according to 2 Samuel 21:8f.

20, 21. Michal, Saul's younger daughter (*cf.* 14:49), is also captivated by David's charms and, as it seems from verse 26, the attraction was mutual. Saul, whose first experiment in bartering his daughter's hand for Philistine heads had come to nothing, accordingly saw a chance to revive his scheme and raise his price. David, he reckoned, could be lured into the most dangerous of undertakings, if Michal were the prize. *the thing pleased him*: see on verse 26.

22. Since Saul had previously reneged on his promise to give Merab to David (v. 19), he forestalls suspicion by making the approach through his *servants*. Their involvement is evidence of his good faith.

23–25. The bait is laid, and David professes his unworthiness as before (v. 18). He also pleads poverty, which, in the circumstances, sounds as if he is amenable to suggestion (23). It was customary for a prospective son-in-law to give the bride's father a marriage present (*cf.* Gn. 34:12; Ex. 22:16f.) – and the youngest son in a large family might well baulk at the thought of providing one worthy of a king's daughter. But Saul is graciously disposed to accept a present that David can afford, provided that he is willing to risk his life in battle with the Philistines. (Note that AV, RV 'dowry' is inappropriate here; for examples of the dowry see Gn. 29:24; Jdg. 1:15, *etc.*)

26, 27. Much to Saul's chagrin, David produces the marriage present, and ahead of time (according to MT).[40] Moreover, our text says that he delivered twice the required amount to Saul (27), though 2 Samuel 3:14, like the LXX here, gives the figure as one hundred. (If, however, in 2 Sa. 3:14 David is merely stating the actual price asked by Saul, the extra hundred would be incidental.) Once more Saul has been thwarted in his attempt to rid himself of David, and what had *pleased* both Saul and David from their respective viewpoints (vv. 20, 26) works out to David's advantage.

28–30. Saul's playing the part of a latter-day Laban (*cf.* Gn. 29:15–30) has rebounded upon himself, for now a second member of his own family has made her special contribution to the theme 'all Israel and Judah loved David' (v. 16). There is nothing that Saul can do to worst his rival, because, as he realizes, *the Lord was with David* (28). But Saul, at least, will be an *enemy* (29) of this man who has so many friends. So the chapter, which treats mainly of the attempts of Saul to destroy David, ends with a heavy underlining of the fact that the intended victim prospers in all that he undertakes.

28. As the RSV translators indicate in their footnote, they have preferred the reading of the LXX to MT 'and that Michal, Saul's daughter loved him'. However, while it is true that the reference to 'Saul's daughter' reads a little oddly in a sentence which has Saul for subject, the wording may be deliberately intended to emphasize the king's dilemma, now that his own daughter has fallen for David (*cf.* NEB, NIV).

30. For the first clause of the verse, NEB has an interesting, but unsupported, suggestion: 'The Philistine officers used to come out to offer single combat.'

DAVID EVADES DEATH (19:1–24)

With the failure of his earlier attempts to eliminate David (*cf.* 18:10f., 25–27), Saul 'goes public' (v. 1) – driven, like Pharaoh (*cf.* on 18:12–16), to more desperate measures. But he reckons without the loyalty of his own family towards David, and Stoebe fairly entitles verses 1–17, 'Saul's children save David'. Most remarkably of all, when Saul himself goes to apprehend his enemy at Naioth, he is rendered powerless by the spirit of Yahweh; there is no way that he can lay hands on David.

1. Since his devious plottings have left David unharmed, Saul turns to the direct method – without recognizing that Jonathan's affection for David is undiminished.

2, 3. It was possibly because of his need for a substantial guarantee of safety that David was advised to hide where he would have a good view of what was going on, and would be able to assess Saul's attitude for himself. Jonathan could then elaborate on the detail. Whether Jonathan's drawing his father into the field would make it easier for him to meet David afterwards without incurring suspicion is less certain. That David stays within ear-shot(?) of the conversation, and yet needs to be informed about it, is not necessarily a sign of a composite narrative, for, even if Jonathan contrived to bring his father within yards of David's hiding-place, he could not tell in advance how much David would hear.

4. *the king . . . his servant*: Jonathan, even though he is Saul's son, begins by using the third person, as the appropriate mode of address to a king.

5. McCarter omits *the Lord* in order to associate the victory more directly with David. But there is no advantage in the omission; Yahweh's operating through David would be the strongest argument in his defence (*cf.* 14:45).[41] *sin against innocent blood*: a crime particularly associated with Manasseh (*cf.* 2 Ki. 21:16; 24:4).

6, 7. At this stage Saul can be reasoned with, and Jonathan achieves the desired rapprochement. True to his usual heavy-handed approach, Saul puts himself on oath (*cf.* 14:24, 39, 44).

8–10. A further success by David against the Philistines ignites Saul's feelings of jealousy – though the text does not say this in so many words – and David survives another murderous assault (*cf.* 18:11). Instead of destroying David, as Saul had hoped (18:17, 25), the Philistines merely provide him with opportunities to enhance his reputation.

9. *an evil spirit*: *cf.* 16:14f.; 18:10.

10. *And David fled*: an ironical touch coming after the reference to his putting of the Philistines to flight (v. 8).

11. *Michal*, no less than her brother Jonathan, is concerned to prevent Saul from harming David. The gulf between Saul and his children is thus an ever-widening one.

12. *Cf.* Joshua 2:15. Paul regarded a similar experience as a prophylactic against spiritual pride (2 Cor. 11:32f., where 'let down' seems to counterbalance 'caught up' in 12:2). From now on David is on the run, and must take refuge in less accessible parts of the country – and beyond.

13. Michal's ruse gives David added time to get well clear of the house. Nothing certain is known about the shape or size of the *terāpîm* (RSV *image*; *cf.* on 15:23), though Genesis 31:34 would suggest that they were not invariably large. They may have been figurines venerated as household or guardian deities, in the manner of the Roman *lares* and *penates*. Laban refers to them as his 'god(s)' in Genesis 31:30. A connection with the Hittite *tarpiš* ('spirit, demon') is possible,[42] in which case we should probably think of a physical representation, or of a mantic device giving access to the 'god'. According to another theory, the term derives from the Hebrew root *r-p-'* ('heal'), with the further suggestion that here the *terāpîm* may have been put, not *on* the bed, but beside it, ostensibly to serve as a protective, or curative, talisman (*cf.* v. 14).[43] *pillow*: the probable derivation of the word (*kebîr*) would favour a meaning like 'cover' or 'rug' (NEB); the apparently related *makbēr* is translated 'coverlet' in 2 Kings 8:15. On the other hand, McCarter, comparing Song of Songs 4:1 ('Your hair is like a flock of goats'), thinks of a wig or some arrangement of goats' hair that would, in the circumstances, pass for a human head.

14. McCarter's claim that verses 11–17 represent the original sequel to 18:27 has the curious side-effect of making Michal pretend that David is ill on his wedding night.

16, 17. Michal's trick is not discovered until the messengers enter the bedroom. When summoned to give an account of herself, she denies complicity; there was no knowing how Saul might react to that (*cf.* 20:32f.).

18–24. Whereas one of the signs confirming Saul's election as king had been his participation in an ecstatic display by a band of prophets (10:5–13), his subjection to the same mysterious power in this section serves only to confirm his rejection by Yahweh. As the spirit of Yahweh neutralizes Saul's attempts to apprehend David, it transpires that the latter enjoys a sacrosanctity which Yahweh himself is underwriting. In outline the story bears a resemblance to the account of Ahaziah's efforts to interview Elijah in 2 Kings 1:9ff. (*cf.* also Jn. 18:6).

18. David's visit to Samuel may represent, among other things, a kind of seeking sanctuary. *dwelt*: 'stayed' would be sufficient. *Naioth* is not known outside this passage, and some scholars (*e.g.* Ackroyd, McCarter) suspect that it may be a plural form of the noun *nāweh*, meaning 'shepherd's dwelling, camp' – a possible location for a prophetic commune, if this is what is indicated by verse 20 (*cf.* 2 Ki. 6:1).[44]

20. Although retired from public life (*cf.* 12:1f., 23), Samuel seems to be portrayed as the doyen of a college of prophets.[45] The later (classical) prophets tended to be more individualistic, though Isaiah seems to have been surrounded by a group of disciples (Is. 8:16).

21–23. When all three of his posses have collapsed in ecstasy, Saul himself sets out for Ramah, only to discover that he is even more susceptible to the mysterious influence than are his messengers; he begins to ecstasize even before he reaches Naioth (23)! *Secu* (22) has been tentatively identified with Khirbet Shuweikeh, two or three miles north of Ramah (er-Ram).[46]

24. If Jonathan's disrobing in 18:4 had its symbolic aspect, the same is probably true of Saul's nakedness here.[47] He no longer has the dignity or the authority of a king,[48] and the divine spirit, which was supposed to be the cachet of a king, is actually operating in the interests of his rival. The section is not, therefore, offering an alternative context for the origin of the proverbial *Is Saul also among the prophets?* (*cf.* 10:12), but is pointing out how fraught with irony that saying is when the full story of Saul is told. Perhaps, as McKane suggests, the two occurrences of the proverb represent two different evaluations of Saul vis-à-vis the ecstatics: on the first occasion they were not fit company for him, whereas now he is not fit company for them.

DAVID AND JONATHAN (20:1–42)

The situation is clear enough to David: Saul wants to kill him. But Jonathan is Saul's son, and a key figure at this stage in David's story; and he reckons to know his father's intentions in this or any other matter. The chapter is, therefore, concerned with the means by which Jonathan establishes Saul's attitude towards his friend, and with the disclosing of that information to him. Apart from 23:16–18, this is all that we hear of Jonathan until his death at Gilboa (31:2), hence it is fitting that here the two look beyond the present exigencies to the time when David will rule over Israel. Most importantly, Jonathan secures from David an undertaking that his family will be treated generously when David's enemies have been put down (vv. 15f.). The story of the redemption of that promise is featured prominently in the account of David's reign, being introduced immediately after the summary of his military conquests in 2 Samuel 8 (*cf.* 9:1). Saul also, in an intemperate outburst, voices the expectation that David will one day be king (v. 31). But that is about all that he has in common with Jonathan, so far as attitudes to David are concerned.

1, 2. Jonathan, who speaks as if he is unaware of the most recent alarms (19:9–24), finds it hard to credit that Saul would renew his attack on David without informing him as before (*cf.* 19:1).

3. But it is David's life that is at stake, and David is not so easily convinced. *replied* (with LXX) is better than MT 'swore again'; there has been no mention of an oath before now.[49]

5–7. *new moon* was observed as an extra sabbath (*cf.* Am. 8:5), and was an occasion for special sacrifices (*cf.* Nu. 28:11–15). The arrangement proposed by David reflects the importance of the 'sign' as an indication of Yahweh's leading in a particular situation (*cf.* 14:8–10). If Saul still bore malice towards David, this minor discourtesy would be sufficient to bring it to the surface.

6. As the verse implies, there were, in addition to the national festivals, other cultic occasions of local importance. *yearly sacrifice*: *cf.* 1:21. *family* (*mišpāḥâ*) would be better rendered as 'clan'.

8. The *covenant* is, doubtless, that noted in 18:3, and it is 'a covenant of the Lord' (RSVfn.) in the sense that Yahweh was witness to it, and was expected to supervise its implementation (*cf.* vv. 23, 42). *kindly* represents the Hebrew *ḥeseḏ*, which describes the relationship of loyalty proper to a covenant partnership (*cf.* vv. 14f.).[50]

9. *Cf.* verses 1f.

12, 13. Jonathan, now convinced of the urgency of ascertaining Saul's intentions in relation to David, solemnly undertakes to pass on the information. This is his answer to the 'Who?' of verse 10. If we do not insert the words *be witness* (*cf.* Peshitta) we should begin Jonathan's speech as in NIV: 'By the Lord, the God of Israel . . .' Verse 13b goes a long way to explaining how Jonathan's loyalty could override even his loyalty to his father. He recognizes that David is Yahweh's choice to succeed Saul – an admission which will eventually be wrung from Saul himself (*cf.* 24:20).[51]

14, 15. It is Jonathan's turn to invoke the covenant between himself and David (*cf.* v. 8), as he contemplates the accession of David and the possible consequences for the disinherited house of Saul. He knew well that usurpers were wont to adopt a root and branch policy towards ousted royal families, lest they became alternative foci of loyalty at a later date (*cf.* 2 Ki. 10:1–11; 11:1). Whether or not David was reckoned a usurper, he was likely to suffer from the same disadvantages if the family of Saul were left unculled. *When the Lord cuts off*: when David makes his famous inquiry, 'Is there anyone still left of the house of Saul?' (2 Sa. 9:1), it is, therefore, a sign both of his intention to honour his promise to Jonathan and of his having achieved military superiority in Syro-Palestine (*cf.* 2 Sa. 8).

16.[52]*David's enemies* is almost certainly euphemistic for David himself, for the *vengeance* which Yahweh is expected to exact is in the event of a breach of covenant by David. For other likely instances of the euphemistic addition of 'enemies' see 25:22 and 2 Samuel 12:14. This phenomenon, which is more common in post-biblical Hebrew, is paralleled in second millennium texts from both Egypt and Mesopotamia.[53]

17. *made David swear* is less obviously an expression of Jonathan's love for David – which is what is in question (*cf.* 18:1) – than 'swore to David', the reading of the LXX (*cf.* NEB 'pledged himself afresh to David').

18–23. Details of the signalling method by which David will learn whether or not it is safe for him to return to Saul's court. There are translational problems, especially in verse 19.

19. The first clause is problematical, and is treated very differently in NEB: 'So go down at nightfall for the third time'. Here 'for the third time' is a straightforward rendering of MT *wešillaštā* (lit. 'and you will do for the third time'), though it is not so obvious how it fits into the story. The translation of *meʾōḏ* (RSV *greatly*) by 'at nightfall' accepts Guillaume's suggestion that the word should be revocalized *māʾōḏ* and treated as cognate with an assumed Arabic *maʾād* ('evening').[54] *when the matter was in hand*: lit. 'on the day of the deed'. Various attempts have been made to elucidate the phrase. Since the occasion to which Jonathan refers is that described in 19:1–6, and the matter was therefore very sensitive, the expression could be deliberately vague.[55]

20–23. Arrows were used in certain kinds of divinatory practices in ancient times ('belomancy'; *cf.* Nebuchadnezzar in Ezk. 21:21),[56] but there is no randomness about the flight of Jonathan's arrows, and therefore no such significance here. *the lad* (21): 'Jonathan's precautions seem designed to provide a witness who can assure Saul that he did not meet David while out shooting' (Ackroyd).[57]

25. *sat opposite* (*cf.* LXX, reflecting an original *wayeqaddēm*) is usually preferred to MT 'stood' (*wayyāqom*), but if the latter is taken in the sense of 'stood in attendance', as possibly in a Ugaritic text describing a heavenly banquet scene in which Baal stands in the presence of El, the head of the pantheon, then the traditional

text may be retained. Jonathan, as Saul's eldest son, may have
fulfilled a role similar to that of Baal, in this earthly court banquet.[58]

26. Since the new moon feast was a religious celebration, certain
rules concerning ceremonial cleanness applied. Saul's first reaction
to David's non-appearance was, therefore, to assume that he
had been guilty of some infringement which had rendered him
temporarily unfit for cultic participation. The main types of infringement, and the appropriate means of purification, are set out in
Leviticus 11–15. A person might be rendered unfit by, for example,
contact with a dead body, and, in the case of Passover, provision
was made for such in the institution of the 'Second Passover', held
one month after the main celebration (*cf.* Nu. 9:6–14).

27. The oblique reference to David as *the son of Jesse* need not
be interpreted as expressing contempt,[59] though such was not far
from Saul's mind.

29. From the mention of David's brother – Eliab the eldest,
presumably – it has sometimes been inferred that Jesse was dead
by now. But compare 22:1 with 22:3. 4QSam[b] and the LXX,
however, have 'my brothers have commanded me' (*cf. brothers*
later in the verse), and may be original. *let me get away* (lit. 'escape',
as in 19:17, *etc.*) sounds almost like a gaffe on Jonathan's part, yet
is perhaps intended to excite a reaction in Saul, if he is at all
antagonistic towards David. Even if, as Driver maintains, the idea
of escape is not basic to the root (*m-l-ṭ*), the usage is striking in
the context.[60]

30. *son of a perverse, rebellious woman*, while strong language,
does not call for the dysphemisms of some of the more carefree
modern versions.[61]

31. A vain appeal to Jonathan's self-interest; for, although Saul
spoke truly, Jonathan had already come to terms with the situation
(*cf.* 18:1–4; 20:14f.). The hereditary nature of monarchical rule is
more or less taken for granted here.[62]

32, 33. Jonathan repeats David's questions (*cf.* v. 1), and finds
himself in a situation which was by no means unfamiliar to his
friend (*cf.* 18:11; 19:10). If there is, as Jobling suggests, a certain
merging of identities and roles in the portrayal of David and
Jonathan in these chapters, it is never more apparent than when
Saul lifts his spear to harm his own son.[63] *cast* (33) is the same
verb as in 18:11 but could, by a change of vowels, be 'raised', as
in the most important of the ancient versions. We cannot be
absolutely sure, therefore, that Saul went so far as to hurl his spear
at Jonathan. In the earlier references to his attempted transfixing
of David it is noted that David evaded the weapon.

34. grieved: *cf.* verse 3.

35–40. The arrangement is carried out more or less as agreed (*cf.* vv. 19–22), though there is no specific mention of the three arrows of verse 20.

41, 42. It is strange that Jonathan and David go through with their elaborate plan, and then permit themselves a hurried meeting when the young lad has returned to the city. Some therefore conclude that verses 41f. are an addition intended to formalize the occasion when the two finally went their separate ways; however, a further meeting is recorded in 23:16–18. Presumably it is a case of strong emotions conflicting with the best laid plans, just as happens in ordinary human experience.

41. *three times*: the numeral 'three' enjoys a certain amount of prominence in the chapter (*cf.* vv. 5, 12, 19, 20). *recovered himself*: a more likely meaning of the Hebrew is that David 'wept to excess'; *cf.* NEB 'until David's grief was even greater than Jonathan's'.[64]

42. *Go in peace*: see on 2 Samuel 3:22–39. *sworn*: *cf.* verses 14–17.

DAVID AT NOB AND GATH   (21:1–15)

There is now no question of returning to the palace, and David's fugitive days have begun in earnest. He must live by his wits, though not necessarily in the cunning, mendacious way described in this chapter. Deception is, indeed, the common theme of the episodes at Nob and Gath. But, whereas the second dissolves into harmless burlesque, with neither David nor Achish distinguishing themselves, the duping of the priest Ahimelech is an entirely different matter. David's play-acting, involving Ahimelech in unwitting compromise, will bring down the wrath of Saul upon the whole priestly connexion at Nob (22:11–19), as he ruefully acknowledges when confronted by the lone survivor of the massacre (22:22).

1. *Nob*, 'the city of the priests' (22:19), apparently came into greater prominence after the débâcle described in ch. 4, and, as seems likely, the destruction of Shiloh. As may be judged from Isaiah 10:32, it lay a short distance to the north (or north-east) of Jerusalem. Superintending affairs at the Nob sanctuary was a great-grandson of Eli, *Ahimelech* son of Ahitub (*cf.* 22:9).[65] For *the priest* meaning 'chief priest', see on 1:9. Ahimelech senses that something is wrong when David arrives unaccompanied. Has the young man fallen foul of Saul?

2, 3. A story of a top secret mission and a rendezvous with others of Saul's servants is enough to take Ahimelech in.[66]

4, 5. Ahimelech is willing to release the 'bread of the Presence' (see v. 6), permitted only to the priests in priestly law (Lv. 24:9; *cf.* Mk. 2:23–28), so that David and his men may not go hungry. The priest acted in all innocency, but his generosity had frightful consequences for the whole priestly community at Nob. There is no further mention of David's young men, though their existence seems to be assumed in the New Testament citation of this passage (*cf.* Mk. 2:25f.).[67]

Ahimelech's permission, however, is subject to one condition, viz. that David's men have not been rendered ceremonially unclean through coitus (*cf.* Ex. 19:15; Rev. 14:4). David, in his answer, points to the common practice of sexual abstinence during military operations;[68] if abstinence was the rule for ordinary expeditions (*cf.* 2 Sa. 11:11, 13), how carefully it would be observed on a special mission like the present one! Consecration of warriors was a common preliminary to military action (*cf.* Jos. 3:5; Is. 13:3), though whether the distinction between engagements so undertaken and others of a more 'profane' nature is being made here is, *pace* Driver,[69] an open question. *vessels* (*kᵉlê*, 5) could denote either weapons (Stoebe) or bodies (*cf.* NEB), or could even be euphemistic for genitalia (Hertzberg, comparing the Greek *skeuos*).[70]

6. *the bread of the Presence* was so called because it was set out 'before the Lord', *i.e.* in his presence, in the holy place of the sanctuary each sabbath (*cf.* Lv. 24:5–9). When the twelve loaves were removed from the holy table they were treated as a priestly perquisite, to be eaten 'in a holy place' (Lv. 24:9). This verse adds an interesting side-light on the Pentateuchal passage. The practice probably symbolized God's provision for his people Israel – a far cry from the crude concept of 'food for the gods' which obtained elsewhere.

7. It was possible for Edomites to 'enter the assembly of the Lord' (Dt. 23:8), and there may even be hints, in the Old Testament, of common cultic ties between Israel and Edom.[71] *Doeg* is one of the few royal officials named in connection with Saul's administration (*cf.* on 14:50). The reason for his detention at the sanctuary cannot easily be divined, especially since proximity to places and things holy is exactly what was forbidden for certain offences (Nu. 19:11–13); the temporary restrictions on Jeremiah (Je. 36:5) and Shemaiah (Ne. 6:10), which are also described by the verb *'āṣar*, are not strictly parallel. Sigmund Mowinckel suggested that Doeg had gone to Nob in the hope of receiving an incubation oracle (*cf.* on 28:6).[72]

Doeg was *the chief of Saul's herdsmen*, which could be taken as incidental evidence that the grasping policies of Israelite kings, as denounced in Samuel's speech (8:11–18), began with the first king. At 22:17, however, Doeg is with the 'runners' (RSV 'guard') who are in attendance on Saul, and some therefore prefer to change *herdsmen* (*rō'îm*) to 'runners' (*rāṣîm*). We might, then, compare David's employment of the non-Israelite 'Cherethites and Pelethites' as his bodyguard (see on 2 Sa. 8:18). Nevertheless, MT is not indefensible. The possibly analogous term *rb nqdm* ('chief of the shepherds') occurs in a Ugaritic text – interestingly, in parallel to *rb khnm* ('chief of the priests').[73] (Shepherds and sheep could be associated with temple affairs, as is sometimes noted in connection with the watchful pastors of Bethlehem at the birth of Christ.)

8, 9. When the Philistines defeated Saul at Gilboa, they deposited his armour in the temple of Ashtaroth (31:10). The same practice – for which there appears to be archaeological illustration (see on 31:10) – is reflected here. For *ephod* see on 2:28. It is possible that *ephod* here represents something distinct from the priestly vestment of 14:3; compare the ornate 'ephod' made by Gideon and venerated in his home-town of Ophrah (Jdg. 8:24–27). According to 17:54, David had put the giant's armour in his tent after his great victory. Now, as he takes flight from Saul, the relic of the earlier success becomes an omen of his ultimate triumph.

10. Are we to suppose that, by a daring irony, David arrives in Goliath's native city with the giant's sword in his hand? Presumably David's intention was to offer his services as a mercenary. Another visit to Gath, with a more satisfactory outcome for David, is recounted in 27:1–12. Since this latter passage makes no reference to the present (abortive) visit, this episode is often explained as a sort of duplicate of ch. 27. Common to both is the theme of the duping of Achish (*cf.* on 27:8–12).[74] The name *Achish* is thought to be of Anatolian origin and, possibly, related to the 'Greek' Anchises, as in the Iliad.[75]

11, 12. David's reputation almost causes his undoing. *king of the land* (11) could, as McCarter notes, describe the ruler of a small city-state (*cf.* Jos. 12:7–24), but it may as easily be a piece of exaggeration such as the 'David legend' seemed to encourage. At any rate, the celebratory couplet of 18:7 is interpreted exactly as Saul had interpreted it (*cf.* 18:8). David cannot so easily escape the dangers inherent in his kingly calling.

13–15. While David's behaviour is certainly not regal, it has the desired effect, and he extricates himself from a dangerous situation.[76] If, as is likely, madness was regarded with superstition, this will have worked to his advantage. Klein (p. 217) notes the 'anti-Philistine bias' of Achish's remark in verse 15: 'Gath was so full of wild men that they had no use for any more!' In later tradition Psalms 34 and 56 were linked with this episode, albeit in the superscription to the former 'Achish' has become 'Abimelech'.

THE DESTRUCTION OF NOB   (22:1–23)

When David retires to Adullam he is joined by a ragged assortment of sympathizers whom he soon welds into an effective private army. It is not at all surprising, therefore, that Saul is confirmed in his suspicion of his arch-rival. In response to his complaints about conspiracy among his own retinue, Saul receives from the Edomite Doeg a report of David's visit to Nob, and a grim sequence of events is set in train. David accepts his share of the blame, as he must (v. 22), yet there is no disputing that the outrage must be debited to Saul's account. He, however, is already so heavily in debt that nothing further is made of his barbarous treatment of the priests of Nob – neither in Samuel nor in Chronicles. As noted in the commentary, the near-annihilation of the Nob priesthood resulted in the identification of Abiathar with David's cause, and paved the way for the elevation of Jerusalem to the status of chief sanctuary-city in Israel.

1. *Adullam*, represented by the modern Tell esh-Sheikh Madhkûr, was situated about sixteen miles to the south-west of Jerusalem. It is listed among Rehoboam's cities 'built (*i.e.* fortified) for defence in Judah', in 2 Chronicles 11:7. Because of the similarity in form between the words for *cave* and 'stronghold', the latter possibly referring to Adullam in verses 4f., 'stronghold' is sometimes favoured here as well.[77] See on verse 5. David's family, themselves at risk now that there was outright opposition between Saul and David, join him on his return from Philistia. (If Saul would attack his own family (20:33), there was no telling what he might do to David's.)

2. Like Essex, in the reign of Elizabeth I, David attracts an assortment of social malcontents and derelicts, who see service with him as a way of venting grievances or avoiding responsibilities (*cf.* 25:10, and also the story of Jephthah, Jdg. 11:3). With this 'list of lawless resolutes',[78] David gives credibility to the conspiracy theory which Saul has propounded, and will propound (vv. 8, 13).

3, 4. In entreating the favour of the Moabite king, David could play on the state of hostility between Saul and the Moabites (*cf.* 14:47, and see 27:12); it would be in the interests of Moab to encourage this rebel-against-Saul. The family's ancestral link with Moab, traced through Ruth 'the Moabitess' in Ruth 4:17–22, possibly accounts for the choice of Moab, as against any of the other states which might likewise have been happy to assist David against Saul. This particular *Mizpeh* is known only from this passage. *what God will do* (3): a traditionally pious manner of speaking, and yet entirely consonant with the presentation of David during his fugitive days. The same outlook is expressed in 2 Samuel 15:25f., in the context of Absalom's rebellion and David's flight from Jerusalem.

5. Some degree of respectability is conferred upon David's company by the presence of the prophet Gad, later to become one of David's so-called 'court prophets' (*cf.* 2 Sa. 24:11–14, 18f.), though not so prominent as his colleague Nathan. *do not remain*: Gad uses a strong form of the negative, characteristic of divine prohibitions and amply illustrated in the Decalogue (Ex. 20:3–17). Gad's injunction to *go into the land of Judah* might seem to suggest that the *stronghold* ($m^e s \hat{u} d \hat{a}$) is not the same as the 'cave' of verse 1, since Adullam belonged to Judah (*cf.* Jos. 15:20, 35). But see the comment on Keilah (lying a few miles to the south of Adullam) at 23:3. If, on the other hand, the *stronghold* of verses 4f. is distinct from the cave of Adullam (v. 1), it may be presumed to have been in Moabite territory. *Hereth* is not mentioned elsewhere in the Old Testament.

6. Movement of the type suggested by verses 1f. is not compatible with well-kept secrecy, and, not surprisingly, news reaches Saul.[79] The picture of the king at the citadel of *Gibeah*, seated under a *tamarisk tree*, is vastly different from the Solomonic ostentation of the late tenth century. See on 14:2. The *spear* symbolizes kingly status (*cf.* 26:11), rather as, in later times, it came to represent the authority of the Bedouin sheikh.[80] In the light of previous references to Saul's spear (19:10; 20:33), there may also be a hint at malevolence.

7. Saul is not above appealing to his men's self-interest, when his own interests are at stake (*cf.* 20:31). Just as he has favoured his fellow-Benjaminites in his patronage, so David, a Judahite, may be expected to favour his fellow-tribesmen, if he gains the throne. Again (*cf.* on 21:7) we are reminded of the 'kingly ways' outlined in Samuel's speech in 8:11–18.[81]

8. The complaint is that a conspiracy has been hatched within

Saul's house – by his own son – yet none of his servants has had sufficient regard for him to let him know. Saul's disturbed mind has fixed on the conspiracy idea, and it will cost lives (vv. 13, 16–19). What he seems to be referring to is, in fact, the loyalty pact between David and Jonathan (18:3; 20:8).

9, 10. Doeg has incriminating evidence wherewith to ingratiate himself with his master. He speaks and acts alone from this point on. Three times his gentilic, *the Edomite*, is given (vv. 9, 18, 22), doubtless to emphasize that it was not an Israelite who was responsible for the foul deeds that follow. *stood by* (*niṣṣaḇ 'al*, 9) could be 'was placed over', as in 1 Kings 4:7 (RSV 'over'), but RSV is probably correct. Ahimelech's inquiry of Yahweh on behalf of David (10) is not mentioned in the account of David's trip to Nob. Whether true or false, it was a particularly damaging allegation in the way that it made Ahimelech appear as if he was trying to secure divine protection for David.[82]

11. *Nob* was situated quite near to Gibeah.

13. Saul cannot see past the notion of a widespread conspiracy to put David on the throne. Ahimelech, if he but knows it, is doomed, and the sentence of verse 16 is a formality.

14, 15. The guileless reply bespeaks the man's innocence. In assisting David he had believed himself to be serving the cause of the king. NEB 'Have I . . . done something profane' represents an alternative sense of the Hebrew verb underlying RSV *Is (today) the first time* (15); normal usage, however, favours RSV.

17, 18. To their credit, none of the Israelites in Saul's retinue would dare wield the sword against the priests of Yahweh. No matter that he had recently visited the Nob sanctuary (see on 21:7), Doeg had no compunction about butchering its ministers. The number of priests, *eighty-five*, is noteworthy; apart from Samuel, only Eli and his two sons are mentioned in connection with Nob's predecessor, the temple at Shiloh. This slaughter marks a further stage in the fulfilment of the judgement oracle of 2:27–36(31), as the survivors of the Elide priestly connexion are all but obliterated. *linen ephod*: as worn by the young Samuel (see on 2:18).

19. Nob was treated like some enemy city that had been put under the 'ban' (*cf.* 15:3). It was a rare case of an Israelite community being destroyed at the instigation of an Israelite – much less of an Israelite king. We have thus moved another step towards the eventual recognition of Jerusalem as the religious capital of Israel.

20. There was a survivor, and, whereas Saul has cut himself off from priestly ministration,[83] David now has Abiathar's services,

and, not least, has access to the oracular ephod (23:6). *Abiathar*
subsequently served as chief priest, jointly with Zadok, until dismissed by Solomon for his complicity in Adonijah's coup (*cf.*
1 Ki. 2:35).

22. *I have occasioned* translates the verb *sābaḇ* which has been
used to describe the physical action involved in *turning* (vv. 17f.)
and slaying the priests of Nob. There is some difficulty with its
occurrence in this verse,[84] and yet the repetition would very effectively make the point that David is indirectly responsible for the
tragedy. Even though the narrator withheld comment on David's
despicable conduct at Nob (21:1-6), it was not that the laws
of morality had been suspended, as this self-condemnation now
shows.

23. Like David, Abiathar is in danger from Saul, and should,
therefore, remain with him for safety's sake. NEB 'he who seeks
your life seeks mine' reverses the pronominal suffixes of MT in
order to obtain a sense which, in implying a guarantee of protection,
is certainly not inappropriate to the context.

SAUL SEEKS DAVID   (23:1-29)

We have just witnessed how Saul, in an outburst of rage, became
responsible for the destruction of the priestly city of Nob. In ch.
23, David, even while on the run from Saul, is shown saving a city
from Philistine attack. For the most part, however, the chapter
depicts David in mortal danger, as Saul relentlessly pursues him,
finally coming within an ace of capturing him. That he fails now
as before is given the theological explanation that 'God did not
give him into his hands' (v. 14). What that meant in practice was
that David sought, and received, oracular guidance at each new
crisis-point. The arrival of Abiathar with his ephod (v. 6) sees him
even better off in this regard. Throughout, Saul is able to rely on
local informers, and yet he is the one who is at a disadvantage;
and even when he is, at last, about to lay hands on his quarry in
the wilderness of Maon, word comes of another Philistine raid,
and he is forced to withdraw. While it is not stated, we are doubtless
intended to trace the hand of Yahweh in this.

1. *Keilah*, listed among the cities of the Shephelah in Joshua
15:44, lay due east of Gath. It is probably the same as the 'Kelti'
of the fourteenth-century Amarna letters; the ancient site is represented by Khirbet Qila, close to the presumed site of Adullam

(*cf.* on 22:1). The Philistines were employing an old tactic in raiding neighbouring territory at harvest-time (*cf.* Jdg. 6:3f.).

2. There is no mention of Abiathar in connection with David's inquiry; according to verse 6, the priest did not join David until the latter had been installed in Keilah.

3, 4. The reaction of David's men is just what we should expect from such an assemblage as is described in 22:2. David, like Gideon before him (Jdg. 6:36–40), needs reassuring that the project is feasible. *here in Judah* (3) clearly implies that Keilah was not within the Judahite ambit at this point (*cf.* v. 12).

5. The relief of Keilah is characterized as a notable 'deliverance'; *delivered*, like 'save' in verse 2, translates the verb *yāša'*, mainly used of deliverance on a grand scale, whether by Yahweh or by someone raised up by Yahweh. *their cattle*: the Philistines evidently had been availing themselves of the local grazing facilities.

6. *Cf.* 22:20–23. David, through the acquisition of Abiathar and the oracular *ephod*, has a more sure means of ascertaining the will of Yahweh, and one which he can put to immediate use.

7, 8. In Saul's reckoning, David's remaining in Keilah presented an opportunity to shut him up 'like a caged bird'.[85] His claim that this was God's doing is contradicted by the turn of events, and is expressly unsaid by the narrator in verse 14.[86]

9–12. For the operation of the *ephod* compare 30:7f., where also a two-part question is put to the oracle (*cf.* v. 11 here).[87] It was not necessarily loyalty to the crown that disposed the citizens of Keilah to act so ungratefully towards their benefactor. The recent example of Nob would have dissuaded almost any community from siding with an opponent of Saul, when that opponent had as limited resources as David had. When, late in David's reign, the rebel Sheba took refuge in Abel-beth-maacah, the local inhabitants saved their town by removing Sheba's head and handing it over to the besieging force (2 Sa. 20:14–22).

13, 14. By now David's band has grown by two hundred (*cf.* 22:2). Residence in Keilah would have made provisioning easier, but Saul's constant harassing forced them to exist in less congenial regions. *Ziph* (14), which gave its name to the surrounding area, was situated further south than Keilah, about five miles south-east of Hebron. Meanwhile, Saul continues to be frustrated in his attempts to apprehend David, because, as the narrator explains, it is not the will of God that he should.

15–18. Fear has now taken hold of David himself (*cf.* v. 3), so that Jonathan's visit comes at the right psychological moment. In this, the last recorded meeting of the two, Jonathan is at his most optimistic.

15. *was afraid* is answered by the reassuring 'Fear not' in verse 17. For this reason RSV is justified in revocalizing MT which, as it stands, reads '(and David) saw (that)'. *Horesh*: probably Khirbet Khoreisa, about two miles from the site of Ziph. While BH *ḥōreš* means 'wood, wooded height', this meaning hardly fits the terrain in question.

16. Just when David is in the 'Slough of Despond' Jonathan arrives to cheer him up. *strengthened his hand in God*: encouraged him (*cf.* Jb. 4:3; Ezk. 13:22). The addition of *in God* is unique in the occurrences of this expression in the Old Testament. David is bidden to consider the power and purposes of God, the more so when the immediate circumstances induce to despair (*cf.* 2 Cor. 1:8–11).

17. *Fear not*: see on verse 15. Jonathan is confident about the course of events, and about his own role when David is elevated to the throne.[88] On the latter point he was wrong (*cf.* 31:2), but the statement is important for the way in which it heightens the contrast between Jonathan's voluntary subordination to David and Saul's determination to get rid of him at all costs. This emphasis on Jonathan's renunciation of his own claim to the throne (*cf.* 18:4; 20:13–16) will have been used to silence those who questioned the legitimacy of David's rule, and who may even have hoped for a return to Benjaminite supremacy. *my father also knows*: confirmed by Saul himself in 24:20.

18. The earlier friendship pact (18:3; 20:8, 12–17) is renewed, with Yahweh as witness and guarantor.[89] So David was 'comforted by the coming' of Jonathan (*cf.* 2 Cor. 7:6). As the next verses show, the danger to his life has not receded.

19, 20. If the instinct of self-preservation in the men of Keilah endangered David, these *Ziphites* seem to have been impelled by outright antipathy towards him.[90] They may not have welcomed the idea of such a large contingent of freebooters in their neighbourhood. Both *Hachilah* and *Jeshimon* are of uncertain location. *Cf.* 26:1.

21–23. Saul, not without a hint of self-pity (*cf.* 22:7f.), declares himself to have found worthy allies in the Ziphites (21). There are translational uncertainties in verse 22,[91] but the sense is not in doubt. *with sure information* (23): or, possibly, 'of a certainty' (*cf.* RV).

24, 25. *Maon*, home-town of Nabal (25:2), is confidently identified with Khirbet el-Maʿîn, approximately eight miles south of

Hebron. The *Arabah* here denotes the arid steppe west of the Dead Sea (*cf. BDB*). *rock*: 'crag' (*sela^c*, 25), perhaps an outcrop of the hill mentioned in the next verse (*cf.* v. 28).

26, 27. *closing in* ('*ōṭ^erîm*) suggests an encircling movement to pen David in. It almost succeeded, but for the providential arrival of a messenger with news of another Philistine *raid*.

28. *Escape*: the Hebrew root in question (*ḥ-l-q*) would more naturally produce the meaning 'divisions': this was the place where David and Saul parted company.

29. *En-gedi* ('Goat's Spring'), the modern 'Ain Jidi, is situated on the western shore of the Dead Sea.[92] An oasis, with caves in the vicinity (*cf.* 24:3), it was a useful temporary refuge. There are no material remains of the *strongholds* mentioned here. David is now some miles to the north-east of the wilderness of Maon (vv. 24f.).

DAVID SPARES SAUL   (24:1–22)

Suddenly, from being hunted and endangered, David has Saul at his mercy, in a cave by En-gedi. We need hardly doubt what Saul would have done, if the roles had been reversed, but the point of this narrative, as of the companion account in ch. 26, is to show that even the very thought of harming Saul was anathema to David. This is, then, Davidic 'apologetic' designed to answer the charge of blood-guilt in relation to the house of Saul – a charge which would not lie down during David's reign, thanks to the likes of Shimei, from Saul's own tribe of Benjamin (2 Sa. 16:8). This theme of non-complicity will recur, usually with heavy underlining, in the remaining chapters of the so-called 'History of David's Rise'.

The points of similarity between chs. 24 and 26 have led many scholars to think of them as sibling versions of the same original episode. But there are many basic differences between the two, and it is probably easier to account for the similarities by assuming a degree of assimilation in their early transmission-history. The apologetic function of the narratives is, in any case, unimpaired, whichever view we adopt.

1, 2. A successful operation against the Philistines (*cf.* 23:27f.) seems to be implied. Saul, with up-to-date information on David's movements, deploys a force equal in size to his standing army at one point (*cf.* 13:2), to seek out the elusive quarry. *Wildgoats'* (*y^e'ēlîm*): the ibex (*capra ibex nubiana*), reportedly still found in the area.[93]

4–7. NEB follows an old suggestion in reordering these verses to make David deliver his rebuke to his men *before* cutting off the piece of Saul's robe. But this transposition, carried out in the interests of logic and orderliness, is unnecessary, and not without its own difficulties.[94]

4. The case for revenge is put by David's henchmen in convincing manner: destiny has contrived this situation so that David can have done with his enemy. Nor are they above fabricating an oracle to drive home their point, and those scholars who try to pinpoint the occasion of an otherwise unmentioned oracle – whether at Bethlehem (16:13)[95] or Nob (22:10)[96] – do pay them too much respect.[97] David does not react as bidden, instead merely removing a part of Saul's robe. Soon the piece will be held aloft as proof of his goodwill towards Saul (v. 5). However, the fact that he immediately regrets this violation of Saul's robe strongly suggests that his initial motivation was not so high-minded, and differed only in degree from the more primitive stirrings in his men. In fact, the tearing of a robe, and especially the hem of a robe, could be a highly symbolic act in the near east. We have already had an instance in 15:27f., where the loss of a kingdom is portended (*cf.* 1 Ki. 11:30f.). In certain circumstances the grasping or releasing of a hem could indicate submission or rebellion on the part of the person responsible. It is thus likely that David's removal of a part of Saul's hem was a symbolic act with some bearing on the issue of the throne and the succession.[98] Coming after Jonathan's assurance in 23:17, such a gesture at this point in the story need cause no surprise.

5, 6. It might be possible to explain David's compunction along the line that violation of Saul's robe was tantamount to violation of Saul's – sacrosanct (6) – person. (In Mesopotamia the hem of a person's garment could be used in the person's absence as a means of authentication. This appears to explain the various references to 'hair and hem (*sissiktu*)', in connection with the verification of prophetic utterances, in letters from eighteenth-century Mari.) However, we have argued, in connection with verse 4, that David had other grounds for regretting his hastiness. *smote him*: a strong expression, paralleled only in 2 Samuel 24:10. Saul's anointing originally signified his election by Yahweh and his initiation into a new sphere of service and obligation (*cf.* Lv. 10:7; 21:10 (of priests)). Though he now lacks the divine spirit symbolized in that anointing (*cf.* 16:14 and see on 16:13), and has supplied ample evidence of his inanition, David still respects him as *the Lord's anointed* (6). David is thus defended, on the narrative level,

against any charges of *lese-majesty* which the Saulide faction in
particular might bring against him.

7. *persuaded . . . with these words*: the Hebrew has 'cleft . . .
with words', which is both more colourful and worthy of better
treatment in the versions, ancient and modern. The addition of
'with words' (not 'with *these* words', as RSV) suggests that we
have a figurative usage comparable with the English 'tear in pieces',
'excoriate', *etc.* NEB 'reproved . . . severely' is dull but adequate.
For the expression we might compare Hosea 6:5 ('I have hewn
them by the prophets, I have slain them by the words of my
mouth'), and perhaps also the use of *dichotomein* ('cut in two') in
Matthew 24:51 and Luke 12:46.

9. David himself has just rejected *the words of men* where they
would have brought him into conflict with the purposes of God
(vv. 6f.).

10. *the Lord gave you*: contrast 23:14, where the positions of
Saul and David are reversed.

11. For *father* as a title of respect see Genesis 45:8; 2 Kings 5:13;
compare 'my son' in verse 16. Any symbolic meaning that the torn
skirt might have (see on v. 4) is, at this point, immaterial, compared
with the proof which it furnished that Saul had been in David's
power and had been let go unharmed.

12. David renounces the way of personal revenge on Saul,
preferring, rather, to invoke divine arbitrament (*cf.* v. 15). As far
as the throne is concerned, he will achieve that by divine appointment, and not by an act of usurpation.

13. The likely point of the old saying, as quoted here, is that
deeds express dispositions. Rather than apply it negatively to Saul,
we may interpret it positively of David, whose treatment of Saul
has been honourable because it has sprung from pure motives. But
the aphorism – just three words in the Hebrew – is tersely phrased,
and some other meaning, such as NEB's 'One wrong begets
another', cannot be ruled out.

14. *The King of Israel* should not be concerned with so incon-
sequential a matter as the pursuit of David! Self-deprecatingly, and
to heighten the contrast between king and quarry, David describes
himself as *a dead dog* (*cf.* 2 Sa. 9:8; 16:9), or even as a *flea* on a
dog's carcass (*cf.* McCarter). *a flea* is lit. 'one (single) flea'; *cf.*
NEB 'a mere flea'.

15. As king, Saul himself should have been the vindicator of the
oppressed – except that he is, in this instance, the oppressor. David
therefore appeals to Yahweh for his vindication. In fact, Saul
pronounces sentence *against himself* in verse 17.

16–22. Saul is emotionally stirred by the realization that David has spared his life, but the discovery affects him no more deeply than this, and he will eventually harry his rival out of the land altogether (27:1ff.).

17–19. *righteous* (*ṣaddîq*, 17) sometimes has the forensic sense of being 'in the right', which is what may be intended here. *good* and *evil* are key terms in the sketching of the relationship between Saul and David in chs. 24–26; see on 25:21.

20–22. This acknowledgement of David's high destiny, and the consequential plea for clemency, echoes Jonathan's speeches in 20:14–16; 23:17. Saul has become the most reluctant convert in all Israel to the idea of a Davidic dynasty (as implied in *established* (20)). *descendants . . . name* (21): two aspects of the same request, inasmuch as the name was kept alive through the descendants. *the stronghold* (22) refers to Adullam (*cf.* 22:1).

NABAL AND ABIGAIL   (25:1–44)

Ostensibly this chapter is about David's acquisition of one of his wives, but it serves a far more important function in the way that it plots a decisive point in David's psychological development. This comes about because, although Saul is not so much as mentioned in the main episode (vv. 1–42), Nabal acts as his surrogate: his attitude towards David replicates Saul's, and his untimely demise prefigures Saul's death at Gilboa.[99] The Nabal story is wedged between two accounts of David's sparing of Saul when he had it in his power to finish him off, and it addresses the same issue: revenge by David's hand, or by God in his own time? In the cave near En-gedi David permits himself only a symbolic act, when incited to kill his master there and then (24:4). A similar opportunity comes later, when David enters Saul's camp by night; but on this occasion he rebukes his tempter with the assertion that God would smite Saul (26:10). While in the camp David does not even perform a symbolic act of the kind executed at En-gedi. The key to his apparent insouciance is found in the present narrative, for, from the contretemps with Nabal, David learns that, if he withholds the avenging sword, God will act on his behalf (vv. 38f.). It is once more the question of blood-guilt, and of how David may reach the throne without incurring Yahweh's displeasure.

There are, in the chapter, interesting glimpses of social conditions in southern Judah in the early monarchy.[100] David's own position has been compared with that of the sometimes parasitical *ḥabiru*

who lived on the fringe of settled community life in various parts
of the near east, and who are frequently mentioned in texts of the
second millennium from as far apart as Egypt and southern Mesopotamia.[101] We also gain some insight into the logistical problems
which must have been a controlling factor in David's movements
during this period.[102]

1. It was, evidently, during David's period of outlawry in the
Judaean wilderness that the old prophet Samuel died. With his
passing, we would rightly conclude, went any hope of the situation
between Saul and David being depolarized. *in his house*: cf. 1 Kings
2:34; Manasseh was buried in the garden of his house, according
to 2 Kings 21:18, and Stoebe (p. 446) interprets the present reference
in the same kind of way. *Paran* usually refers to an area in the
north-east of the Sinai peninsula (*e.g.* Gn. 21:21). Since the places
mentioned in verse 2 are further to the north, there is a case for
accepting the LXX variant 'Maon', as in NIV.

2. *Maon*: see on 23:24f. *Carmel* was where Saul erected his
commemorative stele (15:12, *q.v.*). *shearing*: see on verses 4–8.

3. A description of a perfect mismatch. *Abigail* is delectable, and
fit to marry a king-in-waiting (vv. 39–42). She has good sense as
well as good looks.[103] *Nabal* is correspondingly unattractive; for
his name see on verse 25. The *Calebite* clan to which he belonged
had become affiliated to Judah, and had settled in the area south
of Hebron (*cf.* Jos. 14:13f.; 15:13). Because of the similarity between
the clan name and the Hebrew for 'dog' (*keleḇ*), and in view of
Nabal's conduct in the narrative that follows, some find a pejorative
tone in *he was a Calebite*: 'a real Calebbite (*sic*) dog' (Hertzberg),
'a typical Calebite' (Grønbaek[104]).

4–8. Sheep-shearing was a time for celebration, if not actually a
feast day (*cf.* v. 8), in the religio-cultic sense of the term. Compare
Absalom's festivities in 2 Samuel 13:23–29. The poll would have
shown how well the flocks had fared during the recent grazing,
and David was hoping that Nabal would be in a mood to repay
past favours.

5. *ten young men*: it was a substantial hand-out that David was
requesting.

6. RSV glides over a difficult word that comes near the beginning
of the verse. MT *leḥāy* could mean 'to my brothers' (*cf.* Vulgate),
or could preserve a greeting formula not recorded elsewhere in the
Old Testament. This latter suggestion was advocated by the late
Sir Godfrey Driver, and is represented in NEB's 'All good wishes
for the year ahead!'[105] NIV 'Long life to you!' is on the same track.
There is some support for the idea in the LXX tradition.

10, 11. His parvanimity notwithstanding, Nabal was technically in the right, for he had not asked for David's protection. But a more agreeable individual might have responded differently. And though David's thoughts ran to murder when he heard of the reception his men had received, the initial approach carried no menace. Nabal speaks like one of the later rebels against Davidic rule (compare v. 10 with 2 Sa. 20:1), and therein, from the viewpoint of the narrative, lies his real fault. He fails to recognize who David is, and, when he talks of runaway *servants*, he shows perfect contempt for this erstwhile servant of Saul. We may contrast Abigail's clear perception of David's destiny, as expressed in verse 28. Nabal is extremely possessive as well, as the incidence of *my* in verse 11 makes plain. (In this first-person emphasis he strongly resembles that other foolish farmer in Luke 12:16–20).

13. Like some taciturn cowboy hero, David mobilizes his band and heads for Carmel. *four hundred . . . two hundred*: a wildly exaggerated response to Nabal's rebuff; *cf*. 30:9f.

14–17. Meanwhile, back at the farm, Abigail is informed about her husband's incivility, and about its possible consequences.

14. *railed*: 'flew at' (*cf*. NEB) would be better. In 15:19 the same word is translated 'swoop'.

17. Even a servant may describe his master as a 'son of Belial' (RSV *ill-natured*; see on 1:16), and not receive a cuff from his mistress. This, no doubt, is meant to reflect on Nabal's character, rather than to suggest disloyalty on Abigail's part. There simply is no denying that Nabal is contemptible, so that Abigail herself will describe him to David as a 'man of Belial' (v. 25). This alienation between master and servant is also a feature of the relationship between Saul and his staff, and is one more indication of the way in which Saul and Nabal are psychologically 'twinned' (*cf*. on v. 19).

18–42. From this point on the story is dominated by Abigail who, by tact and charm, saves her household from calamity. Her speech, moreover, looks beyond the present exigency to embrace the future rule of David, in terms of pure Davidic orthodoxy comparable with Nathan's oracle in 2 Samuel 7.

18, 19. Abigail's scheme resembles that of Jacob when he was in a similarly awkward situation: a handsome present (*bᵉrāḵâ*,[106] v. 27; *cf*. Gn. 33:11) to induce mollification is sent on ahead (*cf*. Gn. 32:13–21). (Esau was also approaching with a band of four hundred (Gn. 32:6; *cf*. v. 13 here).) Her present may be seen not merely as repairing Nabal's omission, but also – in line with the speech that she will deliver – as an acknowledgement of David's future kingship (*cf.* 10:27; 2 Sam. 16:1f.). *measures* (18): the seah, about one third of an ephah (approx. one and a half gallons). *did not tell* (19): again it is the isolation of Nabal in his own household (see on v. 17). Compare 14:1, and particularly 22:8 ('No one discloses to me'), in the case of Saul.

21. *evil for good*: compare Saul's 'confession' in 24:17–21. Such correspondences encourage us to think of a measure of role-identification between Saul and Nabal in the present narrative.

22. Thanks to an unexpected turn of events (vv. 23ff.), David actually forswore himself. The possible implications have been dispelled in the Hebrew text by resort to the circumlocution, 'the enemies of (David)'. See on 20:16.

23–25. David, having resolved to kill every *male* (v. 22) in Nabal's household, is confronted by this personable female. Abigail's ploy is to draw the blame on to herself, so making it difficult for David to carry out his intention. This, at least, is what is implied in RSV '*Upon me alone*' (24). But McCarter (p. 398), quoting 2 Samuel 14:9 in support, claims that the opening clause of verse 24 represents merely a conventional way of initiating a conversation with a superior. The *guilt* in question then refers to responsibility for anything that might be considered blameworthy in the ensuing interview.

25. Again Nabal is called a 'Belialite' (RSV *ill-natured fellow*: *cf.* v. 17), a term used of Saul's detractors after his election as king at Mizpah (10:27), and of the rebel Sheba in 2 Samuel 20:1. A degree of moral obliquity seems to be associated with the Hebrew root *n-b-l*, hence the occasional preference for 'Churl' (so NEB), rather than 'Fool', as the meaning of Nabal's name. Since it is unlikely that Nabal's parents christened him 'Churl' (or 'Fool'!), it is possible that his actual name has been suppressed,[107] or – perhaps more probable – that the name has another meaning, in which case what we have here is a 'play of homonyms'.[108] Levenson thinks that Abigail's word-play invokes an old proverb which has been preserved in a variant form in Isaiah 32:6.[109] The characteristics of the 'fool' of Isaiah 32:6 certainly provide a most apt description of Nabal. See below on verse 37 for another probable instance of word-play on 'Nabal'.

26. In this setting, the verse anticipates David's relenting, and also the death of Nabal (*cf.* 2 Sa. 18:32). McCarter, accordingly, relocates it between verses 41 and 42. However, while granting that there is some slight difficulty with Abigail's statements at this point in the narrative, we are not bound to assume that David has formally renounced his decision to kill, or that Nabal is, from the standpoint of the verse, already dead. Abigail's interception of David could have been regarded as sufficient evidence of Yahweh's restraint, while, in the reference to Nabal's death, we may be meant to discern a measure of prophetic foresight in this uncommonly perspicacious woman. On the other hand, it might be possible to interpret Abigail's words as merely 'an imprecation of wrong-headedness' on David's enemies.[110] As for McCarter's reposition-ing of the verse, his own comment about Abigail speaking 'as if David himself were present' (p. 400) shows how unsuited the verse is to the proposed context.

David's avoidance of *bloodguilt* is the key issue in the narrative, just as it is in his relationship with Saul during the whole of his fugitive days. The sparing or killing of Nabal therefore has its symbolic aspect, in that David, consciously or otherwise, is even now laying the foundation of his future rule (*cf.* vv. 30f.). Nor should we forget that the chapter is relating how David acquired one of his wives, and that later, in the case of Bathsheba, he did indeed incur blood-guilt. In Psalm 51, traditionally ascribed to David, after he had been rebuked by the prophet Nathan for his behaviour with Bathsheba, the psalmist prays, 'Deliver me from bloodguiltiness, O God' (v. 14) – as well might David have prayed after his treatment of Uriah, Bathsheba's husband (*cf.* 2 Sa. 11:14–21).[111]

28. *Pray forgive*: McCarter interprets this clause as a conven-tional request for permission to speak further (*cf.* on v. 24), rather than as an acceptance by Abigail of her husband's liabilities. She now proceeds, in what some scholars regard as a Deuteronomistic interpolation,[112] to speak of the dynasty which God will enable David to found. The expression *sure house* (NIV 'lasting dynasty') is as much a product of the royal Davidic ideology as the 'everlasting covenant' of 2 Samuel 23:5; both are rays from the central sun of the dynastic oracle recorded in 2 Samuel 7, in Nathan's speech to David (especially v. 16). *the battles of the Lord*: *cf.* 18:17. Even while Saul is king, it is David who is Yahweh's earthly vicegerent.

29. McCarter, following N. H. Tur-Sinai, takes MT *ṣerôr* (RSV *bundle*) to mean a '(tied up) document', as also in Job 14:17. (The verb *ṣārar* is used of the tying up of Isaiah's 'testimony' in Is. 8:16.) The 'document of the living', as MT may then be rendered, corresponds to the 'book of the living' of Psalm 69:28 (*cf.* Is. 4:3; Rev. 3:5, *etc.*). Alternatively, the idea may be that David's life is kept as securely as the tally stones in a shepherd's bag.[113] This would form a neat contrast with the figure of the sling-stone – with its possible echo of 17:40–50 – which is next used, to describe the fate of David's enemies.

30. For an overlord to 'speak good things' to a vassal can, as various studies of near eastern treaty terminology have shown, imply the offer of a treaty relationship (compare discussions of the possible significance of 2 Ki. 25:28).[114] According to this view, Abigail looks forward to the time when God will have fulfilled his covenanted promises to David in relation to the throne. *prince* (*nāḡîḏ*) is as in 9:16; 10:1, and, according to Grønbaek, presents David as Saul's legitimate successor.[115]

31, 33. The issue of the avoidance of blood-guilt is kept to the fore; see on verse 26.

33. *your discretion*: *cf*. verse 3.

35. *granted your petition*: lit. 'lifted up your face'. The raising of the suppliant's face signifies his or her acceptance by the superior party. Jacob, as he prepares to meet his wronged brother Esau, says, 'Perhaps he will lift up my face' (Gn. 32:20; and see on vv. 18f. above).

36. Nabal, as befits a narrative surrogate for Saul (see the introduction to this chapter), is entertaining like a king (*cf*. on 2 Sa. 13:27). He is totally unaware of the Damoclean sword hanging over his head. *told him nothing*: see on verses 17, 19.

37. *when the wine had gone out* treats Nabal as a *nēḇel* ('wine-skin'). (The expression is legitimate enough; *cf*. 9:7 ('the bread has gone from our sacks').) Soberness and sober facts are too great a shock for his system, which promptly seizes up.

38. Nabal's death is stated as the result of a divine act, and in such a way as to underline the significance of Nabal in the history of David's relationship with Saul. In 26:10 ('the Lord will smite him') what is David doing but extrapolating on his recent experience with Nabal?

39. *has returned the evil-doing*: David's attitude is not for emulation by Christians (*cf*. Mt. 5:43–48; Rom. 12:20f.). In AV of 2 Timothy 4:14 Paul's attitude to his adversary, Alexander the coppersmith, is misrepresented. He states a fact ('the Lord will requite'), rather than invokes revenge (AV 'the Lord reward').

41, 42. Abigail is careful to receive David's messengers in the time-honoured fashion (*cf*. Gn. 18:4). She has no hesitation about becoming David's wife; to what extent she may have been able to transfer her late husband's property and influence to David is hard to judge.[116]

43, 44. The *Jezreel* to which *Ahinoam* belonged was in the same area as Maon and Carmel (*cf*. Jos. 15:55f.), and is to be

distinguished from the northern Jezreel in the region of Gilboa
(29:1).[117] For other marriages contracted by David see 2 Samuel
3:2–5; 5:13; 11:26f.[118] Predictably, Saul had made other arrangements for his daughter *Michal* (44), whom he had previously given
in marriage to David. He may have thought to undermine David's
position by breaking his marriage tie with the royal house. As soon
as the opportunity presented itself, David took steps to have Michal
restored to him (2 Sa. 3:13–16). *Gallim* (44) was apparently some
distance north of Jerusalem (Is. 10:30).

DAVID IN SAUL'S CAMP   (26:1–25)

Encouraged by the near-success of his earlier attempt to lay David
by the heels in the wilderness of Maon (23:24–29), Saul responds
enthusiastically to a second piece of intelligence from the Ziphites.
The sum of his achievement was, however, to leave himself again
at David's mercy (*cf.* 24:1–7). Now, while the bounds of credibility
are not unduly stretched by the suggestion that David twice spared
Saul's life,[119] there are, as we noted in connection with ch. 24,
sufficient points of similarity between the two accounts in chs. 24
and 26 to convince many scholars that the same basic event
underlies the two narratives (compare 23:19 with 26:1, and 24:16
with 26:17, for example). But the more important point to note is
that it is these very similarities that enable us to measure the
development in David's character as he reacts to basically the same
set of data. For now, reinforced by the lesson of the Nabal episode
(*cf.* 25:39), he is more resolved than ever that he will not lay violent
hands upon Saul (v. 10). It is important, in this connection, to note
that the exchange of speeches in verses 17–25 is not simply a flat
repetition of 24:8–21. David's, in particular, prepares us for his
decision (27:1) to leave Judah and seek his fortune with the
Philistines.

1. Since the hill of *Hachilah* is located to the south of Jeshimon
in 23:19, there is advantage in translating MT *'al pᵉnê* (RSV *on the
east of*) by '(which) overlooks (Jeshimon)' (*cf.* NEB, NIV). So also
in verse 3.

2. *Cf.* 24:2.

4. *of a certainty*: a good part of the LXX tradition supports the
reading of a place-name – Hachilah(?) – at this point.[120] NEB 'and
found that Saul had reached *such and such a place*' interprets MT
'el nāk̲ôn to similar effect. MT is as in 23:23.

5. It appears that Saul and Abner have failed to take the precaution of stationing sentries, though the real reason for David's unimpeded access to Saul's sleeping quarters will be given in verse 12 as a supernatural sleep which overwhelmed the whole camp.

6. *Ahimelech* is not mentioned elsewhere. Like Uriah, the husband of Bathsheba, he is described as a *Hittite*. Whether *Hittite* relates him to the Anatolian Hittites who administered an empire extending into Syria, in the fourteenth and thirteenth centuries BC, is not clear.[121] It is possible that at least one smaller tribal group in Palestine was also known by the name 'Hittite'. *Abishai*, David's sister's son (1 Ch. 2:16), was later a member of the élite corps of David's army (2 Sa. 23:18).

7. We may compare the night visit of Gideon and Purah to the Midianite camp, in Judges 7:9–14. *spear*: *cf*. on 22:6. It is also a reminder of Saul's murderous attempts on David's life. This is David's mortal enemy who lies comatose before him.

8. Abishai verbalizes the temptation (*cf*. 24:4), and offers to do David's dirty work for him.

9–11. Again David's attitude is governed by the fact of Saul's *anointed* status; God may deal with Saul, but it would be sacrilege for David to interfere. *the Lord will smite him* (10): as happened to Nabal (25:38). That, so to speak, will be the 'theological' interpretation of Saul's death; the actual historical circumstances were those of the *battle* at Gilboa (31:3–6).[122]

12. Once before, Saul had been immobilized by a supernatural power when he had gone in search of David (19:23f.). On that occasion it was the Spirit-induced ecstasy of the prophetic company that prevented him from apprehending David; now a supernatural sleep (*cf*. Gn. 2:21; 15:12) grips his entire camp.

13. It is the last recorded exchange between Saul and David, and even before it takes place there is 'a great gulf fixed'; the physical distance between them is emblematic of the greatly divergent paths that they are pursuing. The scene is set for the final statements of the two.

14–16. Saul's death (*cf*. v. 10) did not mean the end of Saulide rule, for his son Ish-bosheth retired to Transjordan after the Gilboa tragedy; there he presided over a truncated Israelite kingdom for at least two years (*cf*. 2 Sa. 2:10). However, with Ish-bosheth little more than a figurehead, the power behind the throne and, in effect, the last hope of the *ancien régime*, was Abner. Abner does not figure in the parallel En-gedi incident (ch. 24), and his appearance in this chapter, which has a distinctly forward thrust (*cf*. vv. 19f.), can justifiably be read as an oblique commentary on events after Saul's death. For, just as the combined military and political acumen of Abner could not secure the position of Ish-bosheth on the throne indefinitely (*cf.* 2 Sa. 3:6ff.), so even now, in the simple matter of guarding the king's person, this redoubtable character – 'Who is like you in Israel?' (15; *cf.* 2 Sa. 3:21, 38) – is shown to be incapable of checking David's advance.

17. Saul's question is phrased exactly as in 24:16 and may illustrate the case that, if it is separate incidents that are described, 'there has been at various points assimilation of the two narratives in point of details for the obvious reason that the incidents which they recorded had a general similarity' (Mauchline, p. 173).

19. For the sake of argument, David admits the possibility that he may be in the wrong, and that Yahweh may have stirred up Saul to deal with him. In that case, David should seek to appease Yahweh by means of an offering. *may he accept* (lit. 'smell') *an offering*: *cf.* Genesis 8:21, of Noah's 'soothing' offering presented after the flood had abated. In the second possibility envisaged, David makes his point delicately. It was not *men*, in that generalized sense, who were responsible for Saul's implacable hatred of David, but Saul himself.

The consequences, for David, of Saul's harassment are expressed in striking manner, it being implied that, since (the land of) Israel is Yahweh's *heritage*, the worship of Yahweh is properly confined within its boundaries. In purely practical terms, expulsion from Israel would deny David access to the sanctuaries at which Yahweh was worshipped, as the author of Psalms 42–43 appears to have discovered. There are other Old Testament references which reflect the view that the worship of Yahweh, and even the exercise of his power, may be governed by territorial considerations (*cf.* Jdg. 11:24; 1 Ki. 20:23; Ps. 137:4). But these are not representative of mainstream Old Testament theology, and even what might be regarded as the base text – Deuteronomy 32:8 – places the disposition of the 'sons of God' over the nations firmly within Yahweh's control. That control we have already seen exercised beyond Israel, in the cities of Philistia (chs. 5–6), and its display in Egypt forms an integral part of the hallowed exodus tradition (Ex. 7–12). *the heritage of the Lord* may be either the inheritance that God has given to Israel, or, as we have assumed above, the inheritance that belongs to Yahweh, and which may embrace both people and land; they are his special possession (*cf.* Dt. 32:9).

20. It would be a tragedy, says David, if he were to meet a violent death beyond the borders of Israel, since, presumably, his death would go unavenged. Stoebe usefully compares the lament of Cain (Gn. 4:14) with David's fear as expressed here. According to the later 'land theology' of Judaism, it became exceedingly important that the faithful be buried, or at least reinterred, within the boundaries of the 'Holy Land'; otherwise the blessing of resurrection might be withheld.[123] *to seek my life*: RSV follows LXX (MT 'to look for a flea', as NIV), on the assumption that the present passage has been influenced by 24:14.

21. *I have played the fool*, though expressed by a different verb (*s-k-l*), seems to put Saul on the same level as Nabal who – saving Saul's candidature – is the prime fool in the David saga (*cf.* 25:25).

22. The retort is crushing. 'David knew, and Saul knew, the significance of the spear in their relationship (*cf.* 18:10f.; 19:19f.).'[124] In any case, Saul's is a doomed house, so David does not so much as allude to the offer of reinstatement. We may compare Daniel's reply to Belshazzar on the eve of his overthrow (Dn. 5:17). Some scholars, betraying a Civil Service mentality, conclude that, because there is no mention of the jar of water here, the references in verses 11f. cannot be original.[125] Klein (p. 259) suggests that the jar was of relatively little value, or perhaps would not have been used by Saul after it had been in David's hands.

23. NEB translates the verse to refer directly to David: 'The Lord who rewards uprightness and loyalty will reward the man into whose power he put you today.' But to achieve this sharper focus the syntax of MT has to be strained unduly.

24. *in the sight of the Lord*: we might have expected 'in your sight', except that Saul is manifestly not to be trusted. Moreover, David has decided to put himself beyond Saul's reach for the time being.

25. Saul's last words to David acknowledge, though somewhat more obliquely than at En-gedi (24:20f.), David's high destiny. Like Balaam, who was hired to curse the people of Israel, Saul can only bless God's chosen (*cf.* Nu. 23:8); it is he himself who is under an imprecation (v. 19).

DAVID FLEES TO GATH   (27:1–12)

Though the immediate concern was safety from the relentless hounding by Saul, David also has his eye on the future. While Achish benignly receives his reports of expeditions against his former friends and allies, David is, in fact, engaged in merciless slaughter of the enemies of Judah – against the day when he himself will be the acknowledged ruler in Judah. From the apologetic point of view, these activities also afford valuable evidence that, even while he was under Achish's patronage, David remained loyal to his own people in Judah and Israel. As in 21:10–15, the Philistines, and especially their king, are shown being outwitted by David. This contributes, in a way, to the general theme of 'derision' with respect to non-Israelite peoples; see the discussion of the 'Ark Narrative' in the Introduction.

1. The optimism of 26:10 has subsided, and, with this little soliloquy, David heads for Philistia. The blame for his seeking refuge among Israel's enemies, we are reminded, rests wholly with Saul (*cf.* 26:19f.).

2–4. *Cf.* 21:10–15. David's position has been compared with that of the *ḥabiru* groups who, in return for grants of land, sometimes hired themselves out as mercenaries to local rulers (*cf.* the introductory comments on ch. 25).[126]

5. This may be a request for such a land-grant, since, we may imagine, residence in the royal city would have been on a less secure basis.[127] However, the real advantage of the proposal was that David could avoid surveillance, as he engaged in the piratical adventures described in verses 8–12.

6. According to Joshua 15:31, *Ziklag* came into Israelite hands at the time of the settlement. If so, it must have become a satellite of Gath as a result of more recent Philistine expansion. The most likely identification is with Tell esh-Shari'a, about fifteen miles south-east of Gaza. This site has a 'thirteenth-century palace (eleven hieratic texts, two scarabs of Ramesses II) and, after a significant twelfth-century gap, an abundance of late Philistine pottery.'[128] *belonged to the kings of Judah* is usually interpreted to mean that Ziklag enjoyed the status of crown property, yet the evidence for this is largely confined to this verse. G. Buccellati has argued that nothing more is intended here than that the city afterwards remained within the Israelite domain.[129] It is a natural inference from verse 6b that the Judaean state was still in existence at the time of writing.

7. This datum alone makes it difficult to limit Saul's reign to two years; see on 13:1. The LXX, however, has 'four months' for *a year and four months*.

8–12. While Achish thinks that David is fighting his battles, the wily Judahite is frying his own fish, in anticipation of the time when he will be king of Judah. The benefit to Judah notwithstanding, it is one of the most disreputable episodes in David's career – made worse by the need to lie consistently to Achish about what was going on.

8. *Geshurites* are mentioned as neighbours of the Philistines in

Joshua 13:2. A location in the Negev, quite distinct from the 'Geshur of Aram' of 2 Samuel 15:8, is therefore indicated. The *Girzites* not being mentioned elsewhere, various emendations of the word have been suggested. There is some textual and versional support for 'Gizrites' (*cf*. NEB), *i.e.* the inhabitants of Gezer. This reading is unsuitable, however, in view of Gezer's northerly location in relation to the Negev. *Amalekites*: see on 15:1ff. *from of old*: NEB and McCarter favour the old suggestion of a small emendation to 'from Telaim', the place where Saul mustered his troops before attacking the Amalekites (15:4). It is a reading worthy of consideration, not least because of the awkwardness of the whole clause in MT.[130]

9–11. Achish saw the spoil of war, but never a survivor who might open his eyes as to what was really happening. The official reports were of raids on areas which either belonged to Judah or bordered on Judahite territory. The *Negeb* (10), a large arid region in the south of Palestine, is sometimes divided according to the tribe or group inhabiting a particular area (*cf*. 30:14). *Jerahmeelites*: a clan which was subsequently absorbed into the tribe of Judah (*cf*. 1 Ch. 2:5, 9, 25f.). The *Kenites* had close ties with Judah from the time of the settlement (*cf*. Jdg. 1:16). Far from obliterating these two allies of Judah, David was soon to be courting their support with the help of gifts taken from the spoil of his later Amalekite expedition (*cf*. 30:29).

12. How thoroughly Achish was taken in can be seen from 28:1f.; 29:3, 6f., 9. If his client had been doing as he claimed, he would indeed have earned the everlasting disdain of his own people.

SAUL AT ENDOR   (28:1–25)

This visit to the medium of Endor is cited by the Chronicler as proof positive that Saul deserved the judgement that fell on him at Gilboa (1 Ch. 10:13). That apart, it is a remarkable episode that has caused many an exegete an uncomfortable moment or two, even if few have been driven to conclude with Alexander Heidel that 'the whole affair was a demonic delusion'.[131] But it is no such delusion, and Saul finds himself on the receiving end of a prophetic denunciation as searing as any previously delivered to him. By consulting the dead he has merely given himself a preview of his own impending fate; as a result, the death pall descends on his distraught figure while his life is still in him. The story shows that Saul cannot escape the implications of the prophetic message already delivered to him by Samuel. His recent attempts to obtain prophetic guidance having failed (v. 6), he turns to necromancy – the polar opposite of prophecy (see especially Dt. 18:9–22; Is. 8:19–22) – only to be confronted by the same pronouncement of doom as before.

Chronologically the visit to Endor comes after ch. 29, since by then the Philistines have proceeded from their muster-point at Aphek (29:1) to Shunem in Jezreel (28:4). With this arrangement of his material the narrator is able to continue uninterruptedly the story of David's departure from Aphek, his arrival at the, by now, desolate base of Ziklag, and his expedition against the Amalekite destroyers of Ziklag. For even more important to the narrator than the portrayal of Saul as a rejected king is the depiction of David as the one who, by favour of Yahweh, is successful against all adversity.

1, 2. These verses, which give notice of the coming hostilities between the Israelites and the Philistines, have their continuation in 29:1 (see on v. 4 below).[132] We have, therefore, to wait in some degree of suspense for the solving of David's dilemma, now that he is in danger of being deployed against his own countrymen – the situation which he has so far managed to avoid (27:8–12). Meanwhile, the irony in David's reply (2) is completely lost on Achish. In appointing David as 'the keeper of my head' (RSV *bodyguard*), Achish himself comes dangerously near to unconscious irony (*cf.* 17:54).

3. The death notice of 25:1 is repeated at this point because of the following account of the posthumous meeting of Samuel with Saul. As background, we are also informed about Saul's expulsion of *mediums* and *wizards* from Israel. Since necromancy was proscribed in both Deuteronomic and priestly law (Dt. 18:9–14; Lv. 19:31; 20:27), Saul's action against them could have been inspired by zeal for the Yahwistic religion. On the other hand, Gudea, king of the Sumerian city of Lagash – and certainly no Yahwist – claimed to have rid his kingdom of 'sorcerers and witches', a thousand years before Saul.[133] Within Judah, necromancy flourished under Manasseh (2 Ki. 21:6), but was suppressed by Josiah (2 Ki. 23:24). *mediums* (*'ōḇōṯ*): the fuller expression, 'possessor (lit.) of a ghost' (*baʿᵃlaṯ 'ōḇ*), is used in verse 7. The word *'ōḇ*, which means 'ghost, spirit' (*cf.* Is. 29:4, 'your voice shall come from the ground like the voice of an *'ōḇ*'), has variously been connected with an Arabic verb meaning 'to return',[134] with a Hittite word (*a-a-bi*) meaning 'pit'[135] – whence the ghost will have emerged from the underworld – and with the Hebrew *'āḇ* ('father').[136]

wizards (*yidde'ōnîm*): 'The word may either denote the familiar spirit who acts as a go-between, journeying from the world of death to the world of life and *vice versa*, or the wizard himself who 'knows' how to make contact with the underworld. The spirit is the special guide used by the wizard, his familiar'.[137]

4. The Philistine advance to *Shunem* (mod. Sôlem), on the northern fringe of the plain of Jezreel, threatened to cut Saul off from the Israelite tribes further north. This perhaps explains why he was induced to join battle in an area where the Philistines' chariots and cavalry (*cf.* 2 Sa. 1:6) gave them a decisive advantage. In Hauer's attempted outline of Saul's military strategy during his reign, the Philistine mobilization is seen as a response to an initiative by Saul to gain control of the region north of Jezreel.[138] See on 29:1 in this connection. There is considerable evidence of Philistine occupation at Beth-shan – situated at the eastern end of Jezreel – whether earlier as mercenaries of the Egyptians, or now in their own right. The latter situation is possibly presupposed by 31:10, 12. On the opposite (southern) side of the Jezreel plain from *Shunem* stood the *Gilboa* ridge (*cf.* 2 Sa. 1:21, 'you mountains of Gilboa'). The village of Jelbôn preserves the ancient name. As noted in the introduction to this chapter, these positions mark a later stage in the battle build-up than is indicated in 29:1.[139]

5, 6. Quite apart from Saul's fears arising out of this specific situation, the ancient war-leader preferred, as a rule, to go into battle only after oracular consultation to determine strategy and to be reassured about the chances of success. But none of the conventional methods – the triad (v. 6) is paralleled in a Hittite plague-prayer of Mursilis II[140] – works for Saul, for David is now the one to whom Yahweh reveals such information (*cf.* 30:7f.). Revelation by means of dreams might be induced by spending a night at a shrine, although convincing examples of such 'incubation oracles' are difficult to find in the Old Testament.[141] Saul's earlier use of *Urim* and Thummim is recorded in 14:36–42. The reference to prophecy could mean that there was no accredited prophet of Yahweh in Saul's court (*cf.* Gad's defection to David, 22:5), or that the available prophets (*cf.* 10:5; 19:20–24) could produce no satisfactory answer from Yahweh. 1 Chronicles 10:14 ('and did not seek guidance from the Lord') is probably intended as a generalizing comment on the direction of Saul's life.

7. Despite Saul's measures against the necromancers (v. 3), his servants appear to have ready information on the whereabouts of one of them. *Endor* (*cf.* mod. Endûr nearby) lay behind the Philistine lines, a few miles north-east of Shunem. Joshua 17:11–13 notes that the town retained much of its Canaanite character after the settlement, which is, perhaps, a point of some relevance to the present passage.

8. To avoid discovery by the Philistines, and recognition by the medium, Saul travels incognito, and at night. In the Old Testament, however, royal disguises tend to be ineffective (*cf.* v. 12; 1 Ki. 14:6; 22:30, 34; 2 Ch. 35:22f.). *Divine for me by a spirit*: 'Tell me my fortunes by consulting the dead' (NEB). Saul's request to the woman to conjure up a spirit reflects the common view of the ancients that the dead dwell in the underworld – 'Sheol' or 'the Pit', in Old Testament terms. There the effete spirits of the deceased experience some kind of somnolent existence (*cf.* Ps. 88:3–12; Ezk. 26:20). Here, then, is an account of an approach by illicit means to an unseen world imperfectly conceived. And yet, while the story has some of the terms of spirit conjuration (*e.g.* *bring up*), the manner in which Samuel appears and delivers his last oracle seems to suggest that this interview depended on supernatural powers which the medium did not possess. Beyond this, it is difficult to judge what precisely the narrator thought about his story; but the passage is not alone in that respect (*cf.* 2 Ki. 3:27). There are, to be sure, more positive insights on afterlife elsewhere in the Old Testament (*e.g.* Ps. 16:9–11; 73:23–26).

9–11. The woman is at once on her guard, suspecting that these are *agents provocateurs*. *cut off* (9) implies a more severe treatment of the necromancers than mere expulsion (v. 3; *cf.* *my death*). Nevertheless, 'the oath is final' (Heb. 6:16), and her fears are allayed (10, 11). Klein (p. 271) comments on the irony of Saul's swearing by Yahweh in this situation.

12. How does the appearance of Samuel suddenly enable the woman to penetrate Saul's disguise? A few Greek manuscripts read 'Saul' for *Samuel*, but this is no way to solve the problem. Are we to suppose that there was some communication between Samuel and the woman, which is not scored in the text but which was responsible for the unmasking of Saul? Or is it simply that the king's deceit cannot be sustained in the presence of this visitant from the world beyond? Alternatively, when the woman realized that it was indeed Samuel who had appeared, she may have decided that the old prophet could not be conjured up for anyone less than the king; compare Horatio in *Hamlet* (Act 1, Scene 1): 'This spirit, dumb to us, will speak to him.'[142]

13. As in the most probable interpretation of Isaiah 8:19 (see NEB), the Hebrew *'elōhîm* (RSV *god*) is used for the spirit of a deceased person.[143] Though the accompanying participle (*coming* *up*) is plural, it is not necessarily more than one shade that the woman sees; compare 'his' (v. 14). While *earth* is satisfactory for BH *'ereṣ*, the word can sometimes be translated 'underworld', like its Ugaritic and Akkadian cognates.

14. A 'god' Samuel may be (*cf.* on v. 13), yet what the woman sees bears all the signs of human frailty.[144] The characteristic *robe* (*meʿîl*), with its fateful significance for Saul (*cf.* 15:27f.), helps to confirm that his wish has been granted.

15–19. The part played by the spirit-rapper in the interview is not so much as mentioned; and, indeed, it is implied in verse 21 that the conversation was private. 'He who comes with a message from YHWH does not let himself be manipulated by a medium.'[145] Moreover, Samuel speaks as a prophet, not as a ghost, and the séance becomes the occasion for a sermon.

15. Samuel's complaint that he has been *disturbed* is in keeping with that conception of the afterlife noted above (on v. 8). (The verb (*rāḡaz*) occurs in Phoenician sepulchral inscriptions, in reference to the disturbing of tombs.) It may be significant that Saul speaks merely of *God*, whereas Samuel refers repeatedly to 'the Lord' in the next verses.

16–18. A résumé of previous condemnations of Saul, and especially of Samuel's second denunciation of him at Gilgal (15:13–31).[146] There is an allusion to the *torn* robe (17; *cf.* 15:27f.), and the *neighbour* of 15:28 is now named as *David*. *obey* (18): an echo of the obedience motif of ch. 15.

19. Here is the new element in the speech and, far from unsaying the previous threats, it promises a speedy fulfilment. *with me: i.e.* dead.[147] The resemblance in Luke 23:43 is only formal; the New Testament passage is promissory.

20–25. God is at war with Saul and Israel, and the realization overwhelms the distracted king. He is physically weakened by a fast, observed either in preparation for the consultation, or because his anxious state would not permit it otherwise (20). In the circumstances, even the medium is sympathetically drawn, as she tries to revive her hapless client.

21. *came to Saul*: see above on verses 15–19.

22. *a morsel of bread*: a conventional expression of modesty (*cf.* the use of the phrase in Gn. 18:5).

Achish has been blinded by David's charm, but the Philistine commanders take a more pragmatic view of the situation. It is hard not to agree with their assessment (v. 4), even though we are never given an express statement of David's intention. He was, at any rate, saved considerable embarrassment by their intervention. If he had gone into battle and Saul had still lost, the course of Israelite history could have been greatly affected. Certainly the task of winning over the northern tribes, who maintained loyalty to Saul's house for a time after his death, would have been more formidable than it was.

1. In strict chronology, the verse follows on from 28:1f. The Philistines are again at *Aphek*, as in the days of Eli (4:1), though they move to a more northerly point than on that earlier occasion. Since *Jezreel* is a considerable distance to the north of Aphek, the information given here could be interpreted to mean that Saul made the first move, so provoking a Philistine reaction (*cf.* on 28:4).[148] The *spring* is possibly the 'spring of Harod' (Jdg. 7:1), the modern 'Ain Jālūd, located at the foot of Gilboa. On idiomatic grounds, S. R. Driver suspected that a genitive had been lost after *spring*, and this view is, apparently, reflected in NEB's 'En-harod'.[149]

2. *lords*: the rulers of the five Philistine cities (*cf.* 5:8, 11; 6:16). They are not the same as the 'commanders' of verses 3f., 9. *hundreds* and *thousands*: conventional terms for army units, whether Philistine or Israelite (*cf.* 22:7).

3, 4. If amiable naïveté is the hallmark of Achish, the Philistine *commanders* are not so easily convinced of David's loyalty. The Philistines had previous experience of 'Hebrews' changing sides when their Philistine masters had run into difficulties (14:21). *Hebrews* (3): see on 4:6. *adversary* (4): śāṭān, used here without any of its later metaphysical overtones. *the men here* (lit. 'those men') is probably euphemistic for 'our (heads)', which is the reading in the roughly parallel text in 1 Chronicles 12:19. NEB has 'at the price of our lives'. Compare the occurrence of 'these men' in Numbers 16:14.[150]

5. The second time that Philistines quote the couplet celebrating David's victory over Goliath (18:7; *cf.* 21:11).

6. Apologetically, Achish explains that David has been rejected by the other Philistine leaders.[151] *As the Lord lives*, a characteristically Israelite oath-formula, is remarkable on the lips of a Philistine 'lord', unless the narrator has decided not to let Achish swear by one of his own gods. Since in verse 9 the Philistine also uses the expression 'angel of God', it may be that Achish's language is intended to emphasize the extent of David's acceptance with him. For another instance of Israelite religious phraseology on Philistine lips see 6:3–9.

8. By now a practised deceiver, David protests at the injustice; but his *what have I done?* does not ring true, as it did when addressed to Saul (26:18). Are we to savour an ambiguity in *the enemies of my lord the king*? Compare the note on 28:2. Where David's ultimate loyalty was concerned, Saul was king and the Philistines were the enemies.

9. Achish has some knowledge of Israelite angelology![152] See on verse 6. In 2 Samuel 14:17; 19:27 the expression refers to the preternatural powers of discernment which David as king was thought to possess.

10, 11. Thanks to the Philistine commanders' mistrust of him, David is saved – or is prevented – from being involved in Saul's last battle. He may genuinely have been relieved at this turn of events, and his protest (v. 8) may have been one more piece of play-acting, but he could easily have been disappointed at losing an opportunity to 'smite the Philistine' and rehabilitate himself with his fellow-Israelites.[153] However, as the next chapter discloses, there was good reason for David, in retrospect, to be grateful to the Philistine commanders for sending him back to Ziklag.

ATTACKING THE AMALEKITES   (30:1–31)

It can hardly be coincidence that Samuel's denunciation of Saul in 28:16–19 concentrates on his mishandling of the expedition against the Amalekites (*cf.* 15:1–33), and that so much attention is now paid to David's attack on them ('the enemies of the Lord', v. 26) – when at this stage we might have expected the spotlight to focus on the Israelite lines in Jezreel, as they prepared for Saul's final encounter with the Philistines. When it comes (ch. 31), the report of the Israelite defeat is brief and uninformative, compared with the generous proportions of the present chapter. It does not require much imagination, then, to recognize that Saul's irresolute treatment of the Amalekites is being compared unfavourably with David's expeditious handling of the crisis which confronted him at Ziklag. By his actions David shows himself fit to rule Israel, and, with the prospective authority of a king, he even lays down 'a statute and an ordinance' which remained in force for generations

(v. 25). From the Amalekite point of view, the attack on Ziklag was partly a matter of retaliation (*cf.* 27:8), and in circumstances highly favourable to themselves. Israelite hearers of the story, on the other hand, might reflect that, in the attack on the defenceless Ziklag, history was merely repeating itself (*cf.* Dt. 25:17f.).

1, 2. The distance between Aphek and *Ziklag* was about sixty miles (Hertzberg). If the devastation which met the returning band was not immediately blamed on an Amalekite *razzia*, the Amalekites must have been among the chief suspects (*cf.* on 15:2f.); confirmation would soon be forthcoming (v. 13). Providentially, none of the people in Ziklag had been killed in the raid (*cf.* vv. 18f.). In this emphatic way was David's 'Ziklag phase' brought to an end; the return to Judah is not far off (*cf.* 2 Sa. 2:1-4).

3-6. Strong men weep, if not for their wives, at least for their *sons* and *daughters* (*cf.* 6). As often in such circumstances, there was a tendency to 'blame the command', and David, as well as having to contend with his own private grief (5), had to face up to a death-threat (*cf.* Ex. 17:4). Ziklag, perhaps through lack of foresight, had been left unprotected when he led his men north to Aphek. But, whereas Saul in similar plight had no certain source of help or guidance (28:15), David, whose theology, if not his behaviour, has been refined since his last exchange with Saul (26:19), seeks consolation in God. This encompasses more than the mechanical consultation of the ephod in verses 7f., as is evident from 23:16 where, at another crisis-point in his experience, Jonathan arrived and 'strengthened his hand in God'.

7, 8. One tangible reminder that the advantage had passed from Saul to David was the latter's possession of a priestly *ephod* (see on 2:28), to which he could turn for supernatural guidance. *Abiathar*: *cf.* 23:6.

8. For the inquiry compare 23:10-12.

9, 10. *Besor*: possibly Wadi Ghazzeh, some miles south of Tell esh-Shari^ca (see on 27:6). The *two hundred* who were *too exhausted* (10) found that this additional impost on their strength was too much, so soon after the march from Aphek. They were left in charge of the impedimenta (v. 24), in accordance with an arrangement previously tried out (*cf.* 25:13).

11-15. With the discovery of an abandoned Egyptian slave – possibly acquired by the Amalekites in a similar sort of expedition over the Egyptian border – comes the information that it is more than three days since Ziklag has been fired.

12. *raisins*: 'a welcome food for the hungry, being full of energizing sugars' (*IBD*, p. 1624).

14. Compare 27:10, where other districts of the Negev are mentioned. The *Cherethites*, closely linked with the Philistines in two passages (Ezk. 25:16; Zp. 2:5), are not improbably taken to be Cretans who, like the Philistines themselves, took part in the great movement of Aegean and Mediterranean peoples into the Levant in the late Bronze Age. Note the mention of spoil 'from the land of the Philistines' in verse 16, and see further on 2 Samuel 8:18. *of Caleb*: that is, of the Calebite clan which occupied Hebron and district (*cf.* Jdg. 1:10, 20).

16, 17. Conviviality made bad soldiers of the Amalekites, and a dreadful slaughter ensued. *dancing* (16): in most of its occurrences BH *ḥāḡaḡ* means 'to celebrate a festival'. *Philistines . . . Judah*: these are in contention at Jezreel (29:1, 11), but David flails the spoliators of them both. On the relationship of *Philistines* to Cherethites see above (v. 14). For another reference to Amalekite (and Midianite) cameleering (17) see Judges 6:3–6.[154]

18–20. The extent of the success is emphasized (*all*, 18, 19, 20; *cf.* Gn. 14:16). So too is David's role in the recovery operation; for the moment there is no talk of 'David and his men'. (The matter is viewed in a different light, however, in v. 23.) *This is David's spoil* (20) marks the reversal of the earlier hostility against him, when all seemed hopelessly lost (v. 6). Since David has recovered it by his prowess, it is, in a sense, all his (*cf.* Gn. 14:21).

21. Whereas MT has David asking the baggage-keepers how they had fared (*cf.* NEB; RSV *saluted*), the LXX has the two hundred approach David with anxious inquiries. It is probably best to retain MT and to see this as another aspect of David's depiction as heroic, magnanimous, and solicitous of his men's welfare.

22–24. Not all his men (*cf.* 22:2), however, were imbued with the same spirit, and a different kind of leadership is required from David in an awkward moment (*cf.* 11:12f., of Saul). If the recovery of the goods is first and foremost attributable to *the Lord* (23), then combatants and non-combatants must share the spoil on an equal basis (24). It is an interesting example of Israelite case-law (*cf.* Lv. 24:10–23; Nu. 15:32–36), especially since, in the Old Testament, Israelite rulers – as David effectively is here – are not associated with law-making to anything like the extent of some of their near eastern counterparts.

25. *a statute and an ordinance*: a set phrase (*cf.* Ex. 15:25; Jos. 24:25). *to this day*: *cf.* on 27:6.

26–31. Gratitude for past favours is given as the primary reason for this distribution of Amalekite spoils among various towns in southern Judah (31). Any that had suffered from Amalekite depredations (*cf.* v. 14) could also regard themselves as receiving compensation for losses sustained. But this was also the area where David's claim to the throne was first acknowledged (*cf.* 2 Sa. 2:1–4), so that it is likely that the self-interest motive played a part in these benefactions. In the accompanying message, the reference to *the spoil of the enemies of the Lord* (26) carries with it the assertion that, no matter what Saul may be doing, it is David who is successfully fighting Yahweh's battles (*cf.* 25:28).

26. *present*: lit. 'blessing', as in 25:27.[155]

27.[156]*Bethel* cannot be the Ephraimite town of that name, since it was too far north; possibly Bethuel, mentioned with Hormah and Ziklag in 1 Chronicles 4:30 (Bethul in Jos. 19:4), should be read with NEB. The LXX has 'Beth-zur' (*cf.* Jos. 15:58), possibly a Calebite city (*cf.* 1 Ch. 2:45). *Ramoth of the Negeb*: 'Ramah of the Negeb' in Joshua 19:8. *Jattir*: possibly the modern Khirbet 'Attir, about twelve miles to the south of Hebron.

28. *Aroer*: modern Khirbet 'Ar'areh, twelve miles south-east of Beersheba. *Siphmoth*:[157] apart from the existence of Zabdi the Shiphmite (*sic*), who was in charge of David's wine cellars (1 Ch. 27:27), nothing is known of the place. *Eshtemoa*: represented by the modern es-Semū', some miles to the south of Hebron; see Joshua 15:50; 21:14.

29. *Racal*: otherwise unknown; the LXX has 'Carmel'. *Jerahmeelites . . . Kenites*: see on 27:10. 4QSam[a] and the LXX have 'Kenizzites',[158] a tribe from which the Calebites were descended (*cf.* Jos. 14:6, 14); see also Genesis 15:19.

30. *Hormah*: of uncertain location, though Tell Masos, three miles east of Beer-sheba, is currently favoured.[159] For other references to Hormah see Joshua 12:14; Judges 1:17, *etc*. *Borashan*: possibly the same as Ashan in Joshua 19:7. 'A site that was known to earlier geographers as Kh. 'Asan, said to be 3.2 km north of Beersheba, remains archaeologically unknown; it seems to have been built over by expansion of the modern city.'[160] *Athach*: mentioned only here. A minor consonantal change would produce 'Ether', which is listed with Ashan (see previous note) in Joshua 19:7.

31. *Hebron* was the chief city in the region, and David's capital while he ruled over Judah (2 Sa. 2:1–4; 3:2–5).

THE DEATH OF SAUL (31:1–13)

The grim details are recounted without much elaboration. A special concern is shown for the fate of Saul and his sons, and the treatment of the king's body, by profane Philistines and by loyal Jabesh-gileadites, is the subject of the final shots. One immediate consequence – the settling of Philistines in some Israelite cities – is noted, but on the question of the succession to the throne nothing is said. The parallel passage in 1 Chronicles 10 has a few minor differences in detail, as well as the occasional 'private interpretation' of the Chronicler.

1. When the battle on the Jezreel plain (*cf.* 29:1, 11; 2 Sa. 1:6) began to go against the Israelites they took to the hills. *Gilboa*: see on 28:4.

2. Of Saul's sons, only Ish-bosheth (= Ishvi in 14:49) survived, to become the focus of the traditional loyalty to Saul and his house (*cf.* 2 Sa. 2:8ff.). *Abinadab* is not mentioned in 14:49, but see 1 Chronicles 8:33.

3. *the archers found him*: *cf.* 1 Kings 22:34f. (Ahab). At the end of the verse the LXX has 'and he was wounded *in the stomach*', which reading is accepted by NEB.[161]

4, 5. A different version is given by the Amalekite youth who reports Saul's death to David in 2 Samuel 1:6–10, but there is every reason to think that the Amalekite was trying to do himself a favour by telling David what, as he thought, would earn his commendation. Saul died ingloriously, but not as a coward; he would not become the butt of callous jesting by the Philistines (*these uncircumcised*, 4).[162] Abimelech of Shechem was more successful in his appeal to his armour-bearer in a similar situation (Jdg. 9:54). The statement that the armour-bearer *feared greatly* (4), and therefore would not despatch his master, is, in all probability, related to Saul's sacrosanctity; it comments obliquely on the impiousness of the Amalekite who, according to his own story, had no compunction about killing Saul (2 Sa. 1:10, 14).

6. A bald statement of fact, but with, perhaps, a recollection of Samuel's Endor prediction (28:19; *cf.* 2:34, of Eli's sons). The slight differences in 1 Chronicles 10:6 are probably attributable to the Chronicler's desire to portray the whole *house* of Saul as effectively having been destroyed at Gilboa.[163] The Chronicler is aware of Ish-bosheth (*cf.* 1 Ch. 8:33), but passes from Gilboa to David's anointing at Hebron (1 Ch. 11:1–3), without so much as a reference to the diminished Saulide kingdom over which Ish-bosheth reigned for a time, after his father's death.

7. The *valley* refers to Jezreel. *beyond the Jordan*: *be'ēber* in this expression can mean 'in the region of' (*cf.* NEB).[164] While it is not impossible that the Philistines occupied towns in Transjordan as well as in the Jezreel area, the following initiative by the Jabesh-gileadites, and the fact that Ish-bosheth was able to administer a kingdom of sorts from Mahanaim (*cf.* 2 Sa. 2:8ff.), are points to be borne in mind. Even so, the Philistines have, by their defeat of Saul, made deep inroads into Israel.

8. Stripping the slain was a common way for victorious armies to augment their own weaponry.

9. David had removed Goliath's head 'and brought it to Jerusalem' (17:51, 54). According to 1 Chronicles 10:10, Saul's head was displayed in the temple of Dagon. Far from controlling the events of history, the gods of Philistia, as the narrator wryly points out, are as needful of being informed of the victory as are the ordinary citizens. The extent of the Philistine rejoicing at Saul's death tends to support the claim that he had frequent altercations with them (*cf.* 14:52; 24:1), and had achieved notable successes at their expense (*cf.* 14:47).

10. *Ashtaroth*, a plural form, could represent female deities other than Ashtart (*cf.* on 7:3); she was, nevertheless, a goddess of war (among other things), and the deposition of Saul's armour in a temple dedicated to her would be not inappropriate.[165] Weapons were sometimes kept in temples as trophies of war (*cf.* 21:9); the presence of scale armour in the Deir 'Alla sanctuary might also be explained in this way.[166] *Beth-shan*, situated in the Jordan valley, at the eastern end of the plain of Jezreel, shows evidence of Philistine occupation from the time of Rameses III (twelfth century); the Philistines may, in the first instance, have been stationed there as mercenaries by Rameses. The ancient site is represented by Tell el-Ḥuṣn, while the name survives in Beisân, a village nearby.[167]

11, 12. A fate similar to that threatened by Goliath on David (*cf.* 17:44) had been meted out to Saul's torso. But, in a fitting *inclusio* to Saul's reign, the men of *Jabesh-gilead*, mindful of Saul's rescue of their city when it was besieged by the Ammonites (11:1–11), crossed the Jordan and recovered the bodies of the king and his three sons. If, in rather special circumstances, the Jabesh-gileadites *burnt* the bodies, this would be a rare instance of cremation, by Israelites, in the Old Testament. (The treatment of Achan and his family in Jos. 7:25, involving the execution of a death sentence, is not a true parallel; similarly Lv. 20:14; 21:9.) However, the verb *śārap*, translated *burnt*, is occasionally used, though with the preposition l^e ('for'), to mean 'burn spices (for)' (2 Ch. 16:14; Je. 34:5; *cf.* 2 Ch. 21:19). This is the interpretation of the Targum – which adds that it was a practice local to Jabesh-gilead (!) – and a not dissimilar view is represented in NEB, following G. R. Driver ('and anointed them there with spices').[168] Stoebe thinks that the reference to bones in verse 13 argues against Driver's meliorative construction on what the Jabesh-gileadites did; but mention of Joseph's bones, after his body had been embalmed, seems to present no problems (*cf.* Gn. 50:25f.; Ex. 13:19; Jos. 24:32). The main difficulty with the Targumic interpretation is, as has been noted, syntactic. We can only guess at what the Chronicler may have made of the statement, for he has nothing corresponding to it in 1 Chronicles 10:12. But since he himself uses the expression 'burn spices for' (see above), it is possible that the present passage meant something less acceptable to him, and that he omitted it for the selfsame reason.

13. *tamarisk*: *cf.* 22:6. 1 Chronicles 10:12 makes it an oak (*cf.* Deborah's burial oak, Gn. 35:8). *seven days*: a more protracted period than that observed by David and his associates (2 Sa. 1:11f.). The Jabesh-gileadites were subsequently commended for their action by David, who appended a plea to them to direct their loyalty to him, now that Saul was dead (2 Sa. 2:4–7). Eventually, the bodies were exhumed and reinterred in the family grave (2 Sa. 21:11–14).

2 SAMUEL

6 David King of Judah (1:1–4:12)

If we had only the telescoped history of 1 Chronicles to go on, we should take it for granted that the transition from Saul to David, as king of Israel, was smooth and uneventful (*cf.* 1 Ch. 11:1–3). However, as the more detailed account of the early chapters of 2 Samuel makes clear, Saul's death was followed by a period of civil war during which the succession issue was contested by David and Ish-bosheth, the sole surviving son of Saul. David had been acclaimed king by his fellow-tribesmen in Judah, and Ish-bosheth was ruling the remnants of his late father's kingdom from Mahanaim in Transjordan. This situation was finally resolved by a couple of acts of treachery which saw first Abner, Ish-bosheth's right-hand man, and then Ish-bosheth himself, removed from the scene. Thereafter, the way was open for the northern tribes to transfer their allegiance to David (5:1–3).

THE AMALEKITE MESSENGER (1:1–16)

This messenger is put to death, not because he has brought bad news, but because of the self-incriminating elements that he has woven into his story. He has, he claims, delivered the *coup de grâce* to the dying Saul, and he has hastened to David with the symbols of kingship which, he says, now rightly belong to him. An accurate assessment of where Israel's hope lay, and an impressive declaration of loyalty, we might reckon; but David thinks otherwise. Even when mortally wounded, Saul was still 'the Lord's anointed', and the Amalekite has acted impiously. Once more, then, the model propriety of David, in the matter of the throne, is thrust before our eyes. He who himself has rejected the use of violence against Yahweh's anointed is outraged by the Amalekite's self-regarding tale.

1. As we noted in connection with 1 Samuel 30, Saul's defeat at Gilboa has been subordinated, in a manner of speaking, to David's ravaging of the Amalekites – as if to say that David's (relatively minor) success is more significant in the long run than is the major calamity that befell Saul and his army at Gilboa. In other words, the future lies with David. In this verse, too, Saul's death and David's success are mentioned side by side, in such a way as to divert attention, even if only momentarily, from the gloom of Gilboa and focus it upon David. For the fateful part played by the Amalekites in Saul's biography see on 1 Samuel 28:18. *slaughter* is the same verb (*hikkâ*) as in 1 Samuel 15:3, where Saul is told to 'smite Amalek'. *Ziklag*: see on 1 Samuel 27:6.

2. The messenger's appearance matches the mournful tidings that he brings (*cf.* 1 Sa. 4:12).

3. *Where do you come from?* is not the same expression as in verse 13, despite the identical rendering in RSV. There David is quizzing the Amalekite about his background.

4, 5. Special mention is made of *Saul* and *Jonathan*, the subjects of the elegy which rounds off the chapter.

6–10. Since it would naturally be assumed from 1 Samuel 31:4 that Saul ended his own life, there has been plenty of support for the view that these verses retail a variant tradition concerning the king's last minutes. Others prefer to treat the two accounts as complementary: Saul's attempted suicide not having brought the speedy end that he sought, the Amalekite came upon him *in extremis* and put him out of his misery. Thus McKane takes 'fallen' in verse 10 to correspond to the statement, in 1 Samuel 31:4, that Saul fell upon his sword.[1] But there are difficulties in the way of such a harmonization of the passages. In the first place, Saul's armour-bearer was sufficiently convinced of his master's death to follow his example (1 Sa. 31:5). Thereafter, as the harmonization theory would have it, the Amalekite found Saul *leaning upon his spear* (6) – an unlikely sequel to even a botched attempt at self-impalement. It is, therefore, more likely that the Amalekite is claiming responsibility for something that he never did, in expectation of a reward from David, the supposed beneficiary of the imaginary act (*cf.* 18:22).

6. Adele Berlin comments perceptively on the repeated *wᵉhinnēh* ('and behold'; RSV 'and there was', 'and lo') as more typical of dream reports and a possible hint at the Amalekite's fictionalizing.[2]

spear: 1 Samuel 31:4 mentions only Saul's sword. The plain of Jezreel would have been well-suited for the deployment of *chariots* and *horsemen*, which is probably why the worsted Israelite soldiery made for the hills of Gilboa (1 Sa. 31:1). For Philistine chariotry and cavalry see also 1 Samuel 13:5. The wounding of Saul by an arrow, as in 1 Samuel 31:3, is not necessarily contradicted by the Amalekite's enlisting of the mounted brigades; chariots were often fitted with quivers and arrows (*cf.* 2 Ki. 9:16, 24).

9. 'Instead of shrinking from the abuse of the Philistine, he is willing to give himself to be despatched by an equally despised enemy, an Amalekite'; so Smith, harmonistically, and a trifle sententiously. *anguish* (*šābāṣ*): the word is not otherwise attested in Hebrew and the meaning is uncertain; a couple of the ancient versions render it by 'dizziness' (LXX, Peshitta). Both NEB and NIV opt for 'the throes of death'.[3]

10. That *after he had fallen* refers to Saul's suicide attempt (1 Sa. 31:4) cannot be taken for granted, in view of the various discrepancies between the two accounts of his death (see above). Kennedy understood verse 10a to mean that Saul fell while he was talking with the Amalekite, overcome by the giddiness mentioned in the previous verse. *crown*: possibly a workaday model; in ancient Egypt the monarch might have as many as a couple of dozen crowns designed for specific occasions and functions. The Amalekite presents to David the insignia of office which he had acquired by 'just happening' to be on Gilboa (v. 6) when Saul died. He will be executed as a regicide (vv. 14–16), but he was more probably a common looter with some facility in story-telling.

11, 12. David and his men, though outlawed and harassed by Saul in his lifetime, show their solidarity with their fellow-Israelites by their reaction to the Amalekite's report. *the people*: as in verse 4, and often elsewhere, BH *'am* may mean 'army' (*cf.* NIV).

13–16. The Amalekite is not paid for his news; he himself must pay. David acts as a swift judge – though whether, with Mabee, we can discern the formal elements of a judicial procedure here is another matter[4]– and establishes his own innocence in relation to Saul's death. He neither plotted it nor took pleasure in it. This is the answer to any possible charge that, if allowed, he would have fought on the side of Saul's enemies at Jezreel (see the introductions to chs. 27 and 29).

13, 14. The man identifies himself as the son of an Amalekite resident alien (*sojourner* (*gēr*), 13) – an interesting concept in view of Exodus 17:16; 1 Samuel 15:1–33. As a *gēr* he had limited rights and obligations in common with the native-born Israelite (*cf.* Ex.

12:48; 20:10; 23:9; Lv. 19:10, *etc.*), and as a *gēr* he should have respected the inviolability of the king's person. It is, then, on the ground of the Amalekite's privileged status that David presses his charge. If the Amalekite had not been a *gēr* – or, at least, had not claimed to be one – the charge very probably would have been framed in different terms.

15. *Cf.* 1 Samuel 22:18. In later tradition the Amalekite was sometimes identified with Doeg the Edomite, which, though historically impossible, does suggest a point of comparison between two non-Israelites who had no regard for the sacred offices of Israel, whether the priesthood, as in Doeg's case, or kingship, as here.

16. David pronounces sentence like a judge, perhaps in virtue of his authority as a military commander 'in the field'.[5] A charge, to be upheld, needed the corroboration of witnesses, and this, in part, is supplied by the Amalekite himself, whose *own mouth has testified against* him. *testified against* (*'ānâ be*), as in the ninth commandment (Ex. 20:16), is a forensic term.

DAVID'S LAMENT   (1:17–27)

This elegy (Heb. *qînâ*, v. 17), powerfully evocative, generous in its praise of Saul as well as of Jonathan, is one of the finest specimens of Hebrew poetry in the Old Testament.[6] As Driver notes, 'It is remarkable that no *religious* thought of any kind appears in the poem: the feeling expressed by it is purely *human*.'[7] First the poet expresses his abhorrence at the thought of the victory celebrations in Philistia (v. 20), then puts a curse on Gilboa (v. 21), before he can bring himself to speak of the lost heroes. A particularly intense affection is shown towards Jonathan who is directly addressed, as 'my brother', in the last full stanza (v. 26). Only a rare spirit deeply moved by an event of great moment is likely to have produced a little masterpiece like this. Need we doubt that that spirit was David's, or that his masterpiece was composed in the wake of Gilboa? Finally, a technical point: this lament, in the form in which it has been transmitted to us, shows sovereign disregard for the 3:2 rhythm that is particularly characteristic of the Hebrew *qînâ*.

17, 18. *David lamented*: compare the tradition that the prophet Jeremiah composed a lament for Josiah (2 Ch. 35:25). The word 'bow' (18), which RSV relegates to the footnotes, is indeed puzzling. NIV 'that the men of Judah be taught this lament of the bow', where 'bow' (Jonathan's, *cf.* v. 22) is virtually the title of the lament (*cf.* RV '*the song of the bow*'), represents the best that can be done

with the extant text. Some object to this explanation on the
ground that such titling of Hebrew poems is unknown in the Old
Testament – though there certainly are comparable treatments of
narrative pericopes at a later period (*e.g.* 'The Bush' in Mk.
12:26), and Hertzberg finds a distant parallel in the Quran, the second
sura of which is known as 'The Cow'. Pending a better explanation
of MT, it may be advisable to omit the word with the LXX and
RSV. NEB 'ordered that this dirge over them should be taught'
differs little from RSV, but is based on the supposition that the
consonants of the Hebrew word translated 'bow' are actually the
initial letters of a three-word heading to the lament.[8] This piece of
translational dadaism is not for emulation. The *Book of Jashar*,
also mentioned in Joshua 10:13, appears to have been an anthology
of Hebrew poems commemorating great events in national life.
Jashar ('upright') may be related to 'Jeshurun', an appellation of
Israel in Deuteronomy 32:15.

19. *glory* (*ṣᵉḇî*): or, possibly, 'the gazelle' (BH *ṣᵉḇî* II), perhaps
in reference to the agility of the hero (or heroes) so described (*cf.*
2:18). At verse 25b the name of Jonathan stands in the corresponding position in the colon. Nevertheless, it is unlikely that the lament
begins by singling Jonathan out for mention, and the advantage
of translating as in RSV is that *glory* may embrace both Saul and
Jonathan.[9] *high places*: Mount Gilboa (*cf.* v. 21; 1 Sa. 31:1). *How
are the mighty fallen!*: repeated in verses 25 and 27 as a kind of
irregular refrain.

20. The thought of the victory chants of the Philistine women
celebrating Saul's defeat (*cf.* 1 Sa. 18:7) grates on the elegist. By
contrast, the women of Israel are bidden to mourn their loss in
verse 24. *Tell . . . Gath*: there is a certain amount of assonance in
the Hebrew (*taggîḏû . . . gaṯ*). *publish* (*bāśar*) is used in the prose
reference to the Philistine celebrations in 1 Samuel 31:9.

21. *Gilboa*, apostrophized as if the mountain range itself had
been responsible for the disaster, has a curse laid upon it (*cf.* Mal.
3:9f.). *upsurging of the deep* represents a clever emendation of MT,
proposed by H. L. Ginsberg in 1938, on the basis of a passage in
a Ugaritic text.[10] But it is possible to obtain a satisfactory sense
from MT as it stands, if *tᵉrûmōṯ* is related to BH *rûm*, 'be high':
'you high fields' would have a rough parallel in Judges 5:18.[11] And,
in fact, the margin of a Targumic manuscript already offers the
variant 'mountain field'. NEB 'showers on the uplands' combines
part of Ginzberg's explanation with this interpretation of *tᵉrûmōṯ*.
defiled: perhaps with the carnage of war; but, the reference to
armour in 1 Samuel 31:9f. notwithstanding, the more likely sense

is that the shield is becoming tarnished through neglect. *not anointed*: no longer treated with oil, which was the usual way of preserving leather shields (*cf.* Is. 21:5). Note Millard's reference to an Old Babylonian text from Tell Asmar with the entry: 'one sila of oil to rub shield(s)'.[12]

22. Jonathan is particularly commended for his bravery (*turned not back*),[13] Saul for the number he had put to the sword during his warrior career.

23. An idealized account of relations between Saul and Jonathan, especially as David had witnessed them. *lovely*: the same root (*n-'-m*) is translated 'pleasant' in verse 26, in reference to Jonathan. The traditional division of the first two lines as in AV, RV ('lovely and pleasant in their lives . . . ') has recently been defended by P. A. H. de Boer.[14]

24. The women of Israel, who, in the event of victory, would have led the celebrations (*cf.* 1 Sa. 18:7), are called to mourn because they will no longer enjoy the prizes of war brought back by Saul from his campaigns (*cf.* Jdg. 5:28–30).

25b, 26. The last words, bar the refrain (v. 27), are reserved for Jonathan. For David, he is, in a special way, the 'glory' (or 'gazelle'!) of Israel (*cf.* v. 19). And so, in a final outburst of emotion, he addresses him directly (26). *brother* may refer to the covenantal relationship into which David and Jonathan had entered (1 Sa. 18:3; *cf.* 1 Ki. 9:13; Am. 1:9).

CIVIL WAR   (2:1–32)

For a time after Saul's death Israel had two kings – David, who was acknowledged by his fellow-tribesmen in Judah, and Ish-bosheth, the remaining son of Saul, whom Abner installed in Transjordan as 'king over Gilead and the Ashurites' (*sic*) and Jezreel and Ephraim and Benjamin and all Israel' (v. 9). David's overture to the Judahites was, we are informed (v. 1), subject to divine guidance and approval. Ish-bosheth, by contrast, was beholden to Abner, and would be secure for as long as Abner found advantage in a situation of which he was the principal architect. Meanwhile there was a war on, and contingents representing the two sides met by Gibeon, and much to the disadvantage of Ish-bosheth's men. The most significant event that day was, however, Abner's killing of Asahel, younger brother of Joab and Abishai. Because Joab would not let that deed go unavenged, Abner's life would soon be forfeit.

1–3. Consistent with the portrayal of him in the so-called 'History of David's Rise', David seeks divine guidance before he makes his next move. He has been carefully fostering good relations with the men of Judah (*cf.* 1 Sa. 30:26–31), and now is the time to present himself to them as Saul's legitimate successor. *Hebron*, an ancient city with patriarchal connections, had been a Canaanite royal city in pre-settlement days (*cf.* Jos. 10:3). Located high in the Judaean hills, it was far enough away from the Philistine sphere of control to enable David to strengthen his position without interference. It has, indeed, been surmised that the Philistines did not object to David's rule in Hebron. They could keep an eye on him; and the division of Saul's kingdom into two was a situation with obvious advantage for them. *towns* (3): Hebron was the chief city of the area; its older name was Kiriath-arba ('tetrapolis'; *cf.* Gn. 23:2).

4. This represents the second of three anointings recorded in connection with David (*cf.* 1 Sa. 16:13; 2 Sa. 5:3).[15] *the house of Judah* will include the various clans, such as the Jerahmeelites and Kenites, that had become affiliated to Judah (*cf.* 1 Sa. 30:29).

4b–7. In commending the Jabesh-gileadites for their loyalty to Saul (*cf.* 1 Sa. 31:11–13), David appeals to them to recognize him as Saul's natural successor. It was a shrewd enough attempt on his part to establish a bridgehead in Transjordan, which was to remain loyal to the house of Saul for some time yet (*cf.* vv. 8–10).

6. *steadfast love and faithfulness*: correctly for MT *ḥeseḏ weʾemeṯ*; *cf.* Psalm 85:10 (AV 'mercy and truth').

8–10. Ish-bosheth, with Abner's help, establishes himself in Transjordan as king of 'Israel'. A jurymast of sorts, he cut no regal figure as Saul his father had done; the future of the Saulide house rested largely with Abner.

8. *Ish-bosheth*: also known as Eshbaal (1 Ch. 8:33; 9:39). The usual explanation of the form Ish-bosheth is that *bosheth*, meaning 'shame', was substituted for *baal* ('lord') because of the easy association of the latter with the name of the god Baal.[16] *Mahanaim*: often identified with Khirbet Mahneh, some miles to the north of the river Jabbok in Transjordan, though a site close to the river would better satisfy the biblical data. Tulul ed-Ḏahab is a possibility.[17]

9. *Gilead* is sometimes used for the whole of Israelite Transjordan (*cf.* Dt. 34:1); strictly speaking it is the wooded hill-country on either side of the Jabbok. The *Ashurites* are not known apart from this reference. A couple of the ancient versions (Peshitta, Vulgate) read 'Geshur(ites)', evidently in reference to the inhabitants of the Transjordanian kingdom of Geshur to the north of Gilead (*cf.* Jos.

12:5); the Geshurites, however, had their own king in this period (*cf.* 3:3). The Targum sees a reference to the tribe of Asher, which, though distant from the administrative centre of Ish-bosheth's 'refugee government', cannot be ruled out. J. A. Soggin, for example, includes the northern littoral of Israel in Ish-bosheth's domain.[18] *Jezreel* we might expect to have been in Philistine hands, since it was here that the decisive battle between Saul and the Philistines took place (see especially 1 Sa. 31:7). In fact, the areas listed in this verse may represent no more than the territories to which Ish-bosheth laid claim, irrespective of whether he actually exercised control over them. *Israel* is used in its more restricted sense, approximating to the kingdom later ruled by Jeroboam I and his successors.

10, 11. *Cf.* 5:5. It might be deduced from this information that there was a gap of five and a half years between Ish-bosheth's death and David's recognition by the northerners as their rightful king. We are probably to understand, however, that during those years David ruled both Judah and Israel from Hebron. Other interpretations of the data range from the suggestion that David was acknowledged as king of Judah for the last five and a half years of Saul's reign,[19] to the theory that Ish-bosheth did not become king of 'Israel' until five and a half years after Saul's death.[20]

12–17. These verses describe a quite different type of representative combat from that encountered in the story of David and Goliath.[21] The original intention may have been to avoid excessive bloodshed among brother Israelites (*cf.* Jdg. 20), though, in the event, a full-scale encounter was necessary to decide the issue. The suggestion has also been made that the episode and its sequel (vv. 18-32) make up a kind of combat ordeal in which the rival claims of David and Ish-bosheth are adjudicated by Yahweh. On this view, Yahweh, who is not actually mentioned in the narrative, declares his verdict in the casualty figures recorded in verses 30f.[22]

12. *Gibeon* (mod. el-Jib), in Benjaminite territory, was situated about five miles north of Jerusalem.[23] *went out* (BH *yāṣā'*) is sometimes used of a military expedition (*cf.* on 11:1); in this case Mauchline prefers to speak of 'sharp-eyed reconnaissance' by Abner and his men.

13. *Joab*, the son of David's sister Zeruiah (*cf.* 1 Ch. 2:15f.), became the commander of David's army (*cf.* 8:16) and, to the point of embarrassment, his most zealous servant (*cf.* 3:39). *went out*: the LXX (and probably 4QSam[a]) adds 'from Gibeon', as if the city was under David's control at this stage.[24] The *pool* (*cf.* Je.

41:12) is possibly the same as the large pit excavated at el-Jib in the late 1950s.[25]

14. The opposing commanders agree to a representative contest between small teams of *ne'ārîm* (RSV *young men*), which term, in a military context, may denote a specialist class of warrior.[26] *play* (BH *ṣāḥaq*) has given rise to the view that the teams were meant to engage in a mock contest or 'joust', but the word may be used euphemistically (*cf.* NIV 'fight hand to hand', NEB 'join in single combat').

15. *for Benjamin*: Saul's, and therefore Ish-bosheth's, tribe, from which came the nucleus of the Saulide army (*cf.* 1 Sa. 22:7).

16. There are good glyptic illustrations of the procedure described here, for example on a ninth(?) century relief from Tell Halaf in Syria.[27] Apparently all twenty-four combatants were the worse for their engagement, with the result that the main contingents went into action. *Helkath-hazzurim* may mean 'field of flints' (or 'flint-knives'; NIVfn. 'daggers'), but there are other possible explanations of the *hazzurim* component, none of them entirely suited to the context.

18–28. The confrontation escalates into something far more serious, for Ish-bosheth's men in particular. The story of the pursuit of Abner is told at some length, partly because the protagonists were men of destiny in the respective kingdoms, and partly because Asahel's death at Abner's hand gave Joab and Abishai the justification they needed for the killing of Abner, the strongest rival to Joab in either part of Israel.

18. Zeruiah's sons were doughty warriors all, playing a decisive part in David's rise to power and in the building up of his empire. For *Joab* see on verse 13. *Abishai* and *Asahel* were both members of the warrior corps known as 'The Thirty' (*cf.* 23:18, 24).

19–22. *Abner*, as a seasoned warrior, did not regard the callow Asahel as 'fair game'; he had also to consider *Joab*, for whom he had a healthy regard (22). The mention of Joab is ominous, in view of his subsequent murder of Abner (*cf.* 3:27). *spoil* (*ḥaliṣâ*, 21): the word may refer to the belt worn by soldiers as a symbol of their military prowess (*cf.* Targum, NEB 'belt', and see on 21:16). Étan Levine suggests that behind some of the New Testament references to 'girding up of the loins' lies the figure of the 'wrestling-belt'.[28]

23. Forced to deal with Asahel, Abner runs the young man through with the *butt of his spear* – which is, as much as anything, a testimony to his own brute strength.[29] The sight of the fallen

Asahel was enough to deter the rest of David's men from further pursuit.

24. Asahel's brothers, however, are now more determined than ever to overtake Abner. They assume the role of avengers of blood, and Joab's fault will be that he takes revenge on Abner after the hostilities have ended (3:27; *cf.* 1 Ki. 2:5). Beyond what may be deduced from the present text, nothing is known of either *Ammah* or *Giah*.

25, 26. Abner is forced, like David in his last confrontation with Saul (1 Sa. 26:13–25), to make his appeal from a hill-top. His point is that the bonds of kinship are being denied by the Judahite vendetta, as it is in danger of becoming (26).

27. The more likely sense is: 'if you had not spoken, surely the men would not have given up the pursuit of their brethren until the morning' (*cf.* NEB, NIV).

29. *Arabah*: see on 1 Samuel 23:24. The word translated *forenoon* is of uncertain meaning, and, since the underlying root means 'to divide', could even denote a ravine (*cf.* NIV 'the whole Bithron'; fn. 'morning' or 'ravine'). If it is the latter, the Jabbok valley is possibly intended (*cf.* on v. 8).

30, 31. The much heavier losses suffered by Abner's contingent indicate the shape of things to come (*cf.* 3:1). We should note that, although Joab has abandoned his *pursuit* of Abner, he has not abandoned his intention of killing him (*cf.* 3:27).

THE DEATH OF ABNER   (3:1–39)

Sudden as the conversion of Abner to David's cause may seem, he must have realized for some time that David's progress was irresistible. In that case, the squabble with Ish-bosheth over Saul's concubine was merely the pretext for breaking with this feckless monarch. In particular, Abner was aware of certain pro-Davidic sympathies that were gaining ground among the tribal heads of Israel. But his own part in the rapprochement between Israel and Judah ended abruptly in the gate of Hebron, and it was left to the tribes themselves to negotiate with David. We have only to read the second half of this chapter to realize that there must have been a tendency in certain ('Saulide') quarters to lay the responsibility for Abner's death upon David's shoulders. Rarely in the Old Testament has a narrator gone to such lengths, as has the writer of this passage, to preserve the good name of one of his characters.

In one way and another, he assures us that neither David's heart nor his hand was set against Abner: Joab acted on his own account.

1. The encounter described in ch. 2 was, apparently, one of a number of engagements in which Ish-bosheth's men came off second best.

2. An appropriate point at which to record the domestic prosperity of David's 'house' during his stay in Hebron. The story of *Amnon*, and of how he fell foul of Absalom because of his violation of Tamar, is told in ch. 13. *Ahinoam*: cf. 1 Samuel 25:43.

3. *Chileab* seems to be the same as Daniel in 1 Chronicles 3:1.[30] *Abigail*: cf. 1 Samuel 25 *passim*. Absalom's mother was a princess from *Geshur*, a small Aramaean state to the north-east of Israel (*cf.* 13:37; 15:8). When Absalom, the arch-rebel in David's family (chs. 15–19), displeased his father by having Amnon murdered, he took refuge with his maternal grandfather in Geshur (13:37f.). David's marriage to *Maacah* may have been contracted wholly or partly as a means of gaining a political ally among Israel's neighbours.

4. *Adonijah* tried to pre-empt the succession issue by having himself proclaimed king while his father was still alive, but had to give way to Solomon, who finally had him put to death (1 Ki. 1–2). Nothing else is known of *Shephatiah* (*cf.* 1 Ch. 3:3).

5. *Ithream*: mentioned only here and in 1 Chronicles 3:3. *David's wife*: in fact, according to 1 Chronicles 3:9, all the women mentioned in these verses were wives; the Chronicles reference notes that there were also 'sons of the concubines'.

6–11. The house of Saul, on the other hand, was not favoured with such domestic felicity: Ish-bosheth and Abner are wrangling over a concubine. Abner, who was consolidating his own position all the while that Ish-bosheth's rickety kingdom was in decline (*cf.* v. 1), allegedly made use of one of Saul's concubines.[31] While it is disputed whether such an act might amount to a formal claim to the throne in Israelite palace politics,[32] it is likely that Ish-bosheth's suspicions tended in that direction anyway. He was a true son of Saul (*cf.* 1 Sa. 22:7f.).

7. When Adonijah asked for permission to marry Abishag, his father's concubine, Solomon chose to construe it as an implicit claim to the throne (1 Ki. 2:13–25(22)). *Rizpah* figures again in the 'Samuel Appendix' (2 Sa. 21–24), when her loyalty to the members of Saul's house who were executed by the Gibeonites was brought to David's notice (21:8, 10–14).

8. Abner, white-hot with indignation, attacks Ish-bosheth for petty-mindedness. There is no admission of wrongdoing, since he reckons that he has been scolded for a trifle (*a woman*). At the same time, the indebtedness of Ish-bosheth to Abner is evident to the extent that only the latter stands between him and capitulation to David. *a dog's head*: a singular expression; compare the disparaging use of 'dog' in 1 Samuel 17:43; 24:14, *etc.* Ish-bosheth may as well claim that Abner is a Judahite lackey, says Abner.[33]

9, 10. From now on Abner will work for the unification of Judah and Israel under David. He recognizes that the title-deeds of the kingdom are held by David, and, though we have not so far heard of a divine oath to David, these verses fairly summarize what the Davidic kingship ideology was about (*cf.* 7:11–16; 23:5). The oath signifies the inexorability of David's progress towards sovereignty over all Israel. *from Dan to Beer-sheba* (10): see on 1 Samuel 3:20.

12.[34] His *volte-face* announced, it remained for Abner to enter into negotiations with David about the transfer of Ish-bosheth's kingdom to him. Hertzberg thinks that Abner's question expects the answer, 'Abner'! But GNB 'Who is going to rule this land?' may have caught the sense.[35] In either case, Abner is simply negotiating over Ish-bosheth's head. *Make your covenant with me* suggests that he wanted to exclude all possible rivals from making a deal with David (*cf.* v. 17). He is concerned about both his safety and his status in the reunified kingdom. Not unjustifiably, he claims the ability to be able to divert Israelite loyalties in David's direction.

13. David, conscious of a long-standing injustice against himself (*cf.* 1 Sa. 25:44), lays down the precondition that *Michal*, the first of his wives, be restored to him. Michal had been a loyal partner when David's life was seriously at risk (*cf.* 1 Sa. 19:11–17), and he was unlikely to forget her even when he was the possessor of a harem. There could be political benefits too, if *Saul's daughter* were restored to him; her presence might enlist additional Saulide support for David's cause. *not see my face*: cf. Genesis 43:3.

14, 15. Protocol is observed, and the request is made directly to Ish-bosheth.[36] He tamely complies, not so much, we may suspect, because of the reminder of David's heroics in order to win the hand of Michal, but because he was taking his orders from Abner. *a hundred foreskins* (14): see 1 Samuel 18:25–27.

16. Michal has already suffered as a pawn in Saul's marriage game (1 Sa. 18:20–27; 25:44); now the circle of misery widens to include the devoted *Paltiel. Saul's daughter* (13) – *my wife* (14) – *her husband* (15, 16) reflect the tangled situation which Saul's callousness has brought about. *Abner* obviously was supervising the arrangements for Michal's return. *Bahurim*: the modern Ras et-Ṭmim, close to Jerusalem (*cf.* 16:5; 17:18).

David's repossession of Michal does not come within the terms of Deuteronomy 24:1–4, since his separation from his wife was involuntary. The right of a husband to reclaim his wife after enforced separation – if, for example, he has been taken prisoner and removed from his homeland – is well entrenched in Mesopotamian law, and may be assumed to have operated in Israel.[37]

17–19. Aware of the tide of dissatisfaction with Ish-bosheth's rule, Abner did not have to exert himself in order to fulfil his side of the bargain with David. An influential factor for many of Ish-bosheth's subjects was that, so long as he was king, there was no hope of ousting the Philistines from occupied territory in Israel (18). Once David was in overall control, on the other hand, there soon were victories to be reported (5:1–5, 17–25).

19. *Benjamin* is distinguished from the rest of Israel because it had provided Israel with its first king, and with him a good proportion of the key men in the kingdom (*cf.* 1 Sa. 22:7).

20, 21. Abner now deals with David direct (*cf.* v. 12), and he and his delegation are warmly received. The *feast* possibly has a covenantal significance here (*cf.* vv. 12f., and see Gn. 26:28–30; 31:44, 53f.). *my lord the king* (21) is a clear indication of where Abner's loyalty lies. *a covenant*: see 5:3. *in peace* is repeated in verses 22 and 23 (also v. 24 in LXX); for its significance see the next paragraph.

22–39. Abner did not live to see the fruit of his deliberations, thanks to the vengefulness of Joab, brother of Asahel. It was a critical moment for David, who could not fail to recognize that the northern tribes would probably turn against him, if the word got around that Abner had been murdered at his instigation, or even with his tacit approval. And if it was essential for David to declare his innocence of any involvement in the killing of Abner, it was no less important for our narrator to underline the fact, as he developed his theme of David's accession by divine favour alone. Three times (four in LXX) within a very brief span it is repeated that Abner departed from David *in peace* (vv. 21, 22, 23 (24, LXX)). Relations between the two, it is insisted, were of mutual acceptance such as precluded any sinister design on David's part. These statements about Abner's going away *in peace* may also hint at a covenantal dimension to the agreement between him and David (*cf.* on v. 20, and see Gn. 26:31; 1 Sa. 20:42).[38]

22. *Joab* arrives with a cargo of spoil from an unnamed region; things have changed little since David's Ziklag days (*cf.* 1 Sa. 27:8). Although Judah and Israel are at war (v. 1), we are not necessarily to imagine that Joab has been pillaging in Israelite territory (though compare 4:2).

24, 25. While Joab may have been genuinely suspicious of Abner, it will transpire that his attitude is governed by other considerations (see on v. 27). Despite the LXX addition of 'in peace' at the end of verse 24, its absence in MT may be original; Joab will not be inhibited by any covenantal relationship between David and Abner (see above), so he omits the words 'in peace'.

26. *David did not know*: in what follows Joab acts *ultra vires* and simply to settle a private score. The charge that David was encouraging Abner to Hebron in the expectation that sooner or later Joab would eliminate him goes far beyond the evidence.[39] *Sirah*: Driver mentions an 'Ain Sārah, 'about a mile N. of Hebron, on the road to Jerusalem'.[40]

27. The *gate* (or 'gateway', NEB) of an ancient city could be a quite substantial construction with screen walls and bays; compare the six-chambered gateways at, for example, Megiddo and Hazor. *into the midst*: it is possible to treat the word translated *midst* (*tôk*) as a redundant element, hence, presumably, NIV 'into the gateway'. Or, with emendation, we may read 'into the side of the gateway', as in the LXX. Abner's death is seen as revenge for his killing of Asahel (2:23), but we may also suspect that Joab regarded him as a potentially dangerous rival who, already as it seemed, was in very good standing with David (*cf.* vv. 31–38; 1 Sa. 26:15).

28, 29. David both denies complicity and invokes a curse on the perpetrator and his connexion (*cf.* v. 39). The terms of the curse recall the judgement pronounced upon the house of Eli in 1 Samuel 2:31–36; disease and death are to stalk the family as long as it remains. (*one who has*) *a discharge* (*zāb*, 29): of the type described in Leviticus 15, where *zāb* is frequently used. In Lamentations 4:9, however, the same root denotes wasting away through hunger. *leprous*: *mesōrā'* may refer to various types of skin disease. Leprosy proper (*i.e.* Hansen's disease) is not in question.[41] A similar kind of imprecation appears in Deuteronomy 28:27, as also in some Assyrian treaty texts.[42] *holds a spindle*: *i.e.* is an effeminate (*cf.* the English 'distaff side', 'spindle side', and see Pr. 31:19). D. J. A. Clines has suggested, on the basis of a reference in the Ugaritic Keret Epic, that Joshua's appointment of the scheming Gibeonites as 'hewers of wood and drawers of water' was a judgement not only in that they were condemned to menial tasks, but also in that these tasks were normally performed by women.[43] Since Joshua's sentence is announced as a curse (Jos. 9:23), the parallel with the present passage is noteworthy. The view, as old as the LXX and

Targum, that MT *peleḵ* means 'staff' (*cf.* AV) rather than *spindle*, is less easily defended.[44] *lacks bread*: *cf.* 1 Samuel 2:36; Amos 4:6.

30. A summarizing statement which is anticipated in verse 27, but which adds two new elements. *Abishai* has not been mentioned in connection with Abner's death, but is held guilty of criminal intent (*mens rea*) (*cf.* 2:24). Secondly, the words *in the battle*, which come at the end of the sentence in MT, make the point that the law of revenge should not have operated on this occasion (*cf.* 1 Ki. 2:5).

31. David orders court mourning, but there is no court martial for Joab. Indeed, the contrast between David's treatment of Joab and his summary judgement on the murderers of Ish-bosheth (4:9–12) is striking.[45] But Joab was a relative of David, and was too powerful a man to be treated as he deserved; his excesses did, in the end, catch up with him (1 Ki. 2:5f., 28–35).

32. Abner is buried with honours in David's temporary capital, rather than back in Benjamin (*cf.* 21:14).

33, 34. It is the ignominy of Abner's death that is deprecated in this snatch of funeral elegy. Not for him the posthumous glory of death on the battlefield; Abner fell to a low trick. *fool* translates *nāḇāl*, already familiar from the story of the Carmelite farmer of that name in 1 Samuel 25 (esp. v. 25); the LXX, in fact, sees a direct reference to Nabal here.[46]

35–37. By his public display of grief David ensures that the rapprochement between Judah and Israel does not suffer because of Abner's murder. In particular, those sympathetic towards the house of Saul are assured that David has not plotted Abner's death. *if I taste bread* (35): *cf.* 1:12. *all the people . . . understood* (37): the seventh such reference to 'the people' in verses 31–37; the apologetic intent is obvious.

38, 39. A fine tribute is paid Abner; if Joab was jealous of him perhaps he had good reason. Conversely, the ever-loyal sons of Zeruiah are regarded more as a liability at this stage (39). David had more need of diplomats than of these 'sons of thunder' just now (*cf.* Mk. 3:17; Lk. 9:54–56). Until Joab and Abishai were reined in, it would be difficult for David to cast off the old life-style which had suited an outlaw, but which ill befitted a king. That was his dilemma: *these men . . . are too hard* (*i.e.* ruthless) *for me* (39).

TREACHERY AGAINST ISH-BOSHETH   (4:1–12)

The death of Ish-bosheth was merely the *coup de grâce* for his ailing kingdom. Nevertheless, the suggestion that it was in any sense engineered by David could have had a disruptive effect on his attempt to secure the allegiance of the northern tribes. Acting with full regal authority on this occasion (*cf.* 1:15f.), he has the self-confessed murderers executed and their mutilated bodies put on display, in testimony to his own revulsion at what had befallen Ish-bosheth. That the Be-erothites' deed may, in fact, have hastened the submission of the Israelite tribes to David is neither here nor there. Like the Amalekite who claimed to have killed Saul, and like Joab who did kill Abner, the Be-erothites represent that wrongful means of acquiring the throne which David has hitherto repudiated.

1. With Abner's death, the main prop of the Saulide kingdom was removed. (As we have seen in the previous chapter, Abner was in the process of dislodging himself in any case.) Ish-bosheth was patently incapable of holding his kingdom together unaided; if there is a 'weak' king about (*cf.* 3:39), here he is![47]

2, 3. In continuation of his father's policy (1 Sa. 22:7), Ish-bosheth (or Abner?) appears to have favoured Benjaminites for command positions in his army. *Be-eroth also is reckoned* (2): originally Be-eroth was a member of the Gibeonite league (Jos. 9:17). It is usually identified with El-bireh, about nine miles north of Jerusalem (*cf.* Driver). At some point, possibly in the period of the Israelite settlement (*cf.* Jos. 18:25), the Amorite inhabitants of Be-eroth were driven from their city and found refuge in *Gittaim* (3), another town in Benjaminite tribal territory (*cf.* Ne. 11:33). It is sometimes suggested that the Be-erothites' plight related to Saul's anti-Gibeonite pogrom (*cf.* 21:2), and that Ish-bosheth's assassins took the opportunity to settle an old score.[48] *sojourners*: see on 1:13.

4. There is no-one in the house of Saul who can revive its fortunes. *Mephibosheth*, Jonathan's son, was a minor and a cripple (*cf.* on 1 Sa. 10:23f.); he enters the story at a later stage, as the beneficiary of the covenant between David and Jonathan (9:1–13; *cf.* 1 Sa. 20:14–17). He is also known as Meribbaal (1 Ch. 8:34; 9:40). For the *bosheth* element in the name see on 2:8.

5, 6. There is nothing regal-sounding here. When the Be-erothites arrive it is siesta time, and the janitress, apparently the nearest thing to a bodyguard for Ish-bosheth, has dozed off. RSV correctly follows the LXX in verse 6 where MT must be translated as in the footnote, and not as NIV ('They went into the inner part of the house as if to get some wheat . . . ').

7, 8. They hasten by way of the Jordan rift valley to Hebron with Ish-bosheth's head. Their language has a familiar sanctimoniousness about it, especially in the way in which they claim divine instrumentality for what they have done (*cf.* 1 Sa. 24:4; 26:8).

9. David's *the Lord . . . who has redeemed my life* (*cf.* 1 Ki. 1:29) is his counter to 'your enemy, who sought your life' (v. 8); it recalls 1 Samuel 26:24 where, having spared Saul's life, David affirms his faith in his divine protector.

10, 11. The Be-erothites' crime is comparable with that of the Amalekite who claimed to have hastened Saul's death (1:1–16), so they must expect similar treatment. Their fault was not that they had harmed 'the Lord's anointed', for Ish-bosheth is never dignified in this way; nevertheless, Ish-bosheth was a *righteous* (NEB 'innocent') *man* (11), who deserved better from his subordinates. Far from applauding their deed – as they had expected him to – David will therefore take vengeance on them for Ish-bosheth's murder. And once more he distances himself from an act which, since it could so easily help his cause, might just as easily be laid at his door.[49] *reward* (10): a messenger bearing good news could expect to receive a reward from the recipient of the news (*cf.* 18:22). While Paul's discussion of the rights of the Christian preacher is based on different premises in 1 Corinthians 9:1–18, his references to his personal 'reward' for his preaching of the 'good news' (vv. 16–18) could hint at the custom reflected here.

12. A grisly exhibition is mounted in order to proclaim David's displeasure with the murderers of Ish-bosheth. For a similar case of mutilation – of a live victim – see Judges 1:6f.; for hanging of corpses, see Deuteronomy 21:22f.; Joshua 10:22–27.

7 David King of Israel (5:1–20:26)

The reigns of David and Solomon in the tenth century BC represent
the golden age in Israelite history. Then, briefly, Israel earned a
place among the imperial powers of the near east. (The fact that
the survivors of the traumas of the late Bronze Age were somnolent,
if not actually senescent, during this period was no small factor in
Israel's short-lived greatness!) David, having embarked on a series
of wars of conquest, created a small empire consisting mainly of
subject-states governed through their native rulers. Some impression of the military successes achieved can be gained from this
section, and especially from the summary given in ch. 8. First,
however, we are told how David united the kingdom, lately torn
apart by civil war, in loyalty to himself. The capture of Jerusalem,
its elevation to the status of capital, and the siting of the ark of the
covenant within its walls, were decisive steps aimed at preserving a
national unity which recognized both familial and religious ties.
The greater part of this history of David's reign is taken up,
however, with the personalia and problems of the royal family
itself. This preoccupation, which also takes in the question of the
succession, accounts for the term 'Succession Narrative' as applied
to the bulk of this section (2 Sa. 9–20; 1 Ki. 1–2, with prefatory
material from 2 Sa. 6–7). That 'succession' is too narrow a definition of the theme of these chapters is being increasingly recognized;
but the fact remains that a remarkable proportion of 2 Samuel is
taken up with the rivalries and intrigues of the royal family – with
David himself, in his lamentable affair with Bathsheba, setting the
whole thing in motion.

THE CAPTURE OF JERUSALEM (5:1–25)

Once the northern tribes had sworn allegiance to David, Hebron ceased to be a useful base of operation, if only because the new king must not seem to be favouring his own tribe. The ancient city of Jerusalem, sometimes known as Jebus (*cf.* Jdg. 19:10, *etc.*), represented both an opportunity and a challenge in this regard. It was situated in Benjaminite territory, but close to the border with Judah – and it was still in Jebusite hands.[1] Its capture and designation as David's capital city is one of the more inspired moves for which he is justly remembered.[2] The defeat and expulsion of the Philistines, following two separate engagements on Israelite soil (vv. 17–25), was also a notable achievement, and the one which most of all proved his fitness to sit upon the throne of Israel (*cf.* 3:18).[3]

1, 2. Bereft of credible leadership, the disenchanted followers of Ish-bosheth make their peace with David. Three reasons why he should have their allegiance are advanced. First, there is the tie of kinship, for David was no alien seeking to impose his rule on the northerners; he was, in Deuteronomic parlance, 'one from among (their) brethren' (Dt. 17:15). (We may compare the way in which Abimelech, son of Gideon, played on his consanguinity with the Shechemites, in order to be recognized as their king (Jdg. 9:2f.).[4]) Secondly, it is acknowledged that, even when Saul was king, David had been Israel's foremost military leader (*led out and brought in*, 2). Thirdly, David's right to rule is based on a divine decree; and, while the precise terms given here have not previously been encountered, they are implicit in much of what has already been said about David. The conception of the king as a *shepherd* has many parallels in the near eastern and classical worlds; it is a figure much used by the prophets in their depiction of kingship, both actual and ideal (*e.g.* Is. 44:28; Je. 3:15). *prince*: nāḡîḏ, as in 1 Samuel 9:16 (*q.v.*).

3. The new relationship between king and people is formalized in a *covenant* which will have spelled out the rights and duties of the respective parties. Comparison may be made with the 'political' covenant of Jehoiada, when he acted on behalf of the boy king Joash (2 Ki. 11:17), and perhaps also with the occasion described in 1 Samuel 10:25, though it is not represented as a formal covenant ceremony. *anointed*: *cf.* 2:4, referring to the men of Judah.

4, 5. Information of the kind that usually accompanies an accession notice for a new king in the books of Kings. David is now truly 'king of Israel'. *At Hebron* (5): *cf.* 2:11.

6–9. Jerusalem, an ancient city mentioned in Egyptian execration
texts of the early second millennium, as also in the fourteenth
century Amarna letters, had thus far managed to resist annexation
by the Israelites.[5] Its capture represented, therefore, the sweeping
away of the last vestiges of Canaanite resistance to domination by
the Israelites. (Appropriately, the Jebusites – as the pre-Israelite
inhabitants are called here – bring up the rear in the list of
Canaanite tribes which, according to Gn. 15:18–21, were to come
under the sway of Abraham's descendants.) David's choice of
Jerusalem as his capital city was a master-stroke. Located in
Benjaminite territory, it was, in theory at least, a suitable centre
from which he could govern the whole kingdom without seeming
unnecessarily to favour his fellow-Judahites.

6. Associated with the Israelite capture of Jerusalem is a saying
whose significance is perhaps no longer recoverable; it is omitted
in the parallel account in 1 Chronicles 11:5. Not that attempts at
elucidation have been lacking. One view is that the Jebusites placed
such confidence in the impregnability of their fortress that they
considered even the physically handicapped to be a sufficient
garrison. At a later stage the Israelites themselves came to think
of Jerusalem as indestructible, but then for theological reasons
more linked with the character of Israel's God and his relationship
with his people. It was an attitude fiercely opposed by the prophet
Jeremiah because of the way in which it blinded the citizenry to
the real danger confronting them (Je. 7:4, 8–15). Another explanation of *the blind and the lame* is that the Jebusites were announcing their intention of fighting to the last man; even the disabled
would offer resistance (so Ackroyd). There has also been an attempt
to relate the reference to a sanctions clause in a treaty which David
is supposed to have made with the Jebusites some time before he
decided to take control of the fortress. This suggestion takes its
rise from a Hittite loyalty-oath ceremony in which a blind and
deaf woman was paraded before the assembled army as a warning
of what would befall those who failed to keep the oath.[6] *his men*:
i.e. David's personal army, rather than a more representative
Israelite levy. This may explain the designation of Jerusalem as
'David's city' (*cf.* on vv. 7, 9). *the Jebusites, the inhabitants of the
land*: or, less probably, 'the Jebusite ruler of the land (or "city-
state")'.[7]

7. *Zion*, a name of uncertain meaning, probably denotes the hill
on which the fortress stood, though it has also been suggested that
it originally referred to the fortress itself. It is the south-east hill
of Jerusalem; the modern 'Mount Zion' in the south-west of the

city perpetuates a centuries-old misunderstanding. By deploying his personal army David appears to have laid special claim to Jerusalem as his own precinct (*cf.*, perhaps, 'David's spoil', 1 Sa. 30:20). Later, a psalmist rhapsodizing about this same Zion speaks of it as 'the city of the great King' (*i.e.* Yahweh, Ps. 48:2; *cf.* Mt. 5:35).

8. The stratagem by which the fortress was taken also presents a problem. RSV *water shaft* and NEB 'grappling-iron' represent but two of several attempted explanations of *ṣinnôr*, the Hebrew word in question.[8] Père L. H. Vincent early this century identified the *ṣinnôr* – the word occurs only here and in Psalm 42:7 (RSV 'cataracts') – with the water conduit which ran from the Gihon spring to the inner city.[9] (Jerusalem, like so many ancient cities, was dependent for its water-supply on a spring located outside the city walls.) It is thus often assumed that the Israelites, led by Joab, according to 1 Chronicles 11:6, gained access to the fortress-city by climbing up the shaft; comparison is sometimes made with the Romans' entering Veii by a *cuniculus* (tunnel) in 396 BC.[10] It makes a good story, but it must be admitted with Brunet that this explanation of *ṣinnôr* is far from secure. Brunet himself, taking more notice of the occurrence of the word in Psalm 42:7 than is usual, suggests that David ordered his men to take control of the water-source itself, in this way ensuring that the city would be captured without loss of blood.[11] The translation 'strike a joint' (*i.e.* render lame) was proposed by W. F. Albright,[12] but neither it nor any of the other proposals has been able to replace 'water shaft' in most scholars' affections. *to attack the lame and the blind, who are hated by David's soul*[13]: the meaning will depend on how we interpret the similar reference in verse 6. At the least, David's contempt for the Jebusite jibe of verse 6 is indicated. *the house*: presumably the temple. In this saying the writer perhaps sees justification for some such prohibition as that which prevented deformed priests from serving in the temple (*cf.* Lv. 21:18). In the Matthean reference to our Lord's healing of the blind and lame in the temple precincts, after his acclamation as king of Zion and son of David (Mt. 21:5, 9, 14), a deliberate contrast with the tenth-century conqueror of Zion seems to be drawn. See the Introduction ('King David').

9. David's choice of Jerusalem as his capital compares with the building and relocation enterprises of other great rulers in ancient history, from Sargon of Akkad to Philip of Macedon. There is some evidence to suggest that Jerusalem enjoyed the status of 'federal territory', and was administered separately from the tribal

territory that made up the rest of the kingdom.[14] While building
operations in Jerusalem and elsewhere are associated mainly with
Solomon, some improvement in the city's defences was undertaken
by David. The *Millo*, a concern also of Solomon (1 Ki. 9:15, 24;
11:27), cannot be precisely identified. The probable connection with
the Hebrew *mālē'* ('fill (in)') gives a possible clue; a construction
(tower?) built on a filled-in platform of earth or stones, or a
reference to the artificial terracing on the eastern slope of the hill
on which the ancient city stood, are the main candidates.[15]

10. The glorification of David is put into perspective: his achievement is directly attributable to Yahweh's continuing presence with
him (*cf.* v. 12). With this reiteration of a theme which has been
important in earlier chapters (see on 1 Sa. 16:18) the 'History of
David's Rise', as conceived by some scholars, reaches its conclusion. See the Introduction.

11. This aspect of David's building activity may, strictly, belong
to the later part of his reign, since Hiram I of Tyre did not become
king until about 969 BC. Hiram presided over a commercial empire
based on a maritime monopoly (*cf.* 2 Ch. 8:18), but the prosperity
of his kingdom depended heavily on the situation in the hinterland.
It was important, therefore, that Israelite expansion did not deny
Tyre and her trading partners the use of inland trade routes. Hiram,
it would seem, was guided by self-interest when he made his
generous contribution to David's palace-building. The same Hiram
entered into a trade treaty with Solomon (1 Ki. 5:12), but specific
reference to a similar arrangement with David is lacking. Even so,
relations with David could scarcely have been more amicable (*cf.*
1 Ki. 5:1). Katzenstein sees in Hiram's contribution a hint of a
regular tax paid for commercial privileges in the area ruled by
David.[16] *cedar trees*: the cedarwood of Lebanon was widely used
in building work (*cf.* 1 Ki. 5:8f.).

12. Through his successes and acclaim (*cf.* v. 11) David is
confirmed in the knowledge that he is Yahweh's chosen ruler in
Israel. *his kingdom*: possibly meaning David's own kingly rule (*cf.*
NEB 'royal power').

13–16. More family details, again illustrating the theme of
David's prosperity (*cf.* 3:2–5). With the exception of *Solomon* (14),
none of the offspring named in verses 14–16 is of any historical
interest. A slightly longer list – thirteen to the present eleven – is
given in 1 Chronicles 14:4–7.[17]

17–25. No congratulatory messages were forthcoming from the
Philistines. On the contrary, David's recognition by all the tribes
of Israel was a development which they were bound to contest.

Hitherto, we may imagine, they could view his rule in Judah with equanimity, and, so long as the relationship was not put to the test, they could even have regarded David as their vassal. There has been considerable debate as to when precisely the two engagements described in these verses took place – before or after the occupation of Jerusalem (vv. 1–9)? On the face of it, verse 17 suggests that the Philistine response may have come before David would have had opportunity to seize Jerusalem, but this may be an excessively literalistic reading of the verse. Hauer has argued that it was the capture of Jerusalem, even more than David's coronation, which attracted the Philistines' attention; he therefore accepts the relative chronology of the chapter. A point in his favour is that the Philistines come looking for David in the general area of Jerusalem.[18]

17. If *the stronghold* refers to Jerusalem, as in verses 7 and 9, the statement that David *went down* to it would be problematical. A tactical withdrawal to the stronghold of Adullam (23:14; *cf.* 1 Sa. 22:4f.) is, therefore, more likely.[19]

18. The *valley of Rephaim*, usually located to the south of Jerusalem, was noted as outstandingly fertile in the time of Isaiah of Jerusalem (Is. 17:5). One explanation of the name is that the valley was 'frequently the arena for contests involving "champions" or warriors who belonged to some special military élite or guild known in ancient Israel as *yᵉlîdhê hārāphāh* or *rᵉphā'îm*'.[20]

19. David, in accordance with his regular practice (*cf.* 2:1; 1 Sa. 23:2, 4; 30:7f.), consults Yahweh before engaging the enemy.

20. The name of the locale where the victory was won is given a new significance, for here Yahweh – represented by 'Baal', in the sense of 'master, lord' – broke through (BH *pāraṣ*) the enemy lines (*cf.* Is. 28:21). It is possible that the name *Baal-perazim* originally referred to a spring which 'broke through' the rock at that particular point; Hertzberg compares Luke 6:49 in this regard. We might also compare 'Baalath-beer' ('(Divine) Lady of the Well') in Joshua 19:8.

21. In this contest the Philistine gods have been powerless to help their devotees; they suffer the fate of the ark of the covenant on an earlier occasion (1 Sa. 4:11). Thus, under David, the lost glory of Israel is being restored. The Chronicler adds that, on David's orders, the idols ('gods') were burned (1 Ch. 14:12).[21]

22–24. When the Philistines return David employs a different tactic.

23, 24. Yahweh, the man of war (Ex. 15:3), will go into battle at the head of the Israelite contingents. His signal for attack will be the sound of *marching* (24) – rustling, presumably (*cf.* NEB) – in the tops of the *balsam trees*; compare 'the sound of chariots, and of horses, the sound of a great army' that sent the Syrians on their way (2 Ki. 7:6f.). This will throw the Philistines into confusion, as they imagine themselves caught in a *battue*.

25. After this the Philistines did not offer a serious challenge to Israel again (though see 8:1). Surprisingly, the narrator does not underline the significance of David's two victories, even though the banishment of the Philistine menace was one of the major achievements of his reign. Contrast 1 Chronicles 14:17 in this respect. The episodes recounted in the 'Samuel Appendix' (21:15–22; 23:9–17) are possibly to be dated to this period. *Geba*: the LXX and the parallel reference in 1 Chronicles 14:16 have 'Gibeon'; it may be that Chronicles is influenced by Isaiah 28:21 where, however, 'Gibeon' almost certainly recalls the events of Joshua 10.[22]

THE INSTALLATION OF THE ARK   (6:1–23)

Deposited in the house of Abinadab in Kiriath-jearim, following its return from Philistia, the 'ark of God' remained there 'a long time' (1 Sa. 7:2). However, now that the kingdom is united and the Philistines have been expelled from the land, the time has come for it to be conveyed to a more worthy resting-place in David's capital city. It was, moreover, a politically astute move on David's part, since the presence of the ark in Jerusalem would help to ensure that tribal loyalties, despite their centrifugal tendencies, focused on the capital and the ruling house. This, of course, is not stated in the chapter, which, rather, shows David attending to the regulation of divine worship as befitted one who was both secular and sacral head of state. The ark also played an important part in preserving the link between Israel's religious traditions, especially as they had developed at Shiloh, and the uncertain future under the monarchy.[23] But, whereas continuity of tradition was achievable in the religious sphere, there was one area where it was ruled out. Michal, daughter of Saul – a loyal wife to David in the past – was seriously out of sympathy with the new development and was highly contemptuous of David for his part in it. The final sentence of the chapter, which may imply some sort of judgement on Michal for her sarcasm, forecloses any possibility that David and Michal will produce an heir who will be able to unite Davidide and Saulide loyalties.

2 Samuel 6 has been described as 'undoubtedly the apogee of the ark narratives of the Old Testament',[24] a status which certainly appears to be acknowledged in the Psalter (*e.g.* Pss. 68, 132). Others detect its formative influence in Luke's account of the 'Visitation' (Lk. 1:39–56), when Mary, bearing the Christ-child, stayed with Elizabeth for three months (Lk. 1:56; *cf.* 2 Sa. 6:11).[25] The chapter has a fair number of textual problems, not all of which can be noted within the confines of this commentary. Rarely is the sense unclear; moreover, the parallel, if somewhat divergent, account in 1 Chronicles 13, 15–16 offers welcome assistance.

1. A large military escort for the returning ark is no more than we should expect, given its cultic importance and previous role in Israel's military history. It is therefore unnecessary to regard the verse as a detached introduction to an account of a military expedition such as we have in 8:1. The return of a pagan idol to its own territory could be attended with similar pomp and circumstance; how much more the ark of Yahweh![26]

2. *Baale-judah* is almost certainly a by-form of, or a corruption of, 'Baalah of Judah', another name for Kiriath-jearim (*cf.* Jos. 15:9; 1 Ch. 13:6), the place where the ark had been kept since its retrieval from the Philistines (1 Sa. 7:2). The translation of MT *ba'ªlê* by 'lords' or 'citizens', though supported in the ancient versions, is ill-advised in view of the alternative name for Kiriath-jearim.[27] The ark is that 'upon which the name of the Lord of hosts is called' (lit.), which expression at the least indicates ownership of the ark by Yahweh. In the Deuteronomic literature there is virtually a 'theology of the name', especially in relation to Yahweh's dwelling in the Jerusalem temple (*e.g.* Dt. 12:5, 11). By this means the Deuteronomic writers sought to subordinate belief in God's localized presence in the temple to the truth of his transcendence.[28] *Lord of hosts*: see on 1 Samuel 1:3. *enthroned on the cherubim*: see on 1 Samuel 4:4.

3, 4. The arrangements for the transport of the ark were much as for its journey from Ekron to Beth-shemesh, when also it was carried on a *new cart* (1 Sa. 6:7). It is noticeable that, on the resumption of the journey after Uzzah's death (vv. 12–15), there is no mention of the cart, but only of 'those who bore the ark' (v. 13; *cf.* 15:24). Therein is contained a point of no little importance in the eyes of the Chronicler: 'Because you did not carry it the first time, the Lord our God broke forth upon us, because we did not care for it in the way that is ordained' (1 Ch. 15:13). For the kind of Pentateuchal references that the Chronicler may have had in mind see Exodus 25:12–15; Numbers 4:15; 7:9; Deuteronomy 10:8.

the house of Abinadab: *cf.* 1 Samuel 7:1. *Uzzah and Ahio* are not
mentioned in 1 Samuel 7:1, where Eleazar, also a son of Abinadab,
is the sole custodian of the ark. *Ahio*, if taken as a common noun
with suffix, meaning 'his (*i.e.* Uzzah's) brother', could refer to
Eleazar. But the repetition of 'his brother' (vv. 3f.) without indication that Eleazar is intended seems unlikely.[29] (The problem is
certainly not lessened if this chapter is taken as a direct continuation
of 1 Samuel 7:2.) Uzzah and Ahio may have been younger sons,
or even grandsons, of Abinadab. McCarter (p. 169) presents a
certain amount of evidence for treating Eleazar and Uzzah as
variant forms of the same name.

5. The return of the ark is celebrated with full consort, and in a
manner that recalls the cultic acclamations of the ark in the Psalter
(*e.g.* Pss. 24:7–10; 68:24–27). *with all their might, with songs*: this
is the reading in 1 Chronicles 13:8; MT 'with all kinds of fir trees'
has few defenders.[30] *castanets* (lit. 'shakers'): possibly sistra (so
Vulgate), which are well represented in Egyptian drawings.

6–11. The destructive 'holiness' of the ark is reasserted as Uzzah
suffers the fate of the men of Beth-shemesh (*cf.* 1 Sa. 6:19), and
the project is temporarily abandoned.

6. *the threshing floor of Nacon*: or 'a certain threshing floor' (*cf.*
NEB); it is the same word as in 1 Samuel 23:23; 26:4.[31] *stumbled*:
'let (it) fall' is preferable.

7. Although *Uzzah* may be presumed to have acted on reflex,
and without sacrilegious intention, he suffered nonetheless.[32] In
fact, the clause beginning *because he put forth* is translated from
the Chronicles parallel (1 Ch. 13:10). MT's shorter text is, with
difficulty, rendered 'because of his irreverent act' (NIV), or 'for his
rash act' (NEB);[33] more probably it is a torso of a longer reading
as in Chronicles. We are perhaps intended to understand that
Uzzah's unhappy fate was attributable not simply to his acting on
impulse when the ark seemed endangered, but to the inappropriate
treatment of the ark which made the error possible in the first
place (*cf.* on vv. 3f.). Through this tragedy the men of Israel are
reminded that the ark is not an object to be handled familiarly.
David must not try to make it serve his ambitions as king and
would-be emperor; he must learn that the ark is not for manipulating. It must always command his fear and respect.

8. If David by his anger verges on impiety, the next verse speaks
of his proper fear of Yahweh, in consequence of Uzzah's death.
Perez-uzzah: this is another story which produces a name involving
the Hebrew verb *pāraṣ* ('break through'; see on 5:20). Sometimes
it is the contiguity of such catchwords which gives the clue to an

editor's arrangement of his material (compare the visit to the potter's house and the breaking of the potter's flask in Je. 18 and 19 respectively), though this is hardly necessary to explain the relationship of 2 Samuel 5 and 6.

9, 10. Frustrated in his attempt to install the ark in his capital city – while for the moment it looks less of an asset and more of a liability – David diverts it to the house of *Obed-edom* (10), who must have lived close to the scene of Uzzah's death. The most likely inference from *Gittite* is that Obed-edom (meaning 'servant of (the god?) Edom') came from the Philistine city of Gath, even though this might seem to render him an improbable guardian of the ark and an even less likely candidate for Levitical preferment (1 Ch. 15:18, 21, 24; 26:4–8). But the very improbability of the tradition may, by a familiar manner of reckoning, be the best guarantee of its historicity. Possibly Obed-edom was one of those citizens of Gath who had been attracted to David's cause during the latter's stay in Gath and district (1 Sa. 27–30; *cf.* 2 Sa. 15:18). Or possibly the ark was foisted on him without regard to either his feelings or his credentials. If Obed-edom was indeed a native of Gath, his case sheds light on the way in which foreigners could be co-opted into religious offices in the early days of the monarchy. Isaiah 56:3, 6f. (and 66:21?) is fulfilled some centuries ahead of its time! We should note, finally, that other explanations of *Gittite* are sometimes suggested, for example that Obed-edom was a native of Gath-rimmon (*cf.* Jos. 19:45; 21:24f.), or that he belonged to Gittaim, mentioned in 4:3.[34]

11. Whereas the nature of the blessing enjoyed by Obed-edom is not specified, 1 Chronicles 26:4f. credits him with eight sons, adding the comment, 'for God blessed him' (*cf.* Ps. 127:3). See also on verse 23 below.

12. News of the prosperity lately bestowed on Obed-edom and his family encourages David to think that the ark might now be safely conducted to Jerusalem. *with rejoicing*: as on the occasion of the first, abortive attempt; but now without any tragic mishap.

13. It appears that the new cart is dispensed with, and the ark carried in the prescribed manner (see on vv. 3f.). The information given here differs from that in 1 Chronicles 15:26 ('And because God helped the Levites who were carrying the ark of the covenant of the Lord, they sacrificed seven bulls and seven rams.').[35] The implication of the present verse is that thanksgiving was offered to God for an auspicious beginning to a hazardous undertaking.[36] It may well be that later ceremonies involving the ark reproduced the sort of ritual described here; this may even account for the mention of the *six paces*. David as a priest-king (*cf.* on vv. 17f.) plays the leading role in the ceremony. While it is possible to interpret *he sacrificed* to mean that David had others do it on his behalf, it is an unnecessary resort; see on 1 Samuel 13:8–12.

14, 15. As befits his present function, David wears a priestly *linen ephod* (*cf.* on 1 Sa. 2:18).[37] 1 Chronicles 15:27 also attires him in a robe of fine linen, in company with 'all the Levites who were carrying the ark'. *shouting* (*terû'â*, 15) is the word used in 1 Samuel 4:5 to describe the 'mighty shout' with which the Israelite troops welcomed the ark into the camp. Psalm 47:5 ('God has gone up with a shout, the Lord with the sound of a trumpet') either alludes to this occasion or to a ritual re-enactment of it.

16. *Cf.* verses 20–23. On the analogy of Sisera's window-gazing mother (Jdg. 5:28), Michal should be waiting to welcome a returning hero. But the joyous celebration of the day is lost on her, and she despises David in the same way that certain 'worthless fellows' had despised her own father on the day when he was acclaimed king (1 Sa. 10:27). The basic problem was that Michal did not share her husband's enthusiasm for the ark: 'like father, like daughter' (*cf.* 1 Ch. 13:3).[38]

17. A *tent* was provided for the ark, pending its installation in a permanent structure. *offered*: *cf.* on 'sacrificed' (v. 13). The burnt offering and peace offering (see on 1 Sa. 11:15) were the primordial sacrifices in the Israelite sacrificial system.

18. David, again in priestly capacity, blesses the congregation (*cf.* Nu. 6:23). It has been suggested that David's priestly functions as outlined in this chapter continue an older Jerusalemite priest-king tradition of which traces are preserved in Genesis 14:18–20 and Psalm 110.[39] In 8:18 David's sons are actually described as 'priests' (*kōhanîm*).

19. The victorious monarch dispenses largess among his subjects (*cf.* Jdg. 5:30); compare certain interpretations of Psalm 68:18 (notably Eph. 4:8), which psalm could conceivably 'have been composed for David's procession with the ark "from the house of Obed-Edom to the city of David with rejoicing" (2 Sa. 6:12)'.[40] Compare also Psalm 132:15 ('I will satisfy her poor with bread'). *a portion of meat*: perhaps 'a cake of dates' (NIV).[41] *cake of raisins*: associated with pagan fertility rites in Hosea 3:1 (*cf.* Song 2:5).[42]

20–22. Ostensibly Michal's curtain-lecture is about David's *déshabillé* as he gyrated clad only in his ephod, but her contempt for the whole of the day's proceedings seems to be implied. In reply, David vaunts his election as king in preference to Michal's father, and assures her that the maids of whom she speaks are possessed of a finer religious instinct than she either commands or allows.

20. *came out to meet*: again an echo of the theme of the returning conqueror (*cf.* 1 Sa. 18:6); but Michal has no felicitations to offer. *the king of Israel*: she stands him up to his full height in order to stress the incongruity of his behaviour.

21, 22. David refuses to give up his dancing, for it is in honour of Yahweh who put him on the throne of Israel. Where the honour of Yahweh is concerned, his own dignity is of no account.

23. A not wholly transparent conclusion to the story. Was Michal rendered infertile as a punishment for her reproof of David? Or did David break off conjugal relations with her? Or is this just 'the last painful twist of a wronged woman's fate'?[43] It is hard not to see the statement as in some way implying a punishment on Michal. Certainly, because she remains childless there can be no continuation of the rejected Saulide house (v. 21) in any offspring from her union with David. From such a consideration Leonhard Rost concluded that the so-called 'Succession Narrative' must have begun with these verses (16, 20b–23), which see the final rejection of the house of Saul and pave the way for the succession struggle within David's family.[44]

We may also observe that this apparent judgement on Michal, for the sake of the ark, is in pointed contrast to the blessing, also for the sake of the ark, of Obed-edom and his household (see on v. 11).[45]

THE DYNASTIC PROMISE   (7:1–29)

In response to David's modest proposal to build a permanent 'house' for the ark of the covenant, Yahweh announces his start-lingly generous intention of building a dynastic 'house' for David. This is the obvious way to sum up a chapter which embraces two distinct topics, both of which are represented by the frequently recurring word 'house'. As our chapter heading suggests, it is the so-called 'dynastic oracle' (vv. 8–16) that takes pride of place, and such is its importance that 2 Samuel 7 is rightly regarded as an 'ideological summit', not only in the 'Deuteronomistic History' but also in the Old Testament as a whole. The Nathan oracle constitutes the title-deed of the Davidic house to the rule of Israel and Judah, which rule it did indeed exercise over Judah for fully four centuries. Throughout that period celebration of Yahweh's bestowal of the Davidic house upon Judah figured prominently in the community's

worship, so that, even when the reigning Davidide fell short of
expectation, the remembered greatness of David and the hope of
a glorious restoration remained as a potential source of inspiration.

The hymnic references to the Nathan oracle in the Old Testament
are correct in speaking of a 'covenant', though the word is a
surprising absentee from this chapter (see 2 Sa. 23:5; Pss. 89:3, 28,
34; 132:12). It is, moreover, a promissory covenant, by which it is
meant that Yahweh's favour is not made conditional upon the
fulfilment of certain obligations by David or his successors. In this
respect, as in some points of detail (see the commentary), the
Davidic covenant can be compared with the Abrahamic covenant
as outlined in Genesis 15. Inevitably, the repeated stumblings of
David's successors, culminating in their removal altogether from
power, called in question the validity of the dynastic covenant.
But, long before the final act, the conviction that there must be a
reconstitution of the 'Davidic hope' was being voiced. The looked-
for deliverer would be 'a shoot from the stump of Jesse' (Is. 11:1);
it would be a case of 'back to Bethlehem' (cf. Mi. 5:2). We shall
not be exaggerating the importance of the Nathan oracle, therefore,
if we see it as the matrix of biblical messianism.

To take account of the numerous literary-critical analyses of
2 Samuel 7, and, in particular, of the attempts to discover an
original 'core' within the Nathan oracle, would be impossible
within the limits of this commentary. We may simply take as a
testimonial to the importance of the chapter the wide-ranging
comparisons – many of them fruitful and by no means mutually
exclusive – that have been made with near eastern literary forms
of various types. See the Introduction ('King David').[46]

1. Thematically the chapter follows on naturally from the preceding narrative: the ark has been brought to Jerusalem, and David
wants to provide the appropriate accommodation for it. He is
shown acting in the spirit of Deuteronomy 12:10f., which decrees
that, when peace has been won, the people of Israel must frequent
the central sanctuary as occasion demanded. In terms of strict
chronology the chapter belongs later, for the story of David's wars
and conquests is still largely untold.

2, 3. David, who is a fairly typical near eastern king in this
regard, wants to crown his external achievements with the erection
of a temple to Yahweh who has granted him his victories. In the
ancient world, moreover, a god who lacked a proper temple was
in danger of being regarded as cultically inferior. *in a tent*: 'housed
in curtains' (NEB) is nearer the literal sense. *Nathan*, sometimes
called a 'court prophet' because of his semi-official status in David's

court, readily agrees with the proposition. In other countries it had long been considered the responsibility of kings both to build and to maintain the dwellings of the gods. But for all his prompt complaisance, Nathan is not to be compared with the kind of fawning time-servers who surrounded Ahab and told him what he wanted to hear (1 Ki. 22:6); his subsequent behaviour here, as also in ch. 12, puts him in a different class.

4–17. Permission to build a temple is withdrawn, partly on the ground that Yahweh has never been dependent upon a permanent structure for his well-being, and partly because the 'rest' of verse 1 is only relative, since there are still enemies to be overcome before Israel can attain to what Yahweh has in mind for her (vv. 9f.). It is then disclosed that Yahweh will build a 'house' (*i.e.* dynasty) for David, and that David's son and immediate successor will have the honour of building the temple that David has in mind. It by no means follows from this that the section is racked by contrary evaluations of the innovation that was the temple, though we need not doubt that it had both its supporters and its detractors. Those of a Rechabite cast of mind, for example, will have seen it as a betrayal of traditional Yahwism and a dangerous assimilation to contemporary pagan practice (*cf.* Je. 35:1–17). And their successors could have appealed to history in their defence. Our text, however, is more concerned with safeguards. The transition from tent-shrine to temple will come, but *in God's time*, and not as a favour from David. What held good among Israel's neighbours must apply in Israel: the initiative for temple-building belongs to the deity.[47] This, after all, is how it is in the account of the building of the tabernacle (Ex. 25:8f.).

5. David is let down gently. *my servant*, as a title granted to an exclusive few (*cf.* 'my servant Moses'), underlines the fact that, though David's plan is rejected, his person is not. Nor is the rejection expressed in a blunt negative; it is done obliquely, in the form of a question (contrast the version given in 1 Ch. 17:4).[48]

6, 7. Not only has Yahweh never *dwelt* in a temple since Israel became a nation, he has never given instructions that one should be built. In keeping with what has been said above, we note the emphasis on Yahweh's right to initiate in the matter of temple-building. It is clear that, despite its description as a *hêkāl* ('temple') in 1 Samuel 1:9, the Shiloh sanctuary does not come into the category of 'permanent house' at this point.[49] It is, in any case, associated with the period of 'unrest' which has yet to run its course (vv. 9f.).[50] *judges* (7) differs by a single consonant from MT 'tribes', and is supported by 1 Chronicles 17:6. Some adduce a

similar meaning for MT unemended.[51] While the judges are not
elsewhere described as shepherding Israel, the point of *commanded
to shepherd* may be that *functionally* they were on a par with David
(*cf.* 5:2), and yet none of them felt the same impulse to build a
temple.

8–11. David is reminded of Yahweh's initiatives in the past, as
he has experienced them in his own life, and learns that the future
depends, equally, on Yahweh's 'I will'.

8, 9a. Those who compare the Nathan oracle with the near
eastern vassal treaties draw attention to the correspondence
between these verses and that section of the treaties which records
the past benefits conferred by the overlord upon his vassal.[52]

9b. *a great name*: compare the promise to Abraham (Gn. 12:2).
It is unwise to try to equate the expression with its literal equivalent
in Egyptian, *ren wer*, since, although the latter is used in relation
to kings, it has the technical sense of 'titulary', which is plainly
unsuitable here.[53] The change from past tense to future midway
through this verse – compare also verses 10f. – indicates that there
is a level of achievement which David and Israel, victorious though
they have been, have still to reach (*cf.* 8:13, 'won a name for
himself').[54]

10. 'There remains a sabbath rest for the people of God' (Heb.
4:9). The writer of Hebrews and our present passage have a not
dissimilar view of that 'rest' (*cf.* v. 11) into which Joshua brought
the people of Israel. So here Yahweh speaks as if the entry into
Canaan lay in the future. This perspective will have held special
interest for the generation of the exile, for whom the sequence of
exodus and entry had, literally, to be re-enacted – then in fulfilment
of a promised 'new exodus', as preached in, for example, Isaiah
40–55. *plant*: cf. Psalms 44:2; 80:8, 15; Jeremiah 2:21. If, on
the other hand, *place* (*māqôm*) is given the restricted sense of
'sanctuary', it is possible to interpret the whole verse in relation to
the future building of the temple.[55] '*will plant* it' (lit.) would then
be applying a figure used elsewhere of a tent (Dn. 11:45, MT) to
this more permanent construction, and the reference to *violent men*
would recall the (presumed) destruction of the Shiloh sanctuary.
On balance, however, it is better to interpret *place* of the land.

11. *Moreover*: the main theme of the oracle, Yahweh's building
of a dynasty (*house*) for David, is introduced.

12. The reference is to Solomon, as verse 13 makes clear. *who
shall come forth from your body* parallels an expression in Genesis
15:4 (RSV 'your own son' obscures the parallel) and alerts us to
the reciprocity of the Abrahamic and Davidic covenant traditions

(*cf.* on v. 9). The age of David and Solomon was regarded as, in many respects, fulfilling the promises made to Abraham; compare, for example, 1 Kings 4:20 with Genesis 22:17. Like Abraham, David is receiving promises concerning a son as yet unborn (see 12:24).[56] *offspring*[57] translates the Hebrew *zera'* (AV 'seed'), which usually has a collective sense but which seems to be individualized here, just as in Paul's interpretation of the same word in the promise to Abraham (Gal. 3:16; *cf.* Gn. 12:7); see also on 1 Samuel 1:11.

13. *He* is emphatic in the Hebrew, answering to the similar use of the pronoun in 'Would *you*' in verse 5.[58] Solomon is, therefore, nominated by Yahweh as the builder of his temple. No explicit reason for the passing over of David, in connection with the temple, is offered in this chapter. But in another part of the 'Deuteronomistic History' this decision of Yahweh is explained in terms of the incomplete 'rest' with which our chapter has already associated David (vv. 9b–11a). In 1 Kings 5:3 Solomon tells Hiram of Tyre that his father was unable to build the temple 'because of the warfare with which his enemies surrounded him, until the Lord put them under the soles of his feet'. The Chronicler links the interdict more with the fact that David as a warrior had shed blood and was on that account unfitted for the task of erecting a temple in Yahweh's honour (1 Ch. 22:8f.; 28:2f.). *for my name* is sometimes taken as an expression of the Deuteronomic 'name theology' (see on 6:2). 1 Chronicles 17:12 has simply 'for me'.[59] *and I will establish the throne of his kingdom for ever*: compare the 'messianic' terms of Isaiah 9:7.

14. Formally the language of the verse suggests notions of kingship such as are represented in other parts of the ancient near east – for example, the idea that, on accession, a king was adopted by the chief god of the pantheon as his son.[60] However, while such comparisons permit some insight into the favoured status of the Israelite king, there is never any thought – neither here nor in analogous passages such as Psalms 2:7; 89:26f. – of the deification of the monarch as, most famously, in the kingship ideology of ancient Egypt. As Yahweh's 'son', the Davidic king was to enjoy a unique relationship with Yahweh, but one which would bring him all the more firmly within the constraints of Yahweh's fatherly discipline (*chasten*; *cf.* Heb. 12:7–9). A broad comparison may also be drawn between this father-son relationship and the suzerain–vassal relationships of the near eastern vassal treaties.[61] As Yahweh's 'vassal', the Davidic king had to show the same kind of allegiance to his Lord as had the political vassal to his overlord.

Since it is Solomon who is principally in view at this point, it is
noteworthy that the Chronicler regarded Solomon as having supplied the necessary obedience – so much so that he does not
reproduce the disciplinary clauses of this verse in 1 Chronicles
17:13! This matter of Solomon's obedience has, as far as the
Chronicler is concerned, an important bearing on the vitality of
the Davidic covenant in later centuries.[62] 2 Samuel 7:14 itself was
not lacking in vitality in later times. A fragment of a commentary
on this chapter, found at Qumran, identifies the referent of the
verse with the Davidic Messiah,[63] while the author of Hebrews
finds a common Christological significance in our verse and in
Psalm 2:7 (Heb. 1:5). *with the rod of men*: paraphrased in NEB's
'as any father might'. Or are we to think of Yahweh's discipline
being applied through human agency (*cf.* Is. 10:5)? (As 2 Samuel
proceeds to show, David himself knew as much of the disciplinary
hand of Yahweh as did any of his successors.)

15, 16. The Davidic covenant as defined here is unconditional:
the Davidic king may be disciplined, but he will not be set aside.[64]
Whereas Saul fell because of disobedience (1 Sa. 13:13; 15:22f.),
the Davidic covenant introduces a 'better hope' in that it faces up
to such an eventuality and assures that Yahweh will deal mercifully
with the fallible successor(s) of David. Whatever apparent conditionalizing of the unconditional may subsequently have taken place
(*cf.* 1 Ki. 9:6–9; Ps. 132:12; and see on 1 Sa. 2:30), the Davidic
promise as enunciated in these verses gave birth to a 'Davidic hope'
which even the destruction of Jerusalem and Judah could not
deny – witness, for example, the above-mentioned Qumran text (v.
14) – and which Christians believe to have been fulfilled in Jesus
of Nazareth (*cf.* Lk. 1:69f.). *made sure* (*ne'man*, 16): arguably the
keynote verb as far as the Davidic dynasty is concerned (*cf.* 1 Sa.
25:28). In the famous interview between Isaiah and king Ahaz of
Judah recorded in Isaiah 7, the prophet, by word-play on the same
Hebrew root ('believe' and 'established', v. 9), appears to threaten
the disestablishment of the Davidic house.

17. *vision*: *cf.* 'night' (v. 4); Psalm 89:19 perhaps refers to this
occasion.

18–19. David's prayer makes no allusion to the house that he
had proposed to build for Yahweh. Instead, it concentrates on the
magnificent kindness of Yahweh that thought to establish an
unending dynasty for his servant.

18. David's response to the oracle is possibly made in the tent-
shrine (*before the Lord*) which he had commissioned for the ark of
the covenant (6:17). It at once strikes a self-deprecatory note; this

is far more than the offer of a king's daughter in marriage (1 Sa. 18:18)! It has been suggested that David's *sitting* before Yahweh was in accordance with the prerogative of the Davidic kings (*cf.* Ps. 110:1); contrast the necessity for the Aaronide priests to stand while officiating in the sanctuary (*cf.* Heb. 10:11f.).[65]

19. *and hast shown me future generations*: MT has a compact phrase which translates literally as 'and this (is) the law of men', and which has been interpreted to mean that the ramifications of Yahweh's beneficent covenant with David would be worldwide.[66] But the text is obscure and this is not the only way in which it has been taken (*cf.* NIV 'Is this your usual way of dealing with man?'). 1 Chronicles 17:17 has a conspicuously different reading which itself is not easy to translate. (RSV, representing an emended text foreign to both passages, renders as here.)

21. (*thy own) heart*: or, perhaps, 'will' (*cf.* NIV and see on 1 Sa. 13:14). If there was nothing meritorious in David (vv. 18, 20), then the explanation of Yahweh's kindness must lie in his own will and purpose (*cf.* Dt. 7:7f.).

22. An explicit statement of monotheism – among the first in the Old Testament, according to J. F. A. Sawyer.[67] We have, in fact, met a similar declaration in 'Hannah's Song' (1 Sa. 2:2).

23, 24. The idea of Yahweh's incomparability leads to the realization that Israel, his people, are uniquely favoured. In the eighth century Amos declared that Yahweh was concerned with the welfare of peoples other than Israel: even the Philistines and Syrians had known their 'exoduses' (Am. 9:7). But Amos also recognized Israel's unique status as a nation specially chosen by Yahweh (Am. 3:2). And, as verse 23 maintains, no nation had experienced Yahweh's delivering power as had Israel at the time of the exodus and settlement. This national self-consciousness was, if anything, heightened by the experience of the Babylonian exile: 'Because you are precious in my eyes, and honoured, and I love you, I give men in return for you, peoples in exchange for your life' (Is. 43:4). There are several textual cruces in verse 23, some of them perhaps caused by an editorial, or scribal, aversion to mention of other gods. The same may apply to the variant 'and tents' (4QSam[a], LXX) at the end of the verse.[68] RSV's omission of 'whom thou didst redeem for thyself from Egypt' (*cf.* fn.) is unwarranted (*cf.* NEB, NIV). *thy people . . . their God* (24): *cf.* Leviticus 26:12, *etc.*

25–29. The prayer reverts to the main theme of the dynastic promise, for the prosperity of the nation depends upon the prosperity of its ruling house. By covenanting to establish David's dynasty, moreover, Yahweh has inaugurated an important new phase in his saving purpose for Israel. And through his choice of David and his family he will enhance his own reputation still further (v. 26).

27. Repetition of the key words in Yahweh's communication – *I will build you a house* – serves to 'remind' him of his self-imposed undertaking.

28, 29. Yahweh is called upon to fulfil his promise. The invocation will have had a particular poignancy in the exilic period when Yahweh's will, or capacity, to redeem his promises seemed in doubt. Thus Psalm 89, which begins with a celebration of the covenant with David, switches dramatically to expostulation with Yahweh concerning his renunciation of the covenant, now that Judah lies in ruins (Ps. 89:38ff.). *good thing* (*ṭôḇâ*, 28): a word which has covenantal associations, and which is sometimes virtually a synonym for 'covenant'; see on 1 Samuel 25:30.[69]

DAVID'S CAMPAIGNS   (8:1–18)

David's military and administrative archives provide the raw material for this chapter. The emphasis is on the military, as David campaigns in regions west (v. 1), east (v. 2), north (vv. 3–11), and south (vv. 13f.) of Israel. Twice it is affirmed that his rampant victories came from Yahweh (vv. 6, 14). It undoubtedly was a help that none of the great powers of the near east was able, or was disposed, to contest the areas in which David showed interest.

1. *After this* may have as much of a theological as an historical significance, if it is intended to relate the successes that are about to be described to the personal and dynastic promises of the previous chapter (*cf.* on v. 13). (It is possible that the verse is summarizing the engagements described in 5:17–25 or, perhaps, a subsequent encounter.) *Metheg-ammah* as a place-name is not otherwise attested; 1 Chronicles 18:1 has 'Gath and its villages', which could derive from an interpretation of a text closer to our own than at first sight seems likely.[70] Various explanations of MT *meṯeḡ hā'ammâ*, assuming for both words the status of common nouns, have been attempted without success. Although the Philistines were *subdued* (*cf.* on 1 Sa. 7:13), there does not appear to have been any attempt to reduce them to vassalage as in some of the other cases described in this chapter.

2. This savage and arbitrary treatment of the Moabites comes unexpectedly in view of David's happier relations with Moab at an earlier stage in his career (1 Sa. 22:3f.). (According to the genealogical data at the end of the book of Ruth, he was the great-grandson of Ruth the Moabitess (Ru. 4:17).) In 1 Chronicles 18:2 this feature of the Moabite campaign is not mentioned. The amount of *tribute* is not indicated; for a later period when Moab was subject to Ahab of Israel we have the information given in 2 Kings 3:4. For lot-casting by *line* (or 'cord') see Micah 2:5. In the Old Testament the practice is most often associated with the measuring and allocation of land (Jos. 19:51; Ps. 16:6).

3–10. David's campaigns in regions to the north of Israel are reviewed briefly. Because of its strategic and commercial importance, this area attracted the attention of all the great near eastern powers at one time or another during the last two millennia BC. Late in the second millennium large numbers of Aramaeans, who were of the same Semitic stock as the Hebrews, had settled in Syria, establishing petty kingdoms whose chief claim to fame lay in their trading activity. Zobah (v. 3), Damascus (v. 5), and, after a fashion, the neo-Hittite Hamath (v. 9) were members of this 'Aramaean' bloc which, from the evidence before us, sometimes united against a common enemy (v. 5), and sometimes fell victim to bouts of bickering (v. 10).

3. At this point Zobah was the most powerful of these Aramaean states,[71] and it was while its king was going to reinforce his control in the Euphrates region that David made his attack. *to restore his power*: 1 Chronicles 18:3 has 'to set up his monument' (*cf.* LXX here), referring to the erection of a victory stele (*cf.* NEB and see 1 Sa. 15:12); consonantally the two readings differ by a single letter (*lᵉhāšîb*, 'restore', and *lᵉhaṣṣîb*, 'set up'). For BH *yād*, 'hand, power', in the sense of 'monument' see 1 Samuel 15:12; 2 Samuel 18:18. The implications for the strength of Hadadezer's kingdom are much the same, whichever of the two readings we accept.

4. The hamstringing of all but a hundred or two of Hadadezer's *chariot horses* reflects David's dependence upon his infantry, and may or may not point to a blind spot in his military strategy. The military advantages of horses and chariotry were certainly appreciated outside Israel, as this reference shows. Already in the fifteenth century BC the New Kingdom emperors in Egypt prized the war-horse, relying on their Syrian campaigns to build up their stock: 'a major campaign might produce an average of some two hundred horses and a hundred chariots'.[72] Therefore, and particularly in the light of Joshua 11:6, 9, where Joshua hamstrings the enemies' horses at the command of Yahweh, it may be necessary to read David's action against the background of the 'holy war'.[73]

In Deuteronomic law, moreover, there is a prohibition on the king's acquiring great numbers of horses for himself (Dt. 17:16); part of the rationale for this may be as in Psalm 20:6. In fact, it is David's rebel sons Absalom and Adonijah who are the first in Israel to make use of chariots and horses (15:1; 1 Ki. 1:5). Solomon was the great trader in horses, and the chariot cities which he built formed the backbone of his country's defence (1 Ki. 10:26–29).

5, 6. The kingdom of *Damascus* (*Aram of Damascus* in v. 6) expresses solidarity with its Aramaean brother Hadadezer. *help* (5) resonates here, since the name *Hadadezer* means '(the god) Hadad (is) help' – an ineffectual helper, in contrast with Yahweh (6). Damascus lay to the south of Zobah, and was therefore that much nearer to David's kingdom. Its reward for intervening was to be reduced to tributary status; Israelite *garrisons* (6) were left to check the belligerent tendencies of the Aramaeans. *the Lord gave victory*: *cf.* verse 14.

7, 8. David gains some useful metal at the expense of Hadadezer and his domain. For *shields* (7) NEB has 'quivers', which is the translation favoured by R. Borger after a careful survey of biblical and non-biblical material.[74] 4QSam[a] and the LXX have a long addition which says that these same items were taken away by Shishak, king of Egypt, when he came up to Jerusalem in the days of Rehoboam; the note recalls 1 Kings 14:26, though it is not a simple reproduction of what is stated there.[75] *bronze* (8): used by Solomon for the making of various items in connection with the temple, according to the LXX and 1 Chronicles 18:8; *cf.* on verse 11. Little is known of *Betah* (Tibhath in 1 Ch. 18:8) or *Berothai*. The latter is probably the same as Berothah in Ezekiel 47:16 (perhaps mod. Bereitan, south of Baalbek), and both are probably to be located in the Lebanese Beqa.[76] While the bronze in question could have been imported stock, ancient Lebanon appears to have had its own copper supplies.[77]

9, 10. The little kingdom of *Hamath* lay between Zobah and the Euphrates and may be presumed, in the light of verse 3, to have suffered from Hadadezer's imperialist ambitions. *Toi* had therefore good reason to feel grateful to David. He may also have reckoned that David was now master of the Levant and should be offered sizeable tokens of loyalty. The name of Toi's son appears here as *Joram* ('Yahweh is exalted', Jô/Yô being a shortened form of the divine name), and in 1 Chronicles 18:10 as Hadoram ('Hadad is exalted'). Since it is unlikely that a Hamathite would be named in honour of Yahweh in the first instance, it is possible that Hadoram, on his accession to the throne, had his name changed by either

David or Solomon in token of his vassal status.[78] The obvious comparisons would, in that case, be with the Judaean kings Jehoiakim (originally Eliakim) and Zedekiah (originally Mattaniah) in the Babylonian period. Failing that, 'the divine name Hadad was simply paraphrased with an Israelite one'.[79]

11, 12. The spoils of war and the diplomatic gifts are alike dedicated *to the Lord* as the giver of David's success (*cf.* vv. 6, 14). If this dedication is not to be viewed negatively, as merely the withholding of the material from profane use, then we may see in verse 11 a hint of what becomes explicit in Chronicles, viz. that David made lavish preparations for the building of the temple (*cf.* 1 Ch. 22:2–5). The list of conquests in verse 12 includes most of Israel's familiar enemies (*cf.* Saul's list in 1 Sa. 14:47f.). The mention of victories over *Edom*[80] and *Ammon* is anticipatory: for Edom see verses 13f., and for Ammon chs. 10–12. Successful expeditions against *Moab*, the *Philistines*, and *Zobah* have already been noted in the chapter (vv. 1–8). There is no account of a victory over the *Amalekites* subsequent to that described in 1 Samuel 30.

13, 14. *won a name* (13) seems to view David's achievements against the background of the dynastic promise of ch. 7 (especially v. 9). RSV rightly corrects MT 'Aramaeans' to *Edomites* (*cf.* LXX and 1 Ch. 18:13); the names 'Aram' and 'Edom' can be almost indistinguishable in an unvocalized Hebrew manuscript.[81] This alteration is supported by the mention of the *Valley of Salt* (*cf.* 2 Ki. 14:7), which lay somewhere to the south, or south-west, of the Dead Sea. The same campaign may also be commemorated in the superscription to Psalm 60, though there the number of the slain is given as twelve thousand and the victory is associated with the name of Joab (*cf.* 1 Ki. 11:15; in 1 Ch. 18:12 Abishai is named as the commander responsible). At any rate, the association of a victory now with a king and elsewhere with his commanding officer does not in itself pose a problem (*cf.* 1 Sa. 13:3f.). *Edom* (14), a small country to the south-east of Judah, was easily annexed in periods of Israelite strength. The fact that it could regain its independence while Solomon was still alive therefore augured ill for the empire (1 Ki. 11:14–22). The posting of *garrisons* (*cf.* v. 6) in subject areas meant that trade routes were protected, and that tribute could be levied on a regular basis. *the Lord gave victory*: *cf.* verse 6.

15. David is presented as the ideal ruler administering a unified kingdom in accordance with the principles of *justice* and *equity*. These characteristics of divine rule (Ps. 99:4) were required in Yahweh's earthly representative (Pss. 45:6f.; 72:1f.). Failure in this

regard is later noted as a cause of David's unpopularity, and as a
contributory factor in Absalom's rebellion (15:2–6).

16–18. A list of the chief officials in David's administration.
Bureaucracy is still in its infancy compared with what it became
under Solomon, but the main terms and the trend are already
established. See also 20:23–26.

16. *Joab* was commander of the army, though we still have to
think of David as commander-in-chief. 1 Chronicles 11:6 links
Joab's promotion with his part in the capture of Jerusalem. At the
end of the reign Joab supported Adonijah's bid for the throne and,
inevitably, fell foul of Solomon (1 Ki. 1–2). This is the first reference
to the office of *recorder* (*mazkîr*). Nothing much may be gleaned
from the occurrences of the term in the Old Testament. One
suggestion, based largely on Egyptian analogy, is that the *mazkîr*
was a royal herald.[82]

17. *Zadok* has not previously been mentioned in the books of
Samuel. In 1 Chronicles 6:3–8 he is again described as a *son of
Ahitub*, and his genealogy is traced back to Eleazar and Aaron.[83]
It is surprising that he is not mentioned in the account of Saul's
destruction of Nob; only Abiathar the son of Ahimelech is said to
have escaped that massacre (1 Sa. 22:20). In explanation of this it
has been propounded that Zadok was the chief priest in Jerusalem
before its seizure by the Israelites, and that his retention in office
represents the integration of the old Jerusalemite cultus (*cf.* Gn.
14:18–20; Ps. 110:4) into the Israelite religion.[84] It might not be
coincidental, then, that Zadok's name reproduces an element which
occurs in the names of two early Jerusalemite kings, Melchi*zedek*
(Gn. 14:18) and Adoni*zedek* (Jos. 10:1; perhaps also Adoni-bezek
in Jdg. 1:5–7, if the name originally was Adonizedek). Although
speculative, it is a serious attempt to deal with a real problem.
The mention of *Ahimelech the son of Abiathar* arouses suspicion.
Normally Zadok's colleague is named as Abiathar son of Ahimelech, the survivor of the destruction of Nob (1 Sa. 22:20; 2 Sa.
15:24, 29). It is therefore probable that the names of father and
son have been accidentally transposed (*cf.* NEB).[85] *Abiathar* held
office throughout David's reign, only to be unfrocked by Solomon
because of his identification with Adonijah's cause (1 Ki. 2:35).
Seraiah, the royal *secretary* (*sôp̄ēr*), will have been responsible
for the king's correspondence, both domestic and foreign. This
particular incumbent's name appears as Sheva in 20:25 and as
Shavsha in 1 Chronicles 18:16 (Shisha in 1 Ki. 4:3 is probably
another variant). The form Shavsha has been connected with the
Egyptian *sš-š't* ('letter-scribe'), and, since there is no mention of

the man's father, it has even been suggested that he himself was an Egyptian.[86] In view of the Egyptians' long experience in the scribal and administrative aspects of monarchy, the hiring of an Egyptian for this task would have been a sensible arrangement. If Shisha in 1 Kings 4:3 represents another form of the name, then the family tradition of royal service was continued under Solomon.

18. Royal bodyguards were often made up of foreigners whose personal loyalty to the king was less likely to be adulterated by involvement in national politics (*cf.* 1 Sa. 28:2). The *Cherethites* probably originated in Crete, coming to Palestine as part of that migration of 'Sea Peoples' which also saw the arrival of the Philistines in the Levant at the beginning of the Iron Age (*c.* 1200 BC).[87] See on 1 Samuel 4:1; 30:14. *Pelethites*: the Hebrew $p^e l \bar{e} t \hat{i}$ is possibly a dialectal variant of $p^e l i \check{s} t \hat{i}$ ('Philistine'), or has been assimilated to $k^e r \bar{e} t \hat{i}$ (Cherethite(s)) with which it always occurs. J. Strange offers another explanation, viz. that the two groups are special classes of soldiers – 'butchers' (*cf.* BH *ṭabbāḥ*, 'butcher', 'guard') and 'élite-soldiers'.[88] But 'Cherethites' in 1 Samuel 30:14 must refer to a tribal or ethnic group. *Benaiah* remained loyal during the conspiracies of Absalom and Adonijah, and, by command of Solomon, replaced Joab as army commander (1 Ki. 2:35). *David's sons were priests* ($k\bar{o}h^a n\hat{i}m$): but how did their office or function relate to those of Zadok and Abiathar (v. 17)? If David's kingship also conferred priestly prerogatives upon him (*cf.* 6:17f.), possibly in continuation of a Jerusalemite priest-king tradition (*cf.* on v. 17), the designation of his sons as priests would have a possible explanation.[89] 1 Chronicles 18:17 has a periphrasis, '(were) the chief officials in the service of the king', from which it has been concluded that the original reading here was $s\bar{o}k^e n\hat{i}m$ ('stewards', as of Shebna in Is. 22:15).[90] However, the Chronicler's explanation could as easily be a paraphrase of 'priests' as of 'stewards' (*cf.* Zc. 6:13). The fact that the Chronicler had to acknowledge that David and Solomon performed priestly functions does not automatically mean that he would have been happy with the description of David's sons as 'priests'; even David and Solomon do not have that term applied to them. Moreover, the LXX, far from corroborating an 'Old Palestinian' reading indirectly attested in 1 Chronicles 18:17, may actually be influenced by the Chronicles reference (*aularchai*, 'chiefs of court' for (lit.) 'first (or "chief") at the side of the king'); it would not be the first time that LXX Samuel gave evidence of having been thus influenced.

MEPHIBOSHETH, SON OF JONATHAN   (9:1–13)

'When the Lord cuts off every one of the enemies of David from the face of the earth, let not the name of Jonathan be cut off from the house of David' (1 Sa. 20:15f.). This plea by his friend Jonathan forms the background to David's display of magnanimity towards Mephibosheth, whom he brings from the obscurity of Lo-debar to an honoured place at court. If, as is sometimes argued, the real motive was the desire to keep an eye on Mephibosheth, the plan might easily have backfired (*cf.* 16:3). Discussion of the relationship, if any, between this chapter and 21:1–14 tends to be inconclusive. It is held by some scholars that the events of 21:1–14 are presupposed here, since David's inquiry (9:1) only makes sense if the other members of Saul's house have already been eliminated. D. M. Gunn, on the other hand, regards the deaths of Abner and Ish-bosheth (chs. 3–4) as providing the explanation for David's question: David is asking about figures 'of public or political standing'.[91] The mention of Mephibosheth in 21:7 certainly assumes David's awareness of his existence at the time of that particular episode, though the verse is sometimes taken as a harmonizing cross-reference. We should also note that 2 Samuel 9:1 has usually been regarded as the beginning of the main body of the so-called 'Succession Narrative' (see the Introduction).

1. David is now in a position to fulfil his long-standing promise to Jonathan (1 Sa. 20:14–17). But this is also a gesture towards the disgruntled Saulide faction in general, as the repeated references to *the house of Saul* (*cf.* vv. 2f.) suggest. *kindness* answers to 'loyal love' and 'loyalty' in 1 Samuel 20:14f. where also the Hebrew is *ḥeseḏ*.

3. *the kindness of God* picks up Jonathan's reference to 'the loyal love of the Lord' in 1 Samuel 20:14. It is 'the kindness imposed by God in the obligation of the oath' (Smith); *cf.* NEB 'the kindness that God requires'. The attribution of a superlative force to 'of God', as if the expression meant 'outstanding kindness', is therefore unhelpful.

4. Mephibosheth was living in Transjordan. *Lo-debar*, which is very difficult to locate precisely,[92] was within reasonable distance of Mahanaim, Ish-bosheth's capital (*cf.* 17:27; Jos. 13:26(?)). On the evidence of 17:27–29, *Machir* was a man of means. Other occurrences of the name link it with the tribe of Manasseh and its sub-tribe the Gileadites, who occupied areas in Transjordan (Gn. 50:23; Nu. 26:29; Jos. 17:1).[93] For the name *Mephibosheth* see on 2:8; 4:4.

6, 7. This summons to the palace brings unexpected favours; Mephibosheth is not going to be treated as a rival who had best be destroyed in the interests of David's continued rule. On the contrary, the private property of king Saul, his grandfather, is to be handed over to him. This could have been a substantial benefaction, if the inventory of 'king David's property' in 1 Chronicles 27:25–31 is anything to go by (cf. on v. 10).[94] And further, Mephibosheth is to enjoy the right of 'pension' at the king's table (cf. 1 Ki. 18:19; 2 Ki. 25:29).[95]

8. *dead dog*: cf. 1 Samuel 24:14. For similarly self-deprecating uses of 'dog' see 2 Kings 8:13 and Lachish Ostracon VI ('Who is thy servant (but) a dog?').[96] Conventional though it is, the expression suitably describes Mephibosheth's position of complete dependence upon David's mercy. In 19:28 he amplifies it with the admission that all his father's house 'were but men doomed to death'.

9. Ziba is appointed as Mephibosheth's estate manager. *servant* (*na'ar*) could be translated 'steward' as in the legends of some seal impressions found on Palestinian sites (*e.g.* 'Eliakim steward of Jehoiachin').[97] *son*: used for 'grandson' (*cf.* NEB).[98]

10. The reference to Ziba's *fifteen sons and twenty servants* indicates that a considerable amount of property is involved. *your master's son*: some Greek manuscripts have 'your master's *house*', which has the merit of relieving the tension with the following statement that Mephibosheth would dine at the king's expense. NEB accepts the alternative reading.

12. Nothing further is known of *Mica*, apart from some genealogical details in 1 Chronicles 8:34f.; 9:40f. Since Mephibosheth was five years old at the time of Gilboa (4:4), Mica will not have been born until well into David's reign. Hertzberg thinks that this mention of him is 'intended to indicate how right it was of David to keep watch on this possible claimant to the throne. Events could have gone the same way as in the later history of the kings (II Kings 11), where a child who grew up in secret caused the downfall of the queen.' Stolz, however, attaches a less sinister significance to this reference to Mica: the covenant between Jonathan and David will bring blessing not only upon Mephibosheth, but also upon subsequent generations of Jonathan's descendants.

AMMONITES AND ARAMAEANS   (10:1–19)

An insult delivered by the newly-crowned king of Ammon brings him into conflict with David, who, it may be judged, was not averse to expanding his empire in an eastward direction, especially since outright subjugation of the Philistines to the west appears to have been regarded as unfeasible.[99] However, because of the Aramaeans' rallying to the support of the Ammonites, attention finally fixes on the Aramaean states whose subjection to David has already been noted in 8:3–8. Since it is difficult to imagine how there could have been a recrudescence of Aramaean activity in the aftermath of the defeats of 8:3–8, the relationship of that passage to the present chapter is problematical. One theory is that 8:3–8 and 10:15–19 are parallel, but considerably discordant, accounts of the same events. An alternative view which accommodates the respective sets of data more satisfactorily relates 8:3–8 to a third, and final, Israelite campaign against the Aramaeans (see on vv. 15–19).

1, 2. The *Nahash* whose death marked the end of friendly relations between Israel and Ammon was, presumably, the Ammonite king whom Saul defeated at Jabesh-gilead (1 Sa. 11). The cordiality between David and Nahash may, indeed, be not improbably traced to the time when David was on the run from Saul. There is no reference to a treaty between the two countries, but, just as in the case of Hiram of Tyre (5:11), such a relationship may be presupposed. The sending of messages of condolence or congratulation was a regular feature of inter-state diplomacy in the near east over a wide period.[100] *deal loyally with* (2): lit. 'do kindness (*ḥeseḏ*) with'; the theme of ch. 9 is thus continued here.

3, 4. Hanun's *princes* – perhaps military commanders (*śārîm*), as in 1 Samuel 29:3 – suspect that the Israelite delegation has come for purposes of reconnaissance. They were wrong, but they probably had evidence enough of David's imperialistic designs in other directions to give their suspicions some basis in fact. *and to overthrow it* (3): precisely what they themselves brought about (12:29f.). Hanun, 'the young and arrogant braggart',[101] treated the envoys with contempt (*cf.* Is. 7:20; 20:4), perhaps even to the extent of parodying the conventional signs of mourning (*cf.* 3:31; Is. 15:2). Royal envoys commonly enjoyed a measure of diplomatic immunity in their comings and goings, which made Hanun's treatment of David's messengers all the more reprehensible. David was therefore provided with an unsought *casus belli* and, in the end, an addition to his empire.

5. *Jericho* would have been the envoys' first main stopping-place, on the near side of the Jordan, on their journey back from Rabbah (*cf.* 11:1) to Jerusalem.

6. *saw*: *cf.* verses 9, 14, 15, 19. Having committed the outrage, Hanun had to call on a quartet of Aramaean states to bolster his fighting capacity. *Beth-rehob* (Rehob in v. 8) was situated to the south of Zobah, for Laish (Jdg. 18:28) had been included within its territory. *Zobah*: *cf.* on 8:3–8. *Maacah* (Aram-Maacah in 1 Ch. 19:6) lay to the north of the Manasseh tribal territory in Transjordan (*cf.* Jos. 13:8–13).[102] *Tob* was further south, but still in Trans-jordan (*cf.* Jdg. 11:3, 5; 1 Macc. 5:13).

7. *all the host of the mighty men*: the Hebrew ('all the host, the mighty men') is awkward; at any rate, a large force comprising more than David's élite corps was put under Joab's command.

8. Possession of the capital city of Ammon (Rabbah; *cf.* 11:1; 12:26) is a key factor in the war (*cf.* v. 3; 12:26–31).

9–11. By advancing on the city Joab let himself be boxed in. The Aramaeans had taken up position at Medeba – according to 1 Chronicles 19:7 – and, having noted Joab's movements, may have closed in from the south.[103] His tactics were therefore dictated by the simple necessity of having to fight the battle on two fronts.

12. A rousing call, and here perhaps a sign of desperation (*cf.* 1 Sa. 4:9). The appropriateness of the reference to *the cities of our God* is sometimes questioned, though the philological alternative of 'altars' for *cities* (*cf.* NEBfn.) is a doubtful expedient. It may be that the Aramaean–Ammonite alliance was regarded as potentially destructive of the Israelite hold on the cities of Canaan. But it may be Transjordanian cities associated with Yahweh-worship that are in question (McCarter, p. 272). Earlier commentators (*e.g.* Kennedy) tended to emend 'cities' to 'ark', citing 11:11 – the ark's presence in the camp – in support. We note, in any case, that even Joab, when under pressure, finds comfort in piety.

13, 14. Joab regarded the Aramaeans as posing the greater danger (*cf.* v. 9), so he dealt with them first. It is not claimed that the city was captured at this point; a second campaign was necessary for that purpose (11:1; 12:26–31). *Abishai* (14): see verse 10.

15–19. Further opposition from the Aramaeans necessitates another call to arms and a confrontation in Transjordan. The fact that Hadadezer was able to summon vassal help (*cf.* v. 19(?)) from *beyond the Euphrates* (16) tends to support Malamat's suggestion that these verses relate to an encounter which occurred before the events described in 8:3–5.[104] *Helam* (16, 17) is sometimes identified with Alema, a Transjordanian town mentioned in 1 Maccabees 5:26, 35.

18. The casualty figures are different in 1 Chronicles 19:18: 'men of seven thousand chariots, and forty thousand foot soldiers'. The substitution of 'foot soldiers' for *horsemen* is certainly to be preferred.[105]

19. In consequence of Hadadezer's defeat, the petty kingdoms that had been in vassalship to him transferred their allegiance to David. Changing patterns of alliances were a feature of the Syrian political scene, with the smaller states often enough having to act as described here. With the Aramaeans firmly under control, a second campaign against the Ammonites could be undertaken in relative comfort (*cf.* 11:1).

DAVID AND BATHSHEBA   (11:1–27)

The final stages of the Israelite–Ammonite war provide the framework for the scabrous story of David's adultery with Bathsheba and the murderous intrigue that followed. This basically domestic preoccupation, while typical of the chapters which make up the so-called 'Succession Narrative', is particularly justified here because of the long-term repercussions which it is also the business of the 'Succession Narrative' to describe and enlarge upon. In short, because of his behaviour in the matter of Bathsheba and Uriah, the David of 2 Samuel 12–20 is a man under judgement, reaping publicly, through his family, the fruit of his cloistered sin.

1. Such evidence as there is suggests that the Israelite calendar year began in the *spring*, though advocates of an autumnal New Year, in the pre-exilic period, are not lacking.[106] Spring was the time for launching military campaigns, when the winter rains had stopped and the male population was not yet involved in harvesting (*cf.* 1 Ki. 12:24x (LXX); 20:22, 26; 2 Ch. 36:10). The month of March, named after Mars the Roman god of war, affords a parallel nearer home. In the light of David's decision to stay at home, and of his behaviour while his troops were on campaign, this reference to normal kingly practice may strike us as ironical. It is true that David did sometimes stay behind in Jerusalem (*e.g.* 10:7–14), but never with the consequences described here.[107] Actually, for *kings* (*mᵉlāḵîm*) MT has 'messengers' (*mᵉlā'ḵîm*), which looks like a scribal attempt to shade off the irony and salvage something for David's reputation as a war-lord. (There are other places in the Old Testament where the insertion of the quiescent consonant '*aleph* performs a similar function.[108] Even if the reading 'messengers' is preferred there is still the difficulty that David's envoys are called 'servants' – possibly implying a higher status than 'messengers' – in ch. 10.) *go forth to battle*: the Hebrew is elliptical, omitting the words *to battle*; for BH *yāṣā'* ('go out') in this sense see 1 Samuel 21:5 (*cf.* Jdg. 11:3). Whatever the reason for Joab's withdrawal after his earlier success against the Ammonites (10:14), this was now a full-scale offensive intended to win the submission of the Ammonite capital. *Rabbah* (mod. Amman) is sometimes called by the fuller name 'Rabbah of the Ammonites' (*e.g.* Dt. 3:11); it was situated about twenty-two miles east of the Jordan.

2–5. A story, simply told, of an abuse of kingly power. David rises after his siesta and from his palace roof espies a woman bathing a little lower down in the city. Bathsheba, presumably unaware of the interest of the royal voyeur, is taking a purificatory bath after menstruation (*cf.* v. 4). Inquiry reveals that she is the wife of Uriah the Hittite (see on 1 Sa. 26:6), a member of David's warrior corps 'The Thirty' (*cf.* 23:39) who is currently with Joab in Transjordan.

2. Whybray comments on the irony of the reference to the *roof* in view of 16:22.[109]

3. The Qumran scroll (4QSam[a]) adds that Uriah was Joab's armour-bearer (*cf.* Josephus, *Ant.* vii. 7. 1).[110] *Eliam*: listed among 'The Thirty' is an Eliam, son of the great Ahithophel (23:34; *cf.* 16:23), but it is doubtful whether he can be identified with Bathsheba's father.

4. *purifying herself*: the point of the note is, presumably, that David was without doubt the father of Bathsheba's child.[111] NEB translates the parenthesis: 'though she was still being purified after her period', so adding an infraction of the laws of purity to the more serious offence (*cf.* Lv. 15:24). But the bathing probably marked the end of her period of 'impurity'.

5. There was a death penalty attaching to adultery in Israelite law (Lv. 20:10; Dt. 22:22; *cf.* also the trial by ordeal in Nu. 5:11–31). When Bathsheba discovers her predicament she sends word to David; what she thought of his nefarious schemes thereafter is not disclosed, though a degree of complicity might reasonably be inferred.

6–13. Absolute candour marks this account of David's abysmal attempts to pass off Bathsheba's child as also Uriah's. The despicableness of the king's behaviour contrasts with the noble figure of the wronged Uriah, several times referred to as 'the Hittite' (vv. 3, 6, 17, 24), as if to emphasize that, whereas the king of Israel was

so obviously lacking in principle, the same could not be said of
this foreigner. Uriah was possibly a resident alien, or the descendant
of one. His name, in any case, incorporates a short form of the
name of Yahweh.

6–9. Ostensibly David's summoning of Uriah was in order to
obtain firsthand news of the Ammonite campaign. It is unlikely
that Uriah saw through the stratagem, though Hertzberg notes 'a
ready source of court gossip' in the messengers who knew about
Bathsheba's visit to the palace (*cf.* vv. 3f.). It was the man's sense
of duty, carried almost to the point of obstinacy, which got in the
way of David's plan. *wash your feet* (8) could refer to a ritual
ablution releasing a soldier from the vow of sexual abstinence
during a military campaign (*cf.* McKane and see on 1 Sa. 21:5).
If, however, *feet* is euphemistic for genitalia, the expression refers
more overtly to sexual relations.[112] Even the addition of a *present*
fails to induce in Uriah a feeling of obligation to comply with the
wishes of the giver. Instead, he demonstratively eschews the joys
of peace-time by sleeping at the palace gate where the royal guard
(*servants*, 9) was mounted (*cf.* 1 Ki. 14:27).

11. This reply to David's attempt at cajolery was so effective
that the king did not again try the persuasive power of words.
Uriah's sense of propriety was religiously based. He first mentions
the *ark*, which accompanied the army in their campaigns as the
visible guarantee of Yahweh's presence with them (*cf.* 1 Sa. 4:3f.),
then pleads that he must maintain solidarity with his fellow-soldiers
in the field. For *booths* in connection with a military encampment
see also 1 Kings 20:12, 16. Theories such as that the first half of
the verse refers to the celebration of the 'Feast of Booths' (*cf.* Lv.
23:33–36) by the rest of Israel not engaged in the fighting,[113] or
that MT *sukkôṯ* actually refers to Succoth in Transjordan,[114]
introduce problems foreign to the passage. It might be possible to
interpret Uriah's words to mean that the national militia (*Israel
and Judah*) was being held in reserve, encamped in booths, while
Joab and the professional troops (NEB 'officers') were in the open
field in an advance position; but the two statements could be in a
kind of synonymous parallelism. *As you live*: when Uriah puts
himself on oath David has few ploys left.

12, 13. A little boredom, and then saturation with wine – but
even when Uriah is befuddled he is not inflamed (*cf.* Gn. 19:30–
38). 'Uriah drunk is more pious than David sober' (Ackroyd). *and
the next* (12) may be joined with verse 13 to read, 'And the next
day David invited him' (*cf.* NEB); this agrees better with David's
statement earlier in verse 12.

14, 15. In Joab David had a loyal accomplice who would not scruple to end a life the maintenance of which was not in the king's interest. In retrospect, David's complaint after Abner's murder ('the sons of Zeruiah are too hard for me', 3:38) sounds a trifle hollow. Uriah himself carried the *lettre de cachet* that sealed his fate. (Even if the letter was unsealed he would possibly have been unable to read it anyway.)

16, 17. Joab seems to have adhered to the spirit of the royal missive rather than to the letter – perhaps with good reason, for David's suggestion was so unsubtle as to be bound to raise suspicion among Uriah's comrades. Joab, on the other hand, was willing to cover the tracks by sacrificing a few more men. By inviting a sally by the besieged army he contrived that Uriah and, unfortunately, some others – eighteen, according to the LXX Lucianic tradition (vv. 21, 24) – were killed as they pursued the retreating Ammonites to the city gate (*cf.* vv. 23f.).

18–21. To be sure, David would be annoyed at the loss of other troops in this way. Did not the Israelite army manuals illustrate the folly of approaching too close to city walls from the story of *Abimelech*, whose inglorious end at the tower of Thebez was administered by a woman with a *millstone* (Jdg. 9:50–57)? If the king did become enraged – as he surely would – he was then to be told about Uriah's death. *Jerubbesheth* (21): a variant of the name Jerubbaal (Gideon); for the *besheth* element see on the name Ish-bosheth in 2:8.[115]

22–25. The messenger's report to David appears in its turn to be an improvement on Joab's message. Uriah's death is mentioned directly, so that David has no chance to flare up in the way Joab expected that he might. But the LXX has a longer version of verse 22, in which David reacts angrily to the initial report and repeats the reference to Abimelech's misfortune at Thebez – so making Joab something of a minor prophet! And if MT *kî* (23) is given its frequent sense of 'because', the longer reading (ending with 'Why did you go near to the wall?') would seem to be presupposed. See the Introduction ('The Text') for a comment.

25. David sends a consolatory message to his commander in the field, unctuously attributing the deaths of Uriah and the others to 'the vicissitudes of war'. *Do not let this matter trouble you*: see on verse 27.

26, 27. Bathsheba observed the customary period of *mourning* – seven days (*cf.* 1 Sa. 31:13; Gn. 50:10) – for her husband, though it is impossible to tell how much affection she had felt for him before or since her infidelity. Throughout the sordid story the inner thoughts and feelings of the protagonists have remained a closed book. But Yahweh's attitude is described in an ominous final sentence which points forward to the reproof and discipline of ch. 12 and, indeed, to the string of woes that are visited upon David and his family in the chapters that follow. Verse 27b, as has often been remarked, is one of those few places in the so-called 'Succession Narrative' where the attitude or activity of God is noted as having a determinative effect on the external events being narrated (cf. 12:1, 15, 24f.; 17:14). As a rule, English translations make no attempt to represent the correspondence between David's message to Joab (v. 25) and verse 27b. The former, translated literally, reads: 'Do not let this matter *be evil in your eyes*', while a literal rendering of verse 27b runs: 'But the thing that David had done *was evil in the eyes of the Lord.*'

NATHAN'S PARABLE   (12:1–31)

If it was one of the chief characteristics of the prophets that they challenged monarchical abuses of power, then Nathan is every inch a prophet here. Nor is the reproving finger pointed in vain. It was not that David could easily deny his guilt, but it is accounted to him for righteousness that he bowed to the prophetic word without any of the casuistry or self-justification that marks the confrontations between Samuel and Saul in similar circumstances (e.g. 1 Sa. 15:13ff.). Early Hebrew tradition makes Psalm 51 the heart-cry of David when the prophet exposed his sin on this occasion, and, even though other life-settings have been proposed for the psalm,[116] it gives fit expression to that consciousness of wrong within that is seen in the penitent of this chapter.

1–4 Yahweh makes one of his decisive interventions (cf. on 11:27), this time through the prophet Nathan. The normal language of the royal audience is absent, there are no deferential words of address; David is a man subject to the prophetic word like everyone else in the kingdom. Nathan's parable is of the 'judgement-eliciting' type, formulated in such a way that the hearer is invited to pass judgement on a hypothetical case and so, unwittingly, on a situation in real life to which the teller wishes to draw attention.[117] The story must have resembled many of the cases which were brought before the king in his role as chief justice in the land. Compare the petition of the woman of Tekoa in 14:1–20, or the dispute for which Solomon's arbitrament was sought in 1 Kings 3:16–28. Indeed, some Greek texts preface Nathan's tale with the words, 'Give me a ruling on this.' The parables of the two debtors and of the good Samaritan (Lk. 7:41-50; 10:29-37) achieve a similar effect by asking the hearer to pronounce on a story which in some way reflects his own situation. The genius of Nathan's parable is that it so aptly depicts the baseness of David's behaviour without the latter's realizing it. The detail is intended both to evoke compassion and to excite moral outrage on the part of the man who was authorized to right the wrong. *daughter* (*baṭ*, 3) represents the first element in Bathsheba's name. Is this a hint of the identity of the real 'lamb' whom Nathan has in mind?

Mindful of the obligation of hospitality towards the *traveller* (4), but unwilling to provide anything from his own resources, the rich man violates the rights and property, such as it was, of his impoverished neighbour.[118] He has wealth and influence, and he is guilty of a kind of oppression against which the Hebrew prophets, and especially those of the eighth century, thundered loud and often.

5, 6. David is suitably outraged, to the extent of declaring that the culprit is worthy of death – as if the *fourfold* (6) restitution required in law (Ex. 22:1; *cf.* Lk. 19:8) would be too exiguous an exaction on this occasion. For *fourfold* the LXX has 'sevenfold', which finds a parallel in Proverbs 6:31, in a section which also likens adultery to theft. Some prefer the alternative reading as sounding more spontaneous, in the circumstances, than a statement of the precise legal requirement. But it is not much of an argument. R. A. Carlson not only favours the LXX variant, but also sees the 'sevenfold' as significant for the whole structure of 2 Samuel 13:1–21:14, which allegedly deals with two seven-year cycles within David's reign.[119] Some, for that matter, detect a special significance in *fourfold*, which is taken to refer to the untimely deaths of four of David's offspring – the first child by Bathsheba, Amnon, Absalom, and Adonijah.[120]

7, 8. Nathan no longer speaks obliquely, and David is suddenly and remorselessly confronted with his crimes. The exposé comes in the course of a prophetic oracle complete with sonorous introductory formula. It begins ominously, in the style of Samuel's denunciation of Saul ('The Lord anointed you king over Israel', 1 Sa. 15:17), and reminds David of Yahweh's preservation of him when Saul sought to kill him. Is he about to be written off as in no way better than Saul? Moreover, as Saul's successor he had been given control of Saul's *house* (8) and his wives, a fact which made his behaviour with Uriah's wife all the more disreputable.[121] How literally the reference to Saul's wives is to be taken is hard to judge.

Only one wife, Ahinoam (1 Sa. 14:50), and a concubine, Rizpah (3:7), are mentioned in connection with Saul. On the other hand, a ruler's requisitioning of his predecessor's harem, arguably to bolster the legitimacy of his own rule, cannot be said to lack parallel (*cf.* 16:21; 1 Ki. 2:22).[122] Because Ahinoam was also the name of one of David's wives (1 Sa. 25:43, *etc.*), it has even been conjectured that David had laid claim to Saul's wife before he came to the throne.[123] However, despite the fact that no other women bear the name Ahinoam in the Old Testament, the grounds for identifying the two are far from adequate.

9,[124]10. Further comparison with Samuel's judgement oracle against Saul is prompted by verse 9; compare 1 Samuel 15:23, 26. David's sin, while grievous on the human plane, was primarily against Yahweh; Psalm 51:4, traditionally associated with this episode in David's life, expresses this idea with particular vigour. *sword* (9) is used figuratively as in 11:25; according to 11:24 Uriah fell by an arrow. *have slain* could be stronger (*cf.* NEB 'murdered'), and the despicableness of contriving the act by the hand of the Ammonites is seen as compounding the offence. The judgement of the *sword* (10) will therefore be the condign punishment exacted from David's family. Historically this may be seen as a comment on the deaths of three of David's sons (*cf.* on v. 6), but could be extended to include other traumas of the Davidic dynasty, for example its attempted liquidation by Athaliah (2 Ki. 11:1).

11. Most specifically, the rebellion led by Absalom against his father (chs. 15–19) is brought into causal connection with David's sin. In Absalom's appropriation of his father's concubines (*cf.* 16:21f.) the idea of the punishment being made to fit the crime is taken to the limit (*cf.* Jb. 31:9–12). *neighbour* (NIV 'one who is close to you') is used as in Samuel's condemnation of Saul, where, as it happens, it alludes to David (1 Sa. 15:28; 28:17). *in the sight of this sun*: Absalom pitched a tent on the palace roof when he 'went in to his father's concubines in the sight of all Israel' (16:22). Weinfeld notes a parallel between this judgement and a malediction in an Assyrian vassal treaty text: 'May Venus, the brightest of the stars, make your wives lie in the lap of your enemy before your eyes.'[125]

13. David utters his *peccavi* (*I have sinned*), not that any other response would have been tolerable given the transparency of his guilt. *against the Lord*: see on verses 9f. Although David himself had adjudged the villain of the parable to be deserving of death (v. 5), Nathan announces that such a penalty will not be exacted by Yahweh. Repentance has its reward (*cf.* 1 Sa. 7:3). In law the death penalty was prescribed for adultery (*cf.* on 11:5), though, as McKeating notes, there are no recorded instances of its application in the Old Testament.[126]

14. RSV rightly consigns the words 'the enemies of' to the footnotes.[127] See on 1 Samuel 20:16. Otherwise we must translate as NIV ('you have made the enemies of the Lord show utter contempt'). In both Testaments contrition is a necessary precondition for forgiveness; its lively exercise in David permits some attenuation of the punishment that would fall upon him (compare the cases of Ahab (1 Ki. 21:27–29) and Manasseh (2 Ch. 33:12f.)).

15. *the Lord struck*: *cf.* 1 Samuel 25:38.

16. *and went in and lay*: the choice of tense suggests that this happened each night while the child's life hung in the balance (so NIV). 4QSam[a] and some Greek texts add that David lay 'in sackcloth',[128] which agrees well with the attitude of mourning which he adopted throughout the seven-day period (*cf.* on vv. 18, 20). Verses 17 and 20 indicate that the nights were spent in David's own house rather than in a sanctuary.

18. *the seventh day*: David has thus completed the normal period of mourning (*cf.* on 11:26) by the time the child dies. This partly explains his sudden reversion to normal behaviour as described in verse 20. The *servants* were quite unprepared for his reaction to the news; since the Hebrew merely says 'he may do harm', it was not necessarily the king's own welfare that concerned them.

20. *washed . . . anointed*: compare Matthew 6:16f., where the subject is fasting. Mourners likewise refrained from anointing themselves (*cf.* 14:2), and, as we have noted (vv. 16, 18), David's behaviour hitherto has had the character of mourning. Just when the mourning fast might have been expected to begin, he visits the sanctuary and returns to the palace to eat.

21–23. It is all very perplexing for the palace officials who, now that their master is in a better frame of mind, ask for an explanation. In reply they are given a short sermon on the futility of prayers for the dead. All that verse 23 is saying is that David would one day go to the same shadowy world that the child had entered, and that there was no hope of the child returning to this life; 'but how far this falls short of the Christian hope of the Resurrection of the Body, and the Life Everlasting!' (Kirkpatrick).

24, 25. A historical notice that takes us well beyond the immediate context of the war with Ammon. But it is important as marking a new stage in David's relations with Yahweh.[129]

24. Only now is Bathsheba described as David's *wife*. Then the second child of their union is expressly said to have enjoyed divine

favour: *the Lord loved him.* Since near eastern kings sometimes
claimed divine patronage from birth as proof of the legitimacy of
their rule, we may have already in this statement the suggestion
that *Solomon* was marked out as Yahweh's nominee to succeed
David on the throne. The name *Solomon* is sometimes connected
with the *salem* element in Jerusalem, with both possibly celebrating
a divine name or epithet. A more obvious comparison may be
made with the Hebrew *šālôm* ('peace'), as in the Chronicler's play
on the name in 1 Chronicles 22:9. Others prefer 'his replacement'
(*cf. šillēm,* 'compensate'), *i.e.* Solomon replaced the child that died
(*cf.* McCarter, p. 303). There is no further mention of Solomon
until late in David's reign when the rebellion by Adonijah brought
the succession issue to the forefront of court politics. *and he called*:
a few manuscripts have 'she called'; for instances of naming by the
mother see 1 Samuel 1:20; 4:21.

25. Confirmation of Yahweh's favour comes in a *message*
through the prophet Nathan. The name *Jedidiah* ('beloved of the
Lord') occurs nowhere else. Since on their accession kings sometimes assumed throne-names (*cf.* on 21:19), it might be possible to
see Solomon as the official name and Jedidiah as the personal.
However, it would be truer to the text if we simply took the
additional name as evidence of the child's favoured status, as in
the case of some other (non-royal) biblical worthies (*e.g.* Jacob,
Gn. 32:28).

26, 27. Joab had been entrusted with the siege of Rabbah (11:1)
and had made some headway. The *royal city* (26) seems to be the
same as the *city of waters* (27); both may refer to fortifications
which protected the city's water-supply outside the city wall (*cf.*
NEB 'King's Pool' and 'pool', and see on 5:8). The fall of the
citadel itself could not be long delayed.[130]

28. Joab expresses concern for David's reputation, taking it for
granted that the king in person should receive the submission of
the Ammonite capital. The calling of a person's name over a thing
betokened his ownership of it (*cf.* on 6:2). Zion became known as
'David's city' after he had personally led his men against it (5:7,
9).

30. An exceedingly heavy gold *crown*, weighing in the region of
sixty-five pounds, was among the spoil taken from Rabbah.
Because the word *malkām (their king)* has the same consonants
as Milcom, the name of the chief god of the Ammonites (*cf.* 1 Ki.
11:5, 33), there is some uncertainty as to whose the crown was.
NEB favours 'Milcom', and in support of this it could be argued
that *their*, as in RSV, strictly has no antecedent. However, the

additional argument that the crown was too heavy for a king to
wear loses some of its weight in the face of the statement that *it
was placed on David's head*. (McCarter maintains, nevertheless,
that it must have been the *store*, rather than the excessively heavy
crown, that David wore (p. 313).)

31. Forced labour – or, just possibly, a fate more gruesome –
was imposed on the vanquished Ammonites. If the translation
'brick-kiln' is retained for MT *malbēn* (*Qerê*), then the Hebrew
says that David made his captives 'pass through (*cf.* RSVfn.) the
brick-kiln'. But such evidence as there is requires that the word be
rendered 'brick-mould', and this strongly favours the emendation
of *he'ebir* ('made pass through') to *he'ebid* ('made to serve'). NIV
is most circumspect with: 'he made them work at brickmaking' (*cf.*
Ex. 1:14). For *set them to labour with saws* 1 Chronicles 20:3 has
the less probable 'sawed them with saws'; there is a difference of
but a consonant between the two readings. It is probable that the
macabre tendencies in the tradition came in at some later point
when the Ammonites had incurred the odium of the Israelites in
exceptional measure[131] – though it has to be said that David's
treatment of the Moabites and Edomites, Ammon's neighbours to
the south, was almost as ruthless (*cf.* 8:2; 1 Ki. 11:15f.). S. R.
Driver's remark about the more brutal version being 'alien to all
that we know of the personal character and temper of David'
(*Notes*, p. 296) is surely wide of the mark.

AMNON, TAMAR, AND ABSALOM   (13:1–39)

Herewith begins a tale of woes that dog the royal house throughout
much of the remainder of 2 Samuel. The story of Amnon's violation
of Tamar, with its painful echoes of David's own sexual aberration,
provides the necessary background in that it explains why Amnon
the crown prince was murdered on Absalom's orders, and why
Absalom became estranged from his father – an estrangement
which, despite a formal reconciliation (14:33), eventually embroiled
the kingdom in civil war. That political earthquake and the rum-
blings that preceded it form the subject-matter of the next seven
chapters. Even if we do not view 2 Samuel 9–20 and 1 Kings 1–2
as primarily a 'Succession Narrative' (see the Introduction), the
events described certainly impinge on the succession question. For,
having introduced David's eventual successor with the assurance
that Yahweh's favour rested upon him (12:24f.), the narrative
proceeds to tell how the other candidates disqualified themselves

from appointment to the high office to which they aspired. From one point of view it is a film-freeze of the power-lust and intrigue that still stalk the earth; from the theological standpoint of the previous chapter, and of Nathan's reproof of David, it is the outpouring of Yahweh's displeasure on one who was highly favoured but who deserted his trust.

1, 2. That it is *Absalom* whose part in the story is ultimately the most significant is indicated by the opening sentence of the chapter. Apparently both Absalom and *Tamar* were children of David by Maacah, daughter of Talmai king of Geshur (*cf.* v. 4; 3:3). Tamar's beauty and Amnon's 'love' – a misnomer for lustful passion here – immediately set up a parallel with the preceding narrative of David and Bathsheba. RSV's reference to Tamar's virginity (2) might suggest that she was chaperoned and guarded to an extent that made it difficult for even Amnon to press his attentions upon her. This may have been the case, though $b^e t\hat{u}l\hat{a}$ seems to mean basically 'a girl of marriageable age' rather than *virgin*; in other words, the emphasis is more on her nubility.[132]

3. Amnon's lust might never have found gratification, had it not been for the devious resourcefulness of his cousin *Jonadab*. *Shimeah*: called Shammah in 1 Samuel 16:9; 17:13. *crafty*: $\d{h}\bar{a}\underline{k}\bar{a}m$ takes its colour from the context; ordinarily it is translated 'wise', while often comprehending ideas of native shrewdness and practical skill. An illustration of Jonadab's shrewdness comes in verse 32.

4. *Absalom's sister*: *cf.* on verse 1. Absalom lurks in the background even at this stage in the story.

5, 6. Jonadab's scheme ensured not only that Tamar came to Amnon's bedchamber but also that her presence there was by permission of the king. It was diabolically cunning in the way that it concealed Amnon's illicit passion in the cloak of a sick man's fondness for his half-sister; David would have looked churlish if he had refused the request. The word for *cakes* ($l^e\underline{b}i\underline{b}\hat{o}\underline{t}$, 6) occurs only in this chapter. By derivation it suggests heart-shaped confections – 'well fitted symbolically for the situation'[133] – or, possibly, cakes whose ingredients were likely to stimulate a flagging appetite.

7–9. David unwittingly confers a *nihil obstat* on the plan. The narrator lingers over the detail of the preparation of the cakes, hinting, perhaps, at the loving care with which the task was performed. The description also has the effect of slowing up the narrative and injecting an element of suspense. Amnon's remaining problem is the presence of his attendants, so he puts on a show of

being too ill for even Tamar's cakes to interest him. A man as
poorly as this cannot be bothered with people about him!

10. We are probably to think of the bedchamber as a recess or
partitioned area within a larger room. Tamar is enticed within
through Amnon's professed need of spoon-feeding.

11, 12. Then comes the heat flash of passion. Tamar, far from
proving seducible, is appalled that Amnon would flout the moral
conventions of Israel in this way. 'The old idioms "we do not do
such things in Israel" (2 Sam. 13:12) and "an outrage in Israel"
(Gen. 34:7 and elsewhere) show . . . that Israel drew a clear
distinction between itself and its Canaanite environment, especially
in the realm of sexual conduct.'[134]

13. She appeals first to his humanity and then to his self-esteem.
The crown prince, if he insists on violating her, will reduce himself
to the level of a wanton knave. He can fulfil his desire, she suggests,
within the context of lawful marriage, if he will but ask his father
for the permission to marry. In fact, marriage between a half-
brother and half-sister is forbidden in Pentateuchal law (Lv. 18:9,
11; 20:17; Dt. 27:22), though whether such a law operated in this
period is open to question.[135] (The marriage of Abraham and Sarah
would have been within the forbidden degrees of consanguinity
according to the later law (Gn. 20:12).)

15–17. Self-gratification is followed by a feeling of revulsion at
the act for which it was responsible. The observation that Amnon
loathed his half-sister with an intensity exceeding his earlier passion
for her represents an interesting psychological insight on the part
of the narrator. In her plight Tamar seems to have hoped for a
regularizing of the relationship, if only to cover shame (16). *But
he would not listen to her*: cf. verse 14. Amnon acts with utter
callousness, referring contemptuously to 'this one' (*zō'ṭ*) when he
tells his servant to remove her from his presence.[136]

18. The reference to Tamar's *robe*, not without its antiquarian
interest, is inserted at this point because of the special significance
attaching to Tamar's tearing of it in verse 19. In one of its
distinguishing features it resembled Joseph's robe (Gn. 37:3): it
may have had *sleeves* or, according to another explanation of MT
passîm, may have been particoloured (*cf.* NIV 'richly ornamented').
RSV *of old* represents an emendation of MT *mᵉ'îlîm* ('garments')
to *mē'ôlām*, and is attractive in view of the poor sense yielded by
the standard text ('for thus were the virgin daughters of the king
clad with garments'). If accepted, the revised reading could have
significance for the dating of the narrative, since a time-gap between
the early monarchy and the time of writing seems to be required –

unless we go to the length of treating the whole clause as an interpolation, which is not recommended.[137] *virgin*: see on verse 2.

19. Tamar goes into mourning (*cf.* 1:2; 15:32). *her hand on her head*: also a sign of mourning; compare Jeremiah 2:37 ('hands') and the illustrations in *ANEP* (nos. 634, 640).

20. Absalom, inwardly seething at what Amnon had done, counselled his sister to accept the indignity as philosophically as she could. But, as events proved, he was set on revenge at a convenient time. Tamar took up residence in Absalom's house, living in virtual widowhood (*desolate*), a perpetual reminder to her brother of her unavenged violation. *Amnon*: the form used here is 'Aminon', which has been explained on Arabic analogy as a diminutive – an 'ironic diminutive', according to Hertzberg, who paraphrases with 'Amnon your little brother'.

21. In a short sentence the inadequate reaction of David is summed up. Perhaps disarmed by his own scandalous behaviour with Bathsheba, he was in no position to castigate his son for a similar fault. An additional sentence in 4QSam[a] and the LXX speaks explicitly of fatherly indulgence: 'but he would not hurt Amnon because he was his eldest son and he loved him' (NEB; *cf.* NAB).[138] David's relationship with Adonijah, as described in 1 Kings 1:6, was just as unsatisfactory. A similar problem had similarly catastrophic effects in Eli's family (1 Sa. 2:23–25, 29). If David had exerted himself as the situation required, he might have prevented that initial estrangement between himself and Absalom which was finally to plunge the nation into civil strife.

22. Absalom's silence and inactivity are 'the most ominous result of the whole affair'.[139]

23. He waited *two full years* before settling the score with Amnon. The occasion was a sheep-shearing celebration (*cf.* 1 Sa. 25:2–8, 11, 36) held on his own private estate. *Baal-hazor*: perhaps the same as Ramath-Hazor, a mountain mentioned in the Qumran *Genesis Apocryphon* (XXI. 8). An identification with the modern Jebel el-'Aṣûr, five miles north-east of Bethel, is generally favoured. *near Ephraim*, if referring to the tribal territory, poses a difficulty in that the preposition (*ᶜim*) is normally used 'to denote proximity to a town or other spot' (Driver). For that reason some see a reference to Ephron (so NEB), a town four miles north-east of Bethel.[140]

24–27. Absalom must have counted on his father's declining the invitation. By refusing to go himself David was again in a situation where he was almost bound to accede to a request the real purpose of which he was unable to read (*cf.* v. 6) – though, if we choose to, we may detect an inkling of a suspicion in his mind in verses 26b–27.

28. At the beginning of the verse the LXX, apparently supported by 4QSam[a], has the additional clause, 'and Absalom made a feast like the feast of a king' (*cf.* NEB and see 1 Sa. 25:36)[141] – a hint, perhaps, of the kingly pretensions which Absalom will later display (15:1ff.). The penalty for killing the crown prince would have been severe, hence Absalom's fine talk of valour (*cf.* Jos. 1:9) with those whom he had deputed to perform the cowardly act. Nothing is said in the subsequent narrative about the fate of the assassins.

29–31. Even though the other princes headed home at something more than a Canterbury gallop, a garbled version of what had happened reached David first, with the result that for a short while he was mourning the loss of all those of his sons who had gone to Absalom's estate. Overwhelmed with grief, he prostrated himself on the ground, as in his earlier agonizing for Bathsheba's child (12:16). Murder on this scale by Absalom surely signalled a bid for the throne. *mule* (29): evidently favoured as the royal mount in this period (*cf.* 18:9; 1 Ki. 1:33, 38), though asses were also widely used by near eastern royalty.[142]

32, 33. But Jonadab, with characteristic shrewdness (*cf.* v. 3), quickly sums up the situation; even after an interval of two years he is alert to Absalom's intentions. NEB's 'Absalom has looked black' takes MT *śwmh* not as a verbal form (RSV *determined*) but as a noun cognate with an Arabic word meaning 'ill-luck', whence 'an inauspicious expression' (*cf.* Driver).

34. *Absalom fled*: repeated in verses 37 and 38. The whole of the next chapter is taken up with the delicate matter of his reconciliation with his father. RSV *Horonaim* for MT 'behind him' (NIV 'west of him') has the indirect support of the LXX, whose longer reading in this verse is accepted in full by NEB. The name Horonaim is dual in form, in virtue of the fact that there were two Beth-horons, Upper and Lower (*cf.* 2 Ch. 8:5). Upper Beth-horon was situated about ten miles north-west of Jerusalem. Others prefer to read 'Bahurim' (*cf.* on 3:16) on the ground that the Horonaim road would not have been visible to a watchman in the city (*e.g.* Hertzberg).

37, 38. The place of refuge to which Absalom *fled* was the little principality of *Geshur* in Transjordan, ruled by his maternal grandfather Talmai (*cf.* 3:3).

39. Two factors may have contributed to David's change of heart: the affection which he bore toward all his sons, even to the point of overlooking very serious faults, and the consideration that

Absalom was, if not his eldest surviving son (there is no mention
of Chileab after 3:3), then at least the second in the line of
succession.[143]

THE WISE WOMAN OF TEKOA   (14:1-33)

By now Absalom is a key figure in relation to the succession. This
is the undoubted implication of the wise woman's words to David
in verses 7 and 16. And David's changing attitude towards his
fugitive son may to some extent have been influenced by the same
thought. Joab, eager for a reconciliation, watched for signs of a
thaw in his master, and may already have put in a good word for
Absalom. The manner by which he brought about the rapprochement sounds almost frivolous given the delicacy of the situation,
but the narration rings true to life in ancient Israel; it is also a part
of the narrator's artistry that in this *entr'acte* he offsets the diet of
violence and intrigue (chs. 13 and 15) with this gentler matter.
Joab's ruse obviously reminds us of Nathan's parable in ch. 12. Is
Joab also among the prophets? In both narratives the crucial point
is reached when David as supreme judge in the land gives his ruling
only to discover that he has passed judgement on a case much
nearer home.[144]

1. Joab's concern, as soon becomes evident, is not so much for
David in his grief as for the future of the royal house. When
Amnon died Absalom possibly became heir-apparent (*cf.* on 13:39),
and Joab considers that his presence in Jerusalem is now a necessity.
He senses, too, that David is ready for a reconciliation with his
wayward son.

2, 3. Even so, he settles on an indirect method of broaching the
subject with the king. From *Tekoa*, about six miles south of
Bethlehem, he summons a *wise woman* who will be able to play
convincingly the part of a widow whose clan are threatening to
put to death her one remaining son. The view that Tekoa was
reputed for its fostering of Israelite wisdom traditions is sometimes
supported from this passage, as also from the presence in the
book of the Tekoite prophet Amos of various features that are
characteristic of those traditions. C. D. Isbell even claims to find
a hint of Tekoa's reputation in this connection in the Septuagint's
rendering of Amos 1:1 ('sayings current among the Akkareim from
Tekoa').[145] But neither this particular point, nor the broader case
which it seeks to buttress, can be said to be justified by the evidence.
So that she will look the part, the woman is instructed to put on

widow's weeds and to refrain from anointing herself with oil (*cf.* 12:20). *put the words in her mouth* (3): and so it has become a debating point whether the 'wisdom' displayed in the interview is to be regarded as that of the woman or of Joab.[146] The impression to be gained from the story, despite verse 19, is that the woman was not just a play-actress; see on verse 14.

4. The indications are that, whatever Absalom had to say about his father's administration of justice (15:3), it was possible for the ordinary citizen to gain a hearing from the king.

6, 7. The woman's clan (RSV *family*) are intent upon applying the death penalty to the fratricide, without regard for the drastic effect this will have. Strictly speaking, *and so they would destroy the heir also* (7) should be as in NIV: 'then we will get rid of the heir as well'. There is therefore a clash of duties here – the duty to avenge the first brother's death, and the duty to preserve the name and issue of the widow's late husband. (The institution of levirate marriage was specifically designed to deal with the latter kind of situation (Dt. 25:5–10).) *the man who struck his brother*: the combination of participle and noun in MT *makkēh 'āḥîw* ('the one smiting his brother') is as in the law on homicide in Exodus 21:12 (*makkēh 'îš*, 'the one smiting a man'). Verse 7 may provide an important clue as to why David hesitated to heal the breach with Absalom even when his fatherly emotions impelled him in that direction. Other members of the royal family, and in particular the remaining sons of David, may have been agitating for the implementation of the law just as soon as Absalom crossed the border into Israel again. *quench my coal*: such figures of speech are especially characteristic of the 'wise' (*cf.* v. 14; 17:1–13).

8–11. David agrees to make a special dispensation in favour of the endangered son. But the woman must secure a more binding promise from him before she can confront him with the real meaning of her acted parable. She succeeds, emerging with a promise on oath that blood-revenge will not be exacted on her son.

9. The woman expresses her willingness to shoulder any blame incurrable as a result of the king's dispensation. However, as was noted in connection with 1 Samuel 25:24, this cringing form of address may be a way of asking for permission to speak (or to speak further, in this case).

11. Since the *avenger (of blood)* (*gō'ēl*) did not normally operate within the clan the term may be used loosely here.[147]

12–14. The petitioner turns preacher and charges the king with failure to appreciate the consequences of his own intransigence, not so much for himself as for the nation. He has exercised the royal prerogative in favour of her, yet withholds it from his own son. *his banished one* (13) is a direct reference to Absalom. This is developed in verse 14 in a sententious observation not unsuited to a 'wise woman': death is unavoidable and irreversible when it comes, but God will spare David if he takes steps to reinstate Absalom. So, at least, RSV and NEB, with the help of a transposition of two letters in the second half of the verse. But MT as it stands must be rendered as in NIV: 'But God does not take away life; instead, he devises ways so that a banished person may not remain estranged from him.' In other words, death may be irreversible, but God's disciplinary dealings with his creatures are far from irreversible. Furthermore, if God acts according to the dictates of mercy – as in David's own experience (12:13) – then David is obligated to do likewise.[148]

15–17. The present position of these verses is often attributed to a copyist's error, for the reason that they would come more logically after verse 7. But this may be to miss some of the subtlety in the woman's presentation of her case. It is true that here she reverts to the fictitious situation of verses 4–11, yet we should not assume that she intended dropping her disguise in verses 12ff., when she drew the parallel between her own circumstances and those of the king. It would have suited Joab well if the woman's wise counsel had been heeded without her having to give herself, and Joab, away. In verses 15–17, therefore, she returns to her own problem and her reasons for bringing it before the king, with, perhaps, the implication that it was her own distressing experience which had awakened her to the dangers in the situation involving David and Absalom. *the people* (15), which may not be an ideal way of referring to the woman's clan (v. 7), suggests a parallel between her domestic problem and the national dilemma (*cf.* 'people of God', v. 13). Likewise, the *heritage of God* (16) could refer to family property (*cf.* 1 Ki. 21:4) or to membership of the community of Israel (*cf.* NEB and see 1 Sa. 26:19). Finally, she rounds off her piece with enough flattery to silence any possible rebuke from the king: she has perfect faith in his judgements. (17).

16. *the man*: the avenger of blood (v. 11).

17. *the angel of God*: see on 1 Samuel 29:9.

18–20. It is possible that Joab had previously made out a case for Absalom's return. David, at any rate, sensed his involvement in the woman's little charade. Joab was a 'loyalist' and a pragmatist, always ready to act in the best interests of the kingdom as he happened to conceive of them. The woman's overblown tribute to the monarch's wisdom (20) seizes upon an essential attribute of the ideal ruler (*cf*. Is. 11:2). The full-grown Davidic ideology would portray the king as possessing not only angelic, but also divine, attributes (Ps. 45:6).

21–24. When Absalom returned to Jerusalem it was not to the society of the court or to the full favour of his father.

21. *the young man Absalom* sounds almost like a back-echo of David's plaintive inquiry in 18:29.

24. *Let him dwell apart*: the verb (*sābab*) is the same as in verse 20 ('to change (the course of affairs)'); David has the last word.

25–27. Verses 25f., in speaking of Absalom's physical attractiveness, also hint at the conceit that went with it. Add to this his plausible personality (15:2–6), and it is easy to see why he was later able to command such a following. Nevertheless, the contrast between his persona and his real character is the clue to the developing tragedy of Absalom.

26. Despite the common assumption, it is not at all clear that Absalom's mane was directly responsible for his death; see on 18:9. *two hundred shekels*: between five and six pounds. *the king's weight*: different standards were in vogue; compare the 'shekel of the sanctuary' (Ex. 30:13, 24). There could also be local weights, as 'the weight of Alalakh' and 'the weight of Aleppo', from further afield.[149] Weights according to royal standards might be inscribed 'for (of) the king', or might even be stamped with a symbol having the same significance.[150]

27. Absalom is credited with *three sons* and *one daughter* – called after his sister Tamar – though 18:18 states that because he had no male heir he erected a monument to perpetuate his name. It is noticeable that only the daughter's name is given, so that perhaps, as is sometimes suggested, the sons may have died young.[151] The LXX adds that Tamar 'became the wife of Rehoboam, the son of Solomon, and bore to him Abiathar', no doubt influenced by 1 Kings 15:2 where Abijam (*sic*) is said to have been the son of Maacah 'daughter of Abishalom'.

28–33. After two years Absalom began to chafe at his limbo existence. But when he attempted to use the good offices of Joab he found that his erstwhile champion now observed the official policy of keeping him at a distance. Joab may well have guessed at the reason for the summons and decided that it would be impolitic to comply. However, fire signals – the story has an air of reckless hilarity about it (*cf*. Jdg. 15:4f.) – succeeded where the more conventional approaches had failed. We need not regard Absalom's professed willingness to accept his fate, if he were guilty of death, as seriously meant. He could have pointed to David's failure to deal with Amnon as the explanation of his own action. The reader knows, and Absalom probably guessed, that David had pledged himself not to apply the full rigour of the law.

ABSALOM REBELS   (15:1–37)

By a tragic irony David's rule was almost terminated prematurely, not by the superior power of a foreign enemy but by his own mismanagement of domestic affairs. For that Absalom was able to capitalize on a serious breach between the king and a considerable proportion of his subjects is on the surface of the narrative. The one explanation offered, viz. that David had neglected important matters of justice, represents Absalom's point of view and hardly tells the whole story. Other factors – John Bright speaks of 'a mass of indefinable grievances' – may have been at work, but our sources are silent.[152] There is also the question of Judah, and the fact that many of David's own tribesmen diverted their allegiance to his rebel son. If one thing is clear in relation to the rebellion, it is that this was no neat division between a loyal Judah and a coalition of the north.[153]

The theme of the rebel prince playing upon the alleged short-comings of his father's administration of justice is paralleled in an interesting way in the Ugaritic Keret Epic.[154]

1. Absalom's rehabilitation in Jerusalem allowed him to pursue openly his ambition of replacing his father on the throne. Towards the end of David's reign another son, Adonijah, conducted himself in a similarly high-handed way (1 Ki. 1:5); so too did Jeroboam in the reign of Solomon, according to an old tradition in the LXX at 1 Kings 12:24. It is surprising that Absalom's venture was not nipped in the bud, once he had made such a public declaration of intent.

2–4. The ground for the rebellion was prepared by highlighting certain defects, actual or alleged, in David's administration of justice. In the morning, when aggrieved citizens came seeking justice from the king ('Execute justice in the morning', Je. 21:12), Absalom would intercept them at the city *gate* and, with professed solicitude, would aggravate their sense of grievance. The cases brought to the king would normally be those which were beyond the competence of local elders, doubtless including complaints against the state.[155] Inter-tribal rivalry may also have contributed to the disaffection which Absalom so effectively turned to his own advantage. At least, it could be concluded from verses 2f. that

David was more ready to hear the cases of fellow-Judahites like the Tekoite woman of ch. 14 than those of Israelites from further afield. It is sometimes suggested in this connection that 'Israel' in verses 2 and 6 has its more restricted sense, referring to the northern tribes. While this would be difficult to prove,[156] the fact that Absalom raised his flag in Judah would not necessarily exclude the factor of tribal jealousy from the discussion.

5, 6. Some of the disappointed travellers will have been flattered to find the king's son, if not the king himself, so accessible. To encourage them still further, the 'people's prince' dispensed with the formality usually associated with introductions to royalty. *stole the hearts*: 'stole the affections' (NEB), or, since 'heart' also represents the intellect in Hebrew, 'duped' is possible.

7. *four years* for MT 'forty' is much to be preferred. Even then, and supposing that the figure includes the two years of 14:28, Absalom waited a long time after his return from Geshur before deciding to fulfil his vow.[157] N. H. Snaith's interpretation of MT *miqqēṣ* (*at the end of*; *cf.* 14:26) to mean that Absalom raised his rebellion at the time of the autumnal festival reads too much into the expression.[158] *to the Lord, in Hebron*: the proposal to translate 'to Yahweh-in-Hebron', *i.e.* to Yahweh as he was worshipped at Hebron (*cf.* Ackroyd, possibly influenced by K. Budde[159]) is interesting; nevertheless, the inscriptional *yhwh šmrn* ('Yahweh of Samaria') from Kuntillet 'Ajrud suggests that the preposition (*bᵉ*) would be omitted if we were dealing with an actual title of Yahweh.[160]

8. *at Geshur*: *cf.* 13:37f. His bargain with Yahweh, as described here, recalls Jacob's similar undertaking made while he was on his way to *Aram* (Gn. 28:20–22).

9. David again plays into Absalom's hands, by failing to suspect the true motive for the visit to Hebron (*cf.* 13:5ff., 26f.).

10. By proclaiming the rebellion at *Hebron*, the city which had first welcomed David as king of Judah after the death of Saul (2:1–4), Absalom was striking where loyalty to his father might have been expected to be strongest. From this distance it is hardly possible to explain the switch of allegiance that is implied in Absalom's choice of the city, though attempts have been made.[161] *the sound of the trumpet*: the signal for revolt, as in 1 Samuel 13:3, but also the normal method of announcing a new reign (*cf.* 1 Ki. 1:34, 39; 2 Ki. 11:14). *Absalom is king*: a formula of a kind also used in the Psalms to proclaim the kingship of Yahweh over the world (*cf.* Ps. 96:10); see also 1 Kings 1:18; 2 Kings 9:13.

11. If Absalom lacked support, relatively speaking, in Jerusalem he managed by this piece of cunning to give David the opposite impression. *two hundred men* who thought that they were guests at a votive celebration became unwittingly implicated in the coup. *in their simplicity*: 'in all innocence' (NEB) is better; we may compare, in a superficial way, the 'unwitting' guests invited by Samuel to a meal in honour of Saul at the time of his anointing as king (1 Sa. 9:22–24). There is nothing to suggest that these Jerusalemites were prominent citizens, though the assumption is not unreasonable. Conroy, on the other hand, thinks that they were from the poorer element in Jerusalem.[162]

12. The *sacrifices* may have been offered as part of the coronation ceremony (*cf.* 1 Ki. 1:9), rather than in fulfilment of the supposed vow (*cf.* on v. 7). *while Absalom was offering*: 'when Absalom had offered' would be more correct.[163] By this time *Ahithophel*, counsellor-extraordinary in Israel (16:23), had declared himself on the side of the rebels. *sent for*: MT has 'sent', but LXX (Mss) 'sent and summoned' relieves the difficulty. *Giloh*: one of the hill towns of Judah (*cf.* Jos. 15:51). The suggestion that Ahithophel defected to Absalom because of David's treatment of his granddaughter Bathsheba assumes too readily that the Eliam of 11:3 is the hero mentioned in 23:34. Moreover, since Bathsheba was in the process of becoming the most influential of David's wives, it would not be too difficult to stand the argument on its head.

13–15. David's *Via Dolorosa* begins with the evacuation of the city. To maintain oneself in Jerusalem during a civil war was a different proposition from defending it against a foreign enemy; the presence of even a few of Absalom's sympathizers could have made resistance very difficult. We must also take into account the fact that two hundred Jerusalemites had – as it would have appeared to David – thrown in their lot with Absalom (v. 11). To avoid encirclement (*cf.* 17:13) and to preserve life (14), therefore, the city was abandoned forthwith. Hertzberg notes the historical parallel in the evacuation of Jerusalem by German and Turkish forces in 1917. The rest of the chapter relates how, in one way and another, certain groups and individuals remained loyal; apart from Ahithophel, who seems not to have been in Jerusalem at the time (v. 12), there were no defections among those closest to David.

16. The token occupation of the palace by *ten concubines* created the circumstances in which one element of Nathan's judgement oracle against David would find fulfilment (*cf.* 16:20–23).

17. *the last house* (*bêt hammerḥāq*): possibly the last house on the outskirts of the city. But the expression is a little obscure, and

NIV 'a place some distance away' is a defensible alternative.[164] NEB 'the Far House' thinks of a wellknown landmark.

18. *Cherethites . . . Pelethites*: see on 8:18. As well as these mercenaries we learn of a contingent of Philistines from *Gath*, who evidently were attracted to David's cause during his period of vassalage to Achish (1 Sa. 27:1–12), though, if with NEB we insert a reference to Ittai here ('and Ittai with the six hundred Gittites under him'), their association with David may have begun in the more recent past (*cf.* v. 20). *six hundred* occurs a number of times in military contexts; Malamat suggests that it is used to denote a brigade.[165]

19–23. The first of five 'meeting scenes' during David's flight from the city (15:19–16:13); a certain symmetrical correspondence with the three encounters on his homeward journey (19:16–40) has often been remarked upon.[166]

19, 20. If David had an ulterior motive for trying to coax Ittai back to the city, as he had in the cases of Zadok and Abiathar (v. 28), and Hushai (vv. 33–36), it is not disclosed. He tested the Gittite's loyalty with strong arguments: Absalom was 'king', Ittai was a foreign mercenary who could claim to be disinterested as regards the internal politics of Israel, and the future with David offered only uncertainties. *foreigner* (*nokrî*, 19) carries none of the implications of duty to the host community that are conveyed by the term 'resident alien' (*gēr*; *cf.* 1:13). *exile* reinforces the point that Ittai was under no obligation to become involved in this constitutional crisis. There could be a considerate use of exaggeration in *yesterday* (20). If Ittai's association with David went back to the latter's stay in Gath and Ziklag (*cf.* 1 Sa. 27), he would by now have been resident in Israel for a considerable number of years; but see on verse 18. The restoration of the words *may the Lord show . . . to you* in verse 20 has the authority of the LXX; MT omits by homoioteleuton.

21. In the repeated *my lord the king* Ittai insists that he acknowledges only one king, and in mentioning *death* before *life* he shows that he has counted the cost. This example of steadfast loyalty from a Philistine contrasts vividly with the perfidy of Ahithophel and the rest (*cf.* Lk. 7:9). David ensured that it was rewarded at an early date (18:2).

23. While the decision to abandon the capital was taken in haste (v. 14), the impression of a reluctant, emotion-laden withdrawal is conveyed by the intermittent progress reports (vv. 23, 30, 32; 16:1, 5, 13), and by the accounts of conversations and encounters along the way. *all the country*: *i.e.* the inhabitants of the countryside (*cf.*, in part, Zc. 12:12), though Conroy thinks that the emotion is possibly attributed to the physical land, as sometimes happens in contexts of lamentation.[167] The *Kidron* valley, which separates Jerusalem on its east side from the Mount of Olives (v. 30), is also mentioned in John 18:1 where 'the exact description is probably introduced with a significant reference to the history of the flight of David from Absalom and Ahithophel'.[168] For another parallel between this narrative and the Passion Story see on verse 31. *toward the wilderness*: the text is difficult. NEB 'before him, by way of the olive-tree in the wilderness' is based on the LXX.

24. RSV obscures the fact that *And Abiathar came up* is problematical, occurring in MT after the reference to the setting down of the ark. Another possible translation is 'and Abiathar offered sacrifices' (NIV), though this too is not without difficulty. It may be that the account originally recorded the involvement of Zadok and Abiathar on an equal basis, and that the present state of the text reflects a scribal attempt to attribute a diminished role to Abiathar in view of his subsequent unfrocking by Solomon (1 Ki. 2:26f.). Apart from 1 Samuel 6:15 (*q.v.*), this is the only direct reference to the *Levites* in the books of Samuel. In both places they are the custodians of the *ark of God*. The Chronicler assumes a much more prominent role for them during David's reign. *set down* as a translation of *yaṣṣiqû* has been defended by Hoftijzer,[169] but usually this rendering is obtained by emending to *yaṣṣigû*. Normally *yaṣṣiqû* would mean 'poured out (a libation)', an idea which would suit the context (*cf.* 6:13), though not the syntax.

25, 26. David will not try to use the *ark* as a means of ensuring his ultimate victory and return; he will submit to whatever sentence Yahweh imposes upon him (*cf.* 16:10–12). There is something akin to the resignation of Eli in *let him do to me what seems good to him* (26; *cf.* 1 Sa. 3:18).

27–29. But such resignation as there is in David is balanced by a healthy resolution to do what he can to win back his kingdom. If Zadok and Abiathar returned to the city they could act as intelligence-gatherers, using their sons as runners to pass on the information to David. The same sort of combination of the pious and the prudential as is seen in verses 25–29 was put to good effect by Nehemiah: 'And we prayed to our God, and set a guard as a protection against them day and night' (Ne. 4:9).

27. *Look* is the reading of the LXX. As RSV indicates in the footnotes, MT seems to mean 'Do you see?', or 'Are you a seer?'[170] However, the first does not fit the context very well, and the second suffers from the difficulty that 'seer' refers to prophets (*e.g.* 1 Sa.

9:9), but never to priests. (NIV 'Are you not a seer?' therefore asks for the answer 'No'!) Prophets, it is true, sometimes did engage in the gathering and relaying of intelligence; compare the function of Elisha in 2 Kings 6:11-14 or, at a more lowly level, the unnamed 'postman' prophet of the Lachish letters (no. 3).[171] The insertion of *and Abiathar* is also favoured by NEB as helping to explain the plural *your* and *you* at the end of the verse (*cf.* also v. 29). While MT is tolerable as it stands, see on verse 24 for a comment on Abiathar's status in this paragraph.

28. *the fords of the wilderness* are, in all probability, crossing points on the river Jordan (*cf.* 17:16).

30. David and his followers resemble a funeral cortège as they make their way up the Olivet slope. Some find evidence here that this account of David's ejection from Jerusalem incorporates elements of a festal drama in which the humiliation of the king and his subsequent reinstallation by Yahweh were acted out. It is suggested, for example, that the description in this verse relates more naturally to a cultic procession than to a civil evacuation (Ackroyd). *with his head covered*: there is evidence for a second root *ḥāpâ* meaning 'to uncover', hence NEB 'bare-headed'.[172] For the uncovering of the head and the removal of footwear as signs of mourning see Ezekiel 24:17, 23 (where the prophet is forbidden to perform these mourning acts).

31. The news of Ahithophel's defection was a body-blow; there was no one in the kingdom who could match his sagacity (*cf.* 16:23). Psalm 41:9 has traditionally been interpreted as referring to him and his treachery; in the New Testament it is applied to the arch-traitor Judas (Jn. 13:18). On hearing the news David uttered a prayer the answer to which is recorded in the verses that follow.

32-37. *Hushai* is the one through whom Ahithophel's wise counsel will be brought to nothing. His admission to Absalom's war-council gave the rebellion the kiss of death.

32. There was evidently a sanctuary or 'high place' on the summit of Olivet in the period of the early monarchy, and it has even been suggested that this accounts for the orientation of Solomon's temple toward the east, *i.e.* in the direction of the Mount of Olives.[173] This reference to a place *where God was worshipped* helps us to see Hushai's appearance at this point as being the answer to David's prayer in the previous verse. Hushai, too, was in mourning. The Archites are mentioned in Joshua 16:2 as occupying an area on the northern boundary of Benjamin with Ephraim.

33. David's seemingly uncomplimentary remark about Hushai's being a *burden* to him presumably means that he considered him too old for the rigours ahead.

34–36. But if Hushai will insinuate himself into Absalom's circle of advisers, he can perform invaluable service for the king. So David himself is taking steps to 'turn the counsel of Ahithophel into foolishness' (v. 31). *Zadok and Abiathar* would be able to take advantage of their privileged status as priests, and, as a further link in the chain, their sons would act as messengers.

37. The timing is suggestive; David's agent arrives on his assignment just as Absalom enters the city. Hushai's decisive part in the confounding of Absalom's war plans is recounted in 17:5–14. He is described as David's *friend* (*cf.* LXX already in v. 32), which means more than that he was a supporter or ally of the king (thus the 'friends' of George III). The 'King's Friend' (*cf.* Gn. 26:26; 1 Ki. 4:5) was his special confidant, and the title seems to have been restricted to one individual at any given time.[174]

DAVID'S FLIGHT TO THE JORDAN (16:1–23)

As he makes his way to the Jordan David has two unhelpful encounters with representatives of the Saulide family. In the first scene (vv. 1–4) Ziba adds to the confusion – mischievously, in all probability – by declaring that Mephibosheth has remained in Jerusalem in the hope that Israel will return to its former allegiance to the house of Saul. Then Shimei, a kinsman of Saul, starts to hurl abuse at the fugitive king who, he claims, is being punished by Yahweh for his (alleged) crimes against the house of Saul (vv. 5–14). David, who had by no means abdicated his kingly authority, as may be seen from his pronouncement on Mephibosheth's property (v. 4), declines, however, to deal with Shimei. For, while the latter's accusation might be awry in particulars, David recognizes his afflictions as being indeed a cup of retribution from Yahweh. Meanwhile, back in Jerusalem Hushai is manoeuvring himself into a position where he can sabotage the diabolical schemes of the great Ahithophel (vv. 15–19).

1–4. Appointed to look after Mephibosheth's estate (9:9–13), Ziba apparently saw the upheaval in Jerusalem as an opportunity to improve his own situation at Mephibosheth's expense. This, at any rate, seems the most likely explanation of the behaviour of these two during this critical period for David. Ziba displays the calculated practicality of an opportunist who realizes David's vulnerability to every sympathetic gesture of support. Only by a monumental miscalculation could Mephibosheth have imagined that events would favour him in the way that Ziba suggested. It was Absalom's rebellion, and it was for Absalom that large numbers of Israelites were declaring themselves. And such was the contrast between the charismatic prince and the crippled pensioner that David should never have fallen for Ziba's preposterous claim. But in an evil day full of uncertain allegiances he was easily deceived. We should note, however, that despite the fact that 19:24 absolves Mephibosheth, to all intents and purposes, of the charge of disloyalty, many writers have inclined towards Ziba's version of events.[175] See on 19:29f.

1. *the summit*: cf. 15:32.

3. *son . . . father*: loosely for 'grandson . . . grandfather' (*cf.* NEB, NIV).

4. David later revised this hasty judgement, though even then he may not have been entirely convinced of Mephibosheth's innocence (*cf.* 19:29).

5, 6. There follows an even less happy experience with one of Saul's kinsmen. *Shimei*, a member of Saul's clan (RSV *family*), showers David with missiles and abuse as he and his company make for the Jordan. *Bahurim*: see on 3:16. *Gera* also occurs as the name of a Benjaminite clan (Gn. 46:21), and as the name of the father of Ehud, the Benjaminite judge-deliverer (Jdg. 3:15).

7, 8. For Shimei, of course, David's distress has nothing to do with his sin against Uriah the Hittite (*cf.* 12:10–12); rather, David is a murderous usurper whom nemesis has at last overtaken. In *all the blood of the house of Saul* (8) Shimei may be charging David with responsibility for the deaths of Abner and Ish-bosheth in particular (see on chs. 3–4). Some, on the other hand, see a reference to David's surrender of seven of Saul's family to the vengeful Gibeonites, as described in 21:1–14.[176] The accusation helps to explain why it was considered necessary to defend David's record in relation to Saul and his house, as in the earlier chapters (notably the so-called 'History of David's Rise'). Shimei is doubtless a mouthpiece for all those who resented the ending of the Benjaminite ascendancy and saw David's rise to power as anything but the appointment of Yahweh.

9. In a manner typical of the sons of Zeruiah, Abishai offers radical surgery as the answer to the problem of Shimei (*cf.* 1 Sa. 26:8; 2 Sa. 3:39; 19:21). *dead dog*: cf. 9:8.

10–12. Three reasons for leaving Shimei unharmed are put forward. The first and most important is that he may actually have been instructed by Yahweh to curse David. David, after all, is a man currently under the judgement of Yahweh. Moreover, when David's own son is in rebellion against him it is not so remarkable that one of Saul's connexion should express strong feelings against the king (11). Thirdly, it may be that submission to Shimei's indignities will help expiate David's guilt (12).

10. *you sons of Zeruiah*: the similar tendencies of Joab and Abishai are acknowledged in the use of the plural; *cf.* on 3:30. As in the story of Balaam, who was hired to curse Israel but could only bless (*cf.* Nu. 23:11f., 25f.; 24:10–13), the underlying assumption of the verse is that Shimei's maledictions may be in response to the irresistible power of Yahweh. So they must be accepted without demur.

12. Even in the bleakest of situations David dares to hope in divine mercy (*cf.* 12:22).[177] Not Shimei's curse, but Yahweh himself, has the power to affect his case.[178] *repay* (*hēšîḇ*) translates the same verb as is rendered by 'avenged' in RSV of verse 8; Shimei speaks of one kind of 'repayment', while David hopes for another.

13. To Shimei's boisterous accompaniment the king and his retinue head towards the Jordan, there to wait for the information which Hushai would smuggle out of the palace (*cf.* 15:35f.). Further episodes in the story of Shimei are recounted in 19:16–23 and in 1 Kings 2:8f., 36–46. *dust*: 'In England mud is more frequently available.'[179]

14. With the arrival at the Jordan the narrator turns to events in Jerusalem, and in particular to the critical battle of wits between Ahithophel and Hushai (16:15–17:14).

15. Ahithophel is the key figure in Absalom's entourage – or would have been, but for Hushai's intervention.

16, 17. *David's friend*: see on 15:37. *your loyalty* (*ḥeseḏ*, 17): whereas the loyalty of the Lord is constant (*e.g.* Ps. 118:1–4), human loyalty may be far less durable (*cf.* Is. 40:6 (RSV 'beauty'); Hos. 6:4 (RSV 'love')).[180]

18, 19. Absalom's surprise at Hushai's apparent defection is smothered by a dole of pious flummery which concentrates divine election, popular acclaim, and personal devotion in one compact sentence (18). In any case, argues Hushai, he was not being disloyal in serving David's son. He might have added that the (eventual) transfer of allegiance from father to son was a common experience for royal courtiers. Nevertheless, the inference to be drawn from 17:5f. is that Hushai did not gain immediate access to the war council.

20, 21. If Ahithophel sensed that some of the supporters of the rebellion might entertain thoughts of a reconciliation between

David and Absalom and so might favour half-measures in the
meantime, his advice to his protégé ensured that he quickly passed
the point of no return. Appropriation of David's harem closed the
door on any hope of reconciliation. Whether the act by itself
constituted a claim to the throne – which Absalom had already
seized – is a debated issue (see on 3:7). *made yourself odious*: the
Hebrew word (*bā'aš*) refers here, as in its other occurrences in
Samuel (1 Sa. 13:4; 27:12), to behaviour of a disloyal or rebellious
nature.[181]

22. The narrator refrains from moralizing on David's punishment, leaving his reader to see the connection with Nathan's
prophecy in 12:11f. The *tent* (*'ōhel*) may be compared with the
bridal *ḥuppâ* (*cf.* Joel 2:16) which is still a feature of Jewish wedding
ceremonies.

23. A tribute to Ahithophel's sagacity which puts it on a par with
divine guidance obtained through oracular consultation. There is
no suggestion that this high valuation put upon Ahithophel's
counsel was misplaced; the counsel of the wise, no less than the
prophetic vision and the priestly instruction, could be viewed as a
gift of Yahweh to his people (*cf.* Ezk. 7:26).[182] But the oracular
word remains the standard of measurement, and we should be
wrong to conclude that this verse implies a devaluation of the
oracle in favour of a wisdom ethos.

Verse 23 serves as both a tailpiece to 16:20–22 and an introduction to ch. 17, where it is Hushai's not inconsiderable task to
overturn the counsel of Ahithophel.

HUSHAI PREVAILS (17:1–29)

The decisive contest of the Absalom rebellion took place in Absalom's own war council in Jerusalem. Although, as usual, Ahithophel sized up the situation correctly, it was the advice of Hushai
which won approval. In verse 14 this fatal misjudgement by Absalom and his aides is put down quite simply to Yahweh's manipu-
lation of the decision-making process. Thus the issue between
Absalom and David is settled even before the two sides line up for
battle. While, therefore, the 'Succession Narrative' does not deal
in miracles and supernatural events in the manner of, say, the book
of Joshua, Yahweh is still held to be the controlling lord of history.

The first half of the chapter is noteworthy for the way in which
Ahithophel and Hushai present their cases, for there can hardly
be a comparable stretch of Old Testament narrative so rich in

simile (and hyperbole) as 2 Samuel 17:1–13. Not only is such language appropriate to the utterances of the wise – we might compare the figures of speech in Proverbs, for example – it also has a significant slowing-up effect on the narrative (retardation) which accurately reflects Hushai's aim in relation to Absalom's war plans. This is, then, a piece of literary coloratura which is to be enjoyed for its own sake even while weightier matters are awaiting resolution.

1–4. Absalom's rebellion did not collapse because Ahithophel's skills deserted him at the last. It was Absalom's failure to take the veteran counsellor's advice – described by the narrator as 'good' in verse 14 – which ensured his downfall. Ahithophel rightly judged that quick action was called for; a night attack on the weary evacuees might well have met with success in the way he predicted. One attractive feature of his proposal was that the loss of life would be minimal. It would be a quick, crisp operation, with the sole purpose of eliminating David, whose supporters could then be counted upon to switch their allegiance to Absalom without further resistance.

3. The simile in this verse has been lost in the Hebrew, which reads 'like the return of the whole (or "when the whole returns") (is) the man whom you are seeking'. NIV 'The death of the man you seek will mean the return of all' provides a suitable sense, but is hardly what the Hebrew says. RSV *as a bride comes home to her husband* sensibly follows the LXX. The unusual incidence of similes in Hushai's speech in verses 7–13 is an argument in favour of the LXX; Ahithophel and Hushai are both 'wise' men in whose rhetorical repertoire simile figures prominently. 'Returns' (RSV *comes home*) is, as Kirkpatrick observes, a 'subtle flattery', for Absalom never had been rightful king.

4. *the elders of Israel* are the leaders of the northern tribes, who formed no part of the Jerusalem secretariat but whose support for the rebellion was so important as to secure a place for them in the council of war.

5. 'In an abundance of counsellors there is safety' (Pr. 11:14). So, at any rate, thought the inexperienced Absalom, even though the good sense talked by Ahithophel had commended itself to both Absalom and the tribal elders. As verse 14 notes, the decision to give Hushai a hearing was, in fact, providentially ordered.

7–10. Hushai knew well that Ahithophel's plan was the worst possible from David's point of view, and that he must buy time on the king's behalf. Even the leisurely pace of his speech, with generous use of simile and metaphor, seems intended to contribute to that end. He plays on the reputation for valour of David and his warrior corps, and he points out that David is too experienced a soldier to risk bivouacking with his troops (8; *cf.* 1 Sa. 26:5). In the confusion of a night attack, moreover, it would take only a rumour of spirited resistance by David and company for Absalom's men to weaken at the knees (9, 10).

7. *not good*: contrast the narrator's own comment in verse 14!

11–13. Hushai's counter-motion would take days to implement, which was precisely what he wanted. The mustering of a pan-Israelite army appealed to Absalom's vanity, we may assume, and it offered the virtual certainty of the enemy's annihilation. Then, in a fine metaphorical flourish, Absalom is encouraged to visualize the dismemberment of the opposition when they seek the security of a walled city. A similarly graphic picture of the destruction of a city is given in Benhadad's message to Ahab in 1 Kings 20:10 (*cf.* Mi. 1:6, also of Samaria). We might also compare a passage in a late Babylonian chronicle describing the destruction of Kazalla by Sargon of Akkad: 'He marched against the land of Kazalla and turned Kazalla into mounds of ruins. He utterly destroyed there every bit of ground where a bird could settle'.[183] Again the use of metaphor helps to depress the urgent tone of the war council and enables Hushai's proposal to be seen in a more favourable light.

11. *you go . . . in person*: lit. 'your presence going'; the expression is as in Exodus 33:14f. The sense is much the same whether we read *to battle* with MT or 'in (their) midst' with the ancient versions. Whereas Ahithophel talked as if he would lead the night attack (v. 1), Hushai cajoles the all-too-susceptible Absalom with thoughts of glory on the field of battle.

14. But the decisive factor in Absalom's choice of Hushai's plan, in preference to Ahithophel's confessedly *good* advice, was Yahweh himself. Few though they are, the explicit references to Yahweh's involvement in the events described in the so-called 'Succession Narrative' mark the main turning-points in the story (*cf.* on 11:27).

15, 16. We are possibly to understand that Hushai withdrew from the council after making his speech and before the final decision was reached. But, even if he was aware of the outcome, the mere fact that Ahithophel had urged swift action may have been enough to make him anxious for David's safety. For the priests' part in the relaying of information to the king see 15:27f. *the fords of the wilderness* (16): *cf.* 15:28.

17. *En-rogel* ('Fuller's Spring') must have been close to the city, and is probably to be identified with 'Job's Well' near the junction of the Kidron and Hinnom valleys. The *maidservant* who liaised between the priests and their sons *Jonathan* and *Ahima-az* was probably in the domestic employ of one of the priests. Her actions would have been less likely to arouse suspicion if she had been in the habit of making visits to the well. The priests' sons evidently had left the city to avoid suspicion (*cf.* 15:27, 36).

18–20. But Jonathan and Ahima-az were spotted by a youth sympathetic to Absalom and who, perhaps, had even been posted for the purpose of intercepting messages between David and the capital. The well-owner's loyalty to the king was, presumably, already established, or the priests' sons would have been deep in trouble. Since David had recently passed through *Bahurim* (18; *cf.* 16:5), the couple will have had opportunity to show whose side they were on.

19. The woman's ruse recalls the story of Rahab and her hiding of the Israelite spies (Jos. 2:1–7). *grain (riṗôṭ)*: the precise meaning of the word is not known. It occurs also in Proverbs 27:22 (RSV 'crushed grain').

20. *the brook (mîkal)*: the word occurs only here and again the meaning is uncertain.

21, 22. Whereas the omniscient reader knows that David is not in immediate danger, the king must act in accordance with the information passed on to him. By daybreak, therefore, the fugitives are safely in Transjordan.

23. The far-sighted Ahithophel realizes already that the adoption of Hushai's plan means doom for the rebel cause. He must also have reckoned that there would be no future for himself, the evil genius of the rebellion, once David had been reinstated. Ahithophel was a traitor, and his suicide suggests a comparison with the most notorious traitor of all (Mt. 27:5). *set his house in order*: 'gave his last instructions to his household' (NEB); *cf.* 2 Kings 20:1; Isaiah 38:1, of Hezekiah. With the departure of Ahithophel Absalom's cause was mortally wounded. Delay in giving chase to David had been failure enough; now, without the services of Ahithophel, the chances of repairing the damage were in ribbons.

24–26. The scene is set for military encounter – on terms more favourable to David than if Ahithophel had been heeded. Some time will have elapsed while Absalom's pan-Israelite force was mustered.

24. *Mahanaim* had been Ish-bosheth's capital during his short reign in Transjordan (*cf.* 2:8) and will have been suitably fortified.

25. Joab's position as commander of the Israelite *army* (or 'militia' (ṣābā'; *cf.* 8:16)) had been given to his relative Amasa. *Ishmaelite* for MT 'Israelite' is much to be preferred since, if the man was an Israelite, there would have been no need to note the fact.[184] RSV has the support of a few LXX texts and of 1 Chronicles 2:17. *had married* is literally 'had gone in to', which has been thought to imply a 'marriage' of the Arab *ṣadiqa* type, in which the wife and children lived with the mother's people.[185]

26. *Israel and Absalom*: 'the dishonourable placing of Absalom's name after the mention of his troops . . . foreshadows his dishonourable end'.[186] McCarter thinks that the reference to Absalom is an explanatory addition by a 'helpful ancient' anxious to define 'Israel' more satisfactorily.

27–29. At Mahanaim David receives practical support from three men of substance. *Shobi* (27) is described as a son of Nahash, which could mean that he was a member of the Ammonite royal family (*cf.* 10:2); he may even have been David's appointee in Rabbah following the Israelites' capture of the city (*cf.* 12:26–31). *Machir* had previously extended his hospitality to Mephibosheth (9:4), which must mean that originally he had supported Saul. The kindness of *Barzillai* greatly impressed David who later would have had him live in Jerusalem at royal expense (19:31–39).

28, 29. RSV reads as if the hardware mentioned at the beginning of verse 28 was among the comestibles. Presumably the Hebrew text originally had separate verbs for the two groups of items brought to David. *cheese from the herd* (29): the translation of MT *šᵉp̄ôṯ* by *cheese* (*cf.* NIV) goes back to the Targum and Peshitta, but has no satisfactory philological basis. NEB has 'fat cattle', which is how the Vulgate rendered the expression. A satisfactory explanation has still to be found.

THE DEATH OF ABSALOM (18:1–33)

Whereas David's men prevailed upon him to keep out of the fighting, lest their leader and their cause be extinguished in one fell swoop (vv. 2–4), no such caution was observed on the rebel side. Absalom went into battle and perished. Only the merest account of the battle itself is given (vv. 6–8); all focuses on the fate of the rebel prince and on the anguished state of David – more father than king at this point – as he waits for news from the battle-front. The messenger scene in the second half of the chapter (vv. 19–33) brilliantly represents the ironies and ambiguities of the situation which Joab, by his disregard of the king's instruction, has brought about.

1, 2. The organization of the army into units of *thousands* and *hundreds*, as also the division of the entire force into three 'heads', is conventional (*cf.* 1 Sa. 11:11; 22:7). In the absence of David from the field (*cf.* v. 3), Joab was in overall command (*cf.* 19:13). Ittai's loyalty (15:19–22) was rewarded with a command position (2).[187]

3. The men's insistence on David's remaining at base made good sense (*cf.* 21:17). Ahithophel's strategy had centred on the removal of David, whose men thereafter would have had little to fight for (17:2f.). Conversely, when Absalom was killed in battle the rebellion collapsed (*cf.* 19:8–10).

4. *side (of the gate)*: see on 1 Samuel 4:18.

5. Poignantly, in view of the sequel, the king's final orders concern Absalom. Absalom is a rebel, but to the fatherly heart of David it is youthful rebellion. *young man*: *cf.* verses 12, 29, 32. Joab's previous record (*cf.* 3:22–27) would have been sufficient to fill David with apprehension.

6–8. This is as much as is said about the battle between David's warrior corps (*the army*) and Absalom's Israelite levy; the narrator is far more interested in what happened to Absalom himself, and in how it affected David. The *forest of Ephraim* (6) must refer to a region within reasonable distance of Mahanaim (*cf.* v. 3, though note the implication of v. 23, after the battle had spread). A settlement by the (cisjordanian) Ephraimites in Transjordan could account for the name; Stolz notes the possible significance of Judges 12:4 in this regard. While there is no other instance of the name in connection with Transjordan, it should not be emended on that account (*pace* NEB 'Ephron').[188] The treacherous terrain – which apparently included large pits (v. 17) – over which the battle spread is held responsible for more casualties than the fighting itself. In the light of Joshua 10:11 ('there were more who died because of the hailstones than the men of Israel killed with the sword'), we may see here a suggestion that nature was enlisted on the side of David. Compare also Judges 5:20f. Verses 9–15 relate the contribution of the forest to Absalom's death.

9. We are possibly meant to think of the famous locks of Absalom (14:26) as instrumental in his death.[189] But a more plausible, eyewitness(!), account is offered by G. R. Driver, according to whom Absalom 'was caught by the neck in the fork of two boughs which had been kept low down and held together by the surrounding branches; jolted by the impact of Absalom's weight, the fork became dislodged and its two arms closed round Absalom's neck as they sprang upwards, freed from entangling branches and carrying him with them'.[190] *mule*: *cf.* on 13:29. *a great oak*: or, possibly, '*the* great oak', if a tree traditionally associated with Absalom's death is indicated.

10–13. The unnamed soldier has much more regard for the word of the king than has Joab. Again the public charging of the section commanders concerning the safety of Absalom is emphasized (*cf.* v. 5). Moreover, Joab's informant was sensible enough to realize that, if he had despatched Absalom, he would have received no backing from his chief when the matter was reported to David (13).

11. *I would have been glad* would be better rendered, 'I would have had (to give you)', as in NIV; at the same time, it is far from clear that Joab had put a price on Absalom's head (*cf.* Mauchline). *a girdle*: the warrior's belt (*cf.* 1 Sa. 18:4; 2 Ki. 3:21 (RSV 'armour'), and see on 2:21). In the mention of a possible reward there seems to be a thinly-veiled invitation to go back and strike Absalom dead.

13. *against his life*: the alternative reading, 'against my life' (*Qᵉrê*), is reflected in NIV's 'if I had put my life in jeopardy'.

14, 15. Joab brusquely dismisses the man's objections and goes off to do the job himself. *darts*: RSV prefers the reading reflected in the LXX to MT 'rods' (*cf.* NEB 'stout sticks'). Joab is accompanied by squires whose task is to finish off their master's work (*cf.* 1 Sa. 14:13). He it was who had schemed to have Absalom reinstated in court circles (14:1–24), but Absalom the rebel prince was a different proposition.

16. Now that the rebel leader is dead there is no point in continuing the fighting; an immediate halt to the fratricidal struggle between Israelite and Israelite is called.

17, 18. Two memorials sum up the life-story of Absalom. Whereas his inordinate personal vanity had driven him to the unusual – for an Israelite – expedient of erecting a stele in his own honour, already in his lifetime, at his death he was accorded the memorial of the infamous (*cf.* Jos. 7:26; 8:29). *all Israel fled* (17): the rebellion is at an end. *I have no son* (18) requires explanation in view of the statement in 14:27 that Absalom had three sons and a daughter. Either the present verse preserves a variant tradition of Absalom's family circumstances, or we have to conclude that Absalom's sons predeceased him. The fact that no names are given for the sons in 14:27, though the name of the daughter is, could be taken to support the second alternative. As in many another society, children, and especially sons, were regarded as the appropriate means of perpetuating one's name (*cf.* Ps. 45:16f.).[191] *King's Valley*: *cf.* Genesis 14:17; a location near Jerusalem is required.

The well-known 'Tomb of Absalom' in the Kidron Valley is a much later construction dating from as late as the first century AD.

19–33. One of the notable 'messenger scenes' of Old Testament narrative (*cf.* on 1 Sa. 4:12–18). This one skilfully conveys the delicacy of the situation as the news is brought to David.[192]

19–21. *Ahima-az*, who had already experienced the hazards of relaying information from the capital to David (15:27, 36; 17:17–21), was eager to carry the news of the rebels' defeat. Joab, however, was too aware of David's poor record where the receiving of the bearers of purportedly good tidings was concerned (*cf.* v. 22; 1:11–16; 4:5–12); a *Cushite* life was more expendable (*cf.* v. 27). Ahima-az later shows every sign of having understood Joab's point when he hedges David's question in verse 29. *has delivered him* (19): the verb *šāpaṭ* (traditionally 'judge') probably requires two verbs to convey its true sense here: 'has vindicated him and delivered him'. *Cushite* (21): *i.e.* a Nubian, from Cush to the south of Egypt. AV 'Cushi', as a personal name, is wrong.

22, 23. Finally Joab gives in to Ahima-az, and the young man sets out for Mahanaim by way of the Jordan *plain* to the north of the Dead Sea. 'The meaning of the passage will be that, while the Cushite went straight across the mountains from the "wood of Ephraim" to Mahanaim, Ahima'az made a *détour*, coming down into the Jordan-valley, and then following the high road through it, and up whatever wādy it might be, which led to Mahanaim.'[193] The assumption is that Ahima-az followed a more circuitous but less exacting route. *reward* (22): *cf.* 4:10.

24. David awaits news of the battle in the city gateway, in the area between the inner and outer gates. The gateway was normally a substantial structure, in appearance like a tower, and the area between the gates might include one or more guard-rooms.

25. A runner approaching on his own was probably a messenger; mere fugitives would be more likely to steal into the city as unobtrusively as possible (*cf.* 19:3).

26. Since David is himself in the gateway, *to the gate* is preferable to MT 'to the gate-keeper' (so NEB, NIV). The RSV reading requires only a revocalizing of the Hebrew.

27. David correctly surmises that Joab would not have chosen Ahima-az to be the bearer of bad news, but he does not realize that Ahima-az is virtually a self-appointed herald. An inference from the character of the man to the kind of news which he brings may also be involved, as in 1 Kings 1:42. In other words, Ahima-az is a man of good omen.

28–30. Ahima-az reports only the good news, and evades the question which is uppermost in the king's mind. *your servant* (29): RSV treats MT 'the king's servant and your servant' as containing doublets. As Driver explains, the more courtly 'the king's servant' probably originated as a correction of the less formal 'your servant'.[194] Less probably, we might understand Ahima-az to mean that a more authoritative report will be brought by the Cushite ('the king's servant').

31. *has delivered*: cf. on verse 19.

32. *like that young man*: The Cushite's reply is not so much indirect as conventionally phrased (*cf.* 1 Sa. 25:26).

33. The personal tragedy of David is summed up in the five-times repeated *my son* (*cf.* also 19:4). It is possible to condemn David for his preoccupation with his personal loss when the stability of the kingdom was at stake, yet even in times of crisis and high drama a king may be a father.

THE KING RETURNS   (19:1–43)

If the story of David's withdrawal from Jerusalem is told in exceptional detail (15:13–16:14), the account of his return is only marginally less so. The vicinity of the river Jordan is the setting for much of the chapter, as David is first greeted by a number of earnest entreaters and then bids farewell to the aged loyalist Barzillai. The Jordan also becomes a *symbol* in that not to have been invited to escort the king across the river is interpreted by the northern tribes as certain proof of their inferior standing in David's estimation. It is for this reason that there is no neat and tidy conclusion to the Absalom episode – that, indeed, the aftermath of one rebellion sees the instigation of another (ch. 20).

1–3. Elation gives way to embarrassment as the returning troops hear of David's grief over Absalom. As Conroy notes, the theme of contrast and reversal is particularly evident in 18:33–19:8.[195]

4. *Cf.* 18:33.

5, 6. For Joab, who neither felt compunction for his killing of Absalom nor shared David's sense of loss, the contradiction in the king's behaviour was too great. In the circumstances his brutal frankness was the right medicine for David. Had Absalom succeeded in his coup, David and the rest of the royal family might have paid with their lives, for there is no reason to suppose that Absalom would have behaved any differently from later usurpers like Baasha (1 Ki. 15:27–30), Zimri (1 Ki. 16:11f.), or Jehu (2 Ki.

10:6f.). 'Joab's voice is the voice of duty, the voice of the king, speaking to the father.'[196]

7. Joab even threatens to stage his own rebellion, if David does not come to heel. At the end of the reign he supported the claims of Adonijah to the throne (1 Ki. 1:7), but what he might have done on this occasion if David had failed to recover himself is an open question.

8a. The threat worked, and David *took his seat in the gate* where he had previously reviewed his troops as they marched out to battle (18:4). Now the rebellion is truly at an end, and David may perform his kingly duties again. It was at the city gate (of Jerusalem) that Absalom had launched his bid for the throne, capitalizing on his father's alleged neglect of the business of the gate, namely the dispensing of justice to the aggrieved citizens of Israel (*cf.* 15:2–6). David's sitting in the gate is, therefore, a high point in the story of the recovery of his kingdom. The act represents a return to normality; compare Thomas de Quincey's interpretation of the knocking at the gate in Act II of *Macbeth*, in his famous essay entitled 'On the Knocking at the Gate in Macbeth'.

8b picks up 18:7b.

9–15. Before David can return to Jerusalem he must be assured of the support of the men of Judah in particular. Somewhat surprisingly, the first conciliatory moves come from the northern tribesmen, with the result that the king's return becomes an issue of protocol, and a highly contentious one at that (*cf.* 19:41–20:2).

9, 10. The disappointed supporters of Absalom fall to thinking about the good things that David had done for them. If his domestic policy had defects, there was no denying his success in the foreign field. Now it seemed ironical that the saviour of the land had been driven into a kind of exile – though, strictly, David was still within the borders of Israel when in Transjordan – by his own son (9). *Israel* is to be taken in its more restricted sense of the northern tribes, as is evident from verse 11. *The king*, on the northerners' lips, is significant, though the narrator himself has used the title freely of David throughout the account of the rebellion (*e.g.* 18:2). *Absalom, whom we anointed* (10): there is no reference to the anointing apart from here.

11–15. The Judahite elders are provoked into adopting a more favourable attitude towards David. Their tardiness may be partly explained by the fact that Hebron, one of the chief towns of Judah, had been the rallying-point for the rebellion (15:10).

11. The priests *Zadok and Abiathar*, who had remained in Jerusalem throughout the rebellion, were now to function openly as David's representatives in the capital. *when the word*: the last clause of the verse is probably to be transferred to the end of verse 10 or beginning of verse 11 as in 4QSam[a] and LXX: 'And the word of all Israel came to the king' (*cf.* NEB).[197] The sense is basically the same: when the Israelites' musings were reported to David he sent a message to the elders of Judah asking whether they were going to let themselves be outmanoeuvred by the northerners.

12. *my bone and my flesh*: *cf.* 5:1, where the northerners are making the request.

13. As a sop to the defeated Israelites David announces his intention of transferring Joab's command to Amasa. Amasa had led the rebel forces (17:25), but since these had included Judahites there is no need to regard this decision by David as endangering the negotiations with the Judahite elders (vv. 11f.). And, without doubt, Joab's demotion is also to be seen as retaliation by David for his defiant killing of Absalom. Joab, however, soon found opportunity to remove Amasa out of his way (20:4–10).

14, 15. The *heart* of the people of Judah is won back to David (*cf.* 15:6, 13). *Gilgal* (15): the exact location is not known, but it was quite near the Jordan (*cf.* on 1 Sa. 7:16).

16–40. The story of David's journey back to Jerusalem presents a mirror image of his departure, when he was sent on his way by Hushai (15:32–37), Ziba (16:1–4), and, after a fashion, Shimei (16:5–13). Shimei, now regretting his earlier incivilities, is the first to pay homage to David *redivivus* (19:16–23), closely followed by Ziba (19:17), and then by Mephibosheth on whose behalf Ziba had earlier presumed to speak (19:24–30). Finally Barzillai appears (19:31–40), now too old to return with David to the capital, just as, apparently, Hushai had been too old to leave it (*cf.* 15:33).

16, 17. Shimei and Ziba are bracketed together not only because of their Saulide connections but also because they had both miscalculated David's chances of surviving the rebellion. With Shimei came a representative contingent of Benjaminites anxious to declare their allegiance to the king. During the parleying between David and Abner the latter had gone to Hebron to report on all that 'Israel and the whole house of Benjamin thought good to do' (3:19). So now, even at this late stage in David's career, the attitude of the Benjaminites – Saul's tribe – is considered worthy of special notice. We may observe in this connection the description of Ziba as *the servant of the house of Saul* (17), as also of Mephibosheth as 'the son of Saul' (v. 24), though he was actually Saul's grandson. ('Son' is sometimes used for 'grandson' in the Old Testament.) *rushed down* (ṣāleḥû, 17): a strange use of the verb; normally it

occurs in connection with the spirit of Yahweh coming upon an
individual (*cf.* 1 Sa. 10:6). McCarter, with a modicum of support
from the Aramaic cognate, argues for 'waded through'.

18a. Ziba and company do not wait for David to cross the
Jordan, such is Ziba's desire to improve his account with the king
(*cf.* on v. 24). He and his servants assist David and his followers
to cross the river – without, alas, the help of AV's 'ferry boat',
which is almost certainly a translators' fiction induced by the
unclarity of the Hebrew.[198]

18b–20. If David does not prove a magnanimous victor, Shimei's
prospects are bleak. *as he was about to cross* (18): the actual crossing
is noted in verse 39. However, the more natural sense of the Hebrew
here would be 'when he had crossed'. (This is the interpretation of
NEB and NIV, except that both make Shimei the subject, which
in turn strains the Hebrew word-order to some degree.) It may be
that Shimei's story is told out at this point even though his actual
petitioning of David did not occur until after verse 39. *the house
of Joseph* (20) at its simplest denotes the tribes of Ephraim and
Manasseh, but it also has an extended usage to cover the northern
tribes which followed Jeroboam at the secession (*e.g.* 1 Ki. 11:28;
Zc. 10:6). Here it also includes Benjamin (*cf.* Ps. 80:1f.) even though
Benjamin remained loyal to the house of David after Solomon's
death (1 Ki. 12:21).

21–23. Abishai's vengeful tendencies surface again (*cf.* on 16:9).
He had a point inasmuch as the cursing of a ruler was regarded in
law as a very serious offence (*cf.* Ex. 22:28; 1 Ki. 21:10; Acts 23:5).
But, by inciting David to order Shimei's execution, Abishai is
casting himself in the role of an *adversary* (22), a *śāṭān* whose
business is to entice and accuse a man. Again, as in 1 Samuel 29:4,
there is nothing metaphysical about the term *śāṭān* – a point
possibly to be borne in mind when we interpret our Lord's rebuke
of Peter at Caesarea Philippi (Mk. 8:33). 'Satan' occurs as the
name, or title, of a kind of prosecuting counsel within the heavenly
court in the later Old Testament period (*cf.* Jb 1:6–12; 2:1–6; Zc.
3:1f.). This is not the first time that an Israelite king is depicted in
generous mood after experiencing a singular deliverance in battle
(*cf* 1 Sa. 11:12f.). In this case David's virtual re-installation as king
makes possible a comparison with the beneficent accession acts
with which near eastern kings often began their reigns (*cf.* 2 Ki.
25:27–30).[199] However, although David kept his oath (23), his
deathbed advice to Solomon showed that he had not forgiven
Shimei his insults (*cf.* 1 Ki. 2:8f.).

24. Unless we accuse Mephibosheth of being very devious (*cf.*

Ackroyd), he provides good evidence of his loyalty to David, despite Ziba's calumny (16:3). During the king's absence Mephibosheth has behaved as if in mourning. *beard* is, properly, 'moustache' (*cf.* NIV). *nor washed his clothes*: *cf.* 12:20.

25. There is some doubt as to where precisely Mephibosheth had his interview with David, since the beginning of the verse should be rendered 'And when he came *to* Jerusalem'. But according to 16:3 Mephibosheth remained in the city after David's departure, and the plain inference to be drawn from verse 24 is that Mephibosheth 'came down' to the Jordan (*cf.* vv. 16, 31). It is probably best, therefore, to assume with RSV (*cf.* also NEB, NIV) the loss of a preposition ('from') in the Hebrew.[200] In that case 'home' in verse 30 will have a relative sense. Finally, we should note the possibility that the kind of textual problem which we have observed in verses 18b and 25 has been occasioned by the narrator's desire to present the interviews of verses 16–40 in a particular order (compare the comment above (vv. 16–40) on 'mirror image').

26, 27. Mephibosheth's defence is that, whereas it had been his intention to join David, Ziba had taken advantage of his physical disability. But now that both sides of the story are known to the king, whose discernment in such matters is preternatural (27; *cf.* 14:17, 20), justice will be done. *to him* (26): an addition by RSV. The sense is, rather, as in NIV, 'I said, "I will have my donkey saddled and will ride on it."'

28. Having already experienced mercy from David (9:1ff.), Mephibosheth does not dare – or affects not to dare – to expect more. *right* ($s^e\underline{d}\bar{a}q\hat{a}$), often translated by 'righteousness' in other contexts, implies a claim upon justice by virtue of the integrity of the appellant concerned.

29, 30. David responds somewhat impatiently, though he is moved to the extent of altering his earlier decision (16:4). His compromise solution suggests that he is not entirely sure about Mephibosheth. The latter's reaction to the pronouncement (30) could be a genuine expression of gratitude for the king's safe return, or the utterance of a man happy to have escaped with his life. The evidence tends to point to the former.

31–36. Since Barzillai lived in Transjordan this occasion is one of leave-taking for him. In return for his generous assistance (33; *cf.* 17:27–29), David would have maintained him as an honoured guest at court, but Barzillai was past being attracted by the pleasures of palace life. It is noteworthy that he, the counterpart of Hushai in the story of David's departure from Jerusalem, speaks of himself as a potential *burden* to the king (35; *cf.* 15:33).

31. *to escort him over the Jordan*: 'to send him on his way across the Jordan' may be the intended sense of MT, which is in some confusion at the end of the verse (*cf.* NEB, NIV). *Cf.* also verses 36, 39.

37–40a. *Chimham* was one of Barzillai's sons, as is indicated in some LXX texts (*cf.* NEB). According to 1 Kings 2:7 David gave special instructions to Solomon in relation to the sons of Barzillai, recalling the kindness that they had shown him during Absalom's rebellion. Some have inferred from the name Geruth Chimham ('Chimham's holding') in Jeremiah 41:17 that David made a grant of land to Chimham, hence the perpetuation of his name in the Bethlehem area over several centuries.

37. *my own city*: Rogelim, mentioned in verse 31 and in 17:27, but otherwise unknown.

38. *whatever seems good to you*: Using Barzillai's own phrase (v. 37), David defers to his esteemed subject.

39. *the king went over*: but LXX (Mss) has 'stood still' (*cf.* NEB 'while the king waited'), which makes it unlikely that Barzillai actually accompanied him across the river before returning to Rogelim (*cf.* on v. 31).

40b–43. David's fellow-tribesmen in Judah steal a march over the northerners, whose divided attitude towards him (*cf.* v. 9) is reflected in the statement that only *half the people of Israel* came to escort him back. In this short section we are given an insight into the tensions which existed between Judah and the other tribes and which were finally responsible for the division of the kingdom soon after the death of Solomon (1 Ki. 12). By itself the issue of who escorted the king across the Jordan was of little importance, but to the northerners it afforded more proof of David's bias towards his fellow-Judahites. For their part, the Judahites, while claiming David as one of their own, denied that they had enjoyed any special favours from him (42). Nevertheless, the acrimony hung in the air, and this unbrotherly exchange – in verses 42f. it is conducted in the first person singular in the Hebrew – forms the backcloth to the northerners' temporary defection under Sheba, as recounted in the next chapter. The underlying difficulty is that of making *e duabus unum* – one kingdom out of two distinct parts – and it is in such circumstances that the northerners can at one time lay claim to *ten shares in the king* (43), and at another deny any interest in him ('no portion in David . . . no inheritance in the son of Jesse', 20:1).[201]

43. *and in David also we have more than you*: read instead with the LXX (*cf.* NEB), 'and also we are senior to you' (*i.e.* b^{e}ḵôr, 'first-born', for *bᵉ ḏāwiḏ*, 'in David'). Judah was never accorded the position of 'first-born' among the Israelite tribes, as the northerners point out here (*cf.* Gn. 29:31–35; 1 Ch. 5:1f.). *our king*: see on 20:2. *were fiercer*: the root *qāšâ* also occurs in the account of the wrangling between Rehoboam and the northerners at Shechem (1 Ki. 12:13, RSV '(answered) harshly'). For other elements in the narrative which point forward to, and possibly reflect awareness of, the later division of the kingdom see on 20:1f.

SHEBA'S SECESSION   (20:1–26)

The fragility of the union between Judah and the other tribes, even during David's reign, is underlined by this account of a second 'rebellion' led by the Benjaminite Sheba. However, despite the 'all-Israel' tones early in the narrative, there was little inclination on the part of the northerners to back Sheba militarily, and the 'great schism' simply failed to materialize at this point. The secession is closely linked in the narrative with the events described at the end of ch. 19 (*cf.* 'there' in 20:1), and, though a thematic association of two 'rebellions' more separated in time than appears from the chapter (*cf.*, however, v. 4) cannot be ruled out, there is nothing improbable about the sequence of events which the narrator presents to us.

1. The disgruntled Israelites found a leader in the Benjaminite *Sheba* ben *Bichri*, and David again has to contend with opposition from Saul's old tribe. Bright, noting the similarity between *Bichri* and Becorath in 1 Samuel 9:1 (Saul's genealogy), surmises that Sheba may have been a kinsman of Saul.[202] The *trumpet* blast could signify the rallying of troops for rebellion (15:10; *cf.* 1 Sa. 13:3f.) or their dispersal after battle (v. 22; *cf.* 2:28; 18:16). In fact, Sheba's 'rebellion' is presented more as a secession than as an armed rising. Advance warnings of the eventual secession of the northern tribes for good and all sound clearly in Sheba's jingle; *cf.* 1 Kings 12:16, and see 1 Samuel 25:10 for another slogan from the anti-Davidide faction in ancient Israel. *tents* harks back to Israel's earlier tribal history.[203]

2. Although the reference to the Judahites' adherence to David *from the Jordan to Jerusalem* might seem to imply that the secession was announced before David and his entourage reached Jerusalem, the necessity for a levy of Judahite forces (v. 4) shows that they had already disbanded. The point of the verse is more in the contrast between the behaviour of the respective parties in relation to David. *their king* is significant in the light of the northerners' use of 'our king' (lit. 'my king') in 19:43. The story is written from the perspective of Judah; moreover, such an exclusive association of David with Judah seems to point to a post-Solomonic dating for the chapter and, perhaps, for those chapters which make up the so-called 'Succession Narrative'. See also on verse 1 and on 19:43.

3. *living as if in widowhood* is the best that can be done with an obscure phrase in MT. The LXX has 'living widows' and the Targum 'widows whose husband was alive'.

4, 5. David's original intention was to put a levy of Judahites into the field against Sheba, but Amasa, who had recently replaced Joab as army commander (*cf.* 19:13), failed to act quickly enough. While no reason is given for his dilatoriness, it emerges from verse 11 that his sympathies lay elsewhere than with David.[204]

6, 7. Since the levy had not been raised within the appointed time, *Abishai* was put in charge of the professional army (*your lord's servants*, 6). Joab was still in disgrace! David's fear was that Sheba and his partisans would be able to entrench themselves in some of the fortified cities of Israel and so require a major effort to root them out. *and cause us trouble*: RSV gives the general sense, though it is based on a variant reading for which it claims the support of the Targum. As often, however, the Targum is merely paraphrasing MT. The clause can be translated literally as 'and pluck out our eye', and it has a parallel in Numbers 16:14 where 'Will you put out the eyes of these men?' is euphemistic for 'Will you put out our eyes?'[205] *Joab* (7), though demoted, is still in the action; by the end of the chapter he will have regained his lost command. MT actually has 'the men of Joab', which may refer either to a contingent under his command (*cf.* 18:2) or, more generally, to those who supported him against his rival Amasa. *Cherethites . . . Pelethites*: see on 8:18.

8–10. *Gibeon*, about six miles north of Jerusalem, was in Benjaminite territory and perhaps not where Amasa was supposed to be at this stage. *the great stone*: a landmark possibly also used as an altar (*cf.* 1 Sa. 6:18; 14:33f.). The rest of verse 8 being obscured to some extent by textual problems, it is not clear how Joab performed his trick. The sword in his *hand* (10) may have been the same as the sword which had fallen to the ground (8) and which he had meanwhile retrieved but had not returned to its sheath. Alternatively, it is possible that Joab had brought two swords, one of which he contrived to let fall to the ground in order to give Amasa the impression that he was unarmed. In view of the fact that *did* *not observe* (10) is properly 'did not take heed of' the first alternative is the more likely.[206]

9. Being grasped by the *beard* as a preliminary to the kiss of greeting would not have been likely to excite Amasa's suspicion (*cf.* Kirkpatrick).

10. Joab deals to Amasa a fate similar to that of Abner (3:27), who had also represented a threat to his personal ambitions. From now to the end of the chapter it is the story of 'Joab and his men'; after verse 10b Abishai is not even mentioned again. See also on verse 11.

11. In the henchman's challenge Joab's name precedes David's – an indication, perhaps, of the mixed motivation of Joab and his supporters (contrast Jdg. 7:18). *men* (*na^{ca}rê*): possibly one of Joab's attendants; see on 2 Samuel 2:14 for this meaning of BH *na^{c}ar*.

12. The text from which, as Robert Louis Stevenson recounts, the *curé* of St. Germain de Calberte preached a 'rousing sermon' over the body of the martyr Du Chayla.[207] The *people* are the troops under the command of Abishai and Joab; they must not be distracted from the urgent business of apprehending Sheba (*cf.* v. 13).

14. *Abel of Beth-maacah* (perhaps mod. Tell Abil) was one of the northernmost towns of Israel, situated a few miles to the west of Dan (*cf.* on v. 18).[208] The full form of the name as here may indicate a connection with the Aramaean kingdom of Maacah, which had become tributary to David (*cf.* 10:6–8, 19).[209] *Bichrites*, denoting the members of Sheba's family or clan (*cf.* v. 1), is preferable to MT 'Berites', a name not attested outside this passage.[210]

15. Standard methods of attacking a besieged city are described. The *mound* was intended to act as a ramp enabling the besieging army to attack the upper section of the wall. A parallel operation to undermine another part of the wall was often undertaken (*cf.* NEB; RSV *battering*). *and it stood against the rampart*: the exact sense is unclear, witness the ancient versions. NEB transfers the clause to the beginning of the next verse and makes the wise woman the subject: 'Then a wise woman stood on the rampart . . . '

16–22. These verses recount how a city was saved by wisdom, though hardly in the manner envisaged by the 'Preacher' in Ecclesiastes 9:14f. A couple of elements in the story recall ch. 14: the protagonists are again Joab and a wise woman, and the basic issue is that of conduct prejudicial to the 'heritage of the Lord' (v. 19; *cf.* 14:16).

16. *a wise woman*: the existence of such 'wise women' in early

Israelite society (*cf.* ch. 14) may have been an enabling factor in the personification of wisdom as a female counterpart to the adulteress in the book of Proverbs.

18, 19. The woman evidently quotes a proverb in proof of the city's long-standing reputation for wisdom and good counsel. Since *ask* (18) may have an oracular connotation (*cf.* 1 Sa. 22:10; 2 Sa. 5:19, 23), it may even be significant that *settled* (*hēṭammû*) derives from the same root as the oracular term 'Thummim'. In verse 19 the woman speaks as the representative of the beleaguered city which, she says, occupies too honourable a place in Israel to deserve the fate that Joab is threatening upon it. *a mother in Israel* describes the prophetess Deborah in Judges 5:7, but *mother* is used here in the sense of 'mother-city' (*cf.* 'metropolis'), just as the 'daughters' of a city are its satellite villages (*e.g.* Jdg. 1:27).[211] At the same time, the dual sense of *mother* aids the identification of the woman with the city, and this presumably also accounts for the use of the verb 'kill' (RSV *destroy*). *the heritage of the Lord*: Israel as a whole is viewed as God's heritage in 1 Samuel 26:19 and 2 Samuel 21:3. This may be the sense in 14:16, and possibly here. To destroy Abel, then, would be to impair the integrity of the community of Israel. There may be the further suggestion that the people of Abel held an inalienable title to their land, in accordance with the tradition of Yahweh's allocations to the tribes at the time of the settlement (*cf.* Lv. 25:23, 28; Nu. 27:1–11; 36:7–9; 1 Ki. 21:3f.).

In view of certain translational difficulties in verses 18f., it may be noted that the LXX reflects a divergent text: 'Let them ask in Abel and in Dan if all is over with what Israel's faithful ones have laid down' (JB). At the least the association of Abel and Dan is interesting – Tell el-Qadi (Dan) is a mere four miles east of Tell Abil! – and, in fact, it is very difficult to decide which of the readings, MT or LXX, is to be considered original. The LXX reading credits Abel (and Dan) with a reputation not so much for wisdom as for its loyalty to Israelite traditions.

21. The *hill country of Ephraim* extends south into Benjaminite territory (*cf.* v. 1). *give up him alone*: Joab reasons as Ahithophel had previously done (17:3).

22. A *wisdom* which counsels the beheading of an individual in order to save a city from destruction is no mere ethereal, humanistic abstraction; it is more like the 'wisdom' of Jonadab (*cf.* on 13:3). The liquidation of Sheba's revolt and, incidentally, of Amasa (v. 10), left the way open for Joab to regain his former position, as may be implied at the end of the verse (*cf.* 14:23, referring to

Absalom's (partial) reinstatement in Jerusalem). *blew the trumpet*: see on verse 1.

23–26. A list of David's officials similar to that given at 8:15–18. The two lists probably come from the earlier (8:15–18) and later (20:23–26) parts of David's reign. Compare also 1 Kings 4:1–6 for a list of Solomon's officials.

23. *Joab* is army commander, notwithstanding his temporary set-back when Amasa replaced him (19:13; 20:4). For *Cherethites* the Hebrew consonantal text has 'Carians'. However, although Carians from Asia Minor were in the service of Joash (*cf.* 2 Ki. 11:4, 19), the usual pairing of *Cherethites* and *Pelethites*, as at 8:18, strongly favours the RSV reading.

24. *Adoram* is not mentioned in the earlier list, from which it could be inferred that the institution of the forced levy,[212] which was more a feature of Solomon's administration and a major cause of the schism which immediately followed (1 Ki. 12:4), was introduced in the later part of David's reign. It was by means of the forced levy that Solomon carried out his grandiose building programme. Adoram is probably to be identified with the Adoniram who occupied the same post under Solomon (1 Ki. 4:6; 5:14) and who – now again as Adoram – was stoned to death by the irate northerners when Rehoboam sent him on an impossible mission (1 Ki. 12:18). This would, of course, assume a very long period in office. An alternative possibility is that two or three generations of the same family bearing the same name worked in the service of David and Solomon. Mettinger surmises that Adoram may have been a non-Israelite.[213]

25. *Sheva*: see on 8:17. *Abiathar*: 'Ahimelech the son of Abiathar' at 8:17 (*q.v.*).

26. *Ira* replaces David's sons mentioned at the corresponding point in 8:18. Quite apart from the considerations discussed at 8:18, the omission of a reference to the princes as 'priests' is not at all surprising in view of the intervening narrative. There is no other certain reference to Ira, though two of David's warrior corps, 'The Thirty', went by the same name (23:26, 38). An identification with one of them, Ira the Ithrite (23:38), has occasionally been proposed. *the Jairite*: possibly from one of the villages called Havvoth-Jair after one 'Jair the son of Manasseh' (*e.g.* Nu. 32:41). There is some support in the ancient versions for a connection with the priestly town of Jattir (Jos. 21:14), also mentioned among the places well-disposed towards David during his period of outlawry (1 Sa. 30:27).

8   The Samuel Appendix (21:1–24:25)

Chs. 21–24, also dealing with David's reign, comprise a variety of material which has not been integrated into the narrative of the preceding chapters. On the contrary, the symmetrical (concentric) arrangement of the several sections in the 'appendix' (see the Introduction) gives it an integrity of its own; it is anything but a haphazard assortment of traditions relating to David. At its centre stand two poetic pieces celebrating respectively Yahweh's delivering acts on behalf of David (22:1–51), and the covenantal relationship between Yahweh and the house of David upon which so much of Israel's hope for the future is based (23:1–7). These, we are reminded, are the secret of David's greatness. The lists of heroes and heroic exploits that frame the poetic centre-piece represent human instrumentality, but not the underlying reality, which is Yahweh.

THE GIBEONITES AND THE FAMILY OF SAUL   (21:1–14)

When Shimei fired his invective at David as he withdrew from Jerusalem at the beginning of the Absalom rebellion, he taunted him with the suggestion that Yahweh was now taking vengeance on him for 'all the blood of the house of Saul' (16:7f.). It is possible that Shimei was referring, at least in part, to the execution of seven members of Saul's family as recounted here. But whether the cause of Shimei's rage or not, David's surrender of the Saulides to their fate was bound to be controversial, and the cultic pretext for the executions could all too readily be read as an excuse for a pogrom against remnants of the rival house. However, the Hittite parallel highlighted by Malamat (see on v. 1) shows that Israel was not alone in believing that the covenant breaches of the fathers could be visited upon the children. To the extent, therefore, that David was a child of his age, he had a defence against the conspiracy charge.

The additional question of the relationship of this section to ch. 9, which tells how Mephibosheth was accorded grace and favour status in Jerusalem, has already been broached in the introduction to that chapter.

1. Famine caused by drought was not unfamiliar in Palestine (*cf.* Gn. 12:10; Ru. 1:1, *etc.*). Both were regarded as signs of divine displeasure (*cf.* 1 Ki. 17:1; Ezk. 14:21; Hg. 1:10f.), so that inquiry as to the cause would naturally follow the kind of outbreak described here. In response to the inquiry it was disclosed that Saul had left David a legacy of *bloodguilt* in connection with certain members of the Gibeonite clan. The story of how, by fraudulent means, the Gibeonites had secured a treaty with the Israelites is told in Joshua 9.[1] That treaty, confirmed on oath (Jos. 9:15), should not have been revoked by the Israelites however much they might have wished to do so. Psalm 15:4 makes this a point of honour. With *because he put the Gibeonites to death* we can contrast 'and they did not kill them' (Jos. 9:26). As Malamat has observed in a short discussion of biblical and Hittite doctrines of causality, the (so-called) second plague prayer of the Hittite king Mursilis II (fourteenth century BC) partly blames a twenty-year plague in Hatti-land on a breach, in the previous reign, of a treaty between the Hittites and the Egyptians.[2]

2. The Gibeonites were *Amorites*, which term is used here to denote the pre-Israelite inhabitants of Canaan (*cf.* 1 Sa. 7:14). Because of their treaty relationship with the Israelites they had continued to live in the land, albeit with servile status (*cf.* Jos. 9:23, 27). *had sworn to spare them* is (lit.) 'had sworn to them' (*cf.*, for the same expression, Jos. 9:15, 18, 19, 20). However, the Gibeonites were an affront to Saul's brand of nationalistic Yahwism, and the fact that they were settled in Benjaminite territory cannot have helped.[3] His ruthless action against them is entirely in keeping with what we have already seen of him (*e.g.* 1 Sa. 22:16–19; 28:3). RSV omits the words 'and said to them' (*cf.* fn.) after *called the Gibeonites*, because there is no direct speech immediately following. This situation occurs elsewhere (*e.g.* Gn. 4:8 (MT only); Ex. 19:25) and is not dealt with consistently in modern translations. NIV 'and spoke to them' assumes that the Hebrew does not have to be followed by direct speech and may be correct. Another possibility

is that the rest of verse 2 was added later by way of explanation,
so making necessary a new introductory clause at the beginning of
verse 3.

3. *make expiation*: *kāpar* most often signifies expiation by
sacrificial blood. The Gibeonites' mention of silver and gold in the
next verse may hint at a related meaning of the root *k-p-r*: the
noun *kōper* means 'ransom'. *that you may bless*: Israel are currently
under a curse because of Saul's violation of the Gibeonites' treaty
(*cf.* Dt. 28:18, 22–24). *the heritage of the Lord*: see on 20:19.

4. Though the commutation of capital sentences to monetary
fines was sometimes possible (*cf.* Ex. 21:30), Saul's crime did not
come into this category (*cf.* Nu. 35:31f.). *neither is it for us. . .*
seems to introduce the idea of blood-revenge, with the suggestion
that, since the Gibeonites are in no position to act, the responsibility
for its execution rests with David.

5, 6. *and planned to destroy us*: RSV involves implicit emendation
of the Hebrew. No less plausible is NEB, 'Let us make an end of
the man who caused our undoing and ruined us, so that he shall
never again have his place within the borders of Israel.' *seven* (6)
may be symbolic as well as literal, representing the totality of Saul's
family whose lives were deemed to be forfeit. What the Gibeonites
planned to do to their victims is expressed by a word (*yāqaʿ*) of
uncertain meaning, variously rendered in the ancient versions
by 'expose to the sun' (LXX), 'crucify' (Targum), and 'sacrifice'
(Peshitta). The uncertainty is well reflected in the contrasting efforts
of RSV (*hang them up*) and NEB ('hurl them down').[4] In Numbers
25:4, where the word must bear the same meaning, *hang them up*
fits better with the accompanying phrase, 'before the sun' (*cf.*,
perhaps, Dt. 21:23; Jos. 8:29; 10:26f.). As in Numbers 25:4, *before
the Lord* (lit. 'for the Lord', but see v. 9) underlines the judicial
nature of the killings. *at Gibeon on the mountain of the Lord*: a
reconstruction of the Hebrew based on the LXX. MT reads: 'at
Gibeah of Saul, the chosen of the Lord'. It is the peculiarity of
this latter – on Gibeonite lips! – that has encouraged the RSV
translators to emend. Since *on the mountain of the Lord* (*beʿhar
YHWH*) is graphically similar to 'the chosen of the Lord' (*beʿhîr
YHWH*), and comes again (*grosso modo*) in verse 9, a reasonable
case for its originality can be made out. The alteration of *Gibeon*
to 'Gibeah of Saul', to provide 'chosen' with a referent, would
have naturally followed the misreading of *beʿhar*.

Though David complies with the Gibeonites' request, there is
nothing in the text to suggest that he engineered the situation so
as to be rid of potential rivals from the house of Saul. That he

could have benefited from the Gibeonites' revenge is no proof of machiavellian plotting on his part.

7. The pact between David and Jonathan was an *oath of the Lord* in that Yahweh was its witness and guarantor (*cf.* 1 Sa. 20:12-17, 42). David's acquaintance with *Mephibosheth*, as in 9:1-13, is presupposed in this verse.

8. *Rizpah*: *cf.* 3:7. *Mephibosheth* was evidently the name of a son of Saul, as well as being the name of the grandson mentioned in verse 7. (We could compare the recurrence of the name Tamar in David's family (13:1; 14:27).) *Merab*: MT has 'Michal', but is almost certainly in error. A couple of Hebrew manuscripts, and also some LXX texts, have *Merab*, who was indeed the wife of *Adriel* according to 1 Samuel 18:19. Michal is said to have remained childless (6:23).[5] The Targum tries to satisfy honour with 'the five sons of Merab whom Michal reared'. This is typical Targumic harmonizing which, in its own way, AV sees fit to emulate.

9. *hanged*: *cf.* on verse 6. If the executions were carried out at Gibeon (see on v. 6), it is possible that the *mountain* corresponds to the location of the high place of 1 Kings 3:4. *barley harvest* features in the Gezer Calendar (1. 4), in between flax-cutting and the general harvest, and took place in April (*cf.* also Ex. 9:31f.; Ru. 1:22).[6] 'We are given the impression that the execution of the men at the time when the first-fruits of the barley harvest would normally be offered represents a sacrifice which is intended to have a similar effect to that of Hiel in I Kings 16.34 and of the Moabite king in II Kings 3.27' (Hertzberg).

10. Rizpah lay upon the sackcloth (*cf.* 1 Ki. 21:27; Is. 58:5; Joel 1:13) until, with the descent of rain upon the corpses (*upon them*), she had received a token of Yahweh's favour. We are probably to think of an unseasonable shower, rather than that she maintained her vigil until the autumnal rains in October-November.

11-14. Strangely, the preoccupation of these verses is with the honourable burial of the remains of Saul and Jonathan, as if David hoped to forestall criticism for the harsh treatment of Saul's family by this act of piety towards the memory of its most senior members. It would not have been the first time that he had tried to make political capital out of the bones of Saul and Jonathan (*cf.* 2:4-7).

12. See 1 Samuel 31:1-13. *stolen* implies nothing dishonourable in this context (*cf.* 2 Ki. 11:2). *public square*: 1 Samuel 31:12 mentions the city wall; the *square* (*reḥōḇ*) may have adjoined the wall (*cf.* 2 Ch. 32:6).

13. Nothing definite is stated about the last resting-place of the

Gibeonites' victims, though the LXX of verse 14 says that they were buried with the remains of Saul and Jonathan.

14. *Zela*: one of 'the cities of the tribe of Benjamin' in Joshua 18:28 (*cf.* v. 21). J. M. Miller claims that it was Saul's home village.[7] *God heeded supplications*: the parallel clause in 24:25 underlines the basic similarity in theme between 21:1–14 and 24:1–25. Here it is almost as if the reburial of Saul and Jonathan in the family grave was a factor in the assuaging of Yahweh's wrath.

ENCOUNTERS WITH PHILISTINE HEROES (21:15–22)

This section, which records with telegraphic brevity some successes of David's men against formidable Philistine heroes, makes a fitting preface to David's psalm of praise in ch. 22. The incidents, most or all of which may be presumed to have taken place during David's reign, cannot be given more precise chronological settings (though see on 5:25).

15. *again* suggests that verses 15ff. have been excerpted from a fuller account of the Philistine wars. Hertzberg thinks that the section was originally preceded by a short account of David's encounter with Goliath, and that this latter was omitted in deference to the longer version in 1 Samuel 17. He notes the possible significance of 'by the hand of David' (v. 22) in this regard. *servants*, as in 20:6, *etc.*, refers to David's personal army.

16. *Ishbi-benob* is possibly a corruption of an original reading, 'And Benob took him (*i.e.* David) prisoner' (*cf.* NEB); this agrees well with the references to David's fatigue (v. 15) and to the giant's intention of killing him.[8] *the descendants of the giants*: the $y^e l \hat{\imath} \underline{d} \hat{e}$ $h \bar{a} r \bar{a} p \hat{a}$, the $r \bar{a} p \hat{a}$ element of which may be related to the term $r^e p \bar{a}$ '$\hat{\imath} m$, used for some of the pre-Israelite population of Canaan (Gn. 15:20; Jos. 17:15).[9] In this connection they are represented as abnormally tall (Dt. 2:11, 20; 3:11). Other explanations of $r \bar{a} p \hat{a}$ think in terms of a warrior guild dedicated to a god Rapha, or to a god whose symbol was the Syro-Palestinian scimitar (*cf.*, perhaps, Greek $harp\bar{e}$).[10] This man's spear, weighing approximately $7\frac{1}{2}$ lbs., was light-weight compared with Goliath's (1 Sa. 17:7)! The word *sword* is supplied according to context; NEB opts for '(a new) belt', which is interpreted to mean 'a belt of honour' (*cf.* 2:21 (RSV 'spoil'); 18:11).[11]

17. David thus owed a personal debt to Abishai, even though in other circumstances he might complain about the troublesome sons of Zeruiah (*cf.* 3:39). In the light of this near-tragedy pressure was put on David to desist from the usual kingly practice of leading his troops in battle. *the lamp of Israel*: when a man dies his lamp is extinguished (Jb. 18:6; Pr. 13:9); David's death would be tantamount to the extinction of the life of the community (*cf.* La. 4:20). The figure of the lamp, which came to symbolize the Davidic dynasty as maintained by Yahweh (1 Ki. 15:4; Ps. 132:17), possibly derives from the world of the sanctuary, in which a lamp was kept burning 'continually' (see on 1 Sa. 3:3). McKane surmises that the sanctuary lamp was a royal emblem in the Jerusalem cult, and that its maintenance symbolized the preservation of the community.

18–21. Highlights from three other engagements with the Philistines.

18. *Gob* is unknown apart from verses 18f.; in this verse the LXX and Peshitta have 'Gath', while the Chronicles parallel has 'Gezer' (1 Ch. 20:4). *Sibbecai*: see on 23:27. *Hushathite*: from Hushah (mod. Ḥūsān), about four miles west of Bethlehem (Simons, *GTTOT*, p. 337). *descendants of the giants*: see on verse 16.

19. Some of the details here so obviously recall the story of David and Goliath (1 Sa. 17) as to lead many to suspect that a victory by the comparatively unknown *Elhanan* has been attributed to David in 1 Samuel 17, in keeping with the later tendency to gild the Davidic lily. But first we should note that *Jaareoregim* compounds two words in the original, and that the second (*'ōreḡîm*) is almost universally regarded as resulting from a premature copying of the identical form (RSV *weaver's*) at the end of the verse. *Jaare*, the first element, should perhaps be read as 'Jair' (*cf.* 1 Ch. 20:5 (*Qerê*)).[12] As to the main point at issue, 1 Chronicles 20:5 offers a variant text: 'and Elhanan the son of Jair slew Lahmi the brother of Goliath the Gittite' (*cf.* AV here). But this looks too much like an attempt at harmonization: for instance, 'Lahmi' is the second element of the Hebrew for 'Bethlehemite', the originality of which in the present text need scarcely be doubted. Since the difficulties confronting the harmonizers have been amply expounded by James Barr,[13] comment will be restricted to the least unlikely proposal, viz. that, if the name David was a throne-name (*cf.* on 8:9f.; 12:25), it is possible that *Elhanan* was the *personal* name of Goliath's conqueror.[14] (In 23:24 there is mention of another Bethlehemite who bore the name Elhanan.) *Jaare* might then be explained as a corruption of 'Jesse', since the two names do not differ greatly in the Hebrew square script. At the same time, it must be conceded that such a reference to David in among a summary of exploits by his mighty men reads a little strangely –

even allowing for the terms of verse 22b. Kirkpatrick's invention of a second Gittite giant by the name of Goliath is quite unconvincing, being on a par with Clement of Alexandria's 'other Cephas' in Galatians 2:11ff.[15] The comparison of the spear-shaft with a *weaver's beam* is made in 1 Samuel 17:7, but also occurs in 1 Chronicles 11:23 in reference to the spear of an Egyptian hero.

20, 21. The fourth Philistine combatant is distinguished by a physical abnormality instead of a name. *taunted* (21) is the verb used five times in the Goliath narrative in 1 Samuel 17 (*cf.* on 1 Sa. 17:10). *Shimei*: the same as Shammah (1 Sa. 16:9) and Shimeah (2 Sa. 13:3).

A PSALM OF THANKSGIVING   (22:1–51)

A psalm from the 'Davidic Psalter' celebrates David's achievements, while attributing them to Yahweh's magnificent interventions on his behalf. It corresponds to Psalm 18 – one of the nine psalms classified as 'royal' by the pioneer form critic Hermann Gunkel. Its antiquity and even the possibility of its Davidic authorship are matters which command wide sympathy, as was noted with the faintest hint of tongue-in-cheek by C. S. Lewis: 'I think certain scholars allow that Psalm 18 (of which a slightly different version occurs in 2 *Samuel* 22) might be by David himself.'[16]

There are numerous differences, mainly of a minor sort, between the two versions of the psalm. Some are attributable to copyists' errors and others to the vicissitudes of (independent) transmission and, to a degree, adaptation. As an example of the last-named we may cite the opening verse of Psalm 18 ('I love thee, O Lord, my strength'), for which there is no equivalent in this chapter.

1–4. The superscription in verse 1 is worded similarly to that of Psalm 18. David appears as Yahweh's anointed against whom the kings of the earth array themselves (*cf.* Ps. 2:1ff.) – though in strict historical terms many of his wars were wars of conquest. The theme of the afflicted servant of Yahweh, which is so prominent in the Psalter and never far from the surface of this poem, is particularly evocative of David's earlier career when Saul sought his life; hence the appended *and from the hand of Saul*. *rock* (2, 3) represents the Hebrew synonyms *sela*[c] and *ṣûr*, the latter being especially common as a divine appellative (*e.g.* Dt. 32:4; 1 Sa. 2:2). *fortress* (2) is the word used for the stronghold of Adullam (1 Sa. 22:1–5; *cf.* 23:14, 19, 29), and for the Jebusite fort that became 'David's city' (5:9). But the psalmist's ultimate security is traced to Yahweh himself. *horn* (3) symbolizes strength (*cf.* on 1 Sa. 2:1). However, the leading idea in these opening lines is expressed by the Hebrew root *y-š-ᶜ*: *salvation, saviour, savest* (3), and *saved* (4). So in Zechariah 9:9 the messianic figure of whom David is the prototype approaches Jerusalem 'triumphant and victorious (*nôšāᶜ*, lit. "saved, delivered")'. Compare the use of the same root in 8:6, 14, where David's military conquests are attributed to the delivering power of Yahweh.

5–7. In a fearful experience the psalmist calls upon Yahweh and is heard. A. R. Johnson sought the locus of this psalm in an autumnal festival whose proceedings involved the ritual humiliation of the king prior to his exaltation, but the evidence for such a rite at such a festival is not easily discovered within the Old Testament.[17]

5, 6. The waters of death are virtually a synonym for Sheol (*cf.* Jon. 2:3–6). *cords* (6), as in Job 18:10 and Psalm 140:5, denotes a kind of trap; compare also the parallel *snares*. These are figures for the hostile powers which threaten the psalmist's life (*cf.* v. 18).

7. The *temple* could be either Yahweh's heavenly sanctuary (*cf.* 1 Ki. 8:44f.; Ps. 11:4; Is. 6:1) or the Jerusalem sanctuary towards which the Israelite suppliant might pray (*cf.* 1 Ki. 8:30; Jon. 2:7). The former is the more likely.

8–16. To describe the effect of Yahweh's intervention, the psalmist resorts to the language of theophany as we encounter it in the exodus and Sinai traditions (*cf.* Ex. 19; Jdg. 5:4f.; Ps. 68:8; Hab. 3). The circumstances which called forth this display are lost to view as the terrifying vision of Yahweh unfolds.

8, 9. Earthquake (8) and fire (9) are the heralds of his coming. This is the only mention of the *foundations of the heavens* in the Old Testament – Psalm 18:7 has 'mountains' for *heavens* – but a similar cosmology is reflected in the 'pillars of heaven' in Job 26:11.[18] In a startling use of imagery applied elsewhere to the monster Leviathan (Jb. 41:19–21) *smoke* and *fire* are said to proceed from Yahweh's *nostrils* and *mouth* – here, it would seem, as an expression of his anger. The *glowing coals* (*cf.* Ezk. 1:13; 10:2), like the smoking fire-pot and flaming torch in Genesis 15:17, are simply emblematic of the divine presence.

10, 11. The very heavens are abased at the advent of God. NEB's 'He swept the skies aside' is, if anything, more grand; the Hebrew (unpointed) can tolerate either sense.[19] Cherubim, in the symbolism of the sanctuary, are the bearers of the divine throne (*cf.* on 1 Sa. 4:4); this warrior figure actually flies upon a *cherub. was seen* can by the merest change become 'swooped' (so NEB and Ps. 18:10;

cf. Ps. 104:3). This is a 'coming down' in deliverance (*cf.* Ex. 3:8), though the judgement of the oppressor is necessary for the relief of the oppressed.

12. *darkness . . . his canopy*: *cf.* 1 Kings 8:12. This idea may have been suggested by the absence of natural light in the 'holy of holies' in the temple. *thick clouds, a gathering of water*: the Hebrew is obscure.[20] Psalm 18:11 has '(his canopy) thick clouds dark with water'.

14. In Hebrew 'thunderings' are, literally, 'voices' (*e.g.* Ex. 19:16), so that the two lines of the verse are in parallel. *Cf.* Job 37:2–5. *Most High* is a translation of *ᶜelyôn*, an epithet of the Canaanite high god which was taken over by the Israelites and applied to Yahweh (*cf.* Gn. 14:22).

15. The *arrows* are lightning shafts (*cf.* Ps. 77:17; Zc. 9:14). As a result of this display the psalmist's enemies are thrown into a 'divine panic' (*cf.* 1 Sa. 7:10).[21]

16. In the flight of the sea before Yahweh's *rebuke* – 'roar (of anger)' is a possible rendering[22] – there are echoes of the primeval battle with the waters of chaos (*cf.* Ps. 104:6f.), and, perhaps, of the deliverance at the Red Sea (*cf.* Ps. 106:9).

17–20. This majestic being comes to the psalmist's aid. The *many* (or 'mighty', as NEB) *waters* (17) are those of verse 5; *drew* is the verb on which Exodus 2:10 builds its etymology of the name Moses ('because I drew him out of the water'). *a broad place* (20): in Hebrew psychology distress is viewed as a narrowing, or hemming in, and relief as the opposite. Psalm 4:1 brings the two ideas together: 'Thou hast given me room when I was in distress.' Verse 20b introduces a theme which is developed in verses 21–25. *because he delighted in me* recalls, as far as David's history is concerned, the resigned utterance of 15:25f. and is, in a way, its answer.

21–25. The psalmist is not talking about justification by works, much less about sinless perfection, but about 'a conscience void of offence toward God and men' (Acts 24:16). In the issue between himself and his opponents right was on his side, or Yahweh would not have savingly interposed. As verses 26–28 make clear, Yahweh may intervene for good or ill, and all depending upon the integrity or otherwise of the human element. In a similar moment of exhilaration another psalmist can observe, 'If I had cherished iniquity in my heart, the Lord would not have listened' (Ps. 66:18). It is true that within the shortened perspective of a largely this-world theodicy the absence of vindication could prove almost unbearable, yet it was by this route that a deeper faith was won – as may be seen, for example, in the 'Psalm of Habakkuk', whose indebtedness to our psalm is evident at one point, but whose author goes on to declare himself for Yahweh even if the signs of his approval are withheld (Hab. 3:17f.).

26–28. From personal experience the psalmist moves on to a general statement about the principles governing God's dealings with humanity. The *loyal* (*ḥāsîḏ*, 26) man is the one who maintains 'steadfast love' (*ḥeseḏ*); for *ḥeseḏ* as a human and divine attribute see on 16:17. (*blameless*) *man*: MT has 'warrior' (*gibbôr*), but RSV is guided by Psalm 18:25 (*geḇar*, 'man'). In verse 27 'shrewd' (NIV) would be better than *perverse* (*tittappāl*) since it avoids any hint of a moral aspersion. Carlson suspects a veiled reference, per word-play, to Ahithophel (*cf.* 15:31).[23] *a humble people* (28): possibly referring to Israel, which is, predictably, how the Targum interprets. NEB 'humble folk' thinks more in social, or even spiritual, terms (*cf.* Jas. 4:6).

29–37. Further expressions of what Yahweh means to the psalmist personally.

29. As an utterance of David, the acknowledgement that Yahweh is his *lamp* takes on added interest in the light of 21:17 (*q.v.*).

30. He who enjoys Yahweh's help will perform exploits, whether it is the crushing of a troop (RSV) or leaping over a bank (NEB) in the first line. If it is the latter, the verse may be referring to two stages in the capture of a city – clearing the outer rampart and then the city wall. Kirkpatrick, translating by 'I have run after a troop' in the first colon, sees allusions to David's pursuit of the Amalekite raiders (1 Sa. 30) and to the capture of Zion (2 Sa. 5).

31. *proves true*: a comparison with refined metal is suggested by MT *ṣerûpâ*; God's word stands the test (*cf.* NEB).

32. This is the Israelite credo with its implicit monotheism, counterpart to the Islamic 'There is no God but Allah', but preceding it by centuries. The Targumic paraphrase ('There is no God but the Lord') is so strongly suggestive of the Islamic confession as to have convinced one writer that it was deliberately phrased as a counter-claim.[24] But there is much against this view, and we may compare, already in the New Testament, the assertion of Paul that 'there is no God but one' (1 Cor. 8:4; *cf.* Dt. 6:4).

33. *my strong refuge*: Psalm 18:32 has 'who girds me with strength', which is also the reading of 4QSam[a] and the LXX (Lucianic) here.[25] RSV itself draws on Psalm 18 for *has made*; MT *wayyattēr* is obscure. *safe*: better rendered 'blameless' (NEB) or 'perfect' (NIV).

34. Swiftness is the point of the comparison with hinds (*cf.* Targum, NEB). *heights* (pl. of *bāmâ*) would normally refer to the cultic 'high places', but that is inappropriate here (unless, with Ackroyd, we see a possible reference to the king's role in community worship (*cf.* 1 Ki. 3:3f.)). Probably the figure of the hind extends to this clause as well (*cf.* 1 Ch. 12:8; Song 2:8f.): the swift-footed on the hills – for *bāmâ* in this sense see 2 Samuel 1:19, 25 – is also sure-footed.

35. Skill, of different sorts (*cf.* Ex. 35:30–35), comes from Yahweh. The *bow of bronze* could be one reinforced with bronze or one adorned with bronze carvings (*cf.* Jb. 20:24). NEB 'arrow tipped with bronze' assumes metonymy, as do several of the modern translations in the Job reference.

36. ²⁶*the shield of thy salvation*: compare the 'helmet of salvation' (Is. 59:17), and the 'shield of faith' and 'helmet of salvation' in the Christian panoply (Eph. 6:16f.). *help*, previously only one of a number of emended readings of MT, now has the authority of 4QSamᵃ.[27] Psalm 18:35 has 'meekness' (*i.e.* *'anwāṯᵉḵā* for *'ᵃnōṯᵉḵā* here). NEB 'providence' assumes a Hebrew cognate for a word in Arabic and Aramaic meaning 'care, solicitude'.[28] MT as it stands could be rendered 'thy hearkening' (*cf.* v. 7), in which case we should observe a contrast with verse 42.

37. *a wide place for my steps*: *cf.* on verse 20. Cross and Freedman prefer 'long-striding legs'.[29]

38–43. The complete subjugation of the king's enemies is celebrated in terms which answer most directly to David's wars of conquest.

41. The turning of enemy backs in flight may be intended (*cf.* Jos. 7:8, 12), but the Hebrew is compressed and as likely refers to the 'act of suppression' in which the foot of the conqueror was placed on the neck – so the Hebrew (lit.) for *back* – of the defeated (*cf.* NEB, and see Jos. 10:24).

42. When the failure of the enemies' gods to deliver their devotees becomes manifest, appeal to Yahweh will be of no avail. In isolation, the verse may also embrace Yahweh-worshippers within the nation who are, for all that, opponents of the psalmist. *looked*: Psalm 18:41 has 'cried out', which differs only slightly in form and is often preferred here (*cf.* NEB, NIV).

44–46. Yahweh's king rules the nations. *the peoples* (44): MT has 'my people', which could recall the civil convulsions of David's reign. But the context favours the plural (*cf.* LXX, Targum (Mss)); Psalm 18:43 has 'people'. This conflict is depicted as a trial-at-court (*rîḇ*) in which the divine judge gives the verdict in favour of his earthly vicegerent. *head of the nations* sits ill on anyone other than David and Solomon, under whom Israel achieved the status of an imperial power. *came cringing to me* (45): perhaps better, 'failed because of me'.[30] BH *kāḥaš* is sometimes used of crop failure (Hos. 9:2; Hab. 3:17) and forms a reasonable parallel to 'withered' in verse 46 (RSV *lost heart*) – though in this case NEB, by revocalizing, obtains 'shall be brought (captive)'. *came trembling*: adopting the reading of Psalm 18:45; *cf.* Micah 7:17, where a different verb (*rāḡaz*) is used.

47–51. A final ascription of praise to Yahweh, in which the themes and imagery of earlier sections are given a brief encore.

47. *The Lord lives* is the same kind of cultic affirmation as the familiar 'the Lord reigns' in the Psalter, and its background is perhaps to be sought in Canaanite ritual where the cry, 'Baal the Mighty is alive', proclaims Baal's return from the dead.[31] Yahweh, by contrast, is the ever-living One who pronounces on the entire pantheon of the old order: 'you shall die like men, and fall like any prince' (Ps. 82:7).[32]

48. *vengeance*, a divine prerogative (Dt. 32:35; *cf.* Rom. 12:19), is plural here, representing those judicial acts by which Yahweh vindicates his servants (Dt. 32:36; *cf.* 1 Sa. 25:39).

50. Quoted by Paul in Romans 15:9 as an intimation of the blessing of the nations through the gospel.

51. Thematically the psalm echoes and enlarges upon much that is in Hannah's Song (1 Sa. 2:1–10). Each climaxes with a reference to Yahweh's faithfulness to his anointed king, but with the difference that, since the dynastic oracle has supervened (7:8–16), it is now the whole Davidic succession which is the object of his favour. Fittingly, the next section takes up this theme of the 'everlasting covenant' between Yahweh and David (*cf.* 23:5).

THE LAST WORDS OF DAVID   (23:1-7)

Whereas the psalm in the previous chapter celebrates the delivering acts of Yahweh by which the Davidic supremacy was established, this little poem is composed around the theme of the dynastic covenant through which the continued prosperity of the Davidic house was vouchsafed. What was announced through Nathan the prophet in ch. 7 is now dignified as an 'everlasting covenant, ordered in all things and secure' (v. 5). It is, therefore, of the greatest significance for our understanding of the origin and development of the 'Davidic hope' that the poem is of palpable antiquity. There is, in fact, no reason to deny it to David himself.[33] As J. R. Porter fairly observes, the royal autobiographical report is a common

literary type in the ancient near east,[34] and the existence of something equivalent in Israel should not occasion surprise. We note,
then, at this early stage both the vitality of the dynastic hope and
the idealizing of the Davidic king in inchoately messianic terms
(*cf.* on vv. 3f.).

1. There are other *last words* of David (1 Ki. 2:1–9; *cf.* also
1 Ch. 23:27), but these represent his enduring legacy to Israel.
The fourfold formula of introduction which follows recalls the
introductions to the oracles of Balaam (Nu. 24:3f., 15f.), and has
even been compared with the throne-names of the messianic figure
of Isaiah 9:6.[35] *oracle* (*nᵉ'um*) frequently prefaces divine speech in
the form of prophetic messages. *who was raised on high*: some
prefer to take *'al* (*on high*) as a divine title comparable with *'elyôn*
(*cf.* NEB 'whom the High God raised up').[36] 4QSamᵃ ('whom God
(*'ēl*) raised up') could be cited in support of this alternative explanation.[37] *Cf.* on 1 Samuel 2:10. There is also uncertainty about the
translation of the last line. *the sweet psalmist of Israel* is the
traditional rendering, comporting with the view of David as the
great singer and song-writer of ancient Israel (*cf.* 1 Sa. 16:14–23;
2 Sa. 1:17–27, *etc.*).[38] The footnoted alternative in RSV, 'the
favourite of the songs of Israel', making him the darling of the
Israelite lyricists (*cf.* 1 Sa. 18:7; 21:11), is also possible.[39] However,
there is increasing support for deriving MT *zᵉmirôṭ* from a root
zāmar meaning 'be strong': 'the beloved of the Protector of
Israel'.[40] While it is difficult to choose from among these possibilities, the third does provide a parallel to the preceding line, particularly in the way in which it matches *Israel* with *Jacob*.

2. The *Spirit of the Lord* is here the spirit of prophecy (*cf.* 1 Ki.
22:24, 28; 1 Ch. 12:18; 2 Pet. 1:21). David is ranked as a prophet
in the New Testament (Acts 2:30) by virtue of his inspiration by
the Spirit (*cf.* Mt. 22:43), and also in accordance with a tendency
to extend the range of the term (*cf.* Gn. 20:7 (of Abraham), and
Josephus' reference to Samson as a 'prophet' (*Ant.* v. 8. 4)).[41] *by
me* (*bî*) could be 'to (or "with") me', as when a special intimacy is
indicated (*e.g.* Nu. 12:2, 6, 8; Hab. 2:1). This occasional ambiguity
of the Hebrew *bᵉ* is sometimes mirrored by the Greek *en* in the
New Testament (*e.g.* Gal. 1:16, where NEB opts for 'to me and
through me').

3, 4. The core oracle in verses 3b–4, with its depiction of the
beneficent effect of righteous rule, states gnomically what Psalm
72:1–7 expresses as a prayer.[42] Compare verse 3b with Psalm 72:1,
and verse 4 with Psalm 72:5f. *justly . . . in the fear of God* (3): *cf.*
Isaiah 11:3f., of the ideal Davidic ruler. Such a ruler is compared

with the healthful rays of the sun at dawn (*cf.* Mal. 4:2), and with the life-giving showers which fructify the earth. The last line of the verse is difficult for the reason that, as it stands, it consists of four nouns, three of them prefixed by the preposition *min* (basically 'from'). RSV is probably not far from the intended sense, though the emendation to *like rain* results in an unlikely dependence upon *he dawns*. In fact, both NEB and NIV translate *mimmāṭār* by 'after rain'[43]: 'a morning that is cloudless after rain and makes the grass sparkle from the earth' (NEB).[44]

5. David responds by appealing to the covenant which Yahweh has given to him and his *house*: 'And your house and your kingdom shall be made sure for ever before me; your throne shall be established for ever' (7:16; *cf.* Pss. 89:1–4, 19–37; 132:11f.). *Yea, does not . . . ?*: RSV's rhetorical question is a great improvement on AV's self-deprecating 'Although my house be not so with God'. G. T. Sheppard, thinking of the possible wider hermeneutical function of the section, suggests that the rhetorical questions in this verse invite the reader to look back over the story of David and answer in the affirmative.[45] Others, however, treat *lō'* as an asseverative particle, or similar, and the whole clause as a positive statement (*cf.* NEB 'Surely, surely my house is true to God').[46] The resultant sense is the same as in RSV. *an everlasting covenant*: this is better than taking *everlasting* as a divine title (*cf.* Cross, 'The Eternal has made a covenant with me'[47]). In *ordered in all things and secure* we may have a legal phrase roughly comparable with the English 'signed and sealed'; the verb translated *ordered* (*'ārak*) has a legal connotation in a few other passages (Jb. 13:18; 23:4; Ps. 50:21). *cause to prosper* is (lit.) 'cause to blossom' and picks up the botanical metaphor of verse 4, just as verse 6 paints a contrasting picture from the same field.[48]

6, 7. The *godless* (for MT *beliyaʻal*, 'Belial') are in all probability the enemies of the Davidic dynasty. Their fate is likened to that of thorns which men toss aside (*cf.* NEB) as fit only for burning (*cf.* Is. 33:12; Heb. 6:8). While there are textual problems in both verses, the general tenor is not in doubt.

'THE THREE' AND 'THE THIRTY' (23:8–39)

The rest of the chapter is concerned with two élite groups within David's army – 'The Three' (vv. 8–12) and 'The Thirty' (vv. 13–39). A parallel version, but with a significant number of additional names, is given in 1 Chronicles 11:11–47. Where the Samuel text is especially difficult the Chronicles parallel sometimes offers an intelligible, if not necessarily original, reading. Verses 13–23 describe some of the exploits of the most distinguished of 'The Thirty', in the manner of 21:15–22.

8. *Joseb-basshebeth a Tah-chemonite*: on the basis of LXX Mss both here and in 1 Chronicles 11:11 NEB gives the hero's name as Ishbosheth. MT, however, has 'Jashobeam' in the Chronicles reference (*cf.* also 1 Ch. 12:6).[49] *Tah-chemonite*: 'Hachmonite' in 1 Chronicles 11:11. *three* (*cf.* vv. 9, 23) is the reading of the Lucianic Greek texts; MT has a form which hovers between 'third' and 'captain'. *he wielded his spear*: modern versions wisely turn to 1 Chronicles 11:11, since MT is unintelligible. AV, adopting the schoolboy stratagem already exemplified in LXX – 'When in doubt make it a proper name' – creates a new hero, Adino the Eznite! *eight hundred*: 1 Chronicles 11:11 has 'three hundred', as in verse 18 here.

9, 10. *defied*: the verb which recurs in the story of David and Goliath (see on 1 Sa. 17:10) and which now, with David and Eleazar as subject, would represent a neat reversal of roles. However, 1 Chronicles 11:13 has the place-name Pas-dammim (*cf.* Ephes-dammim in 1 Sa. 17:1), which is probably the original reading since it supplies the required antecedent to *there* (*cf.* NEB).[50] When the Israelite army fell back Eleazar *rose* (10) up that day as a national saviour (*cf.* Jdg. 5:7). NEB 'stood his ground' for *rose* represents another possible sense of BH *qûm*. *the Lord wrought*: *cf.* 1 Samuel 14:23; 19:5. *the men* (lit. 'the people') are the remainder of the army who had been forced into retreat.

11, 12. Shammah's feat was to repel a Philistine raiding party which came up at harvest time to deprive the local community of its crop of lentils (*cf.* Jdg. 6:3–6, 11). *Lehi*, which reading is obtained by revocalizing MT, is the name of a place mentioned in Judges 15:9 in connection with a Philistine incursion into Judah. Because of its omission of verses 9b–11a, 1 Chronicles 11 inadvertently attributes this feat to Eleazar (and David). *Hararite* (11): no place by the name of Harar is known. A connection with the Hebrew *har*, meaning 'hill, mountain', is possible.

13–17. An act of heroism associated with the Philistine wars. It could have taken place during David's 'Adullam phase' (*cf.* 1 Sa. 22:1f.), though some link it with the situation of 5:17–21, early in David's reign, when the Philistines had advanced into the valley of Rephaim.

13. *the thirty*: *cf.* verse 18. The reference to *harvest time* may be seen as a topical link with the vignette of verses 11f., though

1 Chronicles 11:15 has a different reading ('to the rock'). *band* (*hayyâ*), if correct (Chronicles has 'army'), may denote a clan detachment.[51] *Rephaim*: see on 5:18.

14. *the stronghold*: *cf*. 1 Samuel 22:4f.

15. *the well*: the Massoretic pointing favours 'cistern' (*cf*. v. 20) – the Hebrew words are similar in form – though a thirsty man might well hanker after fresher supplies. No such well is now known at Bethlehem.

16, 17. The heroism of the *three mighty men* is also a testimony to the loyalty which David inspired in his followers, and the more so if this incident took place while he was an outlaw with little else but leadership to offer them. But the water obtained at the risk of men's lives was *poured out* before *the Lord* as a libation; *nāsak* regularly describes the pouring out of drink-offerings (*e.g.* Gn. 35:14; Je. 7:18). By equating the precious liquid with the heroes' *blood* (17), the idea of putting it to such a trivial use as refreshment is made sound utterly repugnant. And David's men will have thought no less of him for that.

18, 19. Abishai's name is already familiar from earlier narratives in Samuel (1 Sa. 26:6–11; 2 Sa. 10:10, 14; 16:9; 18:2, 5; 19:21; 20:6–10; 21:16f.). However, despite his long and loyal service, Abishai was not one of 'The Three', though he ranked first among the lesser heroes.

20–23.[52] Three specific feats of *Benaiah* which almost qualified him for inclusion in 'The Three' are noted. *Kabzeel* (20): possibly Khirbet Hora, eight miles east of Beersheba. *ariels* is a despairing transliteration of the Hebrew word which may tentatively be rendered 'champions' (NEB; *cf*. NIV 'best men'). Compare the treatment of MT *'er'ellām* (Is. 33:7) in the modern versions.[53] In Ezekiel 43:15f. the word appears to mean 'altar-hearth' (*cf*. Is. 29:2, and possibly also 1. 12 of the Moabite Inscription). AV, relating the *'ari* element to the Hebrew for 'lion', translates by 'two lionlike men' ('two lions like men' in one earlier edition![54]). As it happens, Benaiah did also have to contend with a *lion*, and in an enclosed area during inclement weather. 'The lion had probably been driven by the severity of the winter into the neighbourhood of some village, to the terror of the inhabitants' (Kirkpatrick). *a handsome man* (21): 'a man of striking appearance' (NEB) would be more to the point. 1 Chronicles 11:23 has 'a man of great stature' (*i.e.* *'iš middâ* for *'iš mar'eh*). Ackroyd suggests that this Egyptian may have been a mercenary in the service of the Philistines; there certainly are instances of the reverse in Palestine in the early Iron Age. Benaiah's captaincy of David's *bodyguard* (23) is noted at

8:18 and 20:23. He remained loyal during Adonijah's rebellion and was subsequently promoted by Solomon to army commander (1 Ki. 2:35). Like Abishai, he is awarded a *proxime accessit* (*did not attain*).

24–39. Thirty-one names of members of the exclusive corps 'The Thirty' are given, which together with Abishai (v. 18) and Benaiah (v. 20) makes a total of thirty-three. The passage of time, not to mention the occupational hazards of a military career (Asahel being a case in point, *cf*. 2:23), would satisfactorily account for the discrepancy. It is also possible that 'thirty' functioned as a round number just as, for example, 'the Seventy' (*cf*. Septuagint) came to denote the translation of the (supposed) seventy-two translators of the Greek Pentateuch. K. Elliger's study of these verses led him to conclude that the names are given in roughly the order in which the individuals concerned attached themselves to David.[55] Most of the first dozen, for example, are Judahites. There is, indeed, a preponderance of Judahites throughout, from which B. Mazar deduces that the list reflects that period when David's rule was largely restricted to Judah.[56]

24. The career of *Asahel*, the third of Zeruiah's warrior sons, ended prematurely after the set-to at Gibeon (2:18–23). *Elhanan* appears for the second time as the name of a distinguished soldier from Bethlehem (*cf*. on 21:19).

25. *Harod* could be the same as En-harod (Jdg. 7:1; *cf*. on 1 Sa. 29:1), but Mauchline follows Grollenberg in locating this place east of Bethlehem (at the site of the mod. Khirbet Khareidân). Simons (*GTTOT*, p. 338) is not so sure about this latter identification. *Elika* is not represented in the LXX or in 1 Chronicles 11:27; the name was probably omitted by homoioteleuton (*Harod* . . . *Harod*).

26. *Paltite* probably points to Beth-pelet, in the Judaean Negev (*cf*. Jos. 15:27), as the home-town of Helez. In Chronicles he is twice called a 'Pelonite' (1 Ch. 11:27; 27:10). *Tekoa*: see on 14:2.

27. *Anathoth*, about three miles to the north-east of Jerusalem, also produced Abiathar (1 Ki. 2:26) and Jeremiah (Je. 1:1). *Mebunnai*: Sibbecai, as in 21:18 and 1 Chronicles 11:29, is usually regarded as the correct reading. A. Zeron, however, noting the name MBN on a seal inscription found at Shechem, argues for the originality of *Mebunnai*.[57] *Hushathite*: see on 21:18.

28. *Ahohite* may indicate a connection with the tribe of Benjamin (*cf*. 1 Ch. 8:4). A Judaean town by the name of *Netophah* is mentioned in Ezra 2:22 and Nehemiah 7:26.

29. For *Heleb* some manuscripts have 'Heled', as in 1 Chronicles

11:30. *Gibeah*: Saul's city. The Chronicler, mindful of Saul's Benjaminite origin, is careful to note the extent of the help that David received from that quarter during his 'Ziklag phase' (1 Ch. 12:2).

30. *Benaiah*, who is to be distinguished from his more illustrious namesake of verses 20–23, came from the Ephraimite town of *Pirathon* (Jdg. 12:15), possibly to be identified with the modern Far^cata, situated a few miles south-west of Nablus. The difference between *Hiddai* and 'Hurai' in 1 Chronicles 11:32 stems mainly from the easy confusion of *d* and *r* in Hebrew. A 'mountain of *Gaash*' in the hill-country of Ephraim is mentioned in Joshua 24:30 and Judges 2:9.

31. *Abialbon*: 'Abiel' in 1 Chronicles 11:32. He came from Betharabah in the Judaean wilderness (Jos. 15:61; 18:18, 22). (In Jn. 1:28 the readings 'Betharaba' and 'Bethabara' (*cf.* AV) are inferior, their popularity being partly attributable to Origen, who thought that there was no 'Bethany' in the region of the Jordan.[58]) *of Bahurim* (*cf.* on 3:16), with transposition of the middle consonants of the MT reading, is probably correct.

32, 33. *Shaalbon*, called Shaalbim in 1 Kings 4:9, was occupied by the Danites after the Israelite settlement (*cf.* Jos. 19:42, 'Shaalabbin'). The remainder of verse 32 and the beginning of verse 33 have suffered in transmission, notwithstanding RSV's adherence to MT. *the sons of* is probably a dittograph of the last three letters of the preceding word in the Hebrew. 1 Chronicles 11:34 has the main elements of the solution: 'Hashem (or *Jashen*, as here) the Gizonite; Jonathan son of Shammah (Chron. 'Shagee') the Hararite'. In that case *Jonathan* was the son of the member of 'The Three' mentioned in verses 11f. *Hararite* (33): *cf.* on verse 11.

34. There are fairly substantial differences between this verse and its parallel in 1 Chronicles 11:35b, 36. *Maacah*: Beth-maacah (*cf.* 20:14–22); it is also possible that the reference is to the Syrian kingdom of Maacah (*cf.* 10:6). *Ahithophel of Gilo*: David's counsellor who defected to Absalom during the rebellion (*cf.* 15:31).

35. *Carmel*: *cf.* on 1 Samuel 15:12. *Arbite*: perhaps from Arab, a town in the region of Hebron (Jos. 15:52–54), possibly represented by Khirbet er-Rabiyeh, seven miles south-west of Hebron (Simons, *GTTOT*, p. 340). The LXX favours 'Archite' (*cf.* 15:32).

36. *Igal* appears as 'Joel' in 1 Chronicles 11:38; the difference in Hebrew square script is a mere tittle! *Zobah*: the Syrian kingdom which became tributary to David (*cf.* 8:3). *Gadite*: from the tribe of Gad.

37. *Zelek* was another foreigner who distinguished himself in

David's cause (*cf.* vv. 36, 39). *Be-eroth*: see on 4:2. *armour-bearer*: singular as in 1 Chronicles 11:39; MT has the plural. In 18:15 Joab has ten armour-bearers.

38. *Ira* and *Gareb* belonged to Kiriath-jearim (*cf.* 1 Ch. 2:53). *Cf.* on 20:26.

39. Poignantly, the last-named is *Uriah the Hittite* (*cf* 11:1–27). There are, in fact, only thirty-six names in the section (vv. 8–39). If the discrepancy is not simply a consequence of the present state of the text, it may be that Joab has to be included in the total even though he has not been mentioned. As the commander of David's forces for most of his fighting life he may have stood above both 'The Three' and 'The Thirty'.

CENSUS AND PLAGUE (24:1–25)

The presupposition underlying this chapter, viz. that census-taking may lead to unpleasant consequences, is also reflected in Exodus 30:11f., where the payment of a ransom fee suffices to avert what is assumed to be inevitable otherwise ('that there be no plague among them when you number them'). There are indications of a similar attitude towards the census in other parts of the ancient world. At Mari, in Mesopotamia, a regular word for 'census' was *tēbibtum*, the literal meaning of which is 'purification'.[59] One theory is that the Mesopotamian census was accompanied by a purificatory ceremony, though the rationale for this is now lost to us. Further evidence of this phenomenon comes from ancient Rome, where *lustratio populi Romani* ('purification of the Roman people') followed censuses taken for military purposes.[60] In general, a census might be held for taxation purposes, or in connection with the allocation of land, or, as in this chapter, to determine the strength of the national militia (*cf.* Nu. 1:3). Y. Yadin claims that the results of this particular census provided the basis for the organization of the national militia described in 1 Chronicles 27.[61] Although no reason for Yahweh's displeasure with the census is suggested, the likelihood is that in this case it is David's aspirations after self-sufficiency that are being censured. His 'great Babylon' (*cf.* Dan. 4:30) is in danger of being regarded as his own creation, the victories as no longer simply 'the Lord's' (*cf.* 22:35–43; 23:10, 12).

In this chapter David's raising of an altar and offering of sacrifices thereon are the means by which Yahweh's anger is placated (v. 25). The Chronicler attaches far greater significance to the story, however, in that he relates it directly to the founding of Solomon's temple – erected on Araunah's threshing floor no less (1 Ch. 22:1).[62] Since it is unlikely that the author of 2 Samuel 24 was ignorant of this tradition, or that he rejected it, the probability is that he is assuming knowledge of this later development. (An analogy might be drawn with the ending of the book of Acts!) It may even be that the association of the census-plague tradition with the founding of the temple was in part responsible for the preserving of the tradition.

1. *Again* links the chapter with 21:1–14 which tells of another divine visitation. The Chronicler, in a notable rewording of his source which, theologically, has more in common with James 1:13 in the New Testament than 1 Kings 22:19–23 in the Old, attributes the incitement to Satan who 'stood up against Israel' (1 Ch. 21:1). As with the afflictions of Job (*cf.* Jb. 1:12; 2:7, 10) and Paul's 'messenger of Satan' (2 Cor. 12:7), we are faced with a complementarity of roles which is unresolvable simply because the biblical writers are grappling with the mystery of evil.[63] The difference between Samuel and Chronicles does, on the other hand, illustrate the increasing tendency to associate evil with Satan, a tendency which is already discernible in the later Old Testament books and which was fully-developed by the time of our Lord and the apostles. In the second-century (BC) book of Jubilees, for example, the action of God in testing Abraham (Gn. 22:1) is said to have been at the instigation of the Satan-figure 'Mastema' (Jub. 17:15–18:19).

Our verse poses a further problem: is the incitement of David to conduct a census to be viewed as a punishment on Israel for previous wrong-doing, or was it simply David's census-taking which incurred Yahweh's wrath? If the clause-structure of MT is interpreted as it normally would be, the former is the meaning (*cf.* RSV, NIV). GNB puts it beyond a peradventure with, 'The Lord was angry with Israel once more, and he made David bring trouble on them.' The second, and more compact, interpretation might claim the support of verse 17 ('but these sheep, what have they done?'), and seems also to be reflected by the Chronicler.

2. The purpose of the census was to establish the number of fighting men in the kingdom, as is evident from verse 9. *from Dan to Beer-sheba*: *cf.* on 1 Samuel 3:20.

3. *Joab* voices what was probably a popular distrust of censuses, for the kind of reason discussed in the introductory comment on the chapter. Kirkpatrick, however, suspects a more pragmatic consideration: 'It is probable that a shrewd practical man like Joab, whose life shews (*sic*) no signs of being influenced by religious

motives, opposed the king's purpose more from the fear of exciting
disaffection among the people by a scheme to increase the burdens
of military service . . . '

5–8. An outline of the journey undertaken by Joab and the
commanders. Only a rough idea of the extent of the kingdom can
be gathered from the information given here.

5. *Aroer*, situated on the north bank of the river Arnon in
Transjordan, is mentioned in several passages – occasionally in the
company of the unnamed *city that is in the middle of the valley*
(possibly Khirbet el-Medeiniyeh) – as marking the southern boundary of Israel in Transjordan (*cf.* Dt. 2:36; Jos. 13:9, 16). This would
be a natural starting-point for the operation. The conjectural *began*
(*wayyāḥēllû*) for MT 'encamped' (*wayyaḥᵃnû*), together with the
other minor adjustments made by RSV on the basis of the Septuagintal Lucianic tradition, is attractive. The tribal territory of *Gad*
lay further north and included *Jazer* (Jos. 13:25), the probable site
of which is Khirbet Jazzir, just over two miles south of es-Salt.

6. The trek through Transjordan continued north into *Gilead*
(*cf.* on 2:9). While *Kadesh in the land of the Hittites* is an improvement on the improbable-sounding 'land of Tahtim-hodshi' of MT
(*cf.* AV, NIV), and has Septuagintal (Lucianic) backing, Kadesh-
on-Orontes lay a long way north of Dan, which more or less
marked the northern boundary of Israel (*cf.* v. 2). Some therefore
see a reference to Kedesh (*sic*) to the north of Hazor (*cf.* Jos. 19:37;
Jdg. 4:6). However, the inclusion of the Phoenician cities of *Sidon*
and *Tyre* (v. 7) is sufficient indication that the itinerary looks
beyond the strict territorial borders of Israel to take in adjacent
areas in the north and west. 'Hermon', for *Kadesh*, also has its
advocates; it would give a location 'a little E(ast) of Dan' (Driver,
who particularly notes Jos. 11:3 where he accepts LXX 'Hittites'
against MT 'Hivites').[64] *from Dan* represents an emendation of an
obscure reading, but NEB, taking up an old suggestion, has '(to
Dan) and Iyyon' – thus introducing a reference to a town mentioned
in conjunction with Dan in 1 Kings 15:20 and with Abel-beth-
maacah, a near neighbour of Dan (*cf.* on 20:18), in 2 Kings 15:29.

7. *the fortress of Tyre*: the mainland city, sometimes called 'Old
Tyre'.[65] Tyre and Sidon were never included within the kingdom
of Israel, nor is this implied in the references to them in verses 6f.[66]
The *Hivites* appear as a minor ethnic group in several Old Testament lists of pre-Israelite inhabitants of Canaan (*e.g.* Jos. 9:7). In
the absence of extra-biblical information little is known about
them; it has even been suggested that 'an early confusion of the
Hebrew consonants *w* and *r* may have given rise to the "Hivites"

as a separate group from the "Horites"'.[67] Horite (or 'Hurrian')
enclaves existed in various parts of Syro-Palestine. Finally the
commission visited *Beer-sheba* in the Judaean desert (the *Negeb*),
the last major urban settlement in the south.

8. Actual travel will have accounted for only a small proportion
of the time spent compiling the census lists.

9. Taken at face value the tally implies a total population in
excess of five million. If, on the other hand, *'elep̄* (*thousand*) means
'tribal unit, contingent' (*cf.* on 1 Sa. 4:2), such calculations are
ruled out. It would seem that, even when the kingdom was united
under David, Israel and Judah were, for some purposes, separate
administrative entities.

10–14. David repents and is visited by the prophet Gad who
confronts him with a grim set of options.

10, 11. *David's heart smote him*: *cf.* 1 Samuel 24:5. This excitation
of conscience came before the intervention of the prophet Gad,
whose visit could be seen as – despite appearances – a sign of
grace. *when David arose* (11): perhaps implying that he had spent
the night in supplication (*cf.* 12:16). *Gad*, like Nathan, enjoyed
some kind of official recognition at court. The type of practical
advice which he gives in verse 18, as also on the other occasion
when he is mentioned in the books of Samuel (1 Sa. 22:5), is
probably more representative of the service that he was accustomed
to render to the king. Useful comparisons in this regard may
be made with non-Israelite forms of prophecy as at Mari, for
example.[68]

12, 13. The prominence of the numeral *three* in these verses
hardly requires pointing out. It is true that MT has 'seven years'
in verse 13, but the combined witness of the LXX and 1 Chronicles
21:12 favours the reading adopted by RSV. *to him who sent me*:
the prophet is 'a man sent from God' (Jn. 1:6; *cf.* Zc. 6:15, *etc.*).
The king is reminded that Gad is subject to a higher authority
than himself.

14. David expresses the conviction that in wrath Yahweh will
remember mercy (*cf.* Hab. 3:2), that his judgement on his people –
his 'strange work' (Is. 28:21) – is moderated by compassion. 'David
did what was quite unexpected, but precisely in so doing he flung
himself through the thick curtain of the divine anger directly on
God's heart.'[69] His faith was vindicated to a degree by what
followed (v. 16). In fact, David's choice of the third option is not
stated in the text (though LXX (v. 15) makes good the omission),
and either famine or plague would have satisfied his criterion.[70]

15–18. Pestilence (*deḇer*) and plague (*maggēp̄â*) were feared as

much in ancient societies as they have been in more recent times.
Reference has already been made to the famous plague prayers of
the Hittite king Mursilis II (late fourteenth century BC), in which
the gods are implored to end a twenty-year plague which threatened
to depopulate Hatti-land.[71] Pestilence and plague are consistently
regarded as the work of Yahweh in the Old Testament, whether
in punishment of Israel (Nu. 14:12; Amos 4:10) or of the enemies
of Israel (Ex. 9:14; 1 Sa. 5–6). Other peoples had specific gods of
plague – for example, Nergal in Mesopotamia and Resheph in
Canaan. (The latter survives as a common noun (RSV 'plague') in
a demythologized reference in Hab. 3:5.)

15. *until the appointed time* would most naturally refer to the
expiry of the three days, yet the next verse seems to suggest a
merciful intervention by Yahweh before that point was reached.
The other proposed meanings for MT *mô'ēḏ* are less satisfactory.
NEB's 'the hour of dinner' derives from the LXX – which actually
talks of the midday lunch – but the Greek does not seem to be a
reliable guide here. Ackroyd moves along Targumic lines with his
suggestion that *mô'ēḏ* may be 'an appointed religious moment,
an hour of sacrifice'. It is not certain, however, that *mô'ēḏ* can
denote so specific a feature of temple service in addition to its
attested sense of 'religious festival'. In 1 Kings 18:29, 36, which
allude to just such a 'moment', the Hebrew is differently phrased.

16.[72]*the Lord repented*: cf. on 1 Samuel 15:11. The *angel who was
working destruction* is the same as the 'destroyer' of Exodus 12:23
and the 'angel of the Lord' of 2 Kings 19:35 (*cf.* Is. 37:36). It was
partly with the help of traditions like the present one that belief in
Zion's impregnability flourished until the Babylonian sack of the
city in 587 BC. This is the Zion of Zechariah's oracle, the apple of
Yahweh's eye, which none can touch with impunity (Zc. 2:8).
Araunah (Ornan in 1 Ch. 21) belonged to the pre-Israelite population of Jerusalem. For the meaning of his name see on verse 23.

17. Presumably David is not privy to the information conveyed
in the previous verse. Mauchline fairly compares Job's situation in
Job 1:6–12. The protective instincts of the shepherd-king are
aroused by the thought of his charges suffering because of his
misdeed, and his confession is accented with emphatic pronouns
the more to distinguish culpable shepherd from innocent flock.[73]
As it happens, one of the technical terms connected with census-
taking was borrowed from the sheep-cote, as may be seen from a
comparison of Exodus 30:13f. (where 'is numbered' is, literally,
'passes over to those numbered') with Leviticus 27:32 and Jeremiah
33:13.

18–25. David purchases the threshing floor of Araunah and raises an altar there. There is no direct evidence in the narrative that Araunah's threshing floor was previously a Jebusite holy place, despite the occasional assertion that this was so.[74]

18, 19. *Go up* (18) and *went up* (19) suggest a location on a hillside; some such exposed area was required in order to obtain wind advantage for winnowing.

20. 1 Chronicles 21:20 mentions that Araunah was threshing wheat. 4QSam[a] agrees, and also has David and his servants clothed in sackcloth.[75]

22–24. The whole exchange between David and Araunah is reminiscent of Abraham's transaction with Ephron the Hittite (Gn. 23:10–16), starting with a generous offer – 'a typical opening gambit in oriental bargaining' (Mauchline) – and concluding in a deal.

22. *the burnt offering . . . the wood*: cf. Genesis 22:7. The *threshing sledges* would have been made of wood and studded with stone or metal.

23. *All this, O king, Araunah gives*: another possible translation is, 'All this Araunah the king gives' (similarly AV), from which it has sometimes been argued that Araunah was none other than the last Jebusite king of Jerusalem, whom David had allowed to live in honourable retirement after Jebus (Jerusalem) had finally come under Israelite control. The name *Araunah* itself has also been brought into the argument. That it is non-Israelite is to be expected, and is additionally indicated by the fact that it exists in several variant forms in Samuel and Chronicles. The most favoured derivation is from the Hurrian *ewri-ne* meaning 'the lord', which leads to the further consideration that *Araunah* may originally have been a title.[76] And, in fact, in verse 16 the Hebrew definite article is prefixed to the 'name', in opposition to Hebrew usage which, however, permits the article where a name originated as a common noun or where it functions as a title. Nevertheless, most scholars find the evidence for Araunah's (sometime) kingly status too insubstantial. Furthermore, both the LXX and Peshitta lack the key words *O king* (or 'the king').

24. *I will not offer burnt offerings . . . which cost me nothing*: this expresses an essential point about worship and service to God, whether Jewish or Christian (see Mal. 1:6–10; 2 Cor. 8:1–5). If we are to think at this stage of Araunah's threshing floor as the site of the future temple, as in the Chronicler's account (1 Ch. 22:1), then it will also have been important to establish that the holy ground was not delivered gratis by a non-Israelite. David says as much in 1 Chronicles 21:24 ('I will not take for the Lord what is yours'; *cf.* 3 Jn. 7).

25. *burnt offerings and peace offerings*: *cf.* on 1 Samuel 1:4; 7:9; 11:15. *So the Lord heeded*: *cf.* 21:14.

This is not quite the end of the story of David, but nothing that is said later does anything for his reputation (1 Ki. 1–2), and the division between Samuel and Kings at this point is no accident. There is a, by now, familiar realism about the presentation of David as saint and as sinner in these final scenes in 2 Samuel. He offends Yahweh, it is true, and his subjects suffer for his unwisdom. And yet, as Schenker has ably demonstrated, this final episode is noteworthy for the way in which it traces David's advance from despotic self-interest to the solicitude of the shepherd-king who is truly fitted to rule God's people.[77] He is even willing to suffer (die?) for the sake of the sheep (v. 17)!

NOTES

Introduction

1 I have discussed this matter briefly in 'Did Moses Write "Second Isaiah"? Reflections on the Authorship and Transmission of Old Testament Books', *TSF News and Prayer Letter* (Summer 1983), pp. 3f.

2 See Eusebius, *Ecclesiastical History*, 6.25.

3 1 Sa. 28:24 marks the mid-point of 'the book'.

4 *Cf.* B. S. Childs, *Introduction to the Old Testament as Scripture* (London, 1979), p. 230.

5 Though in later Jewish tradition these books were attributed to 'prophetic' authors (*cf.* J. Blenkinsopp, *A History of Prophecy in Israel* (London, 1984), p. 22).

6 *Cf.* C. Westermann, *Handbook to the Old Testament* (ET; London, 1969/1975), p. 87; Childs, *Introduction*, p. 236.

7 M. Noth, *Überlieferungsgeschichtliche Studien* (Tübingen, ²1957), pp. 1–110 (ET *The Deuteronomistic History* (Suppl. *JSOT*, 15; Sheffield, 1981)). For a recent survey of research on the Deuteronomistic History see A. D. H. Mayes, *The Story of Israel between Settlement and Exile* (London, 1983), pp. 1–21, 81–105.

8 *CMHE*, p. 284. See also R. D. Nelson, *The Double Redaction of the Deuteronomistic History* (Suppl. *JSOT*, 18; Sheffield, 1981); R. E. Friedman, *The Exile and Biblical Narrative. The Formation of the Deuteronomistic and Priestly Works* (Harvard Semitic Monographs, 22; Chico, 1981), pp. 1–43; McCarter, I, pp. 14–17.

9 *Cf.* G. von Rad, *OTT* I, p. 346; W. Zimmerli, *Old Testament Theology in Outline* (ET; Edinburgh, 1978), pp. 179f.

10 On this aspect of the 'Deuteronomistic History' see H. W. Wolff, 'The Kerygma of the Deuteronomic Historical Work', in *The Vitality of Old Testament Traditions* (ed. W. Brueggemann, H. W. Wolff; Atlanta, 1975), pp. 83–100.

11 R. Rendtorff, *Das Überlieferungsgeschichtliche Problem des Pentateuch* (BZAW 147; Berlin/New York, 1977).

12 See J. Day, 'The Destruction of the Shiloh Sanctuary and Jeremiah vii 12, 14', *SVT* 30 (1979), pp. 87–94.

13 On antecedent traditions and suggested source divisions see M. Noth, *VT* 13 (1963), pp. 391f.; Hertzberg, pp. 43f.

14 *Cf.* Y. Zakovitch, *JSOT* 15 (1980), pp. 41f.; see also my comments in *JSOT* 24 (1982), pp. 110f.

15 *pace* J. T. Willis, *CBQ* 35 (1973), pp. 148–150.

16 On possible pre-monarchical background or origin see G. E. Wright in *Israel's Prophetic Heritage* (Fs J. Muilenburg; ed. B. W. Anderson, W. Harrelson; London, 1962), pp. 57f.; N. K. Gottwald, *The Tribes of Yahweh. A Sociology of the Religion of Liberated Israel, 1250–1050 B.C.E.* (London, 1980), pp. 534–540.

17 *Cf.* Miller-Roberts, pp. 30f., 63.

18 On this see M. Newman, 'The Prophetic Call of Samuel', in *Israel's Prophetic Heritage* (as above), pp. 86–97.

19 R. Gnuse, *ZAW* 94 (1982), pp. 379–390; *idem, The Dream Theophany of Samuel. Its Structure in Relation to Ancient Near Eastern Dreams and Its Theological Significance* (Lanham/London, 1984).

20 Not all scholars accept the entity 'Ark Narrative'; see, for example, Stoebe, pp. 48, 84–88, 127f., 141f.; J. T. Willis, *TZ* 35 (1979), pp. 201–212.

21   Rost, pp. 13f., 116–120. A study of the vocabulary would also raise questions as to the extent of its distinctiveness within 1 and 2 Samuel.

22   A. F. Campbell, *The Ark Narrative (1 Sam. 4–6; 2 Sam. 6). A Form-critical and Traditio-historical Study* (SBL Diss. Series, 16; Missoula, 1975); idem, *JBL* 98 (1979), pp. 31–43.

23   Campbell, *The Ark*, p. 257.

24   P. D. Miller and J. J. M. Roberts, *The Hand of the Lord. A Reassessment of the 'Ark Narrative' of 1 Samuel* (Baltimore/London, 1977).

25   F. Schicklberger, *Die Ladeerzählungen des ersten Samuel-Buches. Eine literaturwissenschaftliche und theologiegeschichtliche Untersuchung* (Forschung zur Bibel, 7; Würzburg, 1973).

26   On this aspect of the 'Ark Narrative' see H. D. Preuss, *Verspottung fremder Religionen im Alten Testament* (BWANT 5/12 (92); Stuttgart, 1971), pp. 74–80. (On passages in Isaiah 40–48 see pp. 192–237.)

27   For the surrogate role of the ark in the 'Ark Narrative' see M. Delcor, *VT* 14 (1964), pp. 136–154 (pp. 30–48 in *Études bibliques et orientales de religions comparées* (Leiden, 1979)).

28   See D. Daube, *The Exodus Pattern in the Bible* (London, 1963), pp. 73–88.

29   Timm, *EvTh* 26 (1966), pp. 509–526.

30   See J. Wellhausen, *Prolegomena to the History of Israel* (ET; Edinburgh, 1885), pp. 245–256; idem, *Die Composition des Hexateuchs* (Berlin, [2]1889), pp. 243–246.

31   Cf. B. C. Birch, *The Rise of the Israelite Monarchy: The Growth and Development of I Samuel 7–15* (SBL Diss. Series, 27; Missoula, 1976), pp. 1–10; J. R. Vannoy, *Covenant Renewal at Gilgal* (Cherry Hill, 1978), pp. 197–239.

32   A. Weiser, *Samuel. Seine geschichtliche Aufgabe und religiöse Bedeutung* (FRLANT 81; Göttingen, 1962), pp. 44, 79, 92, etc.

33   H. W. Hertzberg, *I and II Samuel* (ET; London, 1964), pp. 130–134.

34   T. Ishida, *The Royal Dynasties in Ancient Israel* (BZAW 142; Berlin/New York, 1977), p. 30.

35   F. Crüsemann, *Der Widerstand gegen das Königtum* (WMANT 49; Neukirchen-Vluyn, 1978), pp. 122–127.

36   See now L. Eslinger, 'Viewpoints and Point of View in 1 Samuel 8–12', *JSOT* 26 (1983), pp. 61–76.

37   H. J. Boecker, *Die Beurteilung der Anfänge des Königtums in den deuteronomistischen Abschnitten des I. Samuelbuches* (WMANT 31; Neukirchen-Vluyn, 1969).

38   Birch, *The Rise*, pp. 27, 153f.

39   B. Halpern, 'The Uneasy Compromise: Israel between League and Monarchy', in B. Halpern, J. D. Levenson (eds.), *Traditions in Transformation: Turning Points in Biblical Faith* (Fs F. M. Cross; Winona Lake, 1981), pp. 63f.; idem, *The Constitution of the Monarchy in Israel* (Harvard Semitic Monographs, 25; Chico, 1981), pp. 150f.

40   Halpern, *The Constitution*, p. 155.

41   Halpern, 'The Uneasy Compromise', pp. 72f.

42   D. Edelman, 'Saul's Rescue of Jabesh–Gilead (I Sam 11 1–11): Sorting Story from History', *ZAW* 96 (1984), pp. 195–209.

43   Cf. P. Weimar, *Biblica* 57 (1976), pp. 63–69; McCarter, I, pp. 16, 19, 149f.

44   pace A. D. H. Mayes, *ZAW* 90 (1978), p. 11.

45   See especially R. E. Clements, *VT* 24 (1974), pp. 398–410.

46   I. Mendelsohn, *BASOR* 143 (1956), pp. 17–22.

47 The word is discussed by, among others, Halpern, *The Constitution*, pp. 1–11

48 Birch, *The Rise*, pp. 29–42.

49 Ishida, *The Royal Dynasties*, p. 43.

50 R. Polzin, *Moses and the Deuteronomist* (New York, 1980), p. 183.

51 Z. Ben-Barak, *ZAW* 91 (1979), pp. 30–43.

52 An exception is V. Fritz, *ZAW* 88 (1976), pp. 346–362.

53 Halpern, *The Constitution*, pp. 125–148.

54 *ibid*, p. 174.

55 Noth, *The Deuteronomistic History*, p. 5. T. Veijola, *Das Königtum in der Beurteilung der deuteronomistischen Historiographie* (Helsinki, 1977), pp. 83–99, attributes 1 Sa. 12 to his (Deuteronomistic) nomistic redactor.

56 See D. J. McCarthy, *Interpretation* 27 (1973), pp. 401–412.

57 *Cf.* von Rad, *OTT* I, p. 308.

58 *Cf.* Halpern, *The Constitution*, pp. 155f.

59 For a recent study on the composition of 1 Sa. 15 see F. Foresti, *The Rejection of Saul in the Perspective of the Deuteronomistic School* (Rome, 1984).

60 See already Rost, pp. 109–112.

61 J. H. Grønbaek, *Die Geschichte vom Aufstieg Davids (1. Sam. 15–2. Sam. 5)* (Acta Theologica Danica, 10; Copenhagen, 1971) [15:1]; A. Weiser, *VT* 16 (1966), pp. 325–354 [16:1]; R. L. Ward, *The Story of David's Rise* (diss. Vanderbilt, 1967) [16:14].

62 *Cf.* D. M. Gunn, *The Story of King David* (Suppl. *JSOT*, 6; Sheffield, 1978), pp. 66–68.

63 See H. A. Hoffner, 'Propaganda and Political Justification in Hittite Historiography', in *Unity and Diversity* (ed. H. Goedicke, J. J. M. Roberts; Baltimore/London, 1975), pp. 49–62; P. K. McCarter, *JBL* 99 (1980), pp. 489–504.

64 *Cf.* R. P. Gordon, *TB* 31 (1980), pp. 37–64.

65 *e.g.* J. C. VanderKam, *JBL* 99 (1980), pp. 521–539.

66 Ishida, *The Royal Dynasties*, pp. 55–63.

67 Ward, *The Story*, pp. 214–216.

68 T. N. D. Mettinger, *King and Messiah* (Coniectanea Biblica, OT Series, 8; Lund, 1976), p. 41. This was also the view of J. Conrad, *TLZ* 97 (1972), cols. 325f.

69 For a recent discussion of 'David's Rise' see R. North, *Biblica* 63 (1982), pp. 524–544.

70 *Cf.* Rost, p. 86.

71 *e.g.* J. Gray, *I and II Kings* (London, ³1977), p. 16; M. Noth, *Könige 1* (BKAT 9.1; Neukirchen-Vluyn. ¹968), pp. 9–11.

72 Mettinger, *King and Messiah*, p. 28.

73 Gunn, *Story of David*, pp. 66–84.

74 Reservations about the 'Succession Narrative' are expressed by P. R. Ackroyd, 'The Succession Narrative (so-called)', *Interpretation* 35 (1981), pp. 383–396.

75 R. N. Whybray, *The Succession Narrative. A Study of II Sam. 9–20 and I Kings 1 and 2* (SBT II.9; London, 1968); *idem*, *The Intellectual Tradition in the Old Testament* (BZAW 135; Berlin/New York, 1974), pp. 89–91.

76 Crüsemann, *Der Widerstand*, pp. 180–193.

77 Gunn, *Story of David*, pp. 37–62.

78   C. Conroy, *Absalom Absalom! Narrative and Language in 2 Sam. 13–20* (AnBib 81; Rome, 1978).

79   *Cf.* Conroy, *ibid.*, pp. 101–105; J. W. Flanagan, *JBL* 91 (1972), pp. 172–181.

80   E. Würthwein, *Die Erzählung von der Thronfolge Davids – theologische oder politische Geschichtsschreibung? (Theologische Studien, 115; Zürich, 1974);* T. Veijola, *Die ewige Dynastie* (Helsinki, 1975); F. Langlamet, *RB* 83 (1976), pp. 321–379, 481–528.

81   *Cf.* G. von Rad, 'The Beginnings of Historical Writing in Ancient Israel', in *The Problem of the Hexateuch and Other Essays* (ET; Edinburgh/London, 1966), pp. 166–204; *idem, OTT* I, pp. 313–316.

82   *Cf.* Rost, p. 106.

83   *pace* Rost, p. 111.

84   For discussion of this and other aspects of the 'Appendix' see K. Budde, *Die Büchᵉʳ Samuel* (KHAT VIII; Tübingen/Leipzig, 1902), p. 304; R. A. Carlson, *David, the Chosen King* (Stockholm, 1964), pp. 194–259; Hertzberg, pp. 415f.; Childs, *Introduction*, pp. 273–275; G. T. Sheppard, *Wisdom as a Hermeneutical Construct* (BZAW 151; Berlin/New York, 1980), pp. 144–158.

85   *Cf.* Carlson, *David*, p. 228.

86   *Cf.* W. E. Lemke, *HTR* 58 (1965), pp 349–363; see also section V ('The Text').

87   S. Japhet, *JBL* 98 (1979), pp. 205–218; *cf.* Childs, *Introduction*, p. 650.

88   *Cf.* R. L. Braun, *JBL* 92 (1973), p. 507.

89   On David and the temple see Ishida, *The Royal Dynasties*, pp. 94, 143f.

90   *Cf.* A. Schenker, *Der Mächtige in Schmelzofen des Mitleids* (OBO 42; Göttingen, 1982).

91   See, for example, W. L. Moran, *Biblica* 39 (1958), p. 413; W. G. E. Watson, *Biblica* 53 (1972), p. 197.

92   So Targum Onkelos (ed. A. Sperber, *The Bible in Aramaic*, I (Leiden, 1959), p. 85). The Fragment-Targum (ed. M. L. Klein, *The Fragment-Targums of the Pentateuch*, I (Rome, 1980), p. 158) and Targum Neophyti (ed. A. Diez Macho, *Neophyti 1*, I, *Génesis* (Madrid, 1968), p. 331) have 'all the kingdoms (of the earth) will be subjected to him'. LXX translates by *prosdokia* ('expectation').

93   On the various possible explanations of the genitive in 'the obedience of faith' in Rom. 1:5 see C. E. B. Cranfield, *Romans*, I (ICC; Edinburgh, 1975), p. 66. Our understanding of the expression corresponds to the seventh in Cranfield's list – the one which he himself favours. Note that, in no. vii, the words 'obedience' and 'faith' have accidentally been transposed in the first edition of Cranfield's commentary. I am grateful to John M. G. Barclay for confirming this, and for referring me to the note by N. T. Wright in *Themelios* 6/1 (1980), p. 18n.

94   For the secondary literature see *OTG*, p. 79.

95   *Cf.* von Rad, *OTT* I, p. 343; E. Zenger, *BZ* NF 12 (1968), pp. 16–30.

96   See H. G. M. Williamson, *JBL* 98 (1979), pp. 351–359; *idem, 1 and 2 Chronicles* (NCB; Grand Rapids/London, 1982), pp. 57f.

97   *Commentary on Matthew*, Book 14, sect. 7 (on Mt. 18:23).

98   See *DJD* IV (ed. J. A. Sanders; Oxford, 1965), pp. 48, 91–93.

99   See, for example, TB Baba Bathra 14b. Ps. 96 (LXX 95) has no superscription in MT, but is associated with David 'when the house was built after the captivity' in the LXX! See also the discussion by F. F. Bruce in *OS* 17 (1972), pp. 44–52. The general problem is addressed by A. M. Cooper, 'The Life and Times of King David According to the Book of Psalms', in R. E. Friedman (ed.), *The Poet and the Historian* (Harvard Semitic Studies, 26; Chico, 1983), pp. 117–131.

100   *Cf.* Bruce, *art. cit.*, pp. 45f.

101   B. Johnson, *SEÅ* 41–2 (1976–7), pp. 131f., attributes the deficiencies of MT 1 Sa. 1 to a damaged scroll.

102   Cross, *BASOR* 132 (1953), pp. 15–26.

103   E. C. Ulrich, *The Qumran Text of Samuel and Josephus* (Harvard Semitic Monographs, 19; Missoula, 1978).

104   Cross, *JBL* 74 (1955), pp. 147–172 (165–172) (= Cross–Talmon, pp. 169–176).

105   Ulrich, *BASOR* 235 (1979), pp. 1–25. Further information on readings in the scrolls is available in *Textual Notes on the New American Bible* (Paterson, n.d.), pp. 342–351, in *BHS* (ed. P. A. H. de Boer), and in McCarter's commentary on Samuel.

106   Cross, 'The Evolution of a Theory of Local Texts', in Cross–Talmon, p. 311.

107   *ibid.*, p. 312.

108   This is not to say that in every instance where MT appears to be haplographic it is inferior to the longer LXX text; see D. W. Gooding, *TB* 26 (1975), p. 124. For the view that insertions *were* made in such a way as to make MT appear haplographic see now S. Pisano, *Additions or Omissions in the Books of Samuel* (OBO 57; Göttingen, 1984), pp. 157–242.

109   According to Cross (*BASOR* 132 (1953), p. 19) MT preserves 'the tell-tale remnant of a lengthy haplography due to *homoioteleuton*'. Johnson, *SEÅ* 41–2 (1976–7), pp. 131f., observes that mere haplography will not explain the survival of both occurrences of *na'ar*. He suggests that the omission arose from the loss of two lines at the bottom of the first column of the MT exemplar.

110   '(The canonical approach) would attempt to assess the range of interpretation possible for this mutilated MT text' (*Introduction*, p. 105).

111   McCarter, I, p. 57, accepts that MT is a truncated version of the 4QSam[a] and LXX reading, but regards the longer text as conflate.

112   Driver, *Notes*, p. 302.

113   S. C. Reif, *VT* 20 (1970), pp. 114–116.

114   *Cf.* Ulrich, pp. 41f., 71, 76; see also pp. 42f. on the confusion of Mephibosheth with Ish-bosheth at 2 Sa. 4:1, 2, 12 (*cf.* LXX).

115   Ulrich, p. 86.

116   Driver, *Notes*, p. 378.

117   Ulrich, p. 271.

118   D. W. Gooding, *Current Problems and Methods in the Textual Criticism of the Old Testament* (Belfast, 1979), p. 11; *idem*, *TB* 26 (1975), p. 125. As is well-known, expansions of this kind are characteristic of the Samaritan Pentateuch.

119   E. Tov, *JSOT* 14 (1979), p. 44, claims that Ulrich has overestimated the extent of the agreement between 4QSam[a] and the Lucianic tradition.

120   On this see N. Fernández Marcos, 'The Lucianic Text in the Books of Kingdoms: from Lagarde to the textual pluralism', in *De Septuaginta* (Fs J.W. Wevers; ed. A. Pietersma, C. Cox; Mississauga, 1984), pp. 161–174.

121   So D. Barthélemy, *Les Devanciers d'Aquila* (SVT 10; Leiden, 1963), pp. 126f.; *idem*, *Études d'histoire du texte de l'ancien Testament* (OBO 21; Göttingen, 1978), pp. 271, 294; E. Tov, *RB* 79 (1972), pp. 101–113 (= Cross–Talmon, pp. 293–305). Barthélemy, *Études*, pp. 264f., claims that the same translator's hand is in evidence in the α section of 'Reigns' (*i.e.* 1 Samuel) as in the (Lucianic) text of β γ (2 Sa. 11:2–1 Ki. 2:11).

122   *Cf.* Cross, in Cross–Talmon, pp. 312–315 (see also the important comment on p. 319 (n. 30)); Ulrich, pp. 115–117.

123   Revised to 2 Sa. 10:1 by J. D. Shenkel, *Chronology and Recensional Development in the Greek Text of Kings* (Harvard Semitic Monographs, 1; Cambridge, Mass., 1968), pp. 117–120.

124   In Barthélemy, *Les Devanciers* (*v. supra*); *cf. idem, Études*, p. 255.

125   *The Old Testament in Greek*, II.1 (ed. A. E. Brooke, N. McLean and H. St. J. Thackeray; Cambridge, 1927).

126   E. Tov, *JSOT* 14 (1979), pp. 37–53.

127   *ibid.*, p. 51.

128   At various points all three are found going their own way (*cf.* Ulrich, pp. 119–149).

129   Barthélemy, *Études*, pp. 295–297: *idem*, 'La qualité du Texte Massorétique de Samuel', in E. Tov (ed.), *The Hebrew and Greek Texts of Samuel. 1980 Proceedings IOSCS – Vienna* (Jerusalem, 1980), pp. 1–44.

130   Gooding, *Current Problems*, p. 8.

131   For the genesis of the idea see W. F. Albright, *BASOR* 140 (1955), pp. 27–33 (= Cross–Talmon, pp. 140–146). Discussion by Cross in *HTR* 57 (1964), pp. 281–299 (= Cross–Talmon, pp. 177–195); *idem, IEJ* 16 (1966), pp. 81–95 (= Cross–Talmon, pp. 278–292); *idem*, 'The Evolution', in Cross–Talmon, pp. 306–320. For critical evaluation see S. Talmon, in Cross–Talmon, pp. 36–41; E. Tov, *The Text-Critical Use of the Septuagint in Biblical Research* (Jerusalem, 1981), pp. 254–260.

132   Cross may have been influenced by the 'local texts theory' long in vogue in New Testament scholarship (so Talmon, in Cross–Talmon, p. 39). For another attempt to read Cross's mind see Barthélemy, *Études*, pp. 292f.

133   See Cross–Talmon, pp. 287f.

134   Though on this point Cross has the support of Barthélemy (*Études*, pp. 291f.).

135   *Cf.* Barthélemy, *Études*, pp. 290, 346.

136   *Cf.* Talmon, in Cross–Talmon, p. 39; Barthélemy, *Études*, pp. 346f.; but see Cross in Cross–Talmon, p. 318 (n. 22).

137   Thus Cross (Cross–Talmon, p. 307) describes the Massoretic text of Isaiah as Palestinian, whereas the Massoretic text of the Pentateuch and Samuel is supposed to be Babylonian (*ibid.*, p. 312).

138   D. W. Gooding, *JSS* 21 (1976), pp. 15–25.

139   *Cf.* Talmon, in Cross–Talmon, p. 325. Barthélemy, *Études*, pp. 348f., makes a similar point in relation to the open-ended canon at Qumran. See further E. Tov, 'A Modern Textual Outlook Based on the Qumran Scrolls', *HUCA* 53 (1982), pp. 11–27.

140   See E. Tov (ed.), *The Hebrew and Greek Texts of Samuel*, pp. 105–119.

141   According to the usual convention Nahash should be introduced as 'Nahash king of the Ammonites'. On the other hand, it is most unusual for the gentilic to be used with a royal name, as happens in both MT and 4QSam[a] in 1 Sa. 11.

142   A. Rofé, *IEJ* 32 (1982), pp. 129–133.

143   Cross, *art. cit.* (note 140), p. 111.

144   McCarter, I, p. 199.

145   McCarter, I, p. 202.

146   See H. J. Stoebe, *VT* 6 (1956), pp. 397–413; D. Barthélemy, in E. Tov (ed.), *The Hebrew and Greek Texts of Samuel*, pp. 19f.; McCarter, I, pp. 295–298, 306–309.

147   I have dealt with this subject in an as yet unpublished paper '*Ben trovato* and the Mixed Parentage of Old Testament History', which was read to a study-group in Cambridge in July, 1982.
148   McCarter, I, p. 298.
149   The absence of 17:41, 17:48b, and 17:50 from the LXX may be regarded as cases in point.

The Rise of Samuel (1 Sa. 1:1–4:1a)

1   *Cf.* N. K. Gottwald, *The Tribes of Yahweh* (New York/London, 1979/1980), p. 283.
2   For discussion of the possible significance of 'Ephraimite' in this verse see M. Haran, *Temples and Temple-Service in Ancient Israel* (Oxford, 1978), pp. 307–309. T. Polk, *SBT* 9 (1979), pp. 5f., suggests that Samuel achieved Levitical status (*cf.* 1 Ch. 6:33) by adoption – perhaps posthumously. The problem, it must be said, is related to the larger question of the prominence of the Levites in the books of Chronicles, where not only Samuel but also the like of Obed-edom is presented as a fully-fledged Levite. W. F. Albright, *Samuel and the Beginnings of the Prophetic Movement* (Cincinnati, 1961), p. 13, concluded that Samuel as a Nazirite was 'drawn by Levitic tradition into family attachment to the tribe of Levi'.
3   An annual festival of covenant renewal at Shiloh is envisaged by Bright, *History*[3], p. 171; Noth, *History*[2], pp. 97f.
4   *Cf.* K. A. Kitchen, *The Bible in its World* (Exeter, 1977), p. 86.
5   See M. Haran, *VT* 19 (1969), pp. 11–22; *idem*, *Temples*, pp. 304–307; Gottwald, *The Tribes*, p. 283.
6   For a good summary of views see Joyce G. Baldwin, *Haggai, Zechariah, Malachi* (TOTC; London, 1972), pp. 44f.
7   *CMHE*, pp. 69–71 (70).
8   See G. R. Driver, *JBL* 73 (1954), pp. 125–127. M. Tsevat, on the other hand, explains 'hosts' as appositional (*HUCA* 36 (1965), pp. 49–58). In support of the genitival explanation note especially the titles 'Yahweh of Teman' and 'Yahweh of Samaria' in the Kuntillet 'Ajrud inscriptions, as discussed by J. A. Emerton, *ZAW* 94 (1982), pp. 2–20.
9   See A. Cody, *A History of Old Testament Priesthood* (AnBib 35; Rome, 1969), pp. 70f.; Cross, *CMHE*, p. 209n.
10   McCarter, pp. 51f., notes most of the recent proposals. See also the comment on this crux by James Barr in *The Heythrop Journal* 15 (1974), p. 391f., and the very tentative proposal which he makes in *Tradition and Interpretation* (ed. G. W. Anderson; Oxford, 1979), p. 48.
11   F. Deist, *VT* 27 (1977), pp. 205–208, who reads *^{a}ḥusā* ('fattened', 'selected') and compares the Targum, but not convincingly.
12   *Cf.* Hertzberg, p. 21n.; Stoebe, p. 90.
13   Both of these suggestions are mentioned by Driver (*Notes*, p. 12).
14   We might also compare the use of *awēlu* ('man') in the Amarna letters, where 'the man of x (town)' denotes a prince or kinglet (see *CAH*[3] II.1, p. 469).
15   See W. F. Albright, *Archaeology and the Religion of Israel* (Baltimore, [3]1953), pp. 107f.
16   For discussion see M. Haran, *JBL* 81 (1962), pp. 14–24 (22); *idem*, *Temples*, pp. 201f.

17   For comment on the poetic structure of v. 11 see McCarter, pp. 60f. On the vow in Ugaritic and Israelite literature see S. B. Parker, *UF* 11 (1979(1980)), pp. 693–700.

18   'Seed' referring to an individual is unusual and affords a rare Hebrew parallel to Paul's use of the word in Gal. 3:16.

19   See Ulrich, pp. 39f., and references there. *Cf.* also on v. 22.

20   The prohibition on strong drink is, in fact, addressed to Samson's mother, being repeated three times in Jdg. 13 (vv. 4, 7, 14).

21   G. W. Ahlström, *Biblica* 60 (1979), p. 254, tries to retrieve a suitable sense ('determined', 'persistent') for MT.

22   *Cf.* the similar observation, in relation to the expression 'priests of the Lord' (v. 3), by J. T. Willis, *STh* 26 (1972), p. 39.

23   So J. Scharbert in Botterweck–Ringgren, II, p. 290.

24   J. Weingreen, *VT* 14 (1964), pp. 225–228.

25   McCarter, p. 62, ingeniously tries to show that the explanation of the name (lit. 'because from the Lord I asked for him') represents an alternative etymology ('He-who-is-from-God') within the MT tradition. To this two points may be made in response: (1) even if an alternative etymology is being suggested, it is by no means clear that it is made independently of the occurrence of the accompanying verb *šā'al*; (2) in emphasizing the significance of the word-order in the explanation McCarter overlooks the close formal parallel with the naming of Moses in Ex. 2:10 ('because from the water I drew him'); here there is no question of the word-order being significant in the way that McCarter suggests for the present verse.

26   For the former see Driver, *Notes*, pp. 18f.; Cross, *CMHE*, p. 11 ('the hypostatized name of the god of the family or clan'); for the latter see L. Kopf, *VT* 8 (1958), p. 209.

27   *Cf.* Y. Zakovitch, *JSOT* 15 (1980), p. 42.

28   Hertzberg, p. 26.

29   It might be inferred from the longer text of the LXX that something has fallen out of MT; RSV 'to pay' is added according to sense.

30   J. T. Willis, *STh* 26 (1972), p. 59, doubts the connection.

31   See McCarthy, *Tiqqune Sopherim*, pp. 199f.

32   Details in Ulrich, pp. 40, 165f.

33   For further discussion see Gooding, *Current Problems*, p. 9.

34   See *BHS*; Ulrich, p. 48. But G. J. Wenham, *The Book of Leviticus* (NICOT; Grand Rapids, 1979), p. 79n., thinks that a case can be made out for MT.

35   On the basis of this reference S. E. Loewenstamm concludes that this feature of Gn. 15:9 is 'early' (*VT* 18 (1968), pp. 505f.).

36   See on 2 Sa. 2:14, and the bibliography cited there.

37   See Ulrich, pp. 40f. B. Johnson, *SEÅ* 41–2 (1976–7), pp. 131f., notes that this is not strictly a case of haplography, since both occurrences of *na'ar* have survived; he suggests that damage (the loss of two lines) to an early exemplar of Samuel accounts for the state of MT.

38   See especially McCarter, pp. 65f.

39   J. T. Willis, *CBQ* 35 (1973), pp. 139–154. Willis also notes various pointers to an 'early' date of composition for 'Hannah's Song'. Gottwald, *The Tribes*, pp. 534–540, argues that the original hymn (vv. 2b–10a) celebrates the ascendancy of the 'depressed egalitarian community of Israel' over the Canaanite kings whom they dispossessed in the pre-monarchical era.

40   *Cf.* Childs, *Introduction*, pp. 272f.

41   Rhetorical aspects of the song are discussed by A. D. Ritterspach in J. J. Jackson and M. Kessler (eds.), *Rhetorical Criticism. Essays in Honor of James Muilenburg* (Pittsburgh Theological Monograph Series, 1; Pittsburgh, 1974), pp. 68–74.

42   The translation of BH *ṣûr* by 'mountain' is preferred by some scholars, *e.g.* M. Dahood in his three-volume commentary on Psalms (New York, 1966–70). An alternative etymology producing the meaning 'creator' has occasionally been mooted, being anticipated in the Babylonian Talmud (Meg. 14a), where God is said to be the unique artificer (*ṣayyăr*) who can give breath to what he creates.

43   D. W. Thomas, *SVT* 4 (1957), pp. 14f.; P. J. Calderone, *CBQ* 23 (1961), pp. 451–460; 24 (1962), pp. 412–419; summary in Gottwald, *The Tribes*, pp. 504f. Note that there is nothing in MT corresponding to RSV 'to hunger'.

44   *Cf.* Calderone, *CBQ* 23 (1961), pp. 452–454. The article, 'A Third Root *'dh* in Biblical Hebrew?' by A. A. Macintosh (*VT* 24 (1974), pp. 454–473), could also usefully be integrated into discussion of 1 Sa. 2:5.

45   On Old Testament views of the afterlife see N. J. Tromp, *Primitive Conceptions of Death and the Nether World in the Old Testament* (BO 21; Rome, 1969).

46   Hertzberg, p. 30, speaks well of 'the consciousness of the unconditioned might of Yahweh' as the 'theological starting-point' of the resurrection belief: 'As creator of the world, he is the Almighty; is his power to be limited by what is under the earth?'

47   Willis, *CBQ* 35 (1973), p. 143, notes that in v. 8b God establishes the earth as his sanctuary following upon his conquest of his enemies, in accordance with Canaanite combat motifs and mythical patterns.

48   Gottwald, *The Tribes*, pp. 538–540, holds that 'princes' (*nᵉḏîḇîm*, 8) is a term for the pre-monarchic leaders of Israel, though, from its occurrences, 'no specific technical leadership function can be identified' (p. 540).

49   On 'Jewish Cosmology' see L. Jacobs in *Ancient Cosmologies* (ed. C. Blacker, M. Loewe; London, 1975), pp. 66–86.

50   *Cf.* C. E. L'Heureux, *Rank Among the Canaanite Gods* (Harvard Semitic Monographs, 21; Missoula, 1979), pp. 26–28.

51   4QSam[a] appears to have both (*i.e.* MT and LXX) readings; *cf.* Ulrich, pp. 119f.

52   *Cf.* M. Dahood, *TS* 14 (1953), pp. 452–457.

53   The older emendation to *'elyôn* is therefore unnecessary. For the suggestion of a divine name *'al* in this and other references see G. R. Driver, *ET* 50 (1938–9), pp. 92f.

54   The kingly horn is explained by W. F. Albright, *Yahweh and the Gods of Canaan* (London, 1968), p. 18n., as arising from the depiction of the king as a wild bull.

55   See McCarter, p. 78; F. M. Cross, *BASOR* 132 (1953), pp. 21f.

56   J. Heller, *VT* 20 (1970), pp. 106–108, suggests that the symbolic equation of fat with strength accounts for the premium put on fat ('Im Fett ist die Kraft').

57   McCarter's translation by 'The servants' (sin)' (p. 77) takes account of the fact that *na'ar* has this meaning in vv. 13, 15, but demands a uniformity of usage to which Hebrew writers do not always aspire.

58   McCarthy, *Tiqqune Sopherim*, pp. 206f., suggests that the insertion of 'the men' is a euphemistic device to separate the verb ('despised') from its object ('the offering of the Lord'); this would be more impressive as an explanation had MT lacked 'offering'. For the 4QSam[a] reading see Ulrich, p. 62.

59   *Cf.* Haran, *Temples*, pp. 201f.

60   Cross, *CMHE*, pp. 201–203, compares the story of the Israelites' defection to Baal-peor in Nu. 25:1–18.
61   Discussion in E. F. de Ward, *JJS* 27 (1976), pp. 117–137; C. Houtman, *ZAW* 89 (1977), pp. 412–417.
62   Miller–Roberts, p. 29, find a specific reference to the sacrificial system which Eli's sons have been abusing; *cf.* on 3:14.
63   McCarter, p. 84, prefers to translate MT *ᵉlōhîm* by 'gods': 'gods may mediate for him' ('for him' added with LXX). But would a Hebrew writer associate such a polytheistic idea with an Israelite priest?
64   Haran, *Temples*, p. 87.
65   Cross, *CMHE*, pp. 196f., follows Wellhausen in seeing just such a reference.
66   Altar steps were a common feature of non-Israelite altars; *cf.* Ahaz' altar, based on a Syrian prototype (2 Ki. 16:10–13).
67   See Haran, *Temples*, pp. 231–238.
68   Comparisons have been made with the Ugaritic *'ušn*, which means 'gift' (*cf.* P. C. Craigie, *The Book of Deuteronomy* (NICOT; Grand Rapids, 1976), p. 258, and references there), and with the Ugaritic *'iṯt*, 'gift to a god'(?) (*cf.* J. Hoftijzer, *SVT* 16 (1967), pp. 114–134; G. R. Driver, *Ugaritica* 6 (1969), pp. 181–184).
69   Miller–Roberts, p. 30, ease the problem by recourse to chiasmus, but I am not entirely convinced.
70   Weinfeld, *Deuteronomy*, p. 76n., connects this expression with the 'grant' of priesthood and priestly succession.
71   See Ulrich, pp. 58f.; McCarter, pp. 88f.
72   *Cf.* McCarter, p. 89.
73   *Cf.* Ulrich, p. 74.
74   *Cf.* Stoebe, p. 124. For a discussion of the narrative as a kind of prophetic 'call narrative' see M. Newman, 'The Prophetic Call of Samuel', in *Israel's Prophetic Heritage* (Fs J. Muilenburg; ed. B. W. Anderson, W. Harrelson; London, 1962), pp. 86–97; U. Simon, 'Samuel's Call to Prophecy', *Prooftexts* 1 (1981), pp. 120–132. R. Gnuse, on the other hand, aligns 1 Sa. 3 with near eastern dream theophanies (*ZAW* 94 (1982), pp. 379–390; *idem*, *The Dream Theophany of Samuel* (London, 1984)).
75   G. R. Driver, *JTS* 32 (1930–1), p. 365, suggests the meaning 'ordained'; NEB has 'granted'.
76   See L. Yarden, *JJS* 26 (1975), pp. 45f.
77   Cody, *A History*, p. 79, notes that the Arabian *sâdin* slept in his sanctuary, but rejects this comparison as evidence that Samuel functioned as a priest.
78   *Cf.* McCarthy, *Tiqqune Sopherim*, pp. 77–79.
79   *Cf.* my note entitled 'Aleph Apologeticum' in *JQR* NS 69 (1979), pp. 112–116.
80   See the article '*kōper et expiation*' by A. Schenker, *Biblica* 63 (1982), pp. 32–46, for the view that a *kōper* is 'a means to mollify or placate'.
81   *Cf.* Simon, *Prooftexts* 1 (1981), p. 128.
82   W. G. Blaikie, *The First Book of Samuel* (The Expositor's Bible; London, ²1888), p. 57.
83   See the discussion of this aspect of prophecy in S. J. DeVries, *Prophet against Prophet. The Role of the Micaiah Narrative (I Kings 22) in the Development of Early Prophetic Tradition* (Grand Rapids, 1978), pp. 141–151.
84   For example, Stoebe, p. 126. See W. T. Claassen, *JNSL* 8 (1980), pp. 1–9.
85   *Cf.* G. Pettinato, *The Archives of Ebla* (New York, 1981), pp. 278, 319 (n. 12).

86   See A. Malamat, *SVT* 15 (1965(1966)), pp. 207–227; *idem*, 'A Mari Prophecy and Nathan's Dynastic Oracle', in *Prophecy* (Fs G. Fohrer; BZAW 150; ed. J. A. Emerton; Berlin/New York, 1980), pp. 68–82; W. L. Moran, *Biblica* 50 (1969), pp. 15–56; J. F. Ross, *HTR* 63 (1970), pp. 1–28; E. Noort, *Untersuchungen zum Gottesbescheid in Mari* (AOAT 202; Neukirchen–Vluyn, 1977); F. Ellermeier, *Prophetie in Mari und Israel* (Herzberg am Harz, [2]1977).

The Ark of God (1 Sa. 4:1b–7:1)

1   It is not easy to choose between MT and LXX at this point. Campbell, *The Ark*, p. 59, comes down on the side of MT.
2   Further information in *AOTS*, pp. 405–427; E. E. Hindson, *The Philistines and the Old Testament* (Grand Rapids, 1972); N. K. Sandars, *The Sea Peoples* (London, 1978), pp. 164–170.
3   See M. Kochavi, in *Tel Aviv* 4 (1977), pp. 1–13; *idem, Aphek-Antipatris 1974–1977. The Inscriptions* (Tel Aviv, 1978); *idem, BA* 44 (1981), pp. 75–86. 'Izbet Ṣarṭah lies two miles to the east of Ras al-'Ain (Tell Aphek).
4   For 'clashed' see G. R. Driver, *JTS* 34 (1933), p. 379, for 'fluctuated' see Stoebe, p. 129, and for 'deployed' see McCarter, p. 103. NAB 'was hard' accepts the older emendation to *wattiqeš*, partly on the basis of a similar expression in 2 Sa. 2:17; *cf.* Miller–Roberts, p. 32.
5   On the meaning of *'elep* see G. E. Mendenhall, *JBL* 77 (1958), pp. 52–66, and the discussion by Gottwald in *The Tribes*, pp. 270–282.
6   *Cf.* G. von Rad, *Der Heilige Krieg im alten Israel* (Göttingen, [5]1969), p. 28; P. D. Miller, *The Divine Warrior in Early Israel* (Cambridge, Mass., 1973), pp. 145–160. For further discussion of the ark see R. E. Clements, *God and Temple* (Oxford, 1965), pp. 28–39; M. H. Woudstra, *The Ark of the Covenant from Conquest to Kingship* (Philadelphia, 1965); P. R. Davies, *JNSL* 5 (1977), pp. 9–18. See also the literature cited in the Introduction ('The "Ark Narrative"').
7   Campbell, *The Ark*, pp. 66f., thinks more in terms of the hopes raised by 'the ark of the covenant'.
8   *Cf.* A. C. Welch, *Deuteronomy: The Framework of the Code* (London, 1932), p. 66; Weinfeld, *Deuteronomy*, pp. 208f.
9   See F. M. Cross and D. N. Freedman, *JNES* 14 (1955), pp. 248f.; Gottwald, *The Tribes*, pp. 512–534.
10   *Cf.* W. F. Albright, *BA* I (1938), pp. 1–3. Further discussion of ark and cherubim in Haran, *Temples*, pp. 246–259. For a Mesopotamian cherub-equivalent see the reproduction of the 9th–8th century BC ivory carving from Nimrud (Calah) in *IBD* 1, p. 264.
11   Haran, *Temples*, p. 257. The ark itself does not constitute the earthly throne, according to J. N. Oswalt (*EQ* 45 (1973), p. 14).
12   On the battle-cry see Miller, *The Divine Warrior*, p. 37, *etc.*
13   A useful survey of the *ḥabiru* in relation to the Amarna texts is given by F. F. Bruce in *AOTS*, pp. 6–20; see also N. P. Lemche, *STh* 33 (1979), pp. 1–23; Gottwald, *The Tribes*, pp. 419–425.
14   The Philistines are represented as speaking indiscriminately in vv. 7f. of 'a god' (v. 7) and 'gods' (v. 8). While this inconsistency is not reflected in the LXX, and may therefore have arisen in transmission, we might possibly compare Ex. 32:4 where the Israelites salute the making of the golden calf with, 'These are

your gods, O Israel'. However, the question of possible interaction between Ex. 32:4 and 1 Ki. 12:28 would also have to be taken into account.

15   Some Peshitta texts also have the conjunction. Suspicion is increased with the observation that the Targum goes to some lengths to tidy up the history: 'smote the Egyptians with every plague *and performed wonders for his people* in the wilderness'.

16   See J. Day, *SVT* 30 (1979), pp. 87–94.

17   *Cf.* McCarter, p. 114, referring to K. Budde.

18   See E. F. de Ward, *JJS* 23 (1972), pp. 1–27.

19   Other rabbinic sources identify the messenger with Saul; see L. Ginzberg, *The Legends of the Jews*, 6 (Philadelphia, 1928), p. 223.

20   For this alternative view see P. R. Davies, *JNSL* 5 (1977), pp. 12f.

21   Ackroyd notes the possibility that there was a Mizpah – a relatively common place-name – to the west of Shiloh; Mauchline thinks that Eli assumed that the battle would take place nearer to the Philistine pentapolis and was therefore expecting the messenger to approach from the south of Shiloh.

22   H. W. Hertzberg, *TLZ* 79 (1954), cols. 285–290.

23   Cody, *A History*, p. 71.

24   See A. Marzal, *JNES* 30 (1971), pp. 186–217; J. D. Safren, *HUCA* 50 (1979), pp. 1–15.

25   *Cf.* Schicklberger, *Die Ladeerzählungen*, p. 37; Miller–Roberts, p. 39. MT *lālaṭ* in v. 19 could be a transcriptional error for *lāleḏeṭ*, but there is a similar case of assimilation of the *daleth* in a Ugaritic occurrence of the cognate verb (see text 52, 1. 53, in C. H. Gordon, *Ugaritic Manual* (AO 35; Rome, 1955), p. 144). *Cf.* already de Boer, *Research*, p. 83 ('a contracted form').

26   The name is discussed at some length by McCarter, pp. 115f.

27   Miller–Roberts, p. 42, compare Hos. 10:5 (where the 'glory' of the calf is its precious metal exterior).

28   See Campbell, *The Ark*, pp. 187f.; Miller–Roberts, pp. 9–17.

29   *Cf.* G. Roux, *Ancient Iraq* (London, 1964), pp. 142, 145. According to G. Pettinato, *BA* 39 (1976), p. 48, Dagon is one of the pantheon at Ebla; *cf.* P. Matthiae, *Ebla. An Empire Rediscovered* (ET; London, 1980), pp. 187f.

30   *Cf.* Daube, *The Exodus Pattern*, p. 73.

31   Miller–Roberts, pp. 44–46, argue with the help of Ugaritic parallels that the picture is of Dagon being felled in battle (*cf.* also 17:49).

32   Campbell, *The Ark*, p. 86n. See also Miller-Roberts as in the preceding note.

33   Campbell, *The Ark*, p. 86.

34   *Cf.* B. S. Childs, *JBL* 82 (1963), pp. 287f.

35   See H. Donner, *JSS* 15 (1970), pp. 42–55, for discussion.

36   For the connection between divine hand and plague see Miller–Roberts, p. 48.

37   *Cf.* J. Wilkinson, *ET* 88 (1977), pp. 137–141.

38   See G. R. Driver, *JRAS* (1950), pp. 50–52. J. B. Geyer, *VT* 31 (1981), pp. 293–304, discounts the link with bubonic plague.

39   *Cf.* K. A. Kitchen in *POTT*, pp. 67, 77 (n. 110); Geyer, *art. cit.*, p. 303.

40   Daube, *The Exodus Pattern*, p. 75.

41   On the 4QSam[a] variant 'panic of the Lord' (lit.) for MT 'panic of death' (lit.) see P. A. H. de Boer, *VT* 24 (1974), pp. 233f.

42   On the *'āšām* see B. A. Levine, *In the Presence of the Lord* (Leiden, 1974), pp. 91–101; J. Milgrom, *Cult and Conscience: The 'Asham' and the Priestly Doctrine of Repentance* (Leiden, 1976), *passim*. In an interesting variant that could

be original 4QSam^a and LXX say that the *'āšām* 'will make atonement for you';
see Ulrich, pp. 75f. D. W. Thomas, proposing the translation 'rest will be given'
for BH *yāḏaʿ* in this verse, presents a case for MT (*JTS* NS 11 (1960), p. 52); in
this he is, as he notes, supported by the Targum. Miller–Roberts, pp. 53f., make
another suggestion as to the original reading here.

43   Daube, *The Exodus Pattern*, p. 80.
44   On the number of gold mice see endnote 50 to v. 18. For an attempt to link
mice and 'tumours' (*'plym*) with Apollo (Smintheus) see O. Margalith, *VT* 33
(1983), pp. 339–341.
45   Miller–Roberts, p. 55 (*cf.* McCarter, p. 138); see *ANET*,³ p. 347.
46   *Cf.* J. Morgenstern, *HUCA* 17 (1942–3), pp. 251–255. A Philistine origin is
argued by E. Sapir, *JAOS* 56 (1936), pp. 272–281.
47   See J. A. Emerton in *AOTS*, pp. 197–206.
48   Even such a cautious scholar as J. T. Willis (*JBL* 90 (1971), p. 296n.) is
inclined to treat v. 15 as secondary because of the tensions which it creates with
the surrounding narrative.
49   Cody, *A History*, p. 80, is representative of the general trend in that he
regards v. 15 as a scrupulous insertion to square up the account with later
practice. (In this case a comparison could be made with the insertion of the monk
in David's drawing for *The Oath at the Tennis Court*! *Cf.* Kenneth Clark,
Civilisation (London, 1969), p. 295.)
50   It is, therefore, probably significant that 4QSam^a and LXX omit 'and five
golden mice' in 6:4, so avoiding a possible contradiction. *Cf.* Miller–Roberts, p.
54.
51   *Cf.* N. H. Tur-Sinai, *VT* 1 (1951), pp. 276f.
52   Nu. 4:20 might support the idea that the mere looking *upon* (so MT here)
the ark could bring judgement, but that would introduce obvious difficulties in
the present context. A text like Ex. 19:21 might also be drawn into the discussion.
53   For further discussion of MT in this verse see Tur-Sinai, *VT* 1 (1951), pp.
277–282. It is unlikely that the difficulty can be relieved by positing one of the
other meanings of BH *'eleḏ* (whether as 'clan' or 'captain') in this instance. See also
R. Althann, *Biblica* 63 (1982), pp. 563–565, for a radically different explanation of
the numerals, involving the introduction of the word *yôm* ('day').
54   *Cf. IDB* 3, pp. 37f.; J. Blenkinsopp, *Gibeon and Israel* (Cambridge, 1972), p.
11.
55   *contra* Miller–Roberts, p. 26. Cody, *A History*, p. 81, finds in Eleazar 'one
of the last clear glimpses in the Old Testament of the primitive rural priest, the
solitary attendant of a local sanctuary'. P. R. Davies, *JNSL* 5 (1977), p. 17, joins
J. Dus in surmising that this Eleazar was the father of Zadok, the priest of
David's reign, as in 1 Ch. 24:3.

The Institution of the Monarchy (1 Sa. 7:2–12:25)

1   *Cf.* J. E. Runions, *EQ* 52 (1980), pp. 130f., though I am far from agreeing
with Runions about the positive attitude of the 'redactor of the Books of Samuel'
towards kingship (p. 131).
2   'Samuel's "Broken *Rîb*": Deuteronomy 32', in *No Famine in the Land* (Fs J.
L. McKenzie; ed. J. W. Flanagan, A. W. Robinson; Missoula, 1975), pp. 63–74.
3   *Cf.* H. W. Wolff, *ZAW* 73 (1961), pp. 171–186 (ET in *The Vitality of Old*

Testament Traditions (ed. H. W. Wolff, W. Brueggemann; Atlanta, 1975), pp. 83–100).

4 See the discussion by D. Diringer in *AOTS*, pp. 329–342.

5 Veijola, *Das Königtum*, p. 36, usefully compares La. 2:19.

6 *Cf.* P. Reymond, *L'eau, sa Vie, et sa Signification dans l'Ancien Testament* (*SVT* 6; Leiden, 1958), p. 215.

7 For a discussion of this passage and others of the same genre see P. Weimar, *Biblica* 57 (1976), pp. 38–73 (63ff.).

8 McCarter, p. 146, mentions a place called 'Ain Kârim, three miles west of Jerusalem.

9 MT may be retained with the support of 14:4f., where 'crag' is used as a topographical term.

10 See the chapter on the Amorites by A. Liverani in *POTT*, pp. 100–133.

11 By a slight emendation of MT at the end of v. 8 S. L. Harris, *VT* 31 (1981), pp. 79f., achieves the reading 'so they are also making a king'. There are problems with this reconstruction, however, and the tension between vv. 7 and 8 in respect of Samuel's rejection or non-rejection does not strike me as being as great as Harris makes out.

12 Veijola, *Das Königtum*, pp. 63–65, finds covenant significance in the root underlying 'solemnly warn' (v. 9).

13 On the corvée see I. Mendelsohn, *BASOR* 167 (1962), pp. 31–35; A. F. Rainey in L. R. Fisher (ed.), *Ras Shamra Parallels* II (AO 50; Rome, 1975), pp. 93–95.

14 Mendelsohn, *BASOR* 143 (1956), pp. 20f.; *cf.* Rainey, *Ras Shamra Parallels* II, pp. 96f.

15 *Cf.* R. Hestrin and M. Dayagi, *IEJ* 24 (1974), pp. 27–29.

16 Weinfeld, *VT* 31 (1981), p. 106, and reference there.

17 *Cf.* S. J. DeVries, *Yesterday, Today and Tomorrow* (Grand Rapids, 1975), pp. 289f.

18 J. M. Sasson, *ZAW* 90 (1978), pp. 184f., noting that MT strictly has 'son of a Benjaminite' for RSV 'a Benjaminite', speculates that this replaces a lost name and that the intention is to make Saul the seventh – auspicious ordinal! – in the genealogy. However, conflation of similar readings is a more likely explanation of MT.

19 W. L. Humphreys, *JSOT* 6 (1978), p. 20.

20 J. B. Curtis, *VT* 29 (1979), pp. 491–493. S. Shaviv, *VT* 34 (1984), pp. 108–110, prefers to speak simply of word-play.

21 S. M. Paul, *Biblica* 50 (1978), pp. 542–544. See also the interesting comparison made by P. Xella (*UF* 14 (1982 (1983)), pp. 295–302) with the word *mšr* in 1. 5 of the fifth-century Tabnit inscription.

22 Various terms for prophets and seers are found in ancient near eastern literature. Biblical Hebrew also has *ḥōzeh* as a synonym of *rō'eh*. In general, see the essay by H. M. Orlinsky, 'The Seer-Priest and the Prophet in Ancient Israel', in *Essays in Biblical Culture and Bible Translation* (New York, 1974), pp. 39–63.

23 See above on 3:20.

24 See P. H. Vaughan, *The Meaning of 'Bāmâ' in the Old Testament* (Cambridge, 1974); J. T. Whitney, *TB* 30 (1979), pp. 125–147; W. B. Barrick, *SEÅ* 45 (1980), pp. 50–57.

25 For a detailed study of anointing in relation to king-making see Z. Weisman, *Biblica* 57 (1976), pp. 378–398.

26 *Cf.* Mettinger, *King and Messiah*, pp. 151–184; Ishida, *The Royal Dynasties*, pp. 50f.; Halpern, *The Constitution*, pp. 1–11.

27 So E. Lipiński, *VT* 24 (1974), pp. 497–499.

28 *Cf.* Albright, *Samuel and the Beginnings*, pp. 15f. (quoting a parallel from the Sefire treaty texts); Bright, *History*[3], p. 190; Calderone, *Dynastic Oracle*, pp. 58f.; Cross, *CMHE*, pp. 220f.

29 *Cf.* W. Richter, *BZ* 9 (1965), pp. 71–84; L. Schmidt, *Menschlicher Erfolg und Jahwes Initiative* (WMANT 38; Neukirchen-Vluyn, 1970), pp. 141–171.

30 *Cf.* A. Alt, *Kleine Schriften*, II, p. 23; Grønbaek, *Die Geschichte*, pp. 175–177. Carlson, *David*, p. 52, regards *nāḡîḏ* as a 'pure synonym' for *meleḵ*, on the other hand (so also does the Targum); *cf.* T. C. G. Thornton, *JTS* NS 14 (1963), pp. 1–11. V. Fritz, *ZAW* 88 (1976), pp. 351–353, sees *nāḡîḏ* as expressive of *prophetic* kingship ideology, according to which the king was placed firmly under Yahweh's authority.

31 *Cf.* M. Buber, *VT* 6 (1956), pp. 126, 142; S. Shaviv, *VT* 34 (1984), pp. 111f.

32 *Cf.* Gottwald, *The Tribes*, pp. 327–334.

33 *Cf.* Schmidt, *Menschlicher Erfolg*, pp. 84f.; Mettinger, *King and Messiah*, pp. 71f.

34 *Cf.* G. R. Driver, *JSS* 1 (1956), pp. 100–105.

35 MT is, however, defended by G. R. Driver, who cites a comparable construction in the Kilamuwa Inscription (*JBL* 73 (1954), p. 130).

36 The strength of this suggestion derives from the fact that such scribal alterations did take place from time to time. The text of 4QSam[a] is uncertain at this point; *cf.* conflicting reconstructions by Ulrich, pp. 124f., McCarter, p. 170.

37 RSV 'what was kept' represents an emendation of MT 'what is left'; Hertzberg, pp. 83f., prefers MT as reflecting 'a courtly style native to the East'.

38 For the text see Ulrich, p. 52; *cf.* the 'two loaves of bread to be waved' of Lv. 23:17. On the so-called 'wave-offering' see Driver, *JSS* 1 (1956), pp. 100–105; J. Milgrom, *IEJ* 22 (1972), pp. 33–38 (arguing for 'elevation offering').

39 The verb *ṣālaḥ* ('come mightily upon') is discussed by H. Tawil in *JBL* 95 (1976), pp. 405–413. For possession of the spirit of Yahweh as 'the new point of the Biblical Messianic theology' in the world of the ancient near east see H. Cazelles, 'Biblical Messianism', in E. A. Livingstone (ed.), *Studia Biblica 1978. I. Papers on Old Testament and Related Themes* (Suppl. *JSOT*, 11; Sheffield, 1979), pp. 52f.

40 On music in relation to prophecy see J. Lindblom, *Prophecy in Ancient Israel* (Oxford, 1962), p. 59.

41 On the subject of ecstatic prophecy see Lindblom, *Prophecy*, pp. 4f., 47–65; S. B. Parker, *VT* 28 (1978), pp. 271–285; R. R. Wilson, *JBL* 98 (1979), pp. 321–337 (331–333).

42 *pace* McCarter who describes this reference as 'immaterial at this point and probably secondary, having been added along with the instructions in v 8 as preparation for c 13' (p. 182).

43 The command is then taken to mean that Saul should attack the Philistine garrison of v. 5, as Jonathan later did at Geba (Gibeah?) in 13:3. See, for example, Halpern, *The Constitution*, pp. 155f.

44 Stoebe, pp. 210f., thinks that 10:8 and 13:7ff. were incorporated from a separate Gilgal tradition. *Cf.* the observation by J. M. Miller, *CBQ* 36 (1974), p.

161, that 9:1–10:13 was at one time more closely bound with the Michmash account in chs. 13–14.

45   The reading 'his father' in LXX (and Peshitta) is explained by Ulrich (p. 141) as an *ad sensum* correction; it may well be a 'correction' – though hardly 'superior' (Ulrich) – made without regard to the honorific sense of 'father' in some contexts.

46   For other explanations of the proverb see Schmidt, *Menschlicher Erfolg*, pp. 103–119; V. Eppstein, *ZAW* 81 (1969), pp. 287–304; J. Sturdy, *VT* 20 (1970), pp. 206–213; J. Lindblom, *ASTI* 9 (1973(1974)), pp. 30–41.

47   For an attempt to relate 'uncle' to the Philistine governor (*sic*) of v. 5 see D. R. Ap-Thomas, *VT* 11 (1961), pp. 241–245. The claim by J. Hoftijzer and G. van der Kooij (*Aramaic Texts from Deir 'Alla* (Leiden, 1976), p. 190) that 'uncle' appears in a similar context at Deir 'Alla is very precarious (so also Hoftijzer, *BA* 39 (1976), p. 14); J. M. Miller, *CBQ* 36 (1974), p. 160, attributes the reference to Saul's uncle to a Deuteronomistic redactor's awareness that Saul had by now reached Gibeah and that this was not his father's home-town.

48   *Cf.* B. C. Birch, *CBQ* 37 (1975), pp. 452–454; *idem*, *The Rise*, pp. 48–51. DeVries, *Yesterday*, pp. 195f., notes that vv. 18f. do not have the *form* of a prophetic denunciation: 'Samuel speaks here the language of covenant confrontation'.

49   See also W. Gordon Robinson, 'Historical Summaries of Biblical History', *EQ* 47 (1975), pp. 195–207.

50   *Cf.* DeVries, *Yesterday*, p. 196; Boecker, *Die Beurteilung*, pp. 37f. Both note the 'Deuteronomistic' character of the usage.

51   For discussion see the article by J. Lindblom, 'Lot-casting in the Old Testament', *VT* 12 (1962), pp. 164–178.

52   The 'secondary social-structural divisions' reflected in this verse are discussed by Gottwald, *The Tribes*, pp. 257–284 (259f.).

53   Some scholars have considered that the falling of the lot on an absentee must be explained along literary-critical lines, viz. the combining of originally separate traditions about Saul's election; see Birch, *The Rise*, pp. 43f.

54   The question 'Did the man come hither?' is textually problematical; nevertheless, the alternative proposed by Mettinger, *King and Messiah*, pp. 180f., is rightly rejected by B. Albrektson, *ASTI* 11 (1977–8), pp. 1–5.

55   'Baal and Mot', 6. 1. 56–65; text and translation in J. C. L. Gibson (ed.), *Canaanite Myths and Legends* (Edinburgh, ²1978), p. 76; see also *NERTOT*, p. 217.

56   See Boecker, *Die Beurteilung*, pp. 51–56; Veijola, *Das Königtum*, pp. 71f., explains Samuel's scribal activity here as being, in the view of the Deuteronomistic historian, an 'actualizing' of the law of Moses, and in particular of the 'law of the king' (Dt. 17).

57   The '*mišpāṭ* of the king' in 8:9, 11 and the '*mišpāṭ* of the kingdom' here are clearly to be distinguished; *cf.* Birch, *The Rise*, pp. 51f.; Boecker, *Die Beurteilung*, p. 56.

58   Z. Ben-Barak, *ZAW* 91 (1979), pp. 30–43 (43).

59   Details in Ulrich, pp. 69f. Stoebe, pp. 213f., prefers MT. Even if the longer text of 4QSam³ is followed, the time-reference may still relate to the Mizpah convention, the NAB footnote notwithstanding (*cf.* McCarter).

60   The name 'Ammon' is perpetuated in the mod. Amman, the capital of Jordan and also the site of the ancient Ammonite capital Rabbah (*e.g.* 2 Sa. 12:26).

61   See N. Glueck, *The River Jordan* (London, 1946), pp. 159–167; *idem* in *AOTS*, p. 432. Other possibilities are noted by Klein (p. 105).

62   *Cf.* Ishida, *The Royal Dynasties*, p. 36.

63   Though see D. J. McCarthy, *Treaty and Covenant* (AnBib 21a; Rome, ³1981), p. 58. H. Reviv, in an article entitled 'Jabesh-Gilead in I Samuel 11:1–4: Characteristics of the City in Pre-Monarchic Israel' (*The Jerusalem Cathedral*, 1981, pp. 4–8), notes the distinction between 'men' and 'elders' in vv. 1, 3; this he takes as reflective of the bicameral self-government of towns in Mesopotamia and Syro-Palestine in the second and first millennia BC. Prof. D. J. Wiseman drew my attention to Reviv's article and provided me with a photocopy.

64   See, however, the discussion in the Introduction ('The Text'). *Cf.* Ulrich, pp. 166–170; McCarter, pp. 199f.

65   For the latter see Vannoy, *Covenant Renewal*, p. 49.

66   LXX 'after the *morning*', representing *bōqer* for MT *bāqār* ('oxen'), could conceivably reflect concern for Saul's dignity.

67   See P. W. Lapp, *BA* 28 (1965), pp. 2–10; N. L. Lapp, *BASOR* 223 (1976), pp. 25–42. For a different identification (mod. Jebaʻ) see J. M. Miller, *VT* 25 (1975), pp. 145–166.

68   *Cf.* Miller, *CBQ* 36 (1974), pp. 167f. M. Noth's placing of Saul's action in the context of the tribal 'amphictyony' naturally reflects commitment to his 'amphictyonic hypothesis' (*Das System der zwölf Stämme Israels* (BWANT 52; Stuttgart, 1930), pp. 109f.). Cross, *CMHE*, p. 221, claims that in vv. 6–11 'Saul faithfully followed, in this instance at least, the covenantal ritual of the league'.

69   G. Wallis, *ZAW* 64 (1952), pp. 57–61, cites a parallel from Mari for Saul's dissection of the oxen (*ARM* II, letter 48). See also R. Polzin, *HTR* 62 (1969), pp. 233–240; M. Held, *BASOR* 200 (1970), pp. 32–40.

70   Veijola, *Das Königtum*, p. 40, is representative of the majority view which plays down, or abolishes altogether, Samuel's role in this chapter. See, however, Ishida, *The Royal Dynasties*, pp. 47f.

71   By New Testament times the Roman division into four watches had become standard (*e.g.* Mt. 14:25; Mk. 6:48).

72   LXX gives the credit to Samuel, as does McCarter (p. 201) on the basis of LXX.

73   Vannoy, *Covenant Renewal*, pp. 61–91.

74   *Cf.* A. Alt, 'The Formation of the Israelite State in Palestine', in *Essays on Old Testament History and Religion* (ET; Oxford, 1966), pp. 194f.; Cross, *CMHE*, pp. 253f.

75   For discussion of the 'prehistory' (Ugaritic) of the so-called 'peace offering' (NEB 'shared-offering', NIV 'fellowship offering') see B. Janowski, *UF* 12 (1980(1981)), pp. 231–259.

76   The appropriateness of the terms 'farewell', 'valedictory' in connection with this chapter is questioned by, for example, Vannoy, *Covenant Renewal*, pp. 18–20; A. D. H. Mayes, *ZAW* 90 (1978), pp. 7f.

77   *Cf.* J. Muilenburg, *VT* 9 (1959), pp. 347–365; McCarthy, *Treaty and Covenant*³, pp. 206–221; K. Baltzer, *The Covenant Formulary* (Oxford, 1971), pp. 66–68.

78   Vannoy, *Covenant Renewal*, p. 12.

79   See E. A. Speiser, *BASOR* 77 (1940), pp. 15–20. For a highly critical discussion of the RSV text at this point see O. T. Allis, *Revised Version or Revised Bible?* (Philadelphia, 1953), pp. 19f.

80   See, for example, G. E. Wright, *God Who Acts* (SBT, First Series, 8; London, 1952).
81   The title of ch. II in W. Zimmerli's *Old Testament Theology in Outline* (ET; Edinburgh, 1978).
82   J. A. Sanders, *Torah and Canon* (Philadelphia, 1972), p. 20.
83   G. W. Ahlström, *JNES* 39 (1980), pp. 65–69.
84   Y. Zakovitch, *VT* 22 (1972), pp. 123–125.
85   Further discussion in McCarter, p. 215.
86   Vannoy, *Covenant Renewal*, p. 39.
87   Some LXX Mss provide – as it seems – an apodosis in 'he will deliver you'.
88   R. Weiss, *RB* 83 (1976), pp. 51–54, proposes a slight emendation to produce 'and your houses'.
89   See T. Longman, *WTJ* 45 (1983), pp. 168–171, for the suggestion that the destructive downpour (*cf.* Pr. 26:1f.) is related to a covenant curse.

The Reign of Saul (1 Sa. 13:1–15:35)

1   For discussion see Stoebe, *TZ* 21 (1965), pp. 269–280; J. M. Miller, *CBQ* 36 (1974), p. 164; A. D. H. Mayes in Hayes–Miller, p. 327.
2   The ancient versions disagree among themselves and are of little or no help. The verse is entirely omitted in part of the LXX tradition. The figure of thirty for Saul's age (*cf.* RV, NIV) has the support of the Greek Lucianic Mss, but its value is far from certain.
3   So M. Noth, *The Deuteronomistic History* (ET; Suppl. *JSOT*, 15; Sheffield, 1981), p. 23; A. D. H. Mayes in Hayes–Miller, p. 329.
4   *Cf.* Blenkinsopp, *Gibeon and Israel*, p. 54. For discussion and useful bibliographical references see C. A. J. Pillai, *Apostolic Interpretation of History* (Hicksville, New York, 1980), pp. 98f.
5   *Cf.* G. R. Driver, *Textus* 1 (1960), p. 127; *idem*, *Semitic Writing: From Pictograph to Alphabet* (rev. edn.; London, 1976), p. 271; Brockington, p. 45. For an attempt to treat v. 1 as poetry, with the numerals functioning indeterminately in much the same way as 'for three transgressions and for four' in Am. 1:3, *etc.*, see R. Althann, *Biblica* 62 (1981), pp. 241–246. Althann, incidentally, defends MT's use of a separate numeral for 'two' instead of the normal dual (*pace* S. R. Driver, *Notes*, p. 97; Stoebe, p. 243, also disagrees with Driver on this point).
6   *pace* Miller, *CBQ* 36 (1974), pp. 164f.
7   The re-ordering of the last two clauses in this verse is unnecessary if we accept the case for literary insertion (AXB) patterns in Biblical Hebrew as argued by David T. Tsumura (*VT* 33 (1983), pp. 468–482).
8   On the name see E. A. Knauf, *Biblica* 65 (1984), pp. 251–253.
9   For discussion see Gunn, *The Fate*, pp. 33–40. William Whiston, translator of Josephus, finds in Saul's venturing to sacrifice a lesson for the Christian laity, who in the absence of a clergyman should 'confine themselves within those bonds of piety and Christianity, which belong alone to the laity'! (note on *Ant.* vi. 6. 2).
10   Albright, *Samuel and the Beginnings*, p. 18.
11   See McCarter, p. 229, and compare the Akkadian *šarra šá libbišú ina libbi ipteqid*, 'he (Nebuchadnezzar II) installed a king of his own choice', in the Babylonian Chronicles (ed. D. J. Wiseman, p. 72, l. 13). My thanks to V. P. Long for drawing my attention to this parallel.

12 The omission in MT would be haplographic, which is a point in favour of the longer LXX reading. Stoebe (p. 245), however, regards the LXX plus as secondary and harmonistic.
13 See the comments by Sandars, *The Sea Peoples*, pp. 174, 177. P. R. Ackroyd, *JSS* 24 (1979), pp. 19f., rightly notes that the text refers not to iron but to craftsmen.
14 Cf. J. P. Brown, *VT* 21 (1971), p. 10.
15 Those seeking further enlightenment may read the article by A. Ben-David in *UF* 11 (1979(1980)), pp. 29–45!
16 For further discussion of v. 21 see J. A. Bewer, *JBL* 61 (1942), pp. 45f.; R. Gordis, *ibid.*, pp. 209–211.
17 This chapter has been subjected to a painstaking literary analysis (672 pp.) by H. Madl, *Literarkritische und Formanalytische Untersuchungen zu 1 Sam. 14* (Bonn, 1974); see also J. Blenkinsopp, *CBQ* 26 (1964), pp. 423–449; F. Schicklberger, *VT* 24 (1974), pp. 324–333; D. Jobling, *JBL* 95 (1976), pp. 367–376.
18 *CTA* 17. 5. 4–8; 19. 1. 19–25.
19 NEB follows the Peshitta and G. R. Driver (*ZAW* 80 (1968), p. 174) in reading $k^e h \bar{o} s^e b \hat{e}$ ('like hewers of ') for MT $k^e b a h^a s \hat{i}$ ('as in a half '(?)), but the suitability of BH $h \bar{a} s a b$ in relation to furrowing has still to be properly demonstrated. McCarter prefers to follow LXX ('with darts and with pebbles of the field'), treating the words as a misplaced gloss from the end of v. 13, where they were intended to explain how the ill-equipped armour-bearer (cf. 13:22) managed to dispatch the Philistines.
20 MT is, in any case, in need of correction at the end of the verse, where $\hat{u} b^e n \hat{e}$ cannot mean '*with* the children of (Israel)'; LXX represents $li p^e n \hat{e}$ ('before') and is to be preferred.
21 Further discussion in Schicklberger, *Die Ladeerzählungen*, pp. 56–58. MT is retained by Stoebe, p. 260, DeVries, *Yesterday*, p. 64n., and, in particular, by P. R. Davies, 'Ark or Ephod in 1 Sam. xiv. 18?', *JTS* NS 26 (1975), pp. 82–87 (cf. *idem, JNSL* 5 (1977), pp. 15f.), who holds that the tradition of the capture of the ark in 1 Sa. 4 is a secondary development. Cf. also, in this respect, G. W. Ahlström, *JNES* 43 (1984), pp. 141–149.
22 I have to thank V. P. Long for his grammatical researches on this point.
23 LXX has a substantially different text of vv. 23b–24a: 'and all the people were with Saul, about ten thousand men. And the battle was spread to every city in the hill-country of Ephraim. (24) And Saul committed a great sin of ignorance on that day . . . ' It would be possible to treat MT *niggaś* (v. 24) as the remnant of the longer reading presupposed in LXX, viz. *šāgâ š^e gāgâ g^e dôlâ*, nevertheless MT can be interpreted as it stands. As for the LXX text, the imputation of a 'sin of ignorance' to Saul is ironic when what is immediately described is one such by Jonathan.
24 Reading $d^e b \bar{o} r \hat{o}$ for MT $d^e b a \dot{s}$ (v. 26), on the basis of LXX *lalōn* (= *dōbēr*). I am inclined, however, to think that MT may be retained if the (implied) subject of $h \bar{e} l e \underline{k}$ (or $h \bar{o} l \bar{e} \underline{k}$) is the forest: 'and behold, it was flowing with honey'. Compare the use of the same verb in Joel 4:18 and the following two lines in the Ugaritic text *CTA* 6. 3. 6f. (//12f.):

šmm šmn tmṭrn
nḥlm *tlk* nbtm

The heavens rain oil,
the valleys *flow with* honey.

25 See A. C. Thiselton, 'The Supposed Power of Words in the Biblical Writings', *JTS* NS 25 (1974), pp. 283–299 (293–299).

26 RSV 'became bright' (v. 27) follows the *Qᵉrê wattā'ōrᵉnâ* in preference to the *Kᵉthî'ḥ wattir'enâ* ('saw'), no doubt correctly in view of the occurrence of the verb *'ôr* in v. 29.

27 See the study by T. B. Dozemann, *SBT* 9 (1979), pp. 81–93.

28 RSV 'flew upon' reads *wayya'aṭ* for MT *wayya'aś*, which in the present context is a *vox nihili*. The emended reading is paralleled at 15:19 (*watta'aṭ*, RSV 'swoop'). See further Barr, *Comparative Philology*, pp. 67, 246f.

29 In his discussion of eating on (*sic*) the blood J. M. Grintz (*ASTI* 8 (1970–1(1972), pp. 78–105) links the slaying of the animals 'towards the ground' (lit.) with sacrifice to underworld deities.

30 At the end of v. 33 LXX reflects *hᵃlōm* ('here', *cf.* RSV) for MT *hayyôm* ('to-day'); the difference consonantally is a minor one and LXX is to be preferred.

31 *Cf.* K. W. Whitelam, *The Just King* (Suppl. *JSOT*, 12; Sheffield, 1979), pp. 78, 80.

32 J. Lindblom, *VT* 12 (1962), pp. 172–178, holds that there are two kinds of lot-casting which have been fused in this section; so, after a fashion, Mettinger, *King and Messiah*, pp. 179–182 (*cf.* n. 70). But see Whitelam, *The Just King*, pp. 76f.

33 MT appears to have sustained a sizeable omission by homoioteleuton, lacking all the material between the first and third occurrences of 'Israel'. On the respective merits of MT and LXX see A. Toeg, *VT* 19 (1969), pp. 493–498. E. Noort, *VT* 21 (1971), pp. 112–116, finds support for reading *tummîm*, against MT *tāmîm*, in a Qumran fragment (4Q 175, 14 (Testimonia)). See also Gooding, *Current Problems*, p. 10.

34 E. Lipiński, *VT* 20 (1970), pp. 495f. (on the basis of a text from Asshur).

35 *Cf.* H. H. Rowley, *The Faith of Israel* (London, 1956), pp. 28f.; McCarter, p. 250.

36 Further discussion in E. Robertson, *VT* 14 (1964), pp. 67–74; B. Johnson, *ASTI* 9 (1973(1974)), pp. 23–29; B. Albrektson, *ASTI* 11 (1977–8(1978)), pp. 1–10.

37 LXX has a long addition, of uncertain worth, in v. 42. According to the Greek, Saul announces that whoever is guilty, whether Jonathan or himself, must die; the people declare that this must not happen, but Saul goes ahead with the lot-casting.

38 Whitelam, *The Just King*, pp. 73f.

39 See the comments by P. D. Miscall (*JSOT* 6 (1978), p. 30) on Saul's 'vow' in relation to those of Jephthah and David (1 Sa. 25:22 in the latter case).

40 Compare also the provision for the careless ox-owner in Ex. 21:30.

41 RSV 'put them to the worse' (v. 47) attempts to deal with MT *yaršia'* which should, strictly, mean 'acted wickedly'. LXX presupposes *yiwwāšēa'* ('was victorious'), which involves only a minor consonantal change and should almost certainly be regarded as original. On MT as a scribal dysphemism see McCarthy, *Tiqqune Sopherim*, pp. 234–237.

42   See C. E. Hauer, 'The Shape of Saulide Strategy', *CBQ* 31 (1969), pp. 153–167; A. D. H. Mayes in Hayes–Miller, pp. 326–329.

43   Some LXX Mss reflect the form 'Ishyô' where -*yô* may be a shorter form of the divine name. We should then assume the substitution of -*yô* for the unacceptable *baal* element.

44   For the view that Abner was Saul's *uncle* see A. Malamat, *JAOS* 88 (1968), p. 171 (n. 27).

45   *DOTT*, p. 197. For an attempt to find a parallel conception at Mari see A. Malamat, 'The Ban in Mari and in the Bible', in *Mari and the Bible* (Jerusalem, 1975), pp. 52–61.

46   Reading '(with) the Amalekites' (*hăʿămālēqî*) for MT '(with) the people' (*hā ʿām*); *cf.* NEB.

47   See F. C. Fensham, 'Did a Treaty between the Israelites and the Kenites exist?', *BASOR* 175 (1964), pp. 51–54. *Cf.* also Ishida, *The Royal Dynasties*, p. 109.

48   RSV 'would not' (v. 9) translates *lō' 'ăḇû*, an expression used especially of 'perverse Israel', according to *BDB*, p. 2.

49   *Cf.* J. Jeremias, *Die Reue Gottes. Aspekte alttestamentlicher Gottesvorstellung* (Biblische Studien, 65; Neukirchen-Vluyn, 1975), pp. 17f.

50   For the various possible explanations of Samuel's anger see Gunn, *The Fate*, pp. 146f.

51   In relation to the Heb. 'hand' for 'monument' Stolz, p. 103, notes the occurrence of stones with representations of hands upraised in supplication to divine symbols, *e.g.* at Hazor (*cf.* his illustration on p. 102).

52   *Cf.* Gunn, *The Fate*, p. 50.

53   If the sentence is original – and I am less than certain of this – then we may have yet another case of omission by homoioteleuton in MT (*cf.* McCarter).

54   See, however, J. L. Kugel, *The Idea of Biblical Poetry: Parallelism and its History* (New Haven/London, 1981), pp. 59–95, for a wider discussion of this frequently observable feature of Hebrew prose.

55   'iniquity' (*'āwen*) also has idolatrous connotations in several of its occurrences (*cf. BDB*. p. 20).

56   *pace* Birch, *The Rise*, pp. 105–108 (*cf.* McCarter, pp. 270f.).

57   MT does not actually say that *Saul* took hold of the robe, and some commentators have thought that it was *Samuel* who grasped *Saul's* robe. But 4QSam^a and LXX both have Saul as subject (Ulrich, p. 54), and this, together with the likelihood that the act was a conventional gesture of entreaty (*cf.* R. A. Brauner, *JANES* 6 (1974), pp. 35–38), supports RSV's interpretation. *Cf.* also E. L. Greenstein, '"To Grasp the Hem" in Ugaritic Literature', *VT* 32 (1982), pp. 217f.

58   See D. W. Thomas, *JSS* 1 (1956), p. 109.

59   Ulrich, p. 64, prefers 4QSam^a, LXX 'and he (taken to refer to Samuel) worshipped' to MT 'and Saul worshipped'.

60   See the discussion on text by S. Talmon, *VT* 11 (1961), pp. 456f.

61   *Cf.* B. E. McKnight, 'Sung Justice: Death by Slicing', *JAOS* 93 (1973), pp. 359f.

62   W. Robertson Smith quoted in Driver, *Notes*, p. 131.

63   Jobling, *The Sense*, p. 24 (n. 9).

64   See B. S. Childs, *Exodus. A Commentary* (OTL; London, 1974), pp. 316f.

65   C. S. Lewis, *Reflections on the Psalms* (London/Glasgow, 1958), p. 113.

David and Saul (1 Sa. 16:1–31:13)

1 M. Kessler, *CBQ* 32 (1970), p. 547.

2 Unfortunately I have not been able to consult V. Vilar Hueso's study of the Bethlehem sanctuary in the period of the judges and Samuel, published in *Escritos de Biblia y Oriente* (ed. R. Aguirre, F. Garcia López; Salamanca, 1981).

3 But see the important discussion by J. Macdonald in *Abr-Nahrain* 17 (1977), pp. 52–71.

4 See the studies by J. J. Stamm, 'Der Name des Königs David', *SVT* 7 (1959(1960)), pp. 165–183 (reprinted in his *Beiträge zur hebräischen und altorientalischen Namenkunde* (OBO 30; Göttingen, 1980), pp. 25–43); A. Hoffman, *David. Namensdeutung zur Wesensdeutung* (BWANT 100; Stuttgart, 1973).

5 See the discussion in W. Eichrodt, *TOT* II, pp. 55–57, and the pertinent comments of G. von Rad in *The Message of the Prophets* (ET; London, 1968), p. 124.

6 Saul's unwitting furtherance of Yahweh's purpose is brought out in 'Provide *for me*' (v. 17), answering to Yahweh's 'I have provided *for myself*' (v. 1).

7 *Cf.* J. T. Willis, *ZAW* 85 (1973), p. 297.

8 The LXX Lucianic tradition has both 'ass' and 'omer' ('and he took an ass and put an omer of bread on it'), which McCarter regards as the original reading.

9 *Cf.* J. A. Thompson, *VT* 24 (1974), pp. 334–338.

10 *DJD* IV, pp. 92f.

11 Goliath's armour is worthy of a Homeric hero, according to J. P. Brown, *VT* 21 (1971), p. 3. K. Galling, *SVT* 15 (1965(1966)), pp. 150–169, argues that Goliath's armour as described here is a collection of pieces of diverse origin which have been assembled by the narrator for literary effect.

12 See Y. Yadin, *The Scroll of the War of the Sons of Light against the Sons of Darkness* (ET; Oxford, 1962), pp. 156f. The meaning 'champion' is defended by R. de Vaux, 'Single Combat in the Old Testament', in *The Bible and the Ancient Near East* (London, 1972), pp. 124f. H. A. Hoffner, *CBQ* 30 (1968), pp. 220–225, compares the Hittite *piran ḫuyanza*, which he renders by 'champion'. The term *'iš-habbēnayim* gave rise to a Jewish tradition that Goliath was born of miscegenation, hence the Vulgate *vir spurius*.

13 *Cf.* K. A. Kitchen in *POTT*, p. 67.

14 In connection with Goliath's abnormal height W. J. Martin, *The Biblical Expositor* (ed. C. F. Henry; Philadelphia/New York, [2]1973), p. 263, refers to one John Middleton (*c.* AD 1600) who is reputed to have been nine feet three inches tall. Middleton is buried at Hale, near Liverpool.

15 *Cf.* Brown, *VT* 21 (1971), pp. 3f.; L. Krinetzki, *Biblica* 54 (1973), p. 191.

16 See Y. Yadin, *The Scroll*, pp. 129–131. *Cf.* G. Molin, *JSS* 1 (1956), pp. 334–337; Galling, *SVT* 15 (1965(1966)), pp. 165–167.

17 For the view that *kāṭēp* possibly means 'weapon' here see R. T. O'Callaghan, *Orientalia* NS 21 (1952), pp. 37–46; J. C. L. Gibson, *Canaanite Myths and Legends*[2], p. 79 (text 6. 5. 2 ('broad-sword')). P. C. Craigie, *The Book of Deuteronomy* (NICOT; London, 1976), pp. 396f., would translate the same expression by 'between his weapons' in Dt. 33:12.

18 Y. Yadin, *PEQ* 86 (1955), pp. 58–69; *idem, The Art of Warfare in Biblical Lands* (ET; London, 1963), pp. 354f.

19 On representative combat see the references in note 11 to vv. 4–7 above.

20 See *ANET*[3], pp. 18–22.

21   *Cf.* H. Jason, *Biblica* 60 (1979), p. 67.

22   All the same, the RSV emendation hardly merits description as 'the kind of "reconstruction" which is calculated to shake confidence in the scholarship of RSV' (O. T. Allis, *Revised Version or Revised Bible?*, p. 11).

23   *Cf.* Wiseman in *AOTS*, p. 126; O. Loretz, *UF* 8 (1976(1977)), pp. 129–131; *idem*, *UF* 9 (1977(1978)), pp. 163–167.

24   So N. P. Lemche, *VT* 24 (1974), pp. 373f.

25   NIV is strictly correct at 16:21 when it translates 'one of his armour-bearers'.

26   *Cf.* NIV 'hair', which is a less than literal rendering of BH *zāqān*.

27   H. J. Stoebe, *VT* 6 (1956), p. 408. Note that the LXX B-text has nothing corresponding to the last clause of v. 38.

28   *Cf.* Yadin, *The Art*, p. 159.

29   The sound-play in 'with sticks' (*bammaqᵉlôṭ*) and 'cursed' (*wayᵉqallēl*) may be deliberate.

30   A similar criticism may be made of the manuscript in the Peshitta tradition which has 'with a staff and with a sling'.

31   A. Deem (*VT* 28 (1978), pp. 349–351), comparing Testament of Judah 3:1, wants to translate 'sank into his greave', *i.e.* the stone hit the upper shin or knee where the giant was unprotected.

32   On this question see J. T. Willis, *ZAW* 85 (1973), pp. 302–305.

33   See further Willis, *ibid.*, pp. 295–298. Jobling, *The Sense*, p. 25n., notes how Saul's ignorance of David's background contributes to a general theme of ignorance on Saul's part.

34   *Cf.* J. A. Thompson, *VT* 24 (1974), pp. 334–338; W. L. Moran, *CBQ* 25 (1963), pp. 77–87. P. R. Ackroyd, *VT* 25 (1975), pp. 213f., finds a similar kind of significance in the verb translated 'knit' (*qāšar*) in v. 1, particularly in view of its use in 22:8, 13 (RSV 'conspired').

35   *Cf.* Jobling, *The Sense*, p. 12.

36   On hereditary monarchy in the near east see Ishida, *The Royal Dynasties*, pp. 6–25.

37   N. P. Lemche, *JSOT* 10 (1978), p. 21 (n. 18), maintains that 'the two positions, in 18, 5 and 18, 13, are in fact identical'.

38   See W. L. Moran, *CBQ* 25 (1963), p. 81.

39   On which see G. W. Coats, 'Self-Abasement and Insult Formulas', *JBL* 89 (1970), pp. 14–26.

40   Since there is no other mention of a deadline and LXX lacks the clause (lit. 'and the days were not complete'), the shorter text is often regarded as the original.

41   J. F. A. Sawyer, *VT* 15 (1965), p. 484 (n. 11), comments on a possibly forensic aspect of *tᵉšû'â* here.

42   See H. A. Hoffner, *JNES* 27 (1968), pp. 61–68; *idem* in *POTT*, p. 217.

43   *Cf.* Ackroyd, *ad loc.* W. F. Albright made the (improbable) suggestion that *tᵉrāpîm* should be translated 'old rags' (*BASOR* 83 (1941), p. 40). G. von Rad, *OTT* I, p. 216 (n. 61), thinks of a cultic mask; *cf.* R. P. Carroll, *STh* 31 (1977), p. 57 (n. 15).

44   See A. Malamat, *JAOS* 82 (1962), p. 146. I owe this reference to McCarter (p. 328).

45   Stoebe, pp. 368f., differs on this point. On the word translated 'company' see Barr, *Comparative Philology*, pp. 25f. On the basis of an Ethiopic comparison it is possible to argue that the word means 'eldership'.

46   LXX 'Sephei' has encouraged a number of scholars to postulate an original

šᵉpî ('bare height') for MT *šeḵû*. For 'great cistern' (*bôr haggāḏôl*) LXX has 'cistern of the threshingfloor' (*bôr haggōren*), which is attractive both for the sense that it offers and because, unlike MT, it properly takes account of the definite article.

47   As Driver, *Notes*, p. 160, observes, Saul could have worn his inner tunic and still be described as 'naked' (*'ārōm*; cf. Is. 20:2).

48   Cf. Stoebe, quoted in Jobling, *The Sense*, p. 10.

49   Dittography of the letter *'ayin* accounts for MT's misreading.

50   Cf. K. D. Sakenfeld, *The Meaning of Hesed in the Hebrew Bible: A New Inquiry* (Harvard Semitic Monographs, 17; Missoula, 1978), pp. 82–84.

51   On the syntax of vv. 12f. see Driver, *Notes*, pp. 163f.

52   At the beginning of v. 16 MT reads: 'and Jonathan made (a covenant) with the house of David', but the reversion to direct speech in what follows is a strong argument in favour of the LXX text adopted by RSV.

53   Cf. R. Yaron, *VT* 9 (1959), pp. 89–91; M. Anbar (Bernstein), *Orientalia* NS 48 (1979), pp. 109–111; McCarthy, *Tiqqune Sopherim*, pp. 189–191.

54   Cf. A. Guillaume, *PEQ* 86 (1954), pp. 83–86. NIV ('The day after tomorrow, towards evening') seems similarly influenced. Note that the meeting was arranged for the next *morning*, according to v. 35.

55   RSV 'yonder stone heap' follows LXX (= *hā'argāḇ hallāz*) in preference to MT 'the stone Ezel' (*hā'eḇen hā'āzel*). Cf. v. 41, where MT 'the south' (*hanneḡeḇ*) also seems to be a misreading of an original *hā'argāḇ*.

56   Cf. S. Iwry, *JAOS* 81 (1961), pp. 27–34.

57   For MT 'the Lord is between' (v. 23) the LXX has 'the Lord is witness between' (cf. NEB). The Greek reading is advocated by E. Finkelstein, *JSS* 4 (1959), pp. 356f.; cf. S. Jellicoe, *The Septuagint and Modern Study*, p. 321. MT, which is defended by Stoebe (p. 377), is as in v. 42.

58   Cf. B. A. Mastin, *SVT* 30 (1979), pp. 113–124.

59   *pace* Stoebe, p. 378; see D. J. A. Clines, *VT* 22 (1972), pp. 283f.

60   Driver, *Notes*, p. 255.

61   4QSam[b] and LXX have 'son of rebellious maidens', which involves the interesting reading *n'rwt* ('maidens') for MT *nᶜwt* ('perverse'). McCarter accordingly reads, 'You son of a rebellious servant girl!', an expression paralleled to some extent in Judith 16:12, as, apparently, first noted by Wellhausen.

62   On this subject see W. Beyerlin, *ZAW* 73 (1961), pp. 196f.; G. Buccellati, *Cities and Nations of Ancient Syria* (Studi Semitici, 26; Rome, 1967), pp. 195–200; Ishida, *The Royal Dynasties*, pp. 151–182.

63   Jobling, *The Sense*, p. 14.

64   For 'stone heap' (MT 'south') see note 55, to v. 19.

65   Ahimelech could conceivably be the same person as Ahijah, also described as a son of Ahitub in 14:3, since *melech* may, like *jah*, be a divine element ('the King').

66   RSV 'made an appointment' represents the original as *yā'aḏtî* (MT *yôḏ a'tî*), as in 4QSam[b] (cf. McCarter). See also the discussion in Barr, *Comparative Philology*, pp. 21f.

67   For discussion of the location of this episode 'when *Abiathar* was high priest' in Mk. 2:26 see J. W. Wenham, *Christ and the Bible* (London, 1972), pp. 75–77; C. S. Morgan, *JBL* 98 (1979), pp. 409f.

68   Cf. von Rad, *Der Heilige Krieg*, p. 7. The same rule applies in the Qumran *War Scroll* (col. VII, 1. 3; ed. Yadin, pp. 290f.).

69   Driver, *Notes*, pp. 174f.

70   So already de Boer, *OTS* 6, p. 35; *cf.* also J. Whitton, *NTS* 28 (1982), pp. 142f.

71   See J. R. Bartlett in *POTT*, p. 246; *idem*, *JSOT* 4 (1977), pp. 5–8; *JSOT* 5 (1978), pp. 33f.; M. Rose, *JSOT* 4 (1977), pp. 28–34.

72   *Psalmenstudien* III (Amsterdam, 1966), p. 24. E. Kutsch, *VT* 2 (1952), pp. 65–67, thinks that Doeg had gone to Nob to observe a holy day. The expression 'before the Lord' can, according to context, have a judicial sense (*cf.* D. C. T. Sheriffs, *JNSL* 7 (1979), pp. 63–68).

73   *Cf.* Gibson, *Canaanite Myths and Legends*², p. 81, and see the discussion by M. Dietrich and O. Loretz in *UF* 9 (1977(1978)), pp. 336f. In later Jewish tradition Doeg was recognized as a scholar and debater, and as knowledgeable about David's family pedigree (TB Yeb. 76b–77a).

74   For a recent discussion see F. Crüsemann, *ZAW* 92 (1980), pp. 215–222.

75   *Cf.* T. C. Mitchell in *AOTS*, p. 415; K. A. Kitchen in *POTT*, p. 67.

76   For MT 'made marks' (*way^{e}ṭāw*) LXX has 'drummed' (representing *wayyāṭōp̄*). McCarter accepts the LXX reading, but relates the form to BH *tōp̄eṭ* ('spitting') and translates 'spat (upon the doors)'.

77   NEB's mention of 'the cave of Adullam' in Mi. 1:15 is of no help since MT has, simply, 'Adullam'!

78   Horatio in *Hamlet* I, 1.

79   D. W. Thomas proposes the meaning 'had taken leave' for this occurrence of the verb *yāḏa'* (RSV 'was discovered'). See *JTS* NS 21 (1970), pp. 401f.

80   *Cf.* J. Gray, *The Legacy of Canaan* (SVT 5; Leiden, ²1965), p. 75 (n. 2).

81   Too much should not be made of this verse in discussions of the extent of Saul's kingdom; see Mettinger, *King and Messiah*, pp. 299–301; Whitelam, *The Just King*, pp. 71, 239 (n. 5).

82   See the essay by H. Madl, discussing *inter alia* the 'holy war' associations of the expression 'to inquire of the Lord', in H.-J. Fabry (ed.), *Bausteine biblischer Theologie* (Fs G. J. Botterweck; Bonner Biblische Beiträge, 50; Köln-Bonn, 1977), pp. 45–55.

83   *Cf.* Jobling, who sees vv. 11–19 as lying 'on two axes of divine rejection' (*The Sense*, p. 24 (n. 10); *cf. idem*, *JBL* 95 (1976), pp. 368f., on Saul's association with Ahijah, representing the rejected house of Eli).

84   LXX and Peshitta support *ḥaḇti* ('I am guilty') for MT *sabbōṭi* ('I have occasioned'). For a defence of MT see de Boer, *OTS* 6, p. 43. NEB has 'I have gambled'.

85   So Sennacherib on his besieging of Hezekiah in Jerusalem (*DOTT*, p. 67).

86   On MT *nikkar* (7, RSV 'has given') see Barr, *Comparative Philology*, p. 267n.

87   The question, 'Will the men of Keilah deliver me into his hand?' does not occur in the 4QSam^b version of v. 11. See F. M. Cross, *JBL* 74 (1955), p. 171.

88   *Cf.* Jobling, *The Sense*, p. 21: 'Jonathan receives no revelations, and yet he knows. Mysteriously, the divine plan is open to him. . . in 23:17 he speaks to David as a prophet speaks . . . '

89   On this significance of 'before the Lord' see Sheriffs, *JNSL* 7 (1979), pp. 59–61.

90   MT does not have the definite article with 'Ziphites', hence McCarter's 'Some Ziphites' in v. 19.

91   These are adequately discussed by McCarter, p. 377.

92   See B. Mazar, 'En-gedi', in *AOTS*, pp. 223–230.

93   *Cf.* A. Danin, *BARev* 5 (1979), pp. 50f.; see *OTA* 3 (1980), p. 108.

94   Cf., for example, McKane, pp. 147f. I hope to publish a short paper which touches on the question of the order of vv. 4–7.

95   So Grønbaek, *Die Geschichte*, p. 168.

96   K. Budde, p. 210.

97   Driver, *Notes*, pp. 192f., argues for 'Behold the day on which Yahweh saith unto thee'; *i.e.* the opportunity given is itself the occasion of the oracle.

98   See my comments in *TB* 31 (1980), pp. 55f., and the references noted there. For further significance of the cutting of a hem (in divorce proceedings) see J. J. Finkelstein, *WO* 8 (1975), pp. 236–240.

99   On this aspect of ch. 25 see *TB* 31 (1980), pp. 37–64; Gunn, *The Fate*, pp. 96–103.

100   Cf. Crüsemann, *Der Widerstand*, pp. 139–141.

101   See H. Cazelles in *POTT*, pp. 4–28. N. P. Lemche, *JSOT* 10 (1978), pp. 11f., compares David with Idrimi of Alalakh, who was forced out of his kingdom to take refuge with the *ḥabiru*.

102   See A. Malamat, 'Military Rationing in Papyrus Anastasi I and the Bible', in *Mélanges bibliques rédigés en l'honneur de A. Robert* (Paris, n.d.), pp. 114–121.

103   F. Perles, *JQR* NS 17 (1926–7), p. 233, translates MT *šeḳel* (RSV 'understanding') by 'shape'; but see Barr, *Comparative Philology*, pp. 244f. In v. 33 David praises Abigail's *ṭa'am* ('discretion'), which, in the context, is nearly synonymous with 'understanding'.

104   Grønbaek, *Die Geschichte*, p. 171n.

105   G. R. Driver, *JTS* NS 8 (1957), pp. 272f. See also the comment on a possible Akkadian parallel, by D. J. Wiseman, *VT* 32 (1982), p. 318n.

106   On the term see A. Murtonen, *VT* 9 (1959), p. 173.

107   So J. D. Levenson, *CBQ* 40 (1978), p. 14.

108   Cf. J. Barr, *BJRL* 52 (1969), pp. 21–28 (see pp. 25f. on other possible meanings of 'Nabal'). See further T. Donald, *VT* 13 (1963), pp. 285–292; G. Gerleman, *VT* 24 (1974), pp. 147–158. For the view that Nabal's name, as originally given, meant 'Fool', see L. Köhler, *Hebrew Man* (ET; London, 1956), p. 65: 'There hovers over the life of the child the fear of what might come upon it, and this is expressed in a name which says what the child should not be.'

109   Levenson, *CBQ* 40 (1978), p. 14.

110   Cf. *TB* 31 (1980), p. 49.

111   Though see J. Goldingay, *CBQ* 40 (1978), pp. 388–390. Goldingay interprets the reference to bloodguiltiness along the lines of Ezek. 3:17–19; 33:7–9.

112   Thus McCarter (p. 17) on vv. 28–31; see, however, Mettinger, *King and Messiah*, p. 55, on these verses as integral to the (so-called) 'History of David's Rise'.

113   Cf. A. L. Oppenheim, *JNES* 18 (1959), pp. 123–128.

114   See W. L. Moran, *JNES* 22 (1963), pp. 173–176; E. Zenger, *BZ* NF 12 (1968), pp. 16–30.

115   Grønbaek, *Die Geschichte*, p. 176.

116   Levenson, *CBQ* 40 (1978), pp. 26f., reckons that Nabal may have been the clan chieftain of the Calebites.

117   Levenson, p. 27, notes that the only other Ahinoam in the Old Testament is Saul's wife; and he cannot resist identifying the two. Levenson sees a *quid pro quo* in Saul's marrying off Michal to Palti, in response to David's laying claim to the throne through his marriage to Ahinoam. 2 Sa. 12:8 is cited in support of this ingenious, though perhaps excessively speculative, explanation of the data.

118   J. D. Levenson and B. Halpern, *JBL* 99 (1980), pp. 507–518, argue that

David's marriages to Ahinoam and Abigail were politically motivated: they were decisive steps on the way to the throne.

119 *Cf.* Mauchline, pp. 172f.

120 See the discussion by R. Thornhill, *VT* 14 (1964), pp. 462–466.

121 See H. A. Hoffner in *POTT*, pp. 197–221.

122 For a parallel to 'his day shall come', in a Mari text, see J.-G. Heintz, *VT* 21 (1971), pp. 528–540 (534).

123 *Cf.* W. D. Davies, *The Gospel and the Land. Early Christianity and Jewish Territorial Doctrine* (London, 1974), pp. 63–65, and the present writer in *SVT* 29 (1977(1978)), pp. 117–121.

124 *TB* 31 (1980), p. 60.

125 *e.g.* K. Koch, *The Growth of the Biblical Tradition* (ET; London, 1969), p. 142.

126 N. P. Lemche, *JSOT* 10 (1978), p. 12.

127 For another suggestion see D. J. Wiseman in *AOTS*, p. 125.

128 R. G. Boling, *Joshua* (AB 6; New York, 1982), p. 383.

129 Buccellati, *Cities*, pp. 160–162. The arguments are summarized by J. A. Soggin in Hayes-Miller, pp. 353–355.

130 Moreover, there is a small amount of LXX support (though see McCarter, p. 413) for the emendation.

131 A. Heidel, *The Gilgamesh Epic and Old Testament Parallels* (Chicago, 1946), p. 189.

132 Note that 4QSam^a adds 'to Jezreel' – regarded by Ulrich (p. 171) as original – at the end of v. 1.

133 *Cf.* Stoebe, p. 489.

134 W. F. Albright, *Archaeology and the Religion of Israel*[3], p. 203 (n. 31).

135 H. A. Hoffner, *JBL* 86 (1967), pp. 385–401; *idem* in *POTT*, pp. 216f.

136 J. Lust, *SVT* 26 (1974), pp. 133–142. See further M. Dietrich-O. Loretz-J. Sanmartin, *UF* 6 (1974(1975)), pp. 450f.; J. Ebach and U. Rüterswörden, *UF* 9 (1977(1978)), pp. 57–70; *idem, UF* 12 (1980(1981)), pp. 205–220.

137 J. B. Burns, *TGUOS* 26 (1975–6(1979)), p. 9 (*cf.* pp. 1–14).

138 C. E. Hauer, *CBQ* 31 (1969), pp. 162–167; see also T. Koizumi, *Annual of the Japanese Biblical Institute* 2 (1976), pp. 61–78.

139 For a radical relocation of this final encounter between Saul and the Philistines see H. Bar-Deroma, *PEQ* 102 (1970), pp. 116–136.

140 *Cf. ANET*^{3}, p. 396; *NERTOT*, p. 174.

141 *Cf.* Weinfeld's discussion of 1 Ki. 3:3–14 in *Deuteronomy*, pp. 250–254.

142 Or, again, we may think of the woman as experiencing a general heightening of her powers of perception when she engaged with the spirit world.

143 M. Hutter, *Biblische Notizen* 21 (1983), pp. 32–36, thinks that 'god(s)' is a redundant term formerly used in incantational formulae. See *OTA* 7 (1984), p. 168.

144 There is not much to be said for LXX 'erect' ($=z\bar{a}q\bar{u}\bar{p}$) in place of MT 'old' ($z\bar{a}q\bar{e}n$).

145 W. A. M. Beuken, 'I Samuel 28: The Prophet as "Hammer of Witches"', *JSOT* 6 (1978), p. 8.

146 For 'your enemy' ($'\bar{a}r^e\underline{k}\bar{a}$, 16) LXX and Peshitta have '(and is) with your friend' ($='im\ r\check{e}'e\underline{k}\bar{a}$). MT may be retained, though the form with initial *'ayin* is properly Aramaic.

147 LXX has 'will fall with you'; MT (lit. 'you and your sons with me') is slightly abrupt, but that is perhaps no disadvantage in this context.

148　Smith, *ICC*, pp. 243f., thinks that there may have been an Aphek in the Jezreel area.

149　Some Greek Mss have 'En-dor', which could be by contamination from ch. 28 or could just possibly have resulted from a misreading of 'En-harod', especially in view of the close similarity of ḍ and ṛ in the Hebrew scripts.

150　See McCarthy, *Tiqqune Sopherim*, pp. 179–182.

151　The negative is not in a couple of LXX Mss, according to which David is, therefore, in good standing with the city-state rulers, if not with their army commanders.

152　LXX does not have the reference to the 'angel of God'.

153　NEB follows the longer text of LXX in v. 10: 'and go to the town which I allotted to you; harbour no evil thoughts, for I am well satisfied with you'.

154　There is no justification for emending MT *ᵉmoh⁰rāṭām* ('of the next day', 17) to read *wayyaḥᵃrîmēm* ('and put them to the ban'), as in *BH³*, etc.

155　The revision of 'to his friends' (*ᵉrē'ēhû*) to 'according to their cities' (*ᵉ'ārêhem*; cf. McCarter's *ᵉ'ārāyw*) was dismissed by Driver as 'rather violent' (*Notes*, p. 225).

156　For brief discussion of the cities mentioned in vv. 27–31, as also of the entity 'Judah' in this period, see H.-J. Zobel, *SVT* 28 (1974), pp. 259–277.

157　Some texts have 'Shiphmoth'.

158　*Cf.* Ulrich, p. 80.

159　See Zobel, *SVT* 28 (1974), p. 260; Y. Aharoni, *BA* 39 (1976), pp. 66–76.

160　Boling, *Joshua*, p. 438.

161　MT has *mēhammôrîm*, while the assumed reading of the LXX *Vorlage* is *baḥōmeš*. It is probably better to keep the reading of MT.

162　For a more favourable reading of Saul's life and death (in contrast with David!) see T. R. Preston, *JSOT* 24 (1982), pp. 27–46 (43).

163　*pace* McCarter (pp. 440f.), who tends to treat the Chronicles version as evidence for a shorter account ancestral to both passages.

164　*Cf.* B. Gemser, *VT* 2 (1952), pp. 349–355; E. Vogt, *Biblica* 34 (1953), pp. 118f.; M. A. v.d. Oudenrijn, *Biblica* 35 (1954), p. 138; J. P. U. Lilley, *VT* 28 (1978), pp. 165–171.

165　For Egyptian veneration of Ashtart in a military context see *CAH³* II.1, p. 482.

166　For a Hittite parallel see H. A. Hoffner, *CBQ* 30 (1968), pp. 224f.

167　See *AOTS*, pp. 185–196.

168　G. R. Driver, *ZAW* 66 (1954), pp. 314f., thinks that Hebrew had a verb *sērēp̄/śērēp̄* meaning 'to smear with resin'.

David King of Judah (2 Sa. 1:1–4:12)

1　McKane, p. 175; see further Mauchline, pp. 201f., for an attempt at harmonization.

2　A. Berlin, *Poetics and Interpretation of Biblical Narrative* (Sheffield, 1983), p. 81.

3　*Cf. KB*, p. 944.

4　C. Mabee, *ZAW* 92 (1980), pp. 89–98.

5　*Cf.* Mabee, *ibid.*, p. 94.

6　Special studies include; S. Gevirtz, *Patterns in the Early Poetry of Israel*

(Chicago, 1963), pp. 72–96; W. L. Holladay, *VT* 20 (1970), pp. 153–189; D. N. Freedman, 'The Refrain in David's Lament over Saul and Jonathan', in *Ex Orbe Religionum* I (Fs G. Widengren; ed. C. J. Bleeker *et al.*; Supplements to *Numen*, 21; Leiden, 1972), pp. 115–126; W. H. Shea, *BASOR* 221 (1976), pp. 141–144.

7   Driver, *Notes*, p. 239.

8   *Cf.* Ackroyd, *ad loc.*; Brockington, p. 50.

9   There is some support in Ugaritic for taking 'gazelle' as a title of honour (*cf.* NEB 'prince').

10   Ginsberg, *JBL* 57 (1938), pp. 209–213; for a defence of Ginsberg see Holladay, *VT* 20 (1970), pp. 170–173; T. L. Fenton, *VT* 29 (1979), pp. 162–170.

11   *Cf.* M. Dahood, *Biblica* 53 (1972), pp. 398f.; *Biblica* 55 (1974), p. 392; Freedman, *op. cit.*, pp. 121f.; J. P. Fokkelman, *ZAW* 91 (1979), pp. 290–292.

12   A. R. Millard, *BASOR* 230 (1978), p. 70.

13   Weinfeld, *Deuteronomy*, p. 136 (n. 3), however, cites various biblical and extra-biblical references in support of the idea that it is the reversing of *the direction of the bow* that is in question.

14   P. A. H. de Boer, *Henoch* 3 (1981), pp. 22–25.

15   On the general question of David's anointing see Mettinger, *King and Messiah*, pp. 198–216.

16   For a more recent, but less likely, explanation see M. Tsevat, *HUCA* 46 (1975), pp. 71–87; W. C. Gwaltney, *IDBS*, p. 461.

17   *Cf.* A. Lemaire, *VT* 31 (1981), pp. 53f.

18   J. A. Soggin, *Old Testament and Oriental Studies* (BO 29; Rome, 1975), pp. 41f. For a different explanation of this verse see W. J. Martin in *IBD* 1, pp. 134f.

19   So D. N. Freedman, 'Early Israelite History in the Light of Early Israelite Poetry', in *Unity and Diversity* (ed. H. Goedicke, J. J. M. Roberts; Baltimore, 1975), p. 16; *cf.* J. D. Levenson, *CBQ* 40 (1978), pp. 27f.; J. C. VanderKam, *JBL* 99 (1980), pp. 527f.

20   Soggin, *Old Testament and Oriental Studies*, pp. 34–36.

21   See the studies by Y. Sukenik (Yadin), *JPOS* 21 (1948), pp. 110–116; O. Eissfeldt, *Kleine Schriften* III (Tübingen, 1966), pp. 140f.; H. A. Hoffner, *CBQ* 30 (1968), pp. 220–225; J. M. Sasson, *Orientalia* NS 43 (1974), pp. 404–410.

22   See F. C. Fensham, *VT* 20 (1970), pp. 356f.

23   *Cf.* W. L. Reed in *AOTS*, pp. 231–243 (and references there).

24   For the 'reading' *cf.* Ulrich, p. 54; as often enough with 4QSam^a, it is a matter of spacing rather than of an extant reading.

25   See J. B. Pritchard, *Gibeon, Where the Sun Stood Still. The Discovery of the Biblical City* (Princeton, 1962), pp. 35, 74, 159f.

26   See J. Macdonald, *JNES* 35 (1976), pp. 147–170; *idem* (with B. Cutler), *UF* 8 (1976(1977)), pp. 27–35; *idem*, *JAOS* 96 (1976), pp. 57–68; H.-P. Stähli, *Knabe–Jüngling–Knecht* (BET 7; Frankfurt am Main, 1978), pp. 137–149.

27   See Yadin, *The Art*, p. 267; Stähli, *Knabe–Jüngling–Knecht*, p. 145.

28   É. Levine, *NTS* 28 (1982), pp. 560–564.

29   There is a slight difficulty with MT, and NEB therefore emends to read 'with a back-thrust'.

30   LXX has *Dalouia*; 4QSam^a is uncertain, perhaps reading 'Daluyah' (Ulrich, p. 81).

31   The Lucianic strand of the LXX has the additional words 'and Abner took her' after 'Aiah' (v. 7).

32   *Cf.* D. M. Gunn, *Semeia* 3 (1975), p. 37n.; *idem*, *Story of David*, pp. 137f. (and references there). See also P. R. Ackroyd, discussing 'the daughters of the

king' (Je. 41:10), in *Tradition and Interpretation* (ed. G. W. Anderson; Oxford, 1979), p. 325.

33   The reference to Judah, which reads slightly awkwardly in MT, is not in LXX. For discussion of the various significances of 'dog' in the Old Testament see D. W. Thomas, *VT* 10 (1960), pp. 410–427.

34   RSV follows LXX (Lucianics) in reading 'at Hebron' for MT *taḥtāw*. NIV's 'on his behalf ' provides a suitable sense for MT; *cf.* NEB's 'instead of going to David himself '.

35   NEB 'seeking to make friends where he could' represents a radically different treatment of MT *ʾmi ʾāreṣ*; see Brockington, p. 51.

36   Ackroyd thinks that the reference to Ish-bosheth at this point stems from a variant account of the restoration of Michal to David.

37   On the legal aspects of David's repossession of Michal see Z. Ben-Barak, *SVT* 30 (1979), pp. 15–29.

38   *Cf.* D. J. Wiseman, *VT* 32 (1982), pp. 323–326.

39   So, nevertheless, J. C. VanderKam, *JBL* 99 (1980), pp. 532f.

40   Driver, *Notes*, p. 250.

41   *Cf.*, for example, E. V. Hulse, *PEQ* 107 (1975), pp. 87–105; J. Wilkinson, *SJT* 31 (1978), pp. 153–166. See also S. G. Browne, *Leprosy in the Bible* (London, n.d.).

42   See Weinfeld, *Deuteronomy*, pp. 116–121. Sufferers from either a discharge or 'leprosy' would be cultically unclean (*cf.* Lv. 13, 15); compare the curse in the Assyrian vassal treaties of Esarhaddon: 'May Sin. . . clothe you with leprosy; may he not order your entering into the presence of the gods or king' (11. 419f.).

43   D. J. A. Clines, *UF* 8 (1976(1977)), pp. 23–26. For other parallels see D. R. Hillers, *Treaty-Curses and the Old Testament Prophets* (BO 16; Rome, 1964), pp. 66–68.

44   There is a *possible* parallel to this use of *pelek* in the Phoenician Karatepe inscription where *ʾšt tk lḥdy dl plkm* (A II, 5f.) has been translated 'a woman walked by herself without supports'; see R. S. Tomback, *A Comparative Semitic Lexicon of the Phoenician and Punic Languages* (Missoula, 1978), p. 264.

45   On this point see Lemche, *JSOT* 10 (1978), p. 25 (n. 46).

46   Instead of 'your feet were not fettered' (v. 34), M. Dahood has suggested 'nor your feet tortured by fetters' (*Biblica* 61 (1980), p. 261).

47   On the absence of the name Ish-bosheth from MT in vv. 1f. and related problems see Ulrich, pp. 42–45.

48   So Soggin, *Old Testament and Oriental Studies*, pp. 46–48; *idem*, in Hayes–Miller, p. 348. Ackroyd suggests that the Be-erothites' flight was a consequence of the murder of Ish-bosheth by two of their number.

49   As is done by Lemche, *JSOT* 10 (1978), p. 17; VanderKam, *JBL* 99 (1980), pp. 532f. On the judicial aspects of David's treatment of the Be-erothites see C. Mabee, *ZAW* 92 (1980), pp. 98–107.

David King of Israel (2 Sa. 5:1–20:26)

1   Jdg. 1:8 is problematical in that it speaks of the capture and destruction of Jerusalem some time after Joshua's death, whereas v. 21 of the same chapter notes the inability of the Benjaminites to expel the original occupants (*cf.* Jos. 15:63; Jdg. 19:10, 12). If the city was captured at this early date, it must quickly have reverted to Jebusite control. Some, on the other hand, think that Jdg. 1:8

refers only to the town outside the fortress city; Hertzberg, p. 268, is of the opinion that it merely attests Judahite possession of pasturage in the area.

2   For consideration of the more negative aspects of the relocation of David's capital see J. W. Flanagan, *JAAR* 47 (1979), pp. 223–244.

3   A more critical evaluation of vv. 17–25 as history is presented by N. L. Tidwell, *SVT* 30 (1979), pp. 190–212.

4   D. Daube, *JBL* 90 (1971), pp. 480f., thinks that the Deuteronomic insistence on consanguinity derives from the Abimelech experience, Abimelech being, in fact, half-Canaanite.

5   On pre-Israelite Jerusalem see J. J. Schmitt in *Scripture in Context* (ed. C. D. Evans *et al.*; Pittsburgh, 1980), pp. 101–121. For a general conspectus see D. R. Ap-Thomas in *AOTS*, pp. 277–295.

6   See G. Brunet, *SVT* 30 (1979), pp. 65–72, 81–84. For an earlier study of this problem see Yadin, *The Art*, pp. 267–270; Yadin thinks in terms of a magical constraint laid upon the attackers by the exhibition of the blind and lame.

7   *Cf.* W. G. E. Watson, *VT* 20 (1970), pp. 501f.

8   LXX translates by 'knife'; E. L. Sukenik, *JPOS* 8 (1928), pp. 12–16, prefers 'trident'.

9   L. H. Vincent, *Jérusalem*, 1 (Paris, 1912), pp. 146–161. The translation 'canales' is as old as the sixteenth century; see Brunet, *SVT* 30, p. 74n.

10   *Cf.* R. M. Ogilvie, *Early Rome and the Etruscans* (Hassocks, 1976), pp. 154f.

11   Brunet, *SVT* 30, pp. 79–81. See, for the more traditional view, K. M. Kenyon, *Digging up Jerusalem* (London, 1974), pp. 98f.

12   W. F. Albright, *JPOS* 2 (1922), pp. 286–290.

13   Ulrich, p. 136, notes a distinctive reading of 4QSam[a] which supports the view that it is David who hates rather than is hated (as in the *K^ethîb*).

14   *Cf.* J. A. Soggin in Hayes–Miller, p. 355.

15   The latter is favoured by Kenyon, *Digging up Jerusalem*, pp. 100–103 (*cf. PEQ* 98 (1966), p. 78).

16   H. J. Katzenstein, *The History of Tyre* (Jerusalem, 1973), p. 95.

17   On Eliada (v. 16), appearing in 1 Ch. 14:7 as Beeliada, see McCarthy, *Tiqqune Sopherim*, pp. 223–225.

18   C. E. Hauer, *CBQ* 32 (1970), pp. 571–578.

19   *Cf.* Hauer, *ibid.*, pp. 575–578; K.-D. Schunck, *VT* 33 (1983), pp. 110–113.

20   Tidwell, *SVT* 30 (1979), pp. 203f.

21   *Cf.* W. E. Lemke, *HTR* 58 (1965), pp. 351f.

22   It is not impossible that the LXX here has been influenced by the Chronicler's reading; *cf.* R. Mosis, *Untersuchungen zur Theologie des chronistischen Geschichtswerkes* (Freiburg, 1973), pp. 64f.

23   On this aspect of continuity see E. Otto, *TZ* 32 (1976), pp. 65–77; J.-M. de Tarragon, *RB* 86 (1979), pp. 514–523.

24   G. Henton Davies, *ASTI* 5 (1966–7(1967)), p. 41.

25   *Cf.* A. Hastings, *Prophet and Witness in Jerusalem* (London, 1958), p. 179n.

26   *Cf.* Miller–Roberts, pp. 16f. See also P. K. McCarter, 'The Ritual Dedication of the City of David in 2 Samuel 6', in C. L. Meyers, M. O'Connor (eds.), *The Word of the Lord Shall Go Forth* (Fs D. N. Freedman; Winona Lake, 1983), pp. 273–277.

27   4QSam[a] has 'Baalah, that is Kiriath-jearim' (Ulrich, p. 194); see further *OTG*, pp. 32f.

28   *Cf.* Weinfeld, *Deuteronomy*, pp. 191–209; T. N. D. Mettinger, *The Dethronement of Sabaoth* (Lund, 1982), pp. 38–79, 123–134.

29   The translation 'his brother' – though not necessarily in reference to Eleazar – is favoured by Campbell, *The Ark*, p. 171. It is equally unlikely that 'his brother', if original, would refer to Zadok, who rose to prominence in David's reign (*cf.* Cody, *A History*, pp. 90f.); see *OTG*, p. 33.

30   4QSam^a appears to agree with 1 Ch. 13:8 (Ulrich, p. 195). For a defence of 'fir trees' see J. A. Soggin, *VT* 14 (1964), pp. 374–377.

31   4QSam^a has either *Nwdn* or *Nydn* (Ulrich, pp. 195, 213); in either case a proper name seems to be indicated (*cf.* 'Chidon' in 1 Ch. 13:9).

32   The consideration that the expression 'to stretch out the hand upon (against)' sometimes expresses hostile intent is scarcely relevant here. MT, as it happens, omits 'his hand', though 4QSam^a and the versions have the full reading (*cf.* Ulrich, p. 56).

33   *KB* gives the meaning 'irreverence' for MT *šal*, claiming support from Akkadian (p. 972).

34   For this latter suggestion see T. Polk, *SBT* 9 (1979), pp. 6f.

35   4QSam^a agrees with 1 Ch. 15:26 at this point (*cf.* Ulrich, p. 196). See also W. E. Lemke, *HTR* 58 (1965), pp. 352f.

36   For the sacrificial ritual during a procession see Miller–Roberts, pp. 16f.

37   There is discussion of David's ephod by A. Philips, *VT* 19 (1969), pp. 485–487; N. L. Tidwell *VT* 24 (1974), pp. 505–507; the latter reaffirms that David's was an item of priestly attire.

38   The words translated 'leaping' and 'dancing' are discussed by Y. Avishur, *VT* 26 (1976), pp. 257–261; G. W. Ahlström, *VT* 28 (1978), pp. 100–102.

39   See C. E. Armerding, 'Were David's Sons Really Priests?', in *Current Issues in Biblical and Patristic Interpretation* (Fs M. C. Tenney; ed. G. F. Hawthorne; Grand Rapids, 1975), pp. 75–86. Contrariwise, H. H. Rowley, *JBL* 58 (1939), p. 129 (n. 44).

40   F. D. Kidner, *Psalms 1–72* (TOTC; London, 1973), p. 238.

41   *Cf.* L. Koehler, *TZ* 4 (1948), pp. 397f.

42   R. Patai, *HUCA* 20 (1947), pp. 212f., suggests a connection with the New Year Festival.

43   *Cf.* R. Alter, *The Art of Biblical Narrative* (New York, 1981), p. 125.

44   See Rost, *The Succession*, pp. 85, 87.

45   For discussion of 2 Sa. 6 in terms of 'rite of passage' see J. W. Flanagan, 'Social Transformation and Ritual in 2 Samuel 6', in Meyers and O'Connor (eds.), *The Word of the Lord*, pp. 361–372.

46   *Cf.* also *OTG*, pp. 71–78.

47   *Cf.* M. Ota, 'A Note on 2 Sam 7', in *A Light unto My Path* (Fs J. M. Myers; ed. H. N. Bream *et al.*; Philadelphia, 1974), pp. 403–407 (406).

48   *Cf.* Ishida, *The Royal Dynasties*, p. 95 (referring to Koch, *The Growth of the Biblical Tradition*, pp. 140f.).

49   *Cf.* Haran, *Temples*, pp. 201f.

50   *Cf.* Carlson, *David*, pp. 111f.

51   *e.g.* S. Gevirtz, 'On Hebrew *šēbeṭ* = "Judge"', in *The Bible World* (Fs C. H. Gordon; ed. G. Rendsburg *et al.*; New York, 1980), pp. 61–66. P. V. Reid, *CBQ* 37 (1975), pp. 17–20, retains the consonants of MT but revocalizes to produce the meaning 'staff-bearers, leaders'. For a defence of MT see P. de Robert, *VT* 21 (1971), pp. 116–118.

52   See Calderone, *Dynastic Oracle*, p. 44.

53   See K. A. Kitchen, *Ancient Orient and Old Testament* (London, 1966), pp. 108n., 110f., and references there.

54 On this see further *OTG*, pp. 73f.

55 *Cf.* A. Gelston, *ZAW* 84 (1972), pp. 92–94.

56 On the relationship between the Abrahamic and Davidic covenants see R. E. Clements, *Abraham and David. Genesis 15 and its meaning for Israelite Tradition* (SBT II.5; London, 1967), pp. 47–60. For a different evaluation see N. E. Wagner, 'Abraham and David?', in *Studies on the Ancient Palestinian World* (Fs F. V. Winnett; Toronto Semitic Texts and Studies, 2; ed. J. W. Wevers, D. B. Redford; Toronto, 1972), pp. 117–140.

57 'son' in some RSV editions.

58 *Cf.* M. Noth, 'David and Israel in II Samuel VII', in *The Laws in the Pentateuch and Other Essays* (ET; London, 1966), p. 251.

59 A Greek Lucianic manuscript (Holmes-Parsons 44) has 'for me'. My reference in *OTG*, p. 74, to the 'Lucianic strand' is much too strong and should be corrected accordingly.

60 See the useful comments of J. A. Soggin on Canaanite (Ugaritic, strictly) kingship ideology in Hayes–Miller, pp. 371–373.

61 *Cf.* Calderone, *Dynastic Oracle*, p. 55.

62 *Cf.* H. G. M. Williamson, *TB* 28 (1977), pp. 140–142.

63 See J. M. Allegro, *DJD* V, pp. 53–55; English translation in G. Vermes, *The Dead Sea Scrolls in English* (London, ²1975), pp. 245–247.

64 A different view of the 'original' Nathan oracle is taken by M. Tsevat, *HUCA* 34 (1963), pp. 71–82.

65 *Cf.* F. F. Bruce, *The Epistle to the Hebrews* (London, 1965), p. 8.

66 So W. C. Kaiser, 'The Blessing of David: The Charter for Humanity', in *The Law and the Prophets* (Fs O. T. Allis; ed. J. H. Skilton; Nutley, 1974), pp. 298–318.

67 J. F. A. Sawyer, *From Moses to Patmos* (London, 1977), p. 50.

68 See Ulrich, pp. 161f.

69 *Cf.* Ishida, *The Royal Dynasties*, p. 110.

70 F. S. Frick, *The City in Ancient Israel* (SBL Diss. Series, 36; Missoula, 1977), p. 57, conflates the readings of Samuel and Chronicles to produce: 'he assumed (or took) the authority of the mother-city Gath and its villages'.

71 *Cf.* A. Malamat, *BA* 21 (1958), pp. 96–102 (= *BAR* 2 (1964), pp. 89–98); B. Mazar, *BA* 25 (1962), pp. 97–120 (= *BAR* 2, pp. 127–151).

72 *CAH*³ II.1, p. 478; *cf.* the Ugaritic text discussed by W. F. Albright in *BASOR* 150 (1958), pp. 36–38. Yadin, *The Art*, p. 285, on the other hand, thinks that David's supply of horses was already up to strength.

73 R. G. Boling, *Joshua* (AB; New York, 1982), p. 307, sees Joshua's hamstringing as a tactic to immobilize the enemy chariots. But even if that is the explanation in Joshua 11, it does not fit the present verse.

74 R. Borger, *VT* 22 (1972), pp. 385–398.

75 *Cf.* Ulrich, pp. 45–48.

76 See further *GTTOT*, p. 333.

77 *Cf.* M. F. Unger, *Israel and the Aramaeans of Damascus* (London, 1957), p. 44. See, however, K.-H. Bernhardt, *Der alte Libanon* (Leipzig, 1976), p. 102.

78 See A. Malamat, *JNES* 22 (1963), pp. 6f.; also McCarthy, *Tiqqune Sopherim*, pp. 223f.

79 Hertzberg, p. 289n., quoting K. Budde.

80 MT has 'Aram'; see on v. 13.

81 The reading of MT is not impossible (*cf.* Y. Aharoni, *The Land of the Bible* (ET; London, ²1979), p. 318 (n. 17)).

82   *Cf.* T. N. D. Mettinger, *Solomonic State Officials* (Coniectanea Biblica, OT Series, 5; Lund, 1971), pp. 52–62.

83   NEB's relocation of 'son of Ahitub' after 'Ahimelech' in 2 Sa. 8:17 (*cf.* 1 Ch. 18:16) is therefore not necessarily an improvement.

84   Rejecting the Jebusite hypothesis, Cross, *CMHE*, pp. 207–215, suggests that Zadok was an 'Aaronide' from Hebron. *Cf.* also S. Olyan, *JBL* 101 (1982), pp. 177–193; Olyan prefers to speak of Zadok's 'south-Judahite' origins.

85   See Mauchline, p. 237, for further discussion; Mauchline prefers to emend the text in the way that we have suggested.

86   *Cf.* A. Cody, *RB* 72 (1965), pp. 381–393; Mettinger, *Solomonic State Officials*, pp. 25–51. On the various offices mentioned in vv. 16–18 see J. A. Soggin in Hayes–Miller, pp. 356–359.

87   See M. Delcor, *VT* 28 (1978), pp. 409–422 (= pp. 314–327 in *Études bibliques et orientales de religions comparées* (Leiden, 1979)). Delcor, p. 421, notes the possibility that the 'Cherethites' came to the Levant after the main Sea Peoples migration.

88   J. Strange, *Caphtor/Keftiu. A New Investigation* (Acta Theologica Danica, 14; Leiden, 1980), pp. 120–124. The Targum suggests 'archers and slingers' for 'Cherethites and Pelethites'. W. F. Albright's connection of $p^e l\bar{e}t\hat{\imath}$ with the Greek *peltastēs* ('light-armed soldier') is very dubious (*CAH*[3] II.2, p. 512).

89   *Cf.* Armerding, 'Were David's Sons Really Priests?', pp. 75–86.

90   G. J. Wenham, *ZAW* 87 (1975), pp. 79–82; see Cody, *A History*, pp. 103–105.

91   Gunn, *Story of David*, p. 68.

92   *Cf.* the comments of A. Lemaire, *VT* 31 (1981), pp. 49f.

93   *Cf.* Lemaire, *ibid.*, pp. 39–61.

94   See Z. Ben-Barak, *Biblica* 62 (1981), pp. 73–91, for discussion of David's gift to Mephibosheth as a release of paternal estate which had passed to the crown in the absence of Saulide male heirs.

95   J. P. Fokkelman, *Narrative Art and Poetry in the Books of Samuel*: I, *King David* (Assen, 1981), pp. 29f., thinks that 2 Sa. 9 interacts with 1 Sa. 20 not only in relation to the covenant between Jonathan and David but also in respect of the theme of eating at the king's table – a privilege first given to, and then denied, David when Saul was king.

96   *ANET*[3], p. 322.

97   *Cf.* W. F. Albright, *JBL* 51 (1932), pp. 77–106; *idem*, in *AOTS*, p. 218.

98   T. Veijola, *RB* 85 (1978), pp. 338–361, distinguishes between references to 'Meribaal (*sic*) son of Jonathan' and to 'Meribaal son of Saul'; the references to the latter, in his view, have the 'historical priority' (352).

99   *Cf.* H. J. Stoebe, *ZDPV* 93 (1977), pp. 236–246.

100   See P. Artzi, 'Mourning in International Relations', in B. Alster (ed.), *Death in Mesopotamia* (Copenhagen Studies in Assyriology, 8; Copenhagen, 1980), pp. 161–170.

101   Fokkelman, *op. cit.*, p. 44.

102   See B. Mazar, *JBL* 80 (1961), pp. 16–28.

103   So Y. Yadin, *Biblica* 36 (1955), pp. 332–351 (349–351); *cf.* B. Mazar, *BA* 25 (1962), p. 102. Since, however, Medeba is a considerable distance to the south of Rabbah, and is in Moabite territory, the Chronicles reading is often regarded as a corruption of *mê rabbâ*, 'waters of Rabbah' (*cf.* 12:27); see Williamson, *Chronicles, ad loc.*

104   A. Malamat, *JNES* 22 (1963), pp. 3f.

105 'The number of *horsemen* is disproportionately large' (Driver, *Notes*, p. 289).

106 On this complex issue see D. J. A. Clines, *JBL* 93 (1974), pp. 22–40 (29f.).

107 Nor, in view of 12:27–31, should 21:17 be regarded as a factor (*cf.* Carlson, *David*, p. 226).

108 *Cf.* my note in *JQR* NS 69 (1979), pp. 112–116.

109 Whybray, *The Succession Narrative*, p. 24.

110 *Cf.* Ulrich, p. 173.

111 *Cf.* A. Berlin, *JSOT* 23 (1982), p. 80. For comment on biological aspects of the verse see M. Krause, *ZAW* 95 (1983), pp. 434–437.

112 So M. Pope, *Song of Songs* (AB 7c; New York, 1977), p. 515 (commenting on the same expression in Song 5:3).

113 *Cf.* McKane, pp. 229f.; but see Mauchline, pp. 249f.

114 Yadin, *Biblica* 36 (1955), pp. 341–351; *idem, The Art*, p. 275.

115 And see M. Tsevat, *HUCA* 46 (1975), p. 83, for an alternative (less probable) explanation.

116 *Cf.* J. Goldingay, *CBQ* 40 (1978), pp. 388–390. A. R. Johnson, *The Cultic Prophet and Israel's Psalmody* (Cardiff, 1979), pp. 412–431, attributes the psalm to David during his period in Transjordan, when Absalom held sway in Jerusalem.

117 *Cf.* U. Simon, *Biblica* 48 (1967), pp. 207–242 (Simon uses the term 'juridical parable').

118 On this aspect of the parable see H. Seebass, *ZAW* 86 (1974), pp. 203–211.

119 Carlson, *David*, pp. 163–169; *cf.* P. W. Coxon, *Biblica* 62 (1981), pp. 247–250, for advocacy of the LXX reading from another angle.

120 Levenson, *CBQ* 40 (1978), p. 23. This explanation is very old, being represented, for example, in a Targum text of v. 12 (Sperber's Ms c).

121 For both occurrences of 'house' (*bêṯ*, 8) the Peshitta has 'daughters' (= *bᵉnôṯ*); *cf.* NEB.

122 *Cf.* M. Tsevat, *JSS* 3 (1958), pp. 241f.

123 *Cf.* Levenson, *CBQ* 40 (1978), pp. 27f.; *cf.* Levenson, with B. Halpern, in *JBL* 99 (1980), pp. 513–516.

124 In v. 9 'the word of ' is probably a euphemistic addition to the text (*cf.* McCarthy, *Tiqqune Sopherim*, pp. 204–206).

125 Weinfeld, *Deuteronomy*, p. 131.

126 H. McKeating, *JSOT* 11 (1979), pp. 57–72 (58).

127 *Cf.* McCarthy, *Tiqqune Sopherim*, pp. 184–187; Ulrich, p. 138.

128 Ulrich, pp. 100f.

129 For the view that Solomon was Bathsheba's firstborn, and that the account of the death of the unnamed child is 'legendary', see T. Veijola, *SVT* 30 (1979), pp. 230–250. For criticism of Veijola see McCarter, pp. 301f., 306.

130 Useful topographical information on Rabbah is given by W. H. Shea, *PEQ* 111 (1979), pp. 17–25.

131 So J. F. A. Sawyer, *TGUOS* 26 (1975–6(1979)), pp. 96–107; Sawyer attributes the harsher aspect of the reference to a Deuteronomist living in the exilic period.

132 See M. Tsevat in Botterweck–Ringgren, II, pp. 338–343; G. J. Wenham, *VT* 22 (1972), pp. 326–348 (342f.).

133 Conroy, *Absalom Absalom!*, p. 29n.

134 W. Zimmerli, *Old Testament Theology in Outline*, p. 55. For a definition of *nᵉḇālâ* ('wanton folly') see A. Phillips, *VT* 25 (1975), pp. 237–241 (239).

135 *Cf.* Conroy, *Absalom Absalom!*, p. 17n.

136   The text of v. 16 poses some problems, though the general sense is not in doubt; see the useful discussion in Conroy, *ibid.*, p. 151.

137   Conroy, *Absalom Absalom!*, p. 152, prefers Klostermann's emendation to *mē'ōllîm* (*sic*), 'from childhood on', but his arguments against reading *mē'ōlām* fall short of being convincing. His own preference, moreover, introduces another problem in that 'from childhood on' does not naturally mean 'once the princesses left the age of childhood'. See also Gunn, *Story of David*, pp. 32f.

138   See Ulrich, pp. 84f.; Conroy, pp. 152f., counsels against too ready acceptance of the addition as part of the earliest text.

139   Conroy, *Absalom Absalom!*, p. 36.

140   On the problems raised by the geographical names in this verse see H. Seebass, *VT* 14 (1964), pp. 497–500.

141   *Cf.* Ulrich, p. 85.

142   *Cf.* E. Lipiński, *VT* 20 (1970), p. 51.

143   RSV's substitution of 'spirit' for 'David' as the subject of MT 'longed' (which is in the 3rd fem. sg.) has the support of 4QSam[a] and LXX; see Ulrich, pp. 106f.

144   For a detailed treatment of vv. 2–22, dividing between supposedly non-Deuteronomistic and Deuteronomistic elements, see R. Bickert, *SVT* 30 (1979), pp. 30–51.

145   C. D. Isbell, *JNES* 36 (1977), pp. 213f.

146   Among recent discussions of the chapter see C. V. Camp, *CBQ* 43 (1981), pp. 14–29; Camp sees the wise women of 2 Sa. 14 and 20 as evidence of a significant political role open to women in the pre-monarchical period. G. G. Nichol, *STh* 36 (1982), pp. 97–104, regards the interview with David as essentially expressive of *Joab's* 'wisdom'.

147   See de Vaux, *AI*, p. 12.

148   V. 14 is discussed at length by J. Hoftijzer, *VT* 20 (1970), pp. 434–438.

149   *Cf.* D. J. Wiseman in *AOTS*, p. 129.

150   *Cf.* Y. Yadin, *ScriptHieros* 8 (1961), pp. 1–62.

151   *Cf.* Hertzberg; Gunn, *Story of David*, p. 33.

152   See further J. Weingreen, *VT* 19 (1969), pp. 263–266; Bright, *History*[3], pp. 208–210.

153   For discussion of the role of Judah in the rebellion see H. Bardtke in *Wort und Geschichte* (Fs K. Elliger; ed. H. Gese, H. P. Rüger; Neukirchen-Vluyn, 1973), pp. 1–8.

154   See *ANET*[3], pp. 142–149; *NERTOT*, pp. 223–225.

155   On this see M. Weinfeld, *IOS* 7 (1977), pp. 65–88.

156   See Crüsemann, *Der Widerstand*, pp. 95–98.

157   Some prefer to read 'forty days'; see Conroy, *Absalom Absalom!*, p. 106 (n. 40).

158   N. H. Snaith, *The Jewish New Year Festival* (London, 1947), pp. 76f.

159   K. Budde, *Die Bücher Samuel* (Tübingen, 1902), p. 270 ('dem Jahwe zu Hebron, dem hebronitischen Jahwe').

160   See J. A. Emerton, *ZAW* 94 (1982), pp. 2–20, for discussion of *yhwh šmrn*, *yhwh tmn*, and related matters.

161   *Cf.* Bardtke, in Gese and Rüger (eds.), *Wort und Geschichte*, pp. 1–8.

162   Conroy, *Absalom, Absalom!*, p. 105n., citing Ps. 22:25f. (the attendance of the poor at a meal celebrating the fulfilment of a vow).

163   Because of the sentence structure the NEB translators felt compelled to translate 'to summon Ahithophel the Gilonite, David's counsellor, from Giloh

his city, where he was offering the customary sacrifices'. This is grammatically possible, but it leaves us to puzzle out why Ahithophel was so engaged; 'customary' is a Targumic-style addition by NEB.

164   *Cf.* Targum, AV.

165   A. Malamat, *Biblica* 51 (1970), p. 9.

166   *Cf.* Conroy, *Absalom Absalom!*, p. 89; D. M. Gunn, *VT* 30 (1980), pp. 109–113.

167   Conroy, *Absalom Absalom!*, p. 126.

168   B. F. Westcott, *The Gospel According to St. John* (1882; reprint: Grand Rapids, 1975), p. 250.

169   J. Hoftijzer in *Travels in the World of the Old Testament* (Fs M. A. Beek; ed. M. S. H. G. Heerma van Voss *et al.*; Assen, 1974), pp. 91–93.

170   But J. Hoftijzer, *VT* 21 (1971), pp. 606–609, argues that MT can have the force of an imperative: 'these words are a formula meant to draw the attention of the listener to the following words of the speaker'.

171   *Cf. DOTT*, pp. 214f.

172   *Cf.* R. Gordis, *JQR* NS 27 (1936–7), pp. 41–43; G. R. Driver, *EThL* 26 (1950), pp. 342f.

173   T. A. Busink, *Der Tempel von Jerusalem von Salomo bis Herodes*, I (Leiden, 1970), pp. 252–256.

174   See A. van Selms, *JNES* 16 (1957), pp. 118–123; H. Donner, *ZAW* 73 (1961), pp. 269–277; Mettinger, *Solomonic State Officials*, pp. 63–69.

175   Conroy, *Absalom Absalom!*, p. 106, suggests that, perhaps, 'both Meribbaal (*sic*) and Ziba deserve the reader's contempt'.

176   On the question of Shimei's referents see J. C. VanderKam, *JBL* 99 (1980), pp. 537–539.

177   There is good versional support for RSV 'affliction' against MT 'iniquity' ($Q^e r\hat{e}$ 'eye') in this verse; see McCarthy, *Tiqqune Sopherim*, pp. 81–85.

178   *Cf.* W. Brueggemann, 'On Coping with Curse: A Study of 2 Sam 16:5–14', *CBQ* 36 (1974), pp. 175–192 (189).

179   F. F. Bruce, quoting Lake and Cadbury, in *The Acts of the Apostles* (London, [2]1952), p. 406 (on Acts 22:23).

180   Conroy, *Absalom Absalom!*, p. 114, comments pertinently on the use of irony and *double-entendre* in these verses and in 17:1–14.

181   *Cf.* M. Tsevat, *JSS* 3 (1958), pp. 242f., on BH *bā'aš* as denoting a challenge in a political context. For a different approach see P. R. Ackroyd, *JTS* NS 2 (1951), pp. 31–36 (33).

182   *Cf.* W. Zimmerli, *Old Testament Theology in Outline*, pp. 107f.

183   See *ANET*[3], p. 266.

184   Unless, possibly, 'Israelite' was intended to link Ithra with the northerners who supported Absalom.

185   So Mauchline; *cf.* de Vaux, *AI*, p. 29. For MT 'Nahash' the Lucianic Mss of LXX have 'Jesse', which certainly harmonizes better with 1 Ch. 2:13–17. On the problems of the MT reading see Driver, *Notes*, p. 326.

186   Conroy, *Absalom Absalom!*, p. 141.

187   Instead of MT 'sent forth' in v. 2 the Greek Lucianic tradition has 'divided into three', which is preferred by NEB. For a defence of MT see Conroy, p. 153 (referring to A. Lemaire, *Semitica* 23 (1973), p. 14).

188   LXX (Lucianic Mss) has 'Mahanaim' for 'Ephraim'. No fundamental objection can be made against either reading.

189   MT *wayyuttan* (lit. 'was put') is normally emended to *wayyittāl* ('was left

hanging', RSV). 4QSam[a] seems to support the 'emended' reading (Ulrich, p. 88). For a defence of MT see S. C. Reif, *VT* 20 (1970), pp. 114–116, and Driver as in the next footnote.

190   G. R. Driver, 'Plurima Mortis Imago', in *Studies and Essays in Honor of Abraham A. Neuman* (ed. M. Ben-Horin *et al.*; Leiden, 1962), p. 131.

191   Josephus (*Ant.* vii. 10. 3) has Absalom erect his pillar lest, if his children were killed, his name should be forgotten.

192   See D. M. Gunn, *VT* 26 (1976), pp. 225–228.

193   Driver, *Notes*, pp. 331f.

194   *ibid.*, p. 332.

195   Conroy, *Absalom Absalom!*, p. 51.

196   Conroy, *ibid.*, p. 49.

197   *Cf.* Ulrich, p. 89. The evidence of 4QSam[a] depends upon space-counting.

198   Though see the commentaries on Bethabarah/Bethany in Jn. 1:28.

199   *Cf.* Stoebe, pp. 457f.

200   The LXX tradition offers but very slight support for this expedient.

201   See Z. Kallai, *IEJ* 28 (1978), pp. 251–261, for a discussion of the relationship between the entities 'Judah' and 'Israel' in the period before the disruption of the kingdom.

202   Bright, *History*[3], p. 210.

203   Later Jewish tradition, with a side-swipe at the Samaritan community, claimed that the original reading was 'to your gods' (the one reading can be obtained from the other simply by transposing two consonants). But see McCarthy, *Tiqqune Sopherim*, pp. 85–91.

204   *Cf.* D. M. Gunn, *Semeia* 3 (1975), p. 28: 'What little is said about Amasa both here and elsewhere in the story suggests that the elements of disloyalty, treachery, and incompetence belong to the configuration of this cameo.'

205   *Cf.* McCarthy, *Tiqqune Sopherim*, pp. 179–182. The clause is surely idiomatic, and not deserving of the various emendations that have been proposed.

206   See E. A. Neiderhiser, *JETS* 24 (1981), pp. 209f.

207   R. L. Stevenson, *Travels with a Donkey in the Cevennes* (1879).

208   See J. Kaplan, *IEJ* 28 (1978), pp. 157–159; E. C. B. MacLaurin, *PEQ* 110 (1978), pp. 113f., concludes that 'Abel Beth Ma'akah probably was the name of twin towns, the main town being Beth Ma'akah on one bank of the creek and Abel the designation of the agricultural settlement on the other bank which supplied the city proper with most of its food'.

209   *Cf.* J. A. Emerton, *JTS* NS 26 (1975), p. 134n.

210   The emended reading has good support from LXX.

211   A. Malamat, *UF* 11 (1979(1980)), pp. 535f., proposes the meaning 'clan' for this occurrence of BH *'ēm*.

212   On the meaning of the Hebrew *mas* as 'unskilled labour' see J. A. Wainwright, *ET* 91 (1979–80), pp. 137–140.

213   Mettinger, *Solomonic State Officials*, pp. 128–139 (133).

The Samuel Appendix (2 Sa. 21:1–24:25)

1   On the Gibeonite treaty see F. C. Fensham, *BA* 27 (1964), pp. 96–100.

2   A. Malamat, *VT* 5 (1955), pp. 1–12.

3   For the suggestion that Saul wanted to make Gibeon his capital see K.-D.

Schunck, *Benjamin* (BZAW 86; Berlin/New York, 1963), pp. 131–138; *cf.* J. Blenkinsopp, *VT* 24 (1974), pp. 1–7.

4   Note that the regular word for 'hanged' (*tālâ*) is used in v. 12 of the Philistines' exposure of the bodies of Saul and Jonathan at Beth-shan.

5   J. J. Glück, *ZAW* 77 (1965), pp. 72–81, argues for MT, claiming that David took the opportunity to have executed Michal's five sons by her other husband. This, of course, necessitates the reading of 'Paltiel the son of Laish' (*cf.* 3:15) for MT 'Adriel the son of Barzillai the Meholathite'.

6   LXX seems to conceal a reference to the month Ziv (*cf.* 1 Ki. 6:37); see S. P. Brock, *VT* 23 (1973), pp. 100–103.

7   J. M. Miller, *CBQ* 36 (1974), pp. 159f.

8   A misplaced marginal correction in LXX of v. 11 offers some support for this treatment of Ishbi-benob; so, in outline, McCarter (*q.v.*).

9   On this aspect see J. R. Bartlett, *VT* 20 (1970), pp. 267–270 (269).

10   *Cf.* F. Willesen, *JSS* 3 (1958), pp. 327–335; C. E. L'Heureux, *BASOR* 221 (1976), pp. 83–85; J. C. de Moor, *ZAW* 88 (1976), pp. 323–345; W. J. Horwitz, *JNSL* 7 (1979), pp. 37–43.

11   The Targum translates by 'sword' (*pace* McCarter); see my note, 'The *Gladius Hispaniensis* and Aramaic *'ispāniqê'* in *VT* 35 (1985), pp. 496–500.

12   A. R. Johnson, *Sacral Kingship in Ancient Israel* (Cardiff, [2]1967), p. 21, suggests that *yā'ar* in Ps. 132:6 should be *yā'îr*, referring to David in the manner of 2 Sa. 21:19. For another attempt on Ps. 132:6 see A. Robinson, *ZAW* 86 (1974), pp. 220–222.

13   J. Barr, *Fundamentalism* (London, 1977), pp. 281f.

14   *Cf.* L. M. von Pákozdy, *ZAW* 68 (1956), pp. 257–259; N. P. Lemche, *JSOT* 10 (1978), pp. 4f.

15   Hertzberg's idea that at an early stage 'Goliath' had come to denote a type (we might compare 'Agagite' in Esth. 3:1) is difficult to sustain.

16   C. S. Lewis, *Reflections on the Psalms* (London/Glasgow, 1958), p. 10.

17   A. R. Johnson, *Sacral Kingship*, pp. 116–123. See the criticism of Johnson by S. Mowinckel, *The Psalms in Israel's Worship*, II (ET; Oxford, 1962), pp. 253–255.

18   *Cf.* L. Jacobs, 'Jewish Cosmology', in *Ancient Cosmologies* (ed. C. Blacker, M. Loewe; London, 1975), pp. 68f.

19   F. M. Cross and D. N. Freedman, *Studies in Ancient Yahwistic Poetry* (SBL Diss. Series, 21; Missoula, 1975), p. 145, opt for 'spread apart' (as of a curtain), comparing Is. 63:19.

20   Cross and Freedman, *ibid.*, p. 146, relate *ḥašraṭ* to a root meaning 'sieve'; the clouds are then viewed as 'sieve-like containers'.

21   NEB refers *them* to the arrows ('he sped them far and wide . . . and sent them echoing'), but the verbs in question so often describe Yahweh's discomfiture of his enemies that it is better to retain the traditional rendering. For a defence of NEB see Mauchline, *ad loc.*

22   *Cf.* A. A. Macintosh, *VT* 19 (1969), pp. 471–479 (472f.).

23   Carlson, *David*, pp. 251f.

24   S. H. Levey, *VT* 21 (1971), pp. 192f.

25   *Cf.* Ulrich, p. 109.

26   NEB translates mainly in the present tense in vv. 36b–46. The differences in modern versions stem mainly from uncertainty about the significance of the Hebrew imperfect tense in parts of this psalm. For its use as a past tense (as in

RSV) – and, as such, a feature of early Hebrew poetry – see Cross and Freedman, *Studies in Ancient Yahwistic Poetry*, pp. 127f.

27 *Cf.* Ulrich, p. 140.

28 *Cf.* D. W. Thomas (ed.), *The Text of the Revised Psalter* (London, 1963), p. 7; Cross and Freedman, *op. cit.*, p. 154 (n. 83). In fact, the Hebrew equivalent occurs in Ecclesiastes with the meaning 'task, occupation' (1:13, *etc.*).

29 Cross and Freedman, *Studies in Ancient Yahwistic Poetry*, p. 137.

30 See J. H. Eaton, *JTS* NS 19 (1968), pp. 603f.

31 See *DOTT*, pp. 130f.

32 *Cf.* C. H. Gordon, 'History of Religion in Psalm 82', in *Biblical and Near Eastern Studies* (Fs W. S. LaSor; ed. G. A. Tuttle; Grand Rapids, 1978), pp. 129–131.

33 The last line of the poem, together with a prose addendum purporting to give statistical information on David's literary compositions, survives in a Qumran fragment (11QPs[a], col. 27); see J. A. Sanders (ed.), *DJD* IV (Oxford, 1965), pp. 48 (text), 91–93 (translation and discussion); G. Vermes, *The Dead Sea Scrolls in English* (Harmondsworth, [2]1975), p. 265.

34 J. R. Porter, 'Old Testament Historiography', in *Tradition and Interpretation* (ed. G. W. Anderson; Oxford, 1979), p. 130.

35 *Cf.* O. Kaiser, *Isaiah 1–12* (ET (1st edn.); London, 1972), p. 130.

36 *Cf.* H. N. Richardson, *JBL* 90 (1971), pp. 260f.

37 Ulrich, p. 113.

38 *Cf.* R. J. Tournay, *RB* 88 (1981), pp. 485f.

39 So A. M. Cooper, 'The Life and Times of King David According to the Book of Psalms', in R. E. Friedman (ed.), *The Poet and the Historian*, p. 129.

40 *Cf.* Richardson, *art. cit.*, pp. 261f.; Cross, *CMHE*, pp. 234n., 236.

41 On David as 'prophet' see Tournay, *art. cit.*, pp. 490f.; J. A. Fitzmyer, *CBQ* 34 (1972), pp. 332–339.

42 On David's 'righteousness' see Sheppard, *Wisdom*, pp. 150f.

43 So also T. N. D. Mettinger, *SEÅ* 41–2 (1976–7), p. 152.

44 To obtain this translation NEB emends *minnōgah* to *mangîah*; *cf.* Brockington, p. 57.

45 G. T. Sheppard, *Wisdom*, p. 154.

46 *Cf.*, for example, Cross, *CMHE*, p. 235 (n. 74).

47 *ibid.*, p. 236 (though Cross is more favourably disposed towards the first alternative); *cf.* Richardson, *art. cit.*, p. 263.

48 Following LXX, NEB takes the last clause of v. 5 with v. 6: 'But the ungodly put forth no shoots'. In view of the difficulties presented by the text, the minor adjustments required for this reading are quite defensible.

49 See further M. Tsevat, *HUCA* 46 (1975), pp. 79f.; McCarthy, *Tiqqune Sopherim*, pp. 220f.

50 That is, unless we think that the information given here has been excerpted from a fuller account in which the location was already mentioned.

51 *Cf.* Gottwald, *The Tribes*, pp. 260f.

52 On these verses see A. Zeron, *ZAW* 90 (1978), pp. 20–27.

53 Zeron, *ibid.*, p. 25, notes the claimed occurrence of 'ariel', in transliteration, in the Egyptian Papyrus Anastasi I, there possibly with the meaning 'armed leader'.

54 *Cf.* F. F. Bruce, *History of the Bible in English* (Guildford/London, [3]1979), p. 109.

55 K. Elliger, 'Die dreissig Helden Davids' (= *KSAT*, Munich, 1966, pp. 72–118).

56 B. Mazar, *VT* 13 (1963), p. 318.

57 A. Zeron, *Tel Aviv* 6 (1979), pp. 156f., and references there.

58 *Cf.* L. Morris, *The Gospel According to John* (London, 1972), p. 142, where a translation of Origen's comment is given.

59 *Cf.* E. A. Speiser, *BASOR* 149 (1958), pp. 17–25; J. C. L. Gibson, *TGUOS* 18 (1959–60(1961)), pp. 18–21.

60 *Cf.* von Rad, *OTT* I, p. 317n. See Livy, *Ab Urbe Condita*, I.44.

61 Y. Yadin, *The Scroll of the War of the Sons of Light*, p. 84n. For a different estimation of 1 Ch. 27 see Williamson, *Chronicles, ad loc.*

62 For discussion of 2 Sa. 24 and its parallel in 1 Ch. 21 see P. R. Ackroyd in *The Cambridge History of the Bible*, I (ed. P. R. Ackroyd, C. F. Evans; Cambridge, 1970), pp. 86–90.

63 See H. W. F. Saggs, *The Encounter with the Divine in Mesopotamia and Israel* (London, 1978), pp. 93–124, for a discussion of the divine in relation to good and evil.

64 Driver, *Notes*, p. 374.

65 *Cf.* H. J. Katzenstein, *The History of Tyre* (Jerusalem, 1973), pp. 20, 65. McCarter thinks, however, that 'Fort Tyre' must have been a fortress on the Israelite-Phoenician border (p. 510).

66 See Katzenstein, *History of Tyre*, pp. 105f.; Y. Kaufmann, *The Biblical Account of the Conquest of Palestine* (Jerusalem, 1953), p. 53.

67 H. A. Hoffner in *POTT*, p. 225, summarizing E. A. Speiser. In one or two passages, as Speiser had noted, LXX has 'Horite' for MT 'Hivite' (*e.g.* Jos. 9:7). For further discussion of the 'Hivite problem' see R. North, *Biblica* 54 (1973), pp. 43–62; M. Görg, *UF* 8 (1976(1977)), pp. 53–55.

68 Sample texts in *NERTOT*, pp. 122–128.

69 von Rad, *OTT* I, p. 318.

70 In addition to stating that David chose the plague option, LXX notes that it was the time of the wheat harvest (*cf.* on v. 20).

71 *Cf.* on 21:1, and see $ANET^3$, pp. 394–396; *NERTOT*, pp. 169–174.

72 On the longer text of this verse in 4QSam[a] see Ulrich, pp. 156f.

73 LXX (Lucianic Mss) and 4QSam[a] have 'even I, the shepherd, have done wrong', with 'shepherd' antithetical to 'these (the) sheep'. See Ulrich, pp. 86f.

74 *Cf.* R. E. Clements, *God and Temple* (Oxford, 1965), p. 61; K. Rupprecht, *Der Tempel von Jerusalem. Gründung Salomos oder jebusitisches Erbe?* (BZAW 144; Berlin/New York, 1977), pp. 5–17.

75 *Cf.* Ulrich, pp. 157f.

76 *Cf.* Hoffner in *POTT*, p. 225. For a proposed Hittite derivation see H. B. Rosén, *VT* 5 (1955), pp. 318–320.

77 A. Schenker, *Der Mächtige im Schmelzofen des Mitleids: Eine Interpretation von 2 Sam 24* (OBO 42; Göttingen, 1982).

GENERAL INDEX

INDEX OF AUTHORS

CPSIA information can be obtained at www.ICGtesting.com
Printed in the USA
LVOW08s2150020815

448491LV00004B/12/P